Law and Religion in a Global Context

Volume 6

Series Editor
Frank S. Ravitch, College of Law, Rm 315, Michigan State University,
East Lansing, USA

Law and Religion in a Global Context will focus on law and religion issues from a global perspective at a time when that field is of increasing importance and relevance around the world. Designed to be broad, the scope allows for books on the relationship between religion and government as well as on religious law. Focus will be placed on comparative law issues, but also on issues within single countries. Representative areas of focus will be:

- the relationship between government and religion ranging from laicete to theocracy
- religious freedom in pluralistic societies
- the relationship between religious freedom and other freedoms such as freedom of speech and sexual freedom
- regulation of religion by government
- original contributions on religious law

The series seeks to highlight up and coming voices in the field alongside those of established scholars. We encourage scholars from a wide range of geographic perspectives to apply. Purely doctrinal analysis of law and religion is not preferred. Nor is analysis of religious law issues without any original contribution or insights. The only exception to this rule might be books on legal doctrine from a region that has been under analyzed in English language literature.

Judith Hahn

The Cultures of Canon Law

Global Catholicism, Glocal Legislation, and the Local Churches

Springer

Judith Hahn
Seminar of Canon Law
University of Bonn
Bonn, Germany

ISSN 2946-5931 ISSN 2946-594X (electronic)
Law and Religion in a Global Context
ISBN 978-3-032-14811-7 ISBN 978-3-032-14812-4 (eBook)
https://doi.org/10.1007/978-3-032-14812-4

This work was supported by Volkswagen Foundation (Funding scheme Opus magnum).

This Springer imprint is published by the registered company Springer Nature Switzerland AG
The registered company address is: Gewerbestrasse 11, 6330 Cham, Switzerland

Acknowledgements

I cannot mention all individuals to whom I owe thanks for their inspiration and support. However, I want to name some whose contribution was of major importance for my book. First, I would like to thank all those scholars who inspired me to take a closer look at the church and its law as global phenomena. Writing a book about the culturality of canon law is an idea that developed during my time as a fellow at the Käte Hamburger Center for Advanced Study in the Humanities "Law as Culture" at the University of Bonn in 2015–16. This resulted in my book *Church Law in Modernity*,[1] a legal theory analysing the foundation of canon law between nature and culture. That natural law, despite its claim of supercultural meaning, is always also the expression of a concrete group's search for justice and is thus a deeply cultural phenomenon has accompanied my work since. However, what my study did not discuss was what it means precisely that canon law is profoundly cultural and is, as all law, a human artefact, reflecting a certain time and circumstances. Ecclesiastical jurisprudence tends to stress the divine origin of canon law. But it tends to pay less attention to the fact that, even if one accepts a supernatural foundation of the law, this does not take anything away from the law's culturality. This is particularly challenging with regard to canon law, which endeavours to organise the legal life of a global church that exists in and out of local churches from across the entire world. Hence, undertaking research on the culturality of canon law includes examining the law's striking globality. Both lines of thought intertwine in this book. Consequently, it owes much to research conducted by others in fields such as cultural studies, legal pluralism, human rights, international law, critical legal studies, missiology, and comparative and intercultural theology. I am indebted to Robert Schreiter, whose 1985 book *Constructing Local Theologies* taught me a great deal about interculturality in theology, as it has many theologians before me. One colleague whose 2018 book *Intercultural Theology* has been inspiring to me is Judith Gruber, systematic theologian at KU Leuven. I owe her thanks for many thoughts which I would not have developed without her work. Many thanks also go to Bryan Froehle, Professor of Sociology and Religious Studies at Palm Beach Atlantic University. I talked at length with him about this project and am grateful for his insistence that there is a

[1] Hahn (2019).

major difference between a truly global law and a "globally extensive law". To be reminded that there are diverse ways of approaching the law is an enriching experience when discussing legal issues with colleagues from all over the globe. One of the first scholars who made me pause for thought to consider whether it makes a difference to study canon law from a continental civil law or a British common law point of view was Robert Ombres OP of Blackfriars Hall, Oxford, who as a common lawyer and canonist is versed in both traditions. Getting to know Brendan Daly, canonist at Te Kupenga Catholic Theological College, Auckland, and my common lawyer colleagues from the Thomas More Law School in Sydney helped me to understand these tensions between legal systems better. I am grateful to Elizabeth Ong, an ecclesiastical judge and secular lawyer, for sharing valuable insights into the cross-cultural intricacies of the law at the intersection of European and Asian cultures, common law and civil law, and secular and religious law. I also want to mention the board of Brill Studies in Global Catholicism, a series edited by Bryan Froehle and Massimo Faggioli, where I was honoured to serve with colleagues from Australia, Brazil, Chile, India, Kenya, the Philippines, and the United States for some years. Their shared scepticism about theology's focus on the Global North and their critical views of the law were thought-provoking. Anna-Lena Wolf, ethnologist and legal anthropologist, was not only kind enough to read the manuscript but also to comment on it in order to add the perspective of legal anthropology, helping me to account for findings in empirical social and cultural studies. Ryszard Bobrowicz, practical theologian and scholar of comparative law and religion, has critically examined the manuscript and provided important advice on how to improve it in the light of historical knowledge of the development of canon law and its contemporary setting in plural legal scenarios. My fellow colleagues in the 2024–28 class of McDonald Distinguished Senior Fellows at the Center for the Study of Law and Religion, Emory University, devoted a working session to discussing my draft manuscript during our 2025 fellow meeting. In particular, I would like to thank Sam Bray and Ashley Purpura, who have taken the trouble to prepare critical comments on the draft to stimulate discussion. I would also like to express my gratitude to the anonymous reviewer who provided important feedback on how to improve the manuscript during the peer-review process. As a member of the University of Bonn, I am part of a community of inspiring theologians, philosophers, and legal scholars. By way of example, I would like to mention Susanne Gössl, whose expertise in comparative law has taught me a great deal about how legal rules operate in different contexts, and comparative theologian Klaus von Stosch, whose perspective on law, inspired by Islamic legal thought, offers a valuable alternative to traditional views of religious law. I am grateful to the Volkswagen Foundation for financing one year of research leave to allow me to finish the book as part of the funding programme *Opus Magnum*. I am most obliged to Robert John Murphy for his indispensable help in carefully proofreading my manuscript. Above all, I owe thanks to Thomas for his patience in listening to me talk endlessly about my work throughout the writing process.

Competing Interests The author has no competing interests to declare that are relevant to the content of this manuscript.

Contents

Chapter 1
Introduction

This book seeks to analyse the current status of global Catholic canon law as law emanating from the Roman centre of Catholicism and its application in the local churches across the world. A law deeply impregnated by the continental legal tradition is being applied in churches with both civil and common law backgrounds, in city parishes and rural areas, in cultures which embrace the law as a medium of organising the social and in contexts where it enjoys less support. This can lead to many misunderstandings and disagreements. Canonists are aware of these challenges from their own observations, from educated guessing, and from the complaints raised by many Catholics throughout the world. As yet, however, no study has collected these diverse observations and used them to construct an overall picture which systematises the conflicts connected with the ambition of covering a worldwide church with a uniform law; has analysed the reasons for these conflicts in light of existing research on legal pluralism, legal transfer, and legal colonialism; and has discussed whether, in light of these findings, there can be a future for a global body of ecclesiastical rules. By raising these questions, this study also contributes to the ongoing and intense debate on legal universalism, which asks whether global rules can be established without reproducing colonialist patterns by imposing alien rules on other cultures. At the same time, it supports the observation made by cultural studies that transferring rules across cultural boundaries inevitably gives rise to multiple meanings. In this sense, universal Roman Catholic canon law is more diverse than the term suggests. This book aims to demonstrate why this is the case.

J. Hahn, *The Cultures of Canon Law*, Law and Religion in a Global Context 6,
https://doi.org/10.1007/978-3-032-14812-4_1

1.1 Ambiguous Universalisms

In the 1983 Code of Canon Law (hereinafter abbreviated to: CIC/1983), the ecclesiastical legislator holds: "Universal laws bind everywhere all those for whom they were issued" (canon 12 §1 CIC/1983). The striking use of the term *universal* in Roman Catholic legislation has several implications. Doctrinally, *leges universales* pertain to all subjects of Roman Catholic canon law in all of the local churches belonging to the Roman Catholic Church. Canon law is thus a marker of global Catholicism. Accordingly, church sociologists Bryan Froehle and Mary Gautier in their inventory on *Global Catholicism* define as being part of the Latin Church all those churches which follow the Latin Rite and "a distinct set of practices and norms, including a code of Church law (Canon Law) uniquely designed for it".[1]

Yet, speaking of "universal laws" implies not only that canonical rules extend into the Roman Catholic Churches all over the globe. It also infuses the law with a transcultural significance. The expression suggests that these rules are suitable for all local churches, regardless of their historical context or cultural circumstances. Canonist Ladislas Orsy observed that "the very nature of a universal law postulates that it should make good sense all over the earth".[2] However, what it means for a law to make good sense to Catholics worldwide is a matter of debate. One might rephrase Orsy's proposition by suggesting that laws are universal when Catholics from all over the world can attribute them with meaning. If a law makes sense to the legal subjects, it allows them to create a legal meaning—not necessarily an identical one, but one that speaks to them in their particular context. This observation concords with a finding which systematic theologian Bernard Lonergan made in his book *Method in Theology*, stating: "Now meaning may regard the general or the universal, but most human thought and speech and action are concerned with the particular and the concrete".[3]

But there is more to Orsy's considerations of the law and its universality. He does not refer to laws as being universal when they make *some* sense, but when they make *good* sense to Christians all over the earth. As canon law serves the church as a community of faith, this may be understood as its ability to support the local churches, their members, and their religious life. Canonists James Provost and Knut Walf describe this connection as follows: "[L]aw, while challenging the community to greater fidelity, must be rooted in the life of the community and sensitive to its true needs; it must not fail to address important aspects of the community's life".[4] A law which is universal, including the ethical and religious implications of universality as proposed by Provost and Walf, therefore constitutes meaning in the local churches insofar as it benefits the local communities, their shared beliefs, and practices.

---

[1] Froehle and Gautier (2003), p. 15.

[2] Orsy (1992), p. 79.

[3] Lonergan (1972), p. 178.

[4] Provost and Walf (1986), p. X.

However, speaking of universality from the perspective of legal theory goes even further. For legal theory, laws are not merely universal if they happen to make sense all over the globe, but if they necessarily do so, as they possess an inherent validity everywhere, because they reflect fundamental truths about justice or morality. Canonical jurisprudence considers rules based on natural law to be universally valid. Large parts of secular legal theory would only speak of universality with regard to a small number of laws, such as those pertaining to basic human rights; and even the universal validity of these laws is contested among scholars. The majority of legal rules, including canonical ones, cannot be considered universal in the sense of legal theory. Most *leges universales* of canon law are not universally valid. And only very few of them even claim to have a supercultural significance. Their limited scope is quite apparent given that these laws frequently do not even embrace all Catholic churches. Most of the *leges universales* of the Code of Canon Law are what legislation refers to as "merely ecclesiastical laws", which only apply to Latin Catholics (see canon 11 CIC/1983). This observation does not exclude the possibility that canonical rules can generate meaning in the local churches all over the globe. But they do so not essentially because of their supercultural content, but because their content happens to make sense all over the globe. Philosopher of religion Raimon Panikkar once wrote when discussing the sense in which human rights may be regarded as universal:

> There are no trans-cultural values, for the simple reason that a value exists as such only in a given cultural context. But there may be cross-cultural values, and a cross-cultural critique is indeed possible. The latter does not consist in evaluating one cultural construct with the categories of another, but in trying to understand and criticize one particular human problem with the tools of understanding of the different cultures concerned, at the same time taking thematically into consideration that the very awareness and, much more, the formulation of the problem is already culturally bound.[5]

His considerations also apply to legal values and rules. While they are not supercultural, they may have cross-cultural value and be relevant in different contexts. An example from canon law might help to illustrate this. The Code of Canon Law establishes global rules for canonical elections (see canons 164–179 CIC/1983). While these regulations are clearly not universal in the sense of legal theory, recalling Ladislas Orsy one might say that they make good sense all over the globe as they provide the local churches with a solid framework for handling elections. However, while these rules might prove adequate all over the globe, they are contingent and changeable. If lawmaking were to decide to regulate elections differently, this would not pose a significant problem. While reliable elections can be considered a universal good, the regulations that provide for them are not universal in the same sense.

[5] Panikkar (1982), pp. 87–88.

1.2 Globalised Legislation

Consequently, as with most rules contained in the Code of Canon Law, the rules on elections are less universal than the term *leges universales* suggests. The Code of Canons of the Oriental Churches (hereinafter abbreviated to: CCEO) makes an alternative terminological suggestion to describe these laws. This Code, which provides a legal frame for the Eastern-rite Catholic Churches, refrains from using the term *leges universales*. Instead it speaks of *common law* ("*ius commune*"). Canon 1493 §1 CCEO defines that the Eastern Code understands as common law all those laws and legitimate customs of the universal church ("*universa Ecclesia*") and of the Eastern Oriental Churches. Thus, its terminology connects the quality of universality with the global Catholic Church, but is more careful about raising any supercultural claims with regard to legal rules. However, the canon continues to integrate also those laws and legitimate customs common to all Eastern Churches into the term *ius commune*. "Common law" thus refers to the laws of the entire church, as well as to those that are shared by all Eastern Churches. This represents a significant shift in perspective. It incoporates a horizontal dimension into the concept of shared rules and complements the vertical line of centralised legislation with the notion of laws and customs shared among the churches. Therefore, the term *ius commune* deserves recognition for expressing the idea that rules common to the churches can be established through centralised legislation for all churches, or developed locally and shared among the churches.

Common law can therefore serve as an alternative term to express the global scope of Catholic canon law, avoiding both supercultural implications and asymmetrical power claims between the churches. Nevertheless, this book rather speaks of *global law* to refer to rules that apply to Catholics all over the globe. This is not done to diminish the value of the terminology used in the Eastern Code. The intention is to avoid confusion resulting from the term *common law* being typically used in a different sense, namely to denote the precedent law of common-law legal systems. As this study will deal with conflicts deriving from global canon law in common law cultures, it would be confusing to use the term "common law" as it is applied in the Eastern Code.

It is also important to note that this book refers to "global law" in a descriptive sense,[6] alluding to the fact that Catholic canon law concerns legal subjects around the world. Accordingly, this study is less interested in what Christian thought offers as "power and potential for the process of globalization of law",[7] and more in observing how the agents who deal with canon law respond to its global claim. By

[6] There are also approaches which understand the term normatively as referring to an "emerging common law of humanity that transcends both the law of individual states and the international law between and among nations and regions", thus representing universal claims of "foundational principles such as dignity, equality, solidarity, sovereignty, subsidiarity, pluralism, the common good, and the rule of law", Domingo and Witte (2020), p. 1.

[7] Domingo and Witte (2020), p. 11.

examining the ambition of canon law to serve global Catholicism as a regulatory framework, this book presents it as a unique case study of global legislation from which much can be learnt about global regulation in general. Legal scholar Grzegorz Blicharz observed that "[t]he Catholic Church, with its canon law, is a micromodel of the universal order and should be of greater interest to anyone analysing concepts of global law".[8] It is in this sense of a micromodel that canon law is introduced to readers in this book.

1.3 Legal Eurocentrism

If one studies the global legal rules in the church, one also comes to find that they are particular rules.[9] Not with regard to their scope of validity, which, as explained, is global, but with regard to their origin. All laws come to life in a specific context, a specific legal culture, as one might say with some caution; as speaking of cultures can suggest a homogeneity and stability of groups and their normative frameworks which is misleading, as legal anthropologists have noted. Social anthropologist Julia Eckert therefore sees a certain hesitancy in contemporary anthropology to use the term culture, as it might gloss over the fluidity of creating meaning in groups.[10] With this caution in mind, this study will continue to use the term, not to ontologise or essentialise groups and their legal views, but to emphasise the character of law as a cultural artefact that connects with fluid structures of meaning. Sociologist Boaventura de Sousa Santos notes with regard to global laws: "There is, therefore, no genuine globalism. Under the conditions of the modern world system, globalism is the successful globalization of a given localism".[11] His words allude to the observation that rules are responses to regulative needs in a particular environment and reflect the contexts from which they derive.

International law, for instance, is heavily influenced by its European and Anglo-American context of emergence. As a consequence, there is an ongoing debate among scholars of international law about how to deal with the European and Anglo-American influence on international law. Legal scholar Brian Tamanaha remarks: "All the main doctrines were developed and shaped in the course of the nineteenth and twentieth centuries by Western jurists drawing from domestic bodies of legal knowledge and practice".[12] These regional influences were an influential variable in the development of law, as he notes with respect to international law:

---

[8] Blicharz (2022), p. 171.

[9] In a similar vein, Krämer (1999), p. 48. However, Krämer understands as universal laws legal rules which pertain to the entire global Catholic Church of the West and the East, whilst he understands as particular those with a smaller scope, for instance rules which only pertain to the Latin Church.

[10] See Eckert (2010), p. 118.

[11] De Sousa Santos (2020), p. 213.

[12] Tamanaha (2017), p. 163.

> International law bears the marks of the professional legal culture of the jurists who produce it. If German jurists had exercised greater influence than Anglo-American jurists in the formulation of international doctrines, for example, it would be structured more in terms of public law than in contract terms. If Latin American or Chinese jurists had played formative roles, it would be different in other ways.[13]

However, as it was lawyers from the Global North who had the greatest influence on forming international law, the law reflects their legal traditions to a greater extent than those from the Global South. International law scholar Antony Anghie describes this process of internal law formation less neutrally than Tamanaha, commenting: "By the end of the 19th century European expansion had ensured that European international law had been established globally as the one single system that applied to all societies. It was in this way that European international law became universal".[14] International law scholar Jörn Axel Kämmerer even speaks of a "'birth defect' of universality"[15] with regard to international law, as European lawyers attributed a particular European view of the law with a universal claim and distributed it across the globe. Anghie therefore doubts whether international law can overcome its colonial legacy and imperialist tendency to impose alien legal thought onto traditions from the Global South.[16]

These concerns are at the heart of the debate about how universal international law truly is. This debate is particularly intense with regard to matters pertaining to human rights. Tamanaha holds a certain view: "Much of what is touted as human rights reflects Western liberal values: freedom of expression, right to privacy, equality between men and women, religious freedom, right to property, democracy, to mention a few examples from the Universal Declaration. Since they are Western derived, the critical import of human rights is mostly directed at non-Western countries".[17] In any case, opinions on this are divided, both across the borders of legal cultures and scholarly disciplines. Many critical legal scholars, ethicists, and social scientists argue that human rights were originally a Western product. While some accept this finding as a somewhat neutral observation on the origins of human rights discourse, others understand it as deeply problematic revealing human rights—at least in their present shape—to be a neo-colonial endeavour subjecting political regimes all over the globe to a new imperialism of humanitarianism.[18] Historian Michael Ignatieff interprets human rights talk as idolatry, seeing discourse at work in favour of promoting human rights as a secular religion with the aim of making a new imperialism of the Global North sacrosanct from criticism.[19] Other scholars, often from the Global

---

[13] Ibid., p. 164.

[14] Anghie (2006), p. 746.

[15] Kämmerer (2016), p. 239.

[16] See Anghie (2006), pp. 739–753.

[17] Tamanaha (2017), p. 164.

[18] E.g. Ignatieff (2001), pp. 3–52.

[19] See ibid., pp. 53–98.

South, reclaim human rights as a genuine product of their own traditions.[20] Observing these essentially contested struggles, other scholars reject both "possessive" positions and question whether it makes any sense to pit universal human rights and particular values against each other. In this sense, scholars such as Julia Eckert have argued that such contradictions assume the juxtaposition of more or less homogenous groups with more or less homogenous competing claims. As she argues, this does not represent the more fluid reality in which legal claims are raised.[21]

1.4 Contextualised Rules

Similar conflicts can be discussed with regard to canon law. Canonical rules resemble the local setting from which they originate and address the needs of a specific Catholic community at a particular point in time. This is most evident with regard to the laws of the local churches created by decentralised lawmaking to meet local demands. However, the same contextuality also applies to global rules. James Provost and Knut Walf allude to this by noting that "the effort to legislate for a world-wide Church carries with it the special problems of relation to local churches and cultures which are at different stages in their history, at different degrees of development. Law, as it conserves values, expresses them in a culturally limited, dated fashion".[22] However, the issue is not only that the local churches are at different stages in their history, so that they do not fit neatly under the umbrella of global canon law. Instead, as cultural artefacts legal rules necessarily express values in a culturally impregnated fashion. On that note, many canonists acknowledge that the Code of Canon Law originates from a specific European legal tradition.[23] Canon law has been an influential factor in European legal history, being "an integral part of that culture, contributing to the fundamental structure and modelling of the European legal culture".[24] It has historical roots in ancient Roman law, takes into account the typical circumstances of European churches, and addresses the specific needs of these churches. As law issuing from the Apostolic See as the centre of the Roman Catholic world, Roman Catholic canon law is European law, even though this centre of Catholicism is increasingly becoming a less European and more plural place, influenced by Catholics—particularly Catholic clergy—from all over the world. Yet, despite this increasing globalisation of Catholicism, contemporary canon law still relies heavily on European concepts of law.

This is apparent, for instance, when studying its form. In its current form, the main body of canonical rules presents itself as the legislative result of the European era of

[20] E.g. Panikkar (1982), pp. 75–102; Sharma (2006).

[21] See Eckert (2010), pp. 115–130.

[22] Provost and Walf (1986), p. X.

[23] E.g. Schmitz (2015), p. 86; Althaus (2020), p. 323.

[24] Pihlajamäki (2010), p. 177.

codification. In the comprehensive reform of canon law in the early twentieth century, the law was codified to give it a typical modern continental fashion in line with continental civil law. Canonist Peter Huizing called the 1917 Code "the first codification of the law of the Latin Church in history" and "the last imitation of the Napoleonic type of legislation",[25] insofar as the 1917 Code—and later also the 1983 Code—attempted to provide the church with a dense body of statutory laws regulating all key issues of ecclesiastical life. In contrast, common law, widespread throughout the Anglo-American world, weaves a tight net of rules with the help of precedents, generating a comprehensive system of case law to grant legal certainty. Due to their differing approaches to law, it is often challenging for canon law to fit into common-law contexts. From the perspective of legal history, this may seem surprising, considering the codification debates in the nineteenth-century United States where codification was seen as a Protestant project, while the common law form was associated with Catholicism, its "superstition", and "priestcraft",[26] as legal historian Kellen Funk has pointed out. However, history took a different turn. In the United States today, law comprises statutory and common law, whereas canon law is mostly codified law. This can cause problems for American Catholics, as canonist John Huels notes: "Catholics living in a society with a common law tradition and a literalistic attitude towards interpretation and observance of law often have difficulty comprehending the canonical system and sometimes experience canon law more as a source of conflict rather than as a source of unity in the community".[27] In a similar vein, legal scholar James O'Reilly and canonist Margaret Chalmers, who published a book on the legal responses to the abuse crisis in the United States, note with regard to the frictions between canon law and common-law traditions: "Like learning a second language as an adult, it is possible to learn another legal system. But like learning another language, one will never be quite as comfortable, quite as expert, quite as polished, or quite as accurate as with one's native language or system".[28] Canonist and common lawyer Peter Shannon has compiled a series of rather amusing cases in which canon law and US-American legal understanding have clashed;[29] it would go beyond the scope of this book's argument to retell all his observations, but they are an enlightening read, raising awareness of the fact that cross-cultural legal encounters frequently result in difficulties.

1.5 Cross-Cultural Conflicts

These conflicts have a long-standing history. Canon law was reaching across the borders of languages and cultures long before other transnational orders expanded their scope of validity. Legal scholar Harold Berman made this observation with regard to medieval canon law, which spread across Europe to bind Catholics

[25] Huizing (1982), p. 239.

[26] Funk (2024), p. 190.

[27] Huels (1987), p. 274.

[28] O'Reilly and Chalmers (2014), p. 384.

[29] See Shannon (1985), pp. 618–630.

everywhere. Already at this early stage, these legal transplants created tensions in the receiving churches. Berman, however, did not regard these differences as overly problematic, as the receiving groups were accomplished legal pluralists. He found that "the canon law of the Church of Rome prior to the Reformation was as much English law as it was Italian or German or French law. Canon law was no more foreign to England than the Internal Revenue Code of the United States is foreign to Massachusetts or Missouri".[30] His observation describes that many legal communities have constantly dealt with rules of an alien origin and have developed strategies to incorporate them into their own legal systems. Yet, this process has often been accompanied by tension. And, as one might assume, it is becoming more challenging nowadays in a church that is truly global. The cross-cultural exchanges of canon law in the premodern era were mostly inner-European. Today, they have gained a global character.

Based on this observation, some theologians and missiologists have offered robust criticism of canon law. They have argued that its specific cultural background and characteristics have been a source of conflict in many non-European contexts. Drawing on his experience of African Catholicism, social anthropologist and missionary Aylward Shorter called canon law "a juridical expression of uniformity and of Western cultural superiority".[31] Collecting critical voices levelled against the law, he summed up a "fundamental objection to the operation of a universal law in the communion of particular churches that constitutes the Catholic Church. This is the objection that Canon Law is culturally Western, that its whole spirit reflects its origins in the ancient culture of Rome and that it is intrinsically incapable of expressing the concerns of non-Western cultures".[32] Shorter therefore described canon law as "the most serious instance of cultural bias among the structures of communion in the Universal Church".[33]

Studies addressing why canonical rules fail to make sense in many Latin American contexts have been on the table since the 1980s. Shortly after the promulgation of the new Code of Canon Law in 1983, José Dammert Bellido, bishop of the Diocese of Cajamarca in the Peruvian Andes, published an article on "The New Code in an Andean Diocese" in which he noted:

> It is a very difficult and serious pastoral problem to apply canonical rules in large areas with valleys and mountains between two and four thousand metres above sea level, and roads whose distances are measured in hours not kilometres, or in heavily populated areas with one or two priests. These circumstances make worthy and pious prescriptions on the rights and duties of parish priests go up in smoke.[34]

Dammert Bellido connects his criticism particularly with the parochial design of the Code, which presents as the regular concept of parish ministry that parish priests

---

[30] Berman (1993), p. 24.

[31] Shorter (1988), p. 70.

[32] Ibid., p. 69.

[33] Ibid., p. 70.

[34] Dammert Bellido (1986), p. 115.

are endowed with the parochial care of only one parish (see canon 526 §1 CIC/1983). Only when priest shortage or other reasons make it impossible to apply this model may the bishop endow a priest with the care of several adjacent parishes. In any case, both the rule and the exception prove incompatible in dioceses with huge areas and a drastic shortage of priests, as he observes:

> It should be remembered that a diocese covering an area of 15,000 square kilometres and half a million inhabitants, has twenty-six parishes, about ten of which are vacant. Either the parish priest attends to the urban population living in the parish capital, doing for them what is laid down in the Code, but completely neglecting the people living in outlying villages or scattered over the countryside: or he can embark on a rural missionary programme, only to receive complaints from the town dwellers that they have no priest to look after them.[35]

He consequently finds that the law makes impossible demands on Andean parish priests with respect to fulfilling their duties as prescribed by the Code, for instance in canons 528–530 CIC/1983; these range from abundant sacramental and liturgical duties to administrative obligations such as keeping all the parish records. In a similar vein, Missiologist Sandra Lassak cites a conversation with a Peruvian pastor, who voiced identical concerns and drew his own conclusions from it: "Canon law does not apply 3000 metres above sea level, I was told many years ago by a clergyman, a friend of mine, who had spent a long time living in the Peruvian Andes".[36] As she recounts, this priest realised that he could not follow the rules, particularly those restricting certain liturgical and pastoral duties to clerics, as adhering to these rules would have prevented him from carrying out his ministry effectively. This is a common concern in many Latin American contexts, as evidenced by the attempts of the 2019 Synod of Bishops for the Pan-Amazon region to reform the regulations on lay ministry.[37]

Dammert Bellido also sees the bishops as heads of their administration in a conflict with the expectations of the Code. Commenting on the canonical approach to administration, he attests global legislation with a narrow view of dioceses, as it apparently had modern European urban dioceses in mind when composing the canons on the diocesan curia. Many mutual duties of coordinating administration between the diocesan curias and the Roman Curia are tasks which a well-equipped urban administration might handle, but are beyond the capacities of a small curia in the Peruvian Andes: "There is a danger of getting bogged down in petty bureaucratic rules to the detriment of pastoral work".[38] Dammert Bellido goes on to explain:

> In curias which are poor in personnel and resources, in which the bishop and chancellor as well as fulfilling their own functions, take part in parish and chaplaincy work, teaching and confessions, as well as having national or even continental responsibilities, an attempt to keep in line with the rulings of superior authorities becomes an intolerable burden, unless a large freedom of spirit prevails.[39]

[35] Ibid., pp. 115–116.

[36] Lassak (2020), p. 173.

[37] Pope Francis, in any case, in his 2020 Apostolic Exhortation *Querida Amazonia* following the synod, dashed the hope that the law could be changed profoundly in the near future to meet these concerns, see Francis (2020a). Acta Apostolicae Sedis (2020), pp. 231–273.

[38] Dammert Bellido (1986), p. 113.

[39] Ibid., p. 114.

In any case, the contexts in which many regulations of global canon law seem to be somehow misplaced are much larger than the Peruvian Andes. This book wants to shed some light on these tensions between global legislation and local realities and discusses whether there is a way to address them.

1.6 Argument of this Book

The argument proceeds in nine steps. The introduction—this Chapter—has already provided some terminological clarifications and outlined the problem discussed in the book. After summarising the study's argument in this section, the discussion moves on to the hermeneutical and methodological challenges of analysing the tension between global legislation and its local implementation. It also explores in more depth how the law positions centralised and decentralised legislation, and its contribution to the creation of asymmetrical power relations between global and local agents.

Chapter 2 introduces the research field by providing an overview of the current state of global canon law in the local churches. It presents case studies of conflicts between global law and local agents. These include cases of conflict over procedural standards in ecclesiastical adjudication and the legal policies of the Apostolic See, as well as examples of how local agents respond to challenges posed by global legislation. Many of these observations were made by the author in her home country of Germany. Consequently, they are selective. Yet, they offer some insights into the intricate relationships between the Apostolic See and the local churches with regard to legislation, adjudication, and administration.

Chapter 3 describes the delicate balance that current canon law attempts to maintain between its universal claims and the cultural realities it faces. Many tensions derive from an antimodernist view of the law that struggles to engage with culture. Catholic natural law arguments, for instance, tend to prioritise the universal over the cultural. Analysing this example illustrates why contemporary canon law tends to universalise its claims and to marginalise the cultural and, with it, the plurality of the local churches, the theological value of their diversity, and its relevance for the law. Conversely, the example of natural law demonstrates that alternatives to the marginalisation of culture exist. Adopting a non-exclusive view of nature and culture allows jurisprudence to acknowledge the supernatural basis of natural law while still considering it a cultural artefact. To clarify what it means to interpret legal rules as cultural artefacts, the chapter also discusses the book's use of the term culture and explains its Geertzian approach to the concepts of culture and legal culture.

Chapter 4 analyses contemporary Catholicism in light of the cultural turn. This turn has enabled theologians to recognise the fundamental "intercultural nature of

Christianity",[40] as systematic theologian Judith Gruber explains. However, as she also recognises, theology has yet to grasp the implications of this finding and learn how to reconcile the universal Christian message with its various cultural manifestations.[41] Since the council, the magisterium has been mediating somewhat uneasily between universality and culturality, producing various approaches to inculturation in order to integrate universal Christian truths into plural ecclesiastical cultures. The chapter discusses concepts that have been developed over the last decades, ranging from early twentieth-century missiological concepts to contemporary contextual theologies. Since the Second Vatican Council, the Apostolic See has relied mostly on a neoconservative interpretation of inculturation, which promises to protect the supercultural message while allowing for careful adaptations to be made at a local level. This policy is not without its problems, as is discussed in Chaps. 5 and 6.

Chapter 5 reviews how contemporary ecclesiastical jurisprudence addresses canon law as a subject of inculturation. Particular emphasis is placed on lawmaking for the global church and how legislation is received locally. These processes are structured as the export of global rules to the local churches and are based on the inculturation approach of *translation*.[42] Lawmaking is centralised, with only limited involvement of decentralised agents. Decentralised authorities, such as the diocesan bishops, are responsible for implementing global rules within their jurisdictions. They have limited power to prevent the law from entering their local churches. Despite the doctrine of *receptio legis*, which emphasises the key role of the community in the formation of law, current legal practice pays little attention to the local churches as receivers of global rules. On the contrary, Catholics are obliged to adhere to global legislation, in accordance with the policy of command and obedience. The generation of local customary laws which oppose global rules is limited, resulting in few options for establishing alternative local regulations. These factors demonstrate that the inculturation of canon law is less sensitive to cultural influences than the term suggests and less open to the development of unique local legal traditions that reflect local cultures.

To gain a more comprehensive understanding of how the law responds to the diversity of the local churches, Chap. 6 examines how legal rules address local and cultural issues. Three perspectives in this field require enquiry. Scrutinising the rules in the Code of Canon Law that mention cultural issues reveals an ambiguous picture, showing uncertainty about what culture means for the church and its law. Similarly, it is revealing to study how legislation incorporates local concerns into the law by addressing specific local challenges, such as a shortage of priests. The idiosyncrasies of the local churches are mostly secured through a rule-and-exception policy, which allows local authorities to deviate from a global rule if it poses a significant problem for their church. Cultural issues also come into play when

---

[40] Gruber (2018), p. 14.

[41] See ibid., p. 11.

[42] With *translation*, this study refers to the use of the term common in contextual theologies, e.g. Schreiter (1985), acknowledging that there are different understandings of the term, particularly in legal discourse, see Bray (2020).

applying the law. Although the absence of a doctrine of *stare decisis* allows ecclesiastical tribunals and administration to interpret the law independently, they must apply the canonical rules of interpretation, which support a centralised methodology for deriving legal meaning. It is also instructive to review the instruments of legal flexibility through which global law responds to conflicts between centralised regulations and local demands. In their current form, these instruments, such as the widespread practice of dispensation, are designed to protect the law from fundamental contestation rather than preserve cultural idiosyncrasies.

Based on the analyses of Chaps. 5 and 6, Chap. 7 discusses the local responses to global legislation. It does so by asking whether the current stance of the church towards the inculturation of canon law is sufficient in two respects: sufficient with respect to the law, ensuring its effectiveness in the local churches; and sufficient with respect to the local churches, allowing Catholics to profit from global rules as a support for their churches. Examining these two perspectives sheds light on the reasons why canon law currently faces opposition in many local churches. Current legislation is widely non-transparent and non-participatory. The law is implemented in the local churches through asymmetrical law planting and "imposed reception".[43] This resembles asymmetrical concepts of legal transfer discussed in critical legal studies and studies on legal colonialism. John Huels seems to share this view, referring to the transfer of law into the local churches as the "imposition of a universal canon law"[44]; with systematic theologian Robert Schreiter one might speak of a paternalistic model of imposing centralist solutions onto the local churches.[45] As a result, transplants of global law are often perceived as "legal irritants"[46] in the local churches, met with various forms of non-acceptance ranging from outright rejection to "cool indifference".[47] However, even irritants can be received when they are reconstructed by the receiving group and given new meaning. In any case, with regard to canon law, the local appropriation of transplanted rules is inhibited by various factors. For instance, the lack of autonomy when interpreting rules or the widespread granting of dispensations makes it challenging for local agents to attribute a local meaning to rules.

If canon law is to be a living law that shapes ecclesial practice, this calls for a reform of current inculturation policies; Chap. 8 proposes an outline of this reform and a postcolonial revision of the law based on findings of intercultural theology. On a practical level, the scope of decentralised legislation must be expanded, granting local agents more autonomy in the creation of locally adequate rules. Fundamentally, a discussion is needed whether a uniform set of rules for the whole global church is justifiable and has a future. Taking into account the principle of subsidiarity and the autonomy of groups to legislate for themselves, the sociological

[43] A term coined by Watson (1993), p. 30.

[44] Huels (1987), p. 289.

[45] See Schreiter (1985), pp. 99–100.

[46] A term coined by Teubner (1998).

[47] Teubner (1998), p. 28.

observation that decentralised legislation increases the chances of rules finding acceptance, and the theological demand to strengthen the role of the diocesan bishops in governing their churches, there is reason to reverse the perspective. Rather than imposing uniform rules on the worldwide church through top-down legislation while allowing for some exceptions, the focus should be on decentralised legislation, allowing for the bottom-up creation of shared rules where uniform regulation is essential for the unity of the church. These shared rules must respect subsidiarity, be the result of transparent and participatory legislation, be intelligible, and invite local consent.

Finally, in Chap. 9, the book concludes by suggesting an intercultural approach to canon law and developing a glocal view of it that considers the interconnections between its global and local dynamics. Following Boaventura de Sousa Santos, it suggests that *counterhegemonic globalisation* can challenge hegemonic globalisation, offering alternative strategies to overcome the asymmetrical power relations established by traditional global politics.[48] The chapter merely outlines how this could play out for canon law. It is impossible to say more without reproducing asymmetrical patterns, since the author of this book is not an expert in predicting the outcome of a postcolonial reconstruction on canon law. These evaluations are the responsibility of decentralised agents within their own communities, taking into account their cultural beliefs and local needs. What the book offers is threefold: As a sociological study, it describes the contemporary Eurocentrism of global canon law and the conflicts arising from it. As a theological study, it presents ecclesiological reasons for challenging the hegemony of global legislation. As a study of canon law, it suggests ways in which legislation could permit greater diversity in the law while maintaining the unity of the universal church.

1.7 Homogenising Views

In any case, bearing in mind Julia Eckert's criticism, one might ask whether it makes sense to establish an analytical framework for examining the tensions arising from global canon law in the local churches. This is because, like Eckert's observation regarding human rights discourse, this is a fairly homogenising view of the conflicting sides. It presents global legislation, on the one hand, and the local churches, on the other, in terms that suggest a certain uniformity. This is not entirely appropriate. For instance, it is important to note that global canon law is not exclusively influenced by European legal thought. While lawmaking takes place under the authority of the Apostolic See, the agents involved in creating the law come from a variety of backgrounds. In the reform of the Code of Canon Law before 1983, the working groups preparing the draft law consisted of canonists and church officials from all over the globe. The Commission for the Revision of the Code was composed of

[48] See De Sousa Santos (2020).

bishops and cardinals from all continents.[49] And before 2021, non-European canonists were involved in the reform of ecclesiastical penal law, as Vatican sources convey.

Against this backdrop, an explanation is needed why it makes sense to treat global canon law as a uniform system that bears the dominant cultural imprint of the Apostolic See. This somewhat homogenising view seems justified, in any case, given that global legislation itself supports the homogeneity of the law. The Apostolic See favours the uniformity of global rules over legal diversity.[50] A uniform law is seen as protecting the unity of the church and its faith. Therefore, despite being influenced by agents from various local churches, the Apostolic See exercises centralised control over legislation to ensure legal uniformity. Experts involved in legal reforms, despite coming from different cultural backgrounds, are usually chosen from among scholars and church officials who received a Roman education and formation during their theological and legal studies. Consequently, their contributions tend to reflect a centralised perspective on law, prioritising the protection of the church's unity by maintaining the uniformity of its legislation and preventing too much variance or change. While these agents bring a variety of views on the law to the debates, the policies they advocate do not differ radically.

The priority of uniform rules over legal diversity is also reflected in the position assigned to the local churches in global canon law. In principle, the law acknowledges the ecclesiological dignity of the local churches. The Code, for instance, mentions that particular churches are the constitutive elements "in which and from which the one and only Catholic Church exists" (canon 368 CIC/1983). And it cites conciliar teaching by defining dioceses as particular churches "in which the one, holy, Catholic, and apostolic Church of Christ is truly present and operative" (canon 369 CIC/1983). However, as canonist Joseph Komonchak observes, this acknowledgement does not adequately reflect conciliar teaching:

> There are no canons in the new Code specifically on the relationship between the universal Church and the local Churches. In fact, the terms 'universal' and 'local' Church are never used. The Code prefers to use the term 'particular' Church which always means the diocese and it speaks of the 'Catholic' or of the 'whole' (*universa*) Church. The existence of the one Church 'in and out of the particular Churches' is acknowledged in a subordinate clause of c. 368; but it does not otherwise seem to have influenced the Code's ecclesiology.[51]

With regard to the Code of 1983, Komonchak therefore speaks of a "failure to express the new ecclesiological focus required by the attention to the local Church".[52] James Provost articulates a similar thought. In an article on the papal law *Pastor Bonus* on the Roman Curia, abrogated in 2022, he notes that *Pastor Bonus* pays little attention to the local churches and their ecclesiological dignity of constituting the universal church: "The document does not attempt to explain this mystery of the catholicity of the Church, a communion of particular churches which at the same

[49] See Pontifical Commission for the Revision of the Code of Canon Law (1981), pp. 5–8.

[50] E.g. Lederhilger (2000), pp. 375–387; Lüdecke (2011), pp. 54–55.

[51] Komonchak (1986), p. 114.

[52] Ibid.

time is more than the sum of its parts; rather, it takes it for granted. … But the document does consider one particular church as more significant than all the rest: the Roman church".[53] In *Pastor Bonus*, with its overemphasis on the motif of unity, the Roman church is seen to be the centre of Catholicism, whilst the other churches are regarded as the periphery.[54] This picture is deceptive: "What is at the 'center' is usually viewed as more significant, more important, indeed more truly whatever the reality may be; those things which are at the 'periphery' are secondary, marginal, not so essential to the reality itself. The connotation is that one church is at the center of the action, the others are peripheral to it".[55]And it has immediate consequences for the legal practice of the Roman Curia, which Provost analyses with regard to the Vatican's handling of issues in the local churches. In *Pastor Bonus*, as he finds, unity through centralist uniformity has triumphed over plurality.

It is notable that Pope Francis sought to counterbalance this development. His 2022 Apostolic Constitution *Praedicate Evangelium*, which replaced *Pastor Bonus*, may be read as an attempt to reform the curial structures to render them of better service to the local churches.[56] In the introduction to *Praedicate Evangelium*, the local churches play a greater role than they did in *Pastor Bonus*. Francis stressed repeatedly that the dicasteries are designed to be of help, on the one hand, to the papacy in governing the global church and protecting its unity, and, on the other hand, to the bishops and their mission to lead their churches. And he seemed aware that being of service to the churches requires the representation of the local cultures within the curia. Regulations, such as the provision that curial officials should "come from different regions of the world, as far as possible, so that the Roman Curia reflects the universality of the church",[57] attempt to give plural voices a say in curial contexts. However, it remains to be seen if diversifying curial recruitment "as far as possible" will lead to success. In this sense, reading the Apostolic Constitution is a similar experience to studying other recent papal documents. Whilst the introduction has a more synodal tone and reflects a greater awareness of the global nature of Roman Catholicism, the actual norms do not depart radically from the established structures. While they change the operation of the Roman Curia to some degree, they are not designed to alter the relationship between the curia and the local churches significantly. Hence, there is reason to doubt whether the 2022 reform will remove the dominance of centralised over decentralised structures and overcome the problematic model of centre and periphery.

Global laws such as the Code of Canon Law—and also *Praedicate Evangelium*—therefore institutionalise an imbalanced ecclesiology. In contrast to what conciliar teaching suggested, the law's primary focus is on the Roman church as one church which dominates the other local churches. This is ecclesiologically questionable

[53] Provost (1992), p. 311.

[54] See John Paul II (1988), introduction, no. 12. Acta Apostolicae Sedis (1988), p. 855.

[55] Provost (1992), p. 312.

[56] See Francis (2022). Acta Apostolicae Sedis (2022), pp. 375–455.

[57] Francis (2022), art. 14 §3. Acta Apostolicae Sedis (2022), p. 388.

and practically conflictive, as Peter Huizing observed when stating that "the issue of the local church is at the center of the institutional and cultural crisis in the Church".[58] Ladislas Orsy similarly commented on the Apostolic See's dominance over the local churches by explaining it in the light of the Hegelian dialectic, noting: "There is no need to be a Hegelian to see that humanity in general, and human institutions in particular, often develop dialectically; that is, not through uniform steady growth but by first going too far in one direction and then by moving in the opposite one".[59] Extreme political systems, such as authoritarianism or anarchy, frequently bring about progress in the form of counter-reactions which turn political constellations into their opposites, as Orsy suggests. In church, he sees the Reformation and the Tridentine reform as "centrifugal forces in particular churches" that "provoked increased centralization in the universal church".[60] Orsy sees the role of the law as supporting these changes: "Law can be instrumental in the bringing about, or in the strengthening, of such dialectical movements".[61] The law responds to these extremes by trying to correct them and in doing so often tends to overact, as he observes with regard to the example of Tridentine legislation, noting that "many of the disciplinary decrees of the Council of Trent were dialectical replies to corrupt practices in the church, or to the excesses of the Reformation; their purpose was to restore the correct balance in practice and doctrine".[62] Catholicism's current centralism is also a reaction to a fundamental loss of power in society and secular politics. Having lost the political power struggle against the modern nation states and experienced a loss of relevance in secular societies, the church has consolidated its forces in Rome in an attempt to compensate the losses in the local churches. Hence, one can understand the current legislation with its centralised accumulation of power at the Apostolic See as a response to this experience. Therefore, while it is not advisable to speak of the Apostolic See or its legal culture as monolithic entities, it seems reasonable to focus on the church's centralist legislation and to study it as one current factor of church politics.

1.8 Avoiding Essentialisations

Bearing in mind Julia Eckert's criticism not to ontologise or essentialise groups and their legal views, it is also necessary to consider whether it is feasible to speak of the local churches as if they all shared similar concerns with regard to the law. It is clearly impossible to understand the local churches as a homogenous body in conflict with global canon law. There are over 3000 Catholic ecclesiastical jurisdictions

[58] Huizing (1982), p. 268.

[59] Orsy (1992), p. 82.

[60] Ibid.

[61] Ibid.

[62] Ibid.

worldwide, spanning all continents. They are composed of multiple agents. And the legal conflicts they encounter are diverse too. For instance, the German and the Nigerian Church have different concerns regarding the law. This was evidenced by their respective responses to the liberalisation of liturgical law introduced by the Dicastery for the Doctrine of the Faith in the Declaration *Fiducia Supplicans*, which allows for liturgical blessings of homosexual couples.[63] Many German bishops applauded this decision; the President of the German Bishops' Conference expressed his gratitude to the Dicastery for moving forward in this direction.[64] In contrast, the Catholic Bishops' Conference of Nigeria criticised the change and stated that there is "no possibility in the Church of blessing same-sex unions and activities. That would go against God's law, the teachings of the Church, the laws of our nation and the cultural sensibilities of our people".[65] So neither the local churches nor their opinions on legal issues are homogeneous. One must therefore be careful not to present an overly harmonised view of the conflicts between global law and local concerns.

Yet, while their concerns differ, what is less different is that many local agents indeed experience the law as conflicting. And there are structural reasons for this, which allow researchers to identify the local churches, despite their diversity, as agents affected by global legislation. The ecclesiological imbalance and its impact on the law, as discussed in the previous section, are among the reasons for this. However, when studying the current law of the church, one can observe some cautious attempts to correct some of the asymmetries laid down in the former Code of 1917. The 1917 Code had attracted criticism for its attempt to regulate the life of the church too tightly[66] and for failing to consider the social and political idiosyncrasies of the local churches.[67] For instance, in the 1917 Code, diocesan bishops were only permitted to dispense their legal subjects from general laws after a higher authority had granted them the power to do so (see canon 81 CIC/1917). The Second Vatican Council changed this approach of concession to an approach of reservation,[68] so that the diocesan bishops acquired the authority to dispense their legal subjects regularly from global laws as well. The 1983 reform of the Code extended the bishops' rights of dispensation accordingly, so that they may now dispense their subjects from most global laws, with few exceptions.[69] In a similar vein, the reformers of the Code revised many rules of the old Code in accordance with the teaching of the Second Vatican Council and removed overly detailed regulations. The reform therefore

---

[63] See Dicastery for the Doctrine of the Faith (2023).

[64] See German Bishops' Conference (2023).

[65] Catholic Bishops' Conference of Nigeria (2023).

[66] E.g. Shorter (1988), p. 167.

[67] E.g. Althaus (2020), p. 331.

[68] See Second Vatican Council (1965a), no. 8b. Acta Apostolicae Sedis (1966), p. 676.

[69] Exceptions being procedural and penal laws and those laws the dispensation of which is expressly reserved to the Apostolic See or another ecclesiastical authority (see canon 87 §1 CIC/1983).

downsized the law to release the local churches to some extent from the grip of centralised law.

It also sought to give decentralised legislation more authority in accordance with the principle of subsidiarity. According to church teaching, subsidiarity is a core principle guiding social organisations. Pope Pius XI, in his 1931 Encyclical *Quadragesimo Anno*, had emphasised that it is a demand of justice that all aims which can be achieved at a lower level of a social body should be left at this level and not handed over to a superior agent: "Just as it is gravely wrong to take from individuals what they can accomplish by their own initiative and industry and give it to the community, so also it is an injustice and at the same time a grave evil and disturbance of right order to assign to a greater and higher association what lesser and subordinate organisations can do".[70] The pope went on to exhort his readers to follow the principle of subsidiarity when organising any social bodies. The church as a social body is consequently bound to implement subsidiarity, with consequences for its legislation. Reacting to this, the Pontifical Commission for the Revision of the Code referred to subsidiarity in their "Principles guiding the revision of the Code",[71] which directed the reform procedures before 1983. This embedded subsidiarity as a principle in the reform process and endowed the reformers with the task of realising it in the new law. Accordingly, the Preface to the reformed Code emphasises subsidiarity as one major guideline and target of the reform.[72]

In any case, studying the 1983 Code reveals it to be less concerned with subsidiarity than its Preface suggests. Unlike the Preface, the legal rules do not mention subsidiarity once. Moreover, they do not implement subsidiary mechanisms to any great extent. One can discover this, above all, in the regulations on the relationship between global and particular law, as reflected in constitutional law in the supreme legislator's—the pope's—broad and the local legislators'—mostly the diocesan bishops'—restricted authority. One might detect a reason for this also in the Preface to the Code. The Preface, namely, counters the demand for more subsidiarity with the concern to protect the unity of the church by providing it with a uniform body of rules: "In virtue of this principle [of subsidiarity, author's addition] one may defend the appropriateness and even the necessity of providing for the welfare especially of individual institutes through particular laws and the recognition of a healthy autonomy for particular executive power while legislative unity and universal and general law are observed".[73] Instead of emphasising the value of subsidiary legislation, the Preface places emphasis on the tension between decentralised and centralised legislation, whilst attributing global law with the function of protecting the unity of the church. It refers to the danger of *disgregation* as a threat to this unity, warning of the

---

[70] Pius XI (1931), no. 79. Acta Apostolicae Sedis (1931), p. 203.

[71] Pontifical Commission for the Revision of the Code of Canon Law (1969), no. 5. Communicationes (1969), pp. 80–82.

[72] See Preface to the Code of Canon Law (1983). Acta Apostolicae Sedis (1983), p. XXII.

[73] Ibid.

"danger of division into or the establishment of national churches".[74] Whilst musing about "a healthy 'decentralization'"[75]—an expression which Pope Francis adopted—[76] the Preface restricts particular legislation to those matters "not necessary for the unity of the discipline of the universal Church".[77] In consequence, a more subsidiary organisation of the church and its law has not progressed much since the times of the old Code.

Adding to this restricted role of local regulation is that the 1983 Code continues to attribute particular laws with a minor status compared to global law, similar to the old Code. Whilst global regulations are less dense than they used to be and consequently provide some space for local law,[78] they also tend to interfere with decentralised legislation and even tend to suppress the emergence of local laws. The Code avoids the general subjugation of particular law to global law, by protecting earlier particular laws from later global laws in those cases in which the new legislation does not explicitly state that those particular laws have been abrogated (see canon 20 CIC/1983). However, when the Code itself came into force in 1983, it abrogated all particular laws contrary to the codified provisions, unless expressly provided for otherwise (see canon 6 §1 no. 2 CIC/1983). The same happened to all customary laws contrary to the Code (see canon 5 §1 CIC/1983). Centenary or immemorial customs were accorded protection. However, the bar was set high to prevent new customary laws from developing in the future by disallowing the revival of any reprobated customs (see canon 5 §1 CIC/1983) and by setting extensive periods of time for customs to receive the force of law (see canon 26 CIC/1983). By regularly requiring observance for thirty continuous years before acquiring the force of law, the current standard is high for a custom to become customary law.

This priority of global law over local legislation is reflected in ecclesiastical constitutional law. Diocesan bishops have to support compliance to global laws in their churches, as each bishop, as part of his service to the unity of the universal church, "is bound to promote the common discipline of the whole Church and therefore to urge the observance of all ecclesiastical laws" (canon 392 §1 CIC/1983). Legislators below the supreme legislator, such as the diocesan bishops, cannot validly issue a law contrary to higher law (see canon 135 §2 CIC/1983). Diocesan bishops and those who preside over other communities of the faithful are divested of their legislative authority in matters reserved to the supreme authority of the church or to another ecclesiastical authority by papal command (see canon 381 CIC/1983). Even greater restrictions pertain to the bishops' conferences, which are competent solely to legislate in those matters in which the global law or the Apostolic See grant them

[74] Ibid.

[75] Ibid.

[76] See Francis (2015). Acta Apostolicae Sedis (2015), 1143.

[77] Preface to the Code of Canon Law (1983). Acta Apostolicae Sedis (1983), p. XXII.

[78] See Althaus (2020), pp. 332–333.

explicit legislative authority (see canon 455 §1 CIC/1983).[79] Laws issued by bishops' conferences require the Apostolic See's review before entering into force (see §2). One might go on to extend the list of examples where the law prioritises centralised over decentralised legislation by including other legislative bodies, such as the particular councils (see canon 445 CIC/1983). However, it seems that the asymmetry between global and local legislation has been sufficiently proven.

These power asymmetries established by canon law between centralised and decentralised agents makes it possible to identify the local churches as both agents of the law and entities affected by global legislation. In line with Julia Eckert's warning, they cannot be considered as a single homogeneous body of institutions, nor as entities with similar legal interests. Both the churches and their concerns regarding global legislation vary widely. However, given the structural nature of the asymmetry between global legislation and the local churches, it seems reasonable to discuss their relationship more generally, while bearing in mind the need to avoid over-generalisation.

From a social studies perspective, one might think of anthropologist Sally Merry's more generalising description of the *vernacularisation* of women's rights in diverse Asian and Pacific countries. She found that through their process of translation into the diverse cultures, human rights remain a somewhat alien yet successful concept for fighting violence against women: "It is not their ability to blend into preexisting cultural systems. Adopting human rights locally does not build on a preexisting similarity of cultural beliefs any more than introducing bureaucracy or traffic lights does. But proponents do dress them in familiar costumes".[80] There is no full indigenisation of human rights, as Merry observes, nevertheless they can take on a certain form acceptable to the local agents so that they are integrated into local practice. This similar structure in which diverse cultures respond—very differently—to transnational ideas, as she notes, allows us to speak about these processes in a general way.[81] Hence, it is with the same caution that one can speak about the relationship between global canon law and the local churches, without assuming that the tension inherent in this relation is the same in all places. Yet, as there is a tension in many encounters between global rules and local practice, it is possible to make some generalising observations.

1.9 State of Research

Canon law, as a specific legal tradition, is an example of the challenges connected with cross-cultural law in general. This is reflected in the literature on which this book draws, including contributions of the humanities, social sciences,[82] and legal

---

[79] On the bishops' conferences' legislative function for the local churches e.g. de Mûelenaere (1985b), pp. 46–49.

[80] Merry (2009), p. 268.

[81] See ibid., p. 297.

[82] In general e.g. Merry (1991); Merry (2009); Eckert (2010); with a particular focus on Roman Catholicism e.g. Angrosino (1994); Joncheray (1997).

studies, particularly from international law, comparative law, critical legal studies, and the extensive debates on legal universalism, legal pluralism, legal transfer, and legal colonialism.[83] Its analysis of the status of global canon law following the Second Vatican Council focuses largely on literature from the field of Catholic theology. As proposed by Bernard Lonergan, the council helped theology to develop from Neo-Scholasticism—with its tendency to refer to the supertemporal and unchangeable—and move towards an understanding of the church more in terms of its historicity and culturality.[84] Subsequently, over the past decades, much has been written about theology and culture after the council. Literature on inculturation and intercultural theology is legend. Many books have influenced this study, some even profoundly.[85] It is interesting to note, however, that many books which deal with the church and inculturation ignore the issue of canon law completely or touch upon it only briefly.[86] Yet, even contributions which leave the law aside have something to say about the challenges of inculturating canon law in a global church. Studies on the inculturation of the liturgy after the Second Vatican Council, for instance, are also instructive with regard to the law.[87] They allude to the top-down approach of *translation* with which the Roman-Catholic liturgies are implemented in the local churches all over the globe, protecting the unity of the Roman Rite by allowing for only minor local variances. Whilst books on the liturgical reform after the council barely even mention the law, they are a rich source of insight for understanding the law in the light of the paradigm of inculturation as an object of translation. On the question of whether this paradigm is appropriate, there is also much to be learned from current debates on theological ethics, which discuss whether and how a global ethics can be developed for a worldwide church.[88]

Whilst there is a rich literature on faith and inculturation, much less has been written about canon law in the light of the paradigm of "law as culture". However,

---

[83] Examples of studies influential on this book include Watson (1993); Robertson (1997); Legrand (1997); Burgess (1997); Teubner (1998); Örücü (2002); Smits (2003); Anghie (2006); Menski (2006); Foljanty (2015); Tamanaha (2017); de Sousa Santos (2020).

[84] E.g. Lonergan (1972); Lonergan (2016).

[85] E.g. Schreiter (1985); Shorter (1988); Bevans (2002); Gruber (2018).

[86] One exception is the edited collection Miñambres (2019). Most articles from this volume study canon law through a historical lens to ponder the cultural background of the canonical legal tradition and of the two codifications of Latin canon law of 1917 and 1983. Some of the articles also examine cultural conflicts deriving from the secular context of modern canon law, while others focus on ecumenical and interfaith legal encounters. Most interesting for this book are those articles which address the impact of canon law in different ecclesiastical cultures. Some of these are referenced later on in this section.

As a monograph from systematic theology which refers to canon law, I want to mention by way of an example systematic theologian Evelyn Monteiro's *Church and Culture* (Monteiro [2004]), in which the author briefly mentions the law by pointing at the Code of 1917 (pp. 19, 56). For Monteiro, the 1917 Code presents a highly centralistic law, due to the centralised dynamic of the *societas perfecta* ideology, insensitive to cultural issues. Monteiro, in any case, refrains from commenting on the current law with respect to cultural issues.

[87] E.g. Chupungco (1992).

[88] E.g. Schockenhoff (2007); Hogan and Heyer (2019); Keenan (2020).

some contributions deserve mention, such as John Huels's article "Interpreting Canon Law in Diverse Cultures",[89] one of the few works which examines canon law in the light of the findings of cultural studies. Whilst Huels's article is not flawless from the view of contemporary cultural studies, it was perhaps the first endeavour by a canonist to address canon law as culture in a profound way and to identify the need to establish a hermeneutics for canon law which gives consideration to cultural diversity: "The challenge remains for canonical science to develop an effective cross-cultural hermeneutic, and for the Church at large to develop a cross-cultural consciousness and sensitivity, which foster cultural pluralism and change and enable Christians of all cultures to respond in their own authentic ways to their gospel vocation".[90] One more recent contribution to this topic is an article by Burkhard Berkmann which discusses inculturation with regard to canon law. It is interesting to note, though, how the article avoids the dark side of this topic by focusing on inculturation merely in the context of mission and evangelisation. Nevertheless, at the beginning of his article, Berkmann makes some remarks about the challenge of understanding canon law with regard to inculturation:

> In accordance with the doctrine of the Roman Catholic Church, this church is not restricted to a specific culture. On the contrary, it is open to all cultures and is able to transcend boundaries. This in turn affects its legal system. It has to implement the principle of subsidiarity in order for local specificities to be taken into consideration. The Catholic Church is not a monolithic block. Rather it consists of several autonomous churches. The biggest amongst them is the Western Church, also designated as the 'Latin Church'. In addition, there are a further 22 Eastern Catholic Churches, that follow their own rites and traditions and are connected to specific cultures. Accordingly, there is a code for the Latin Church, the 'Code of Canon Law' and a code for the Eastern Churches, the 'Code of Canons of the Eastern Churches'. Both codes of Canon Law only provide a framework, which for instance, is then fleshed out by the legislation passed by the bishops for each one of the particular churches. Thus, the cultural diversity within the Catholic Church is reflected in the highly differentiated legal system. Furthermore, some regulations exist, such as those applying to ethnic and linguistic minorities, that provide for their own individual pastoral structure.[91]

Thus, the author promotes the frame-like structure of the Codes as the key instrument of subsidiarity which allows for particular rules to grow to protect the cultural idiosyncrasies of the plural churches of the West and East. He finds this thought explicitly articulated in canon 584 §2 of the Eastern Code. Here, the legislator clarifies that evangelisation needs to protect the cultures of the evangelised with the purpose of enabling the Gospel to express itself in their cultures, that is in their own liturgies, their own sacred art, and in their own law. Berkmann concludes his article by noting: "Thus, the Canon law is, on the one hand, part of a culture and on the other hand, it allows peaceful co-existence of diverse cultures and promotes respect for all cultures".[92] And he adds: "Catholic Canon Law allows for quite a high level of cultural diversity and thus becomes a tool for the management of cultural

---

[89] See Huels (1987).

[90] Ibid., p. 290.

[91] Berkmann (2016), p. 30.

[92] Ibid., p. 38.

diversity".[93] While the observation that canon law is sensitive to the plural cultures of the local churches and allows for the growth of local laws with a high-level of diversity is debatable, the article recognises that canon law is a cultural artefact. Support for exploring this matter also comes from much that Ladislas Orsy has written on law and its reality between Roman centralism and local Catholicism.[94] Other canonists have devoted attention to the relationship between ecclesiastical universal law and particular law and have discussed it critically.[95] They have criticised the domination of the universal perspective with its tendency to ignore or override local idiosyncrasies. For instance, canonist Severin Lederhilger tackled the question of whether canon law should pay more attention to the local churches and demanded the development of what he called a *contextual law*, laying emphasis on local synodal structures and locally established lay ministries.[96] In suggesting that the term *global law* replace the term universal law when speaking of ecclesiastical laws pertaining to the global church, this book makes a terminological choice that canonist Norbert Lüdecke has made before. He published an article in which he posed the question whether a uniform global Catholic law is essential for Catholicism.[97]

Other contributions focus of the reception of the law, particularly the Code of 1983, in the local churches,[98] for instance by discussing specific problems deriving from the application of the law in certain local churches. Of particular help are those studies which show that tensions deriving from global law in the local churches often parallel the boundaries between legal cultures, as in those cases where civil canon law permeates into common law cultures.[99] Other contributions focus on specific conflicts deriving from certain canonical matters, such as canonical marriage law or the procedural law of the nullity procedures, when applied in the local churches.[100] Some of these studies merely note how strongly canon law resonates with certain cultures, for instance by pointing at the impact of reverential fear for marriage nullity between Indian Christians,[101] at canonical rules adequate to meet Japanese concerns,[102] or by collecting how the Roman Rota decides marriage cases

[93] Ibid.

[94] E.g. Orsy (1969); Orsy (1984); Orsy (1995).

[95] E.g. Krämer (1999); Pree (1999).

[96] See Lederhilger (2000); Philipp Thull borrowed this term and the idea presented by Lederhilger: see Thull (2024).

[97] See Lüdecke (2011).

[98] E.g. Dammert Bellido (1986), and also other contributions from the same volume, such as Bwana (1986); Mwaungulu (1996); Mwiti (2015); Pudumai Doss (2019), and other contributions from the same volume, such as Betengne (2019); Salinas Araneda (2019).

[99] For insights into cultural frictions between the Australian legal experience and Roman Catholic canon law e.g. Robinson (1983); for observations with regard to the United States e.g. Shannon (1985); Beal (1996); Martens (2019).

[100] E.g. Robitaille (1999).

[101] See Marattil (2009).

[102] See LaBelle (2002).

from Asia.[103] Others reveal disagreements and collisions. South African canonist Marc de Mûelenaere, for instance, in his dissertation on the canonical implications of marital fidelity among the Bantu, discusses canonical marriage and procedural law with regard to a certain Catholic population of South Africa and its different view of marriage.[104] These studies are important from a comparative point of view insofar as they show how certain canonical rules when entering the local churches collide with legal, moral, or social norms effective in these contexts. Most studies, in any case, refrain from criticising the hegemonic structure of global canon law in general and focus merely on those rules which create conflicts, either suggesting an awareness campaign in the local churches in favour of making canon law more accepted, or proposing a modified application of those laws in cases of cultural incompatibility. Some applaud the law as a unifier, serving a plural global church as a guarantee of unity.[105] Hence, most contributions do not challenge the power imbalances inherent in global legislation. This book seeks to explore these asymmetrical structures. In examining how global laws operate in the local churches, it attempts to describe the mechanisms at work to submit the plural churches to a uniform body of rules and the responses and counter-reactions developed in the local churches. From these dynamics, it is possible to see the limits of understanding canon law in terms of a binary of the *global* versus the *local*. As an alternative, the study of the complex processes between the global ambitions of Catholicism and its local representations proposes a *glocal* view of the law, which examines canon law through the lens of its local mechanisms and effects.

[103] See Mendonça (1995).

[104] See de Mûelenaere (1985a); see also de Mûelenaere (1985b).

[105] E.g. Otaduy Guerin (2018); Otaduy Guerin (2019).

Chapter 2
An Exploration of Current Conflicts

The following chapter is a collection of cross-cultural conflicts related to canon law. It presents some of the author's observations, primarily from her native German context, as well as from international contexts in which she has worked as a scholar. Consequently, it does not offer a comprehensive overview of the current state of global canon law. There are many more and very different experiences that canonists, church officials, administrative professionals, and legal laypeople from all over the globe might contribute. However, commencing with some of the author's findings gives a first impression of the variety of cross-cultural challenges connected with contemporary canonical legislation and legal practice. These examples will provide a starting point for collecting further examples presented by other scholars and for discussing the structural reasons underlying these conflicts.

2.1 Procedural Standards

Many of the current tensions between the Apostolic See and the local churches are rooted in culture clashes based on opposing understandings of how justice is served best in terms of procedural rules. In many churches, these controversies originate from differing procedural standards in secular and ecclesiastical administration and adjudication. Being familiar with secular procedures, many Catholics demand similar standards in ecclesiastical proceedings. As a consequence, their reception of ecclesiastical procedures is critical whenever these differ from their secular counterparts to any significant extent. These conflicts are not new. Canonist John Beal has shown that procedural standards were already at the heart of disputes between the US-American bishops and their clergy in the nineteenth century, when the United States was still a mission country.[1] The clerics demanded from their bishops due

[1] See Beal (1996), pp. 51–52.

J. Hahn, *The Cultures of Canon Law*, Law and Religion in a Global Context 6,
https://doi.org/10.1007/978-3-032-14812-4_2

process of law—as common in secular procedures—whenever the bishops prosecuted clerical misconduct. The bishops, on the contrary, were reluctant to give up the degree of flexibility they enjoyed when treating these cases and even undermined the procedure established by the Congregation for the Propagation of the Faith. Beal has an explanation for this phenomenon. He believes that the status of the churches as entities of private law according to US-American law supported a certain business-like approach among bishops in the way they governed their dioceses. The bishops had become accustomed to this form of church leadership, as Beal concludes: "Thus, it is not surprising that bishops viewed efforts by the Propaganda to introduce canonical protections for the rights of priests with the same hostility with which businesses greeted governmental intervention in private employment practices".[2]

This is certainly different in Europe, where the churches were and are frequently treated by the states as public institutions. Here, the disputes over different procedural standards in church and state tend to arise from the churches being public or quasi-public institutions. They must therefore accept constant comparison with the state and are considered responsible for providing their members with similar procedural standards as common in state law. Recent examples show that many conflicts originate in the procedural right to be heard. Here, ecclesiastical procedural law differs from what is common in the procedural rules of many states. Two examples of controversies between German Catholics and the Apostolic See reveal these dissimilarities and their potential for conflict. The first example is a case which evolved between the diocesan bishop of the German Diocese of Regensburg and the lay organisations of his diocese in 2005–06. The then-diocesan bishop of Regensburg, Gerhard Ludwig Müller (who later became the Prefect of the Congregation for the Doctrine of the Faith), had reorganised the bodies of lay participation in his diocese in 2005, thereby restricting the laypeople's rights to participate in ecclesiastical decision making. One Catholic affected by this regulation, Johannes Grabmeier, appealed to the Roman Curia against the bishop's reform, taking legal recourse to claim his rights (see canon 1737 CIC/1983). This recourse was unsuccessful. In 2006, the Congregation for the Clergy reaffirmed the bishop's decision.[3] Following the events, Grabmeier wrote a book revealing his frustration with the curia's decision and its procedural standards.[4] In particular, he expressed his discontent with his treatment as a plaintiff, above all with the congregation's refusal to talk to him personally. In his book, he describes the curia as protecting the official church, immunising it against the church members' claims, disallowing individual Catholics a right to speak up and to explain their position in person.

A similar complaint was raised in another case which serves as a second example. In May 2019, the Apostolic Signatura acquitted a priest and high-ranking

[2] Ibid., p. 55.

[3] See Congregation for the Clergy (2006). Archiv für katholisches Kirchenrecht (2006), pp. 156–158.

[4] See Grabmeier (2012).

official of the Congregation for the Doctrine of the Faith from the charge of having sexually harassed a penitent, a former member of a religious order, in the context of the sacrament of penance; the alleged offence, *crimen sollicitationis*, is a major crime under canon law (see 1385 CIC/1983). The news of the priest's acquittal was received critically by many Catholics and the general public in the German-speaking dioceses. However, criticism centred less on the fact that the priest had been acquitted, and more on the procedure that had brought about the verdict. Many voices expressed disapproval that the Signatura had passed its sentence through a body consisting exclusively of priests and that it had failed to hear the alleged victim personally. This course of action accords to the procedural standards of the administrative penal procedure. In cases against priests, it is standard to entrust only priests with the investigation and decision.[5] The alleged victims are not considered to be parties in the procedures; it is therefore not a requirement to involve them personally. Whilst victims and witnesses are regularly invited to testify in regular penal trials, this is not necessarily the case in administrative procedures, where the officials investigating and deciding the case collect whatever evidence they find sufficient to decide the case (see canons 1717 §1, 1718 §1 no. 3, 1720 CIC/1983). In the case mentioned, the alleged victim, according to her own statement, had initially been invited to testify in person, but the invitation had been withdrawn two days before the scheduled hearing. In its place, she contributed a written statement. This evidently seemed sufficient to the Signatura to decide the case. The alleged victim, for her part, was not content with this approach to the investigation. She accused the congregation of having violated her right to be heard, calling the verdict "embarrassing evidence of a deficient legal culture in church".[6] Her assessment was supported by many canonists; one German canonist criticised the procedure for its potential to undermine the Catholics' trust in ecclesiastical adjudication.[7] This view was also widely supported in the public debates. One may read a journalist's commentary, covering the story for the church magazine of the Dioceses of Fulda, Limburg, and Mainz, as a typical reaction. The journalist concluded her article by posing three rhetorical questions:[8] First, she asked how it could still be justified to conduct proceedings without hearing both sides; second, if there is a credible explanation for why only priests are allowed to return verdicts on priests; third, if it is adequate for a tribunal to refrain from publishing its verdicts. The journalist answered all of these three questions negatively. She concluded by noting that verdicts such as the one discussed justify public opinion in its belief that the church is an unjust place.

[5] For the legal basis at that time, see Congregation for the Doctrine of the Faith (2010), nos. 10–14. Acta Apostolicae Sedis (2010), pp. 425–426; for the current legal basis, see Congregation for the Doctrine of the Faith (2021b), no. 13.

[6] Original quote: "ein beschämendes Zeugnis für die mangelnde Rechtskultur in der Kirche", quoted by Lehnen (2019).

[7] See ibid.

[8] See ibid.

2.2 Limited Subsidiarity

Another example from Germany alludes to the disagreements that can arise from differences between centralised and decentralised regulations and the centralist policies of the Apostolic See that impact local churches. In 2019, the Bishop of Trier issued a law on the organisation of parishes in his diocese introducing major structural reform in response to the increasing lack of diocesan priests.[9] His legislation foresaw drastically reducing the number of parishes in his diocese and allowing for teams of clerics and laypeople to lead the parishes. One month later, the Prefect of the Congregation for the Clergy sent a letter to the bishop, informing him that following some priests' and laypeople's hierarchical recourse to the dicastery, he could not proceed with his reform (see canon 1737 §3 CIC/1983).[10] Adding to this intervention, the Congregation for the Clergy in 2020 published an instruction generally relating to the organisation of parishes. The instruction obviously relates to Trier and similar situations in other German dioceses,[11] yet it dealt with the issue of parish reform in a more general way.[12] In this instruction, the congregation strictly pointed to the global rules on the organisation of parishes and on the role of the priests in leading the parishes, urging the diocesan bishops to abide by the law when intending reforms.

The instruction prompted an outcry among many German Catholics, among bishops, clerics, and laypeople alike. Reacting to the German bishops' protest, the Congregation for the Clergy invited them to come to Rome and to meet with the curial officials in charge. The President of the German Bishops' Conference in turn accepted this invitation but suggested including the president and vice-president of the Catholic lay organisation of the Central Committee of German Catholics (ZdK), with the argument that the instruction pertains to the laity as much as to the clergy. The dicastery refused to accept the proposal. In a letter to the President of the German Bishops' Conference, the Prefect of the Congregation for the Clergy argued that as the instruction primarily addressed the bishops, it would be more suitable to speak to them alone. It goes without saying how the German Catholics and the German public received his answer. Even *katholisch.de*, the online news portal of the German Bishops' Conference, posted a critical article with a headline reading: "Cardinal Stella [the then-prefect of the dicastery] does not want to talk about the instruction on parishes with laypeople".[13]

These events of 2019–20 allude to a number of issues concerning the church in Germany—and probably elsewhere too. For instance, they show how weak the position of subsidiarity and decentralised legislation is in church. Following current canon law, the Apostolic See may easily correct a bishop's legislation for his

---

[9] See Diocesan Bishop of Trier (2019).

[10] See Prefect of the Congregation for the Clergy (2019).

[11] The original document was in fact published in German.

[12] See Congregation for the Clergy (2020).

[13] Neumann (2020).

diocese; and it evidently has no scruples in doing so. Also, in a similar vein, the Roman dicasteries do not hesitate to correct bishops' conferences, as another example shows. In 2020, the Prefect of the Congregation for the Doctrine of the Faith wrote to the President of the German Bishops' Conference to inform him that the Apostolic See did not support the decision of the German bishops to allow Catholics and Protestants to share communion,[14] a decision that had been made in anticipation of the German Ecumenical Church Convention in 2021. The dicastery requested that the bishops wait for further studies and instructions applicable to the entire church before publishing their own rules. Although the German bishops acknowledged the need for general clarification, they also emphasised the importance of continuing the ecumenical process. What was striking and new, however, was their open and indignant reaction to these Vatican interventions, many of them closing ranks with the laity to protest centralist politics. This episcopal change in tune included the publication of the Apostolic See's correspondence. While Roman rebukes used to be kept hidden in bishops' poison cabinets in the past, the President of the German Bishops' Conference published the letter which he had received from the Prefect of the Congregation for the Doctrine of the Faith on the conference's website. This new transparency in addressing conflicts with the Apostolic See deserves scholarly attention as one example of how local churches respond to the Vatican's centralist legal policies.

2.3 "Allora facciamo così"

A further source of conflict are different views of the law, as another case illustrates. A few years ago, the author of this book had a meeting with a German bishop. The meeting was unrelated to the topic of this study, but they soon started to talk about the current status of canon law and about a legal conflict the bishop had experienced. He had issued a new law for his diocese, responding to a pressing local need for regulation. However, his legislation did not fully align with global canon law. It did not conflict with it to any great extent either, but did not fully accord with it. Perhaps it would be more accurate to say that the new local law diverged from a certain Vatican *interpretation* of global law. From the bishop's point of view, his legislation had been a necessary decision meeting the needs of his church. However, not all affected Catholics received the news well. A small group complained to a Roman dicastery. Their protest moved the Apostolic See to dismiss the new law. In trying to understand this interference and to avoid further interventions into diocesan legislation, the bishop decided to travel to Rome to discuss the issue with the Vatican official in charge. He emphasised how desperate he was before the meeting with the official as he had no idea how to proceed with the matter after the Apostolic See's rejection. However, contrary to his expectations, the talk with the Vatican

[14] See Prefect of the Congregation for the Doctrine of the Faith (2020).

official went fairly well. After the bishop had explained his intentions, the official nodded amicably and instantaneously brought up a legal solution: "*Non è un problema, Eccellenza, facciamo così*..." He assured the bishop that he would procure for him all necessary dispensations from global canon law so that the bishop could legislate according to the specific demands of his diocese without violating global rules.

Analysing the situation, outsiders may wonder why the Apostolic See had stopped the diocesan legislation in the first place. And they may wonder why the dicastery intervened to come up with the same result, a specific regulation for the bishop's diocese to meet the needs of his church. Yet, whilst the outcome might be the same, the means of approaching it are different, as the bishop himself observed. The new regulation might be the same as the initial version, but it is no longer based on his independent acting as a legislator. Instead, it results from his successful negotiation with the Roman Curia and from the concession granted to him by the Apostolic See. This approach binds the local authorities closely to Rome. It weakens their role as legislators and strengthens the Apostolic See's power. This is a peculiar situation, from an ecclesiological as well as from a legal point of view. From the point of ecclesiology, it seems odd that diocesan bishops as proper pastors of their dioceses have to seek the support of a third party to handle the regulative needs of their dioceses. From the perspective of the law, particularly ecclesiastical constitutional law and the laws on ecclesiastical offices, it is puzzling that the diocesan bishops who are endowed with all ordinary, proper, and immediate *legislative* power to govern their churches (see canons 381 §1, 391 §1 CIC/1983) are constrained by an *administrative* authority when doing so. The curia makes use of their administrative power to allow the bishops to depart from global law once this seems necessary to care for the specific needs of a local church. This modus operandi is somehow at odds with ecclesiastical power theory. However, one might find it well suited to protect the unity of global canon law. By preventing local legislators from creating laws that are in conflict with global rules (or with a certain curial *interpretation* of these rules), this approach preserves the uniformity of the law. Yet, whenever an urgent need demands local legislation to depart from global law, the Apostolic See can still provide local authorities with some flexibility, for instance by granting dispensation.

The bishop in the mentioned case was well aware of this structural dimension. And he was aware of how the Apostolic See had corrected him—not by changing his regulation but by giving him a lecture on authority. Most interestingly, in any case, this finding was not what bothered him most. With regard to the result, he expressed relief that everything had worked out well for his diocese. Yet, he was also wondering how to explain the decision to the local Catholics and the general public. "You can't possibly explain that to the people",[15] he mused: "We simply do not do things that way over here. It just does not seem right to the people. They want

[15] Direct quotations here and in the following are taken from the author's memory protocol of the conversation which she wrote down a day after the meeting based on her notes taken during the meeting.

clear and reliable laws, not Roman concessions". He agreed with the author's suggestion that many German Catholics are currently particularly sensitive to "*gutsherrliches Entscheiden*", decisions made in a lordly manner with an absolutist flavour. This criticism is not restricted to particularly liberal circles. It includes *katholisch.de*, the online news portal of the German Bishops' Conference. Here, the Vatican's opaque approach to decision making is frequently criticised. One author called the Vatican a "slow and non-transparent … system", where one hand does not know what the other is doing, or even where this non-transparency is a systemic feature enabling absolutist rule. The author concludes: "This would be all right maybe for a tiny principality of the eighteenth century, but it is fully inappropriate for a world church of the twenty-first century—and unprofessional".[16]

In the mentioned case, the bishop found it troublesome that the legal solution for his diocese proved less to be the result of reliable rules and procedures and more the result of lucky coincidence. Without his own education in Rome, which provided him with fluent Italian and some knowledge of the curia's conventions, he could not have resolved the conflict easily. "You need to know the culture to survive there", he acknowledged. His story could have ended quite differently without his acquaintance with the cultural signs and codes of curial language and protocol—namely with a full-stop embargo of diocesan law, leaving him incapable of procuring a vital regulation for his diocese. Recognising this, in any case, the bishop seemed less proud of himself and more worried for others. He deemed it virtually impossible that any other local bishop with a similar legal problem could have reached a comparable solution without possessing proficient Italian language skills. He found this problematic, as it conflicts with the idea of equality under the law. If an identical problem does not receive an identical solution because local agents are more or less capable of negotiating with the Apostolic See, law becomes a matter of diplomacy, an approach highly incompatible with a modern understanding of law.

2.4 When in Rome…

To show that these conflicts are not merely a matter of German sensitivities, the author wants to provide a further example of a similar disagreement with the Apostolic See's legal practices, as reported to her by a fellow canonist from a different cultural background. As a legal expert in charge of a major procedure of her church, this canonist had to undertake legal business with the Apostolic See. Her national bishops' conference had appointed her with conducting the procedure in collaboration with the offices of the Apostolic See in charge. As an experienced legal professional, she felt the pressure of her official mission, but also empowered to fulfil her duty and to get everything done in due time, as she retold. However, this

[16] Original quote: "Das wäre für ein winziges Fürstentum im 18. Jahrhundert vielleicht noch in Ordnung, für eine Weltkirche im 21. Jahrhundert ist das völlig unangemessen—und unprofessionell", Hartmann (2021).

proved to be more challenging than she had expected, as she found herself in the awkward position of being highly dependent on the Vatican officials' willingness to support her case, whilst they were in no hurry to do so. Over the first months, she could not move the respective Vatican officials to respond to her mails or answer the phone. Finding it impossible to achieve anything from a distance, she then relocated to Rome. However, this did not solve her problems. Despite being a distinguished academic, as a woman—and therefore excluded from the higher clergy's circles—she still found it difficult to get through to the Vatican clergy to support her project. In contrast to her expectations, the Roman Curia is not merely an administrative agency following the technical rules of administration, but an aristocratic institution which abides by the rules governing the holding of court. In court, one does not get through to the men in charge without access to the courtiers. Thus, she developed a workaround, as she shared with a smile. Her strategy was to hook up with some *Eccellenze* and *Eminenze* to get into the vital circles, using higher clergy as door openers. Hence, she attached herself to a cardinal or a bishop and dragged her chaperones along with her to meet the key persons. And she also urged these cardinals and bishops to praise her project as especially dear to them in front of the officials in charge. Once she and her request had gained some "eminent" importance in the respective officials' eyes, everything proceeded smoothly.

Her story reduced the author to tears of laughter. Her fellow canonist is an excellent narrator. However, they both agreed that some parts of her experience are only funny when told light-heartedly and in retrospect. Being raised in a culture where equality between genders but also between classes is of a high value, the canonist was particularly appalled by the open display of inequality which she had encountered in the Vatican. As a woman, she was upset by the fact that her sex had proved to be an obstacle in fulfilling her duty despite her official authorisation. As a layperson, she was appalled to find that being excluded from the clerical circles had proved to be a hindrance too. As a professional canonist, she was startled to discover that dealing with the Apostolic See proved to be less about what you know and more about whom you know. Like the bishop mentioned in the previous section, she was astonished to find how profoundly the success of her mission did not depend on knowing the law and following the legal procedures but on her cultural knowledge and language skills. Despite the existence of an established legal procedure, she believed that she would have failed had she been less determined to decipher the cultural signs and Vatican codes and use them in her favour.

2.5 What is Law, Actually?

Both the canonist and the bishop who negotiated his legislation with the Apostolic See were successful because they played by the curial rules. So many misunderstandings between the Apostolic See and local churches can be attributed to differing cultural expectations. However, the bishop's case reveals that there is more to these disagreements. His analysis of the underlying problems is noteworthy, as he offered an interpretation of his encounter with the curial official, suggesting that a different interpretation of the nature of the law lay at the root of their conflict. From his experience with the Roman legal culture, his conclusion was that the Apostolic See has a specific understanding of what the law is—an understanding which differs from what most German Catholics think: "They [the curia, addition by the author] have clear principles. It is not so much about the statutes themselves; it is about the principles behind them. These principles are clear. They are stable, fairly unchangeable. But when applying them, it is possible to adapt them to cover very different and very specific situations". Hence, the legal understanding of the Apostolic See perceives of the law more as a system of principles than as a system of rules enclosed in positive norms. The principles behind the rules are unwavering; the rules themselves are flexible. These principles are brought to life through legal practice, which can accord to the specific needs of the respective situation. Those who apply the law in particular circumstances are the ones who truly create the law. Accordingly, there is much flexibility in applying the law. At the same time, the decision of who is competent to apply the law and to decide in which way to apply it takes on eminent importance. As *the law* emerges only through the act of its application, the focus on determining what constitutes the law is less on the legislator and more on the administrative authorities who instruct those who apply the law on how to do so; who enforce or modify a law or dispense from it to answer to the legal needs of local churches; and who correct local legal practices when they fail to answer to the Apostolic See's understanding of the law.

This understanding of law differs profoundly from the German view to the law, as the bishop noted. Here, the focus is more on the statutes, the legal norms from which to derive rules on authority, rights, and duties. According to this view of the law, laws need to be certain. Most Germans, including Catholics, understand laws as written-down, unambiguous, and clear-cut rules. They rely on them and refer to them to demand their rights and to identify their duties. They believe in rights granted to them by the law and dislike privileges granted to them by concession. They have trust in the law itself—and not so much in legislation and administration. They actually understand the law as an instrument to defend their rights *against* the administration. A law, consequently, seems helpful to them if it protects individuals and groups and allows them to fight for their rights. This view, on the contrary, is partly incompatible with the Apostolic See's approach. To put it a little simplistically, one might argue that from the Roman point of view, the primary purpose of law is to protect the church by safeguarding its unity. While many German Catholics primarily focus on individuals and groups and their rights as protected by laws, the Apostolic See is more concerned about the church and its unity, which finds protection through the application of the law supervised by the Roman Curia. The conflicts deriving from these different perceptions of what the law is are enjoyable from a scholarly distance. But they are troublesome to local legal practitioners. To legal laypeople, these divergences can have a Kafkaesque quality. Many Catholics may even find the manoeuvres of the Apostolic See pointless and irritating, prompting them to question the value of global legislation. It requires some in-depth study to decipher these conflicts by uncovering the sources responsible for mutual incomprehension.

2.6 Extrajudicial Creativity

Some further observations on contemporary conflicts concern different approaches to organising a more synodal church. Many of these disputes are based on differing views on the type of legislation needed to reform the church. Studying the current situation of the German Church reveals that many German Catholics are still absorbed with processing the results from the *MHG Study* and other diocesan studies which investigated the sexual abuse of minors as committed by priests, deacons, and members of the religious orders in the German dioceses.[17] The extent of the abuse uncovered, together with the way in which many bishops dealt with the accusations, has shattered many Catholics' trust in the church authorities. Contributing to their estrangement is their belief that the authorities impede reform and fail to address the systemic reasons behind the abuse cases, such as absolutist structures, clericalism, and the ecclesiastical stance on sexuality and gender. Reacting to this crisis, the German bishops and laypeople organised a discussion process "Living in Faith Today" in 2011–15.[18] To many laypeople, this endeavour remained largely meaningless because it did not produce a concrete strategy for overcoming the systemic shortcomings that caused the crisis. Following the publication of the *MHG Study*, the German bishops initiated a new reform process in 2019 and approached the Central Committee of German Catholics (ZdK), a lay organisation, as potential partners. In any case, the Central Committee, with the failure of the former dialogue process in mind, made its readiness to consult with the bishops conditional on the consultations taking place at eye level. It emphasised that the lay organisation would not convene again without their vote being decisive and without the results of their deliberations having a binding effect. After having discussed the various institutional frameworks as provided by the Code of Canon Law, such as a local synod, the bishops and the Central Committee found no adequate institutional format for their consultation in canon law, as those formats provided by the law either fully exclude the laity or endow them only with limited rights. This in mind, they decided to create a bespoke format and engage in the so-called *Synodal Path* to allow for an open debate on church reform, including issues such as the life and role of the clergy and of the laity—and particularly of women—and the cooperation between clergy and laity in the parishes and diocesan curias.

[17] See Dreßing (2018).

[18] See German Bishops' Conference (2011–15).

Subsequently, the German Bishops' Conference and the Central Committee set out together to organise the bodies of the consultation process,[19] to invite clerics and laypeople to join the Synodal Assembly and the four Synodal Forums, and to compose their rules of procedure.[20] The dialogue format commenced in December 2019. Even before it took off, Vatican officials had voiced some reservations. In a letter sent to the President of the German Bishops' Conference in September 2019, the Prefect of the Congregation for Bishops expressed his concerns, referring to an expert opinion of the Pontifical Council for Legislative Texts which he attached to his letter. The assessment raises concerns particularly with regard to the statutes of the Synodal Path, allowing the laypeople to participate in the synodal bodies by giving them half of the seats in the assembly and attributing them with a decisive vote. The Vatican's document considers this to be impossible as it suspects the Synodal Path of being in fact a particular council and the German bishops of neglecting the canonical regulations of particular councils (see canons 439–446 CIC/1983). It, in consequence, demanded conformity with global canon law and a Roman examination and authorisation of the statutes before they could become binding for the synodal process, as well as the Roman recognition of the synodal decisions.[21] Responding to the letter and the expert opinion attached, the President of the German Bishops' Conference rejected these demands.[22] Besides refuting it on some technicalities, he emphasised that the Synodal Path was a consultation process *sui generis*. Because of its non-canonical nature, it would not require Roman inspection according to the rules of the law. Unlike particular councils (see canon 439 CIC/1983), the Synodal Path could therefore proceed without the Apostolic See's approval and could invite laypeople to participate in decisive votes—unlike particular councils which reserve decisive votes to the higher clergy and endow their few lay members with a consultative vote only (see canon 443 CIC/1983).

This incident is not relevant here as evidence of the ongoing dispute between the German Bishops' Conference and the Apostolic See. It is referenced because it provides insight into how local churches deal with unsuitable global law. In fact, the president argued that, in order to facilitate productive dialogue between the hierarchy and laity of the German Church, the organisers of the Synodal Path deemed it necessary to bypass canon law and its global institutions. He frankly admitted that, in order to move forward in the German Church, it was necessary to establish an extrajudicial consultation format. This format leaves the question of the institutional character of its procedures somewhat unanswered. The term *Synodal Path* insinuates that the layout is closely related to synods but is not exactly a synod. The preamble of the statutes describes the Synodal Path as a synodal concept "of a special

---

[19] See Plenary Assembly of the German Bishops' Conference/Plenary Assembly of the Central Committee of German Catholics (2019).

[20] See Synodal Assembly (2020).

[21] See Prefect of the Congregation for Bishops (2019).

[22] His letter to the Prefect of the Congregation for Bishops is unpublished, but a major German newspaper paraphrased its content and quoted some sections, see Deckers (2019).

kind",[23] which departs from global canon law to some extent, particularly with regard to its composition and the issue of decision making. According to canon law, synods of bishops consist mainly of bishops (see canon 346 §1 CIC/1983). Diocesan synods encompass clerics and laypeople, the latter chosen by the pastoral council in a manner and number to be determined by the diocesan bishop (see canon 463 §1 no. 5 CIC/1983). However, the focus of canonical regulation is on clerics, as canon 463 §1 CIC/1983 provides a full list of clerics who are obliged to participate in a diocesan synod, including the coadjutor bishop and auxiliary bishops, the vicars general, episcopal vicars, and the judicial vicar, the canons of the cathedral church, the members of the presbyteral council, the rector of the diocesan major seminary, vicars forane, at least one presbyter from each vicariate forane, and selected superiors of religious institutes and of societies of apostolic life. Departing from this approach, the main body of the Synodal Path was the Synodal Assembly. It consisted of the members of the German Bishops' Conference, 69 members of the Central Committee of German Catholics, 10 representatives of religious orders, 27 representatives of diocesan councils of priests, 15 Catholics below the age of 30, 4 permanent deacons, 4 representatives of the professional association of pastoral workers, 4 representatives of the Federal Association of local parish assistants, 3 representatives of the Association of Faculties of Catholic Theology, 3 representatives of New Spiritual Communities, 2 vicars general, up to 10 Catholics nominated by the German Bishops' Conference and up to 10 Catholics nominated by the Central Committee of German Catholics. The organisers also attempted to ensure the gender- and generation-equitable composition of the assembly.

The composition of the Synodal Path also parted ways with canon law with regard to decision making. According to canon law, synods regularly discuss issues with non-binding results, as canon 343 CIC/1983 states with regard to the synod of bishops: "It is for the synod of bishops to discuss the questions for consideration and express its wishes but not to resolve them or issue decrees about them". There is an exception, as the canon states, as the pope can endow a synod with deliberative power to make specific decisions. These decisions only take force when ratified by the pope. The Synodal Path, on the contrary, was—at least initially—expressly designed to produce decisions (see art. 3 sect. 2 of the Statutes), and it attributed laypeople with a decisive vote. All members of the Synodal Assembly shared equal voting rights (see art. 3 sect. 2 of the Statutes). The Synodal Assembly decided their resolutions with a two-thirds majority of its members, including an essential two-thirds majority of the bishops (see art. 11 of the Statutes). One may debate, in any case, of how binding these resolutions truly were, as they did not enter into force without the bishops' involvement as the statutes state: "The authority of the Bishops' Conference and of the individual diocesan Bishops to issue legal norms and exercise

[23] Plenary Assembly of the German Bishops' Conference/Plenary Assembly of the Central Committee of German Catholics (2019).

their magisterium within their respective spheres of competence remains unaffected by the resolutions" (see art. 11 sect. 5). Resolutions which touched upon issues pertaining to the global church were transmitted to the Apostolic See as a vote by the Synodal Path (see art. 12). Hence, whilst the format seemed eager to defend its decisive nature, one may ask in which sense its character as a decisive body was truly so different from synods which require the respective authorities' ratification. Many German Catholics are therefore sceptical as to whether the Synodal Path, which ended with a fifth meeting in March 2023 and is currently transitioning into a new form, should be considered a success. The story is not yet complete enough to make a final judgement on this question. Nevertheless, it is striking to consider what it reveals about the controversial status of canon law in mainstream German Catholicism.

2.7 Faraway Rome

An alternative approach responding to the need for debate between the bishops and the local Catholics was the Australian Plenary Council of 2021–22. Unlike the German Church, the Australian Church organised a plenary council in accordance with the canonical rules. This difference of institutional approaches to enabling dialogue is somewhat surprising, considering that both the Australian and the German Church were addressing similar issues. Both institutions, the Synodal Path and the Australian Council, allowed for dialogue between Catholics, clergy and laity, about the future of their church in their respective countries, and both reacted to similar challenges as the churches rapidly lose their traditional relevance in their respective countries, not least due to the massive abuse scandals in both churches. The Australian Plenary Council was a reaction to the results of the Royal Commission into Institutional Response to Child Sexual Abuse,[24] the German Synodal Path to the findings of the *MHG Study* mentioned above.[25] However, unlike the Synodal Path, the Australian Council chose to follow the canons of the Code of Canon Law on particular councils. The Code defines as a plenary council those councils which convene all local churches under the roof of one bishops' conference (see canon 439 §1 CIC/1983). Plenary councils convene when convoked by the bishops' conference. They are based on the approval of the Apostolic See. Members of the particular councils with a decisive vote always include the diocesan bishops of the respective bishops' conference, the coadjutor and auxiliary bishops, and other titular bishops with a designated function in the territory (see canon 443 §1 CIC/1983). Members with a merely consultative vote include the vicars general and episcopal

[24] See Royal Commission into Institutional Responses to Child Sexual Abuse (2017).

[25] See Dreßing (2018).

vicars, a selection of major superiors of religious institutes and societies of apostolic life, rectors of ecclesiastical and Catholic universities and deans of faculties of theology and of canon law, selected rectors of major seminaries, presbyters and other church members, with the restriction that their number does not exceed half the number of all those aforementioned (see canon 443 §3 CIC/1983). As a council, the particular council is equipped with legislative power and can thus take binding decisions in the form of conciliar decrees (see canon 445 CIC/1983). These decrees require a review by the Apostolic See before being promulgated (see canon 446 CIC/1983).

It is interesting to compare the two approaches, the Australian Council and the Synodal Path, with each other. And it is likewise instructive to study how both were handled in the Catholic media. There was no shortage of voices trying to play the two formats off against each other. Many conservative voices praised the Australian approach for having remained faithful to canon law, whilst criticising the German format as a departure from the law—and hence from Catholicism itself. When speaking about the Australian Council, the then-President of the Australian Bishops' Conference, Archbishop Mark Coleridge, had to repeatedly explain how the Australian model differs from the German one. While promoting the Australian format, he seemed eager to avoid dismissing the German one, stating: "I have been following der synodale weg in Germany and I certainly hope that it will end up being a great gift to the universal Church, and all this talk about heresy I think is alarmist and deeply unhelpful".[26] He added: "I don't share the great anxiety about the synodal way in Germany. I have great confidence in the Church in Germany, and I think the dialogue, even the tension, between the Holy See and the Church in Germany is a very creative thing".[27] Following Coleridge's words, disagreement—even between a local church and the Apostolic See—appear to be a regular phenomenon in discernment, even if the creative tension between the German Church and the Apostolic See is "one of the messy and challenging parts of discernment".[28] However, even though Coleridge seemed eager to erase the spectre of any potential schism, he did stress a certain dichotomy between the Australian and the German approach, for instance by mentioning: "People have warned us about the German contamination, I'm not sure it's a great threat to us here".[29]

Without going into an exegesis of what a "German contamination" might imply, it is interesting to note the context in which Coleridge posed that argument, namely to explain why the Australian bishops had opted for a council. He acknowledged that the Synodal Path might be "a little more flexible" than the Australian format

[26] Quoted by Lamb (2021).

[27] Ibid.

[28] Ibid.

[29] Ibid.

and might provide the German Church with "greater freedom".[30] However, he was quick to add that even though abiding by the canonical rules for a plenary council is somewhat restricting "we haven't found that to be too much of a constriction".[31] He also cited reasons why the rules of a plenary council were less burdensome on the Australian Church by stating: "We have a different history from Germany, dare I say, and the other thing is, of course, the fact of geography: We're a long way away, and we don't figure terribly much on the radar screen of the church universal; we're small, and distant and young".[32] This reference to their peripheral location from a European point of view and their former status as mission churches seems to be a typical Australian response to conflicting demands. The author of this book heard the same reply numerous times from Australian canonists when they were explaining how they deal with Vatican directives. Australian canonist Geoffrey Robinson condensed that answer in his observation: "In the convict society of the 19th century Australia it took at least two years to obtain a reply from Rome, so bishops and priests had become accustomed to doing things their own way".[33] If this analysis is also applicable with regard to the Australian decision to adhere to the canonical rules on the plenary council in organising the synodal process, one is tempted to speculate whether the Australian bishops might have opted for the stricter rules because they do not feel their grip to be overly limiting. German Catholics, on the contrary, under the watchful eye of the Apostolic See, felt compelled to escape the influence of global law and the Apostolic See's control over it by choosing a para-canonical procedure.

2.8 Lack of Participation

Many of the conflicts mentioned involve the issue of denying laypeople substantive participation in ecclesiastical decision making. The Grabmeier case, for instance, evolved between the diocesan bishop of Regensburg and the lay organisations of his diocese after the bishop had restricted the laity's rights to participate in ecclesiastical decision making—in accordance with current canon law. Hence, the bishop had curbed locally established rights and cut them back according to canonical constitutional law. Similarly, the struggle to find a suitable legal frame for the German Synodal Path derived from the fact that current canon law does not allow laypeople to substantially participate within the synods. This motif that canon law is troublesome because it curbs lay participation, is a recurring feature in the ongoing debates

[30] Quoted by Diocese of Tucson (2021).

[31] Ibid.

[32] Ibid.

[33] Robinson (1983), p. 47 fn. 2.

in many contexts. That said, it is less exclusive to the German debates than the previous examples suggest; and neither is it new, but has affected Catholics from democratic and liberal political traditions for a long time. John Beal, in his observations on how canon law has been received in the United States, refers to the conflicts deriving from the US-American trustee system of laypeople running their parish financial administration.[34] This system developed in the late eighteenth century at a time when the American Church was still a mission church without any canonical parishes and therefore also without the canonical structures for the administration of ecclesiastical goods. In their place, the local Catholics formed religious societies following regional secular law and its rules on associations. These societies were led by laypeople usually elected by their members. The trustees built churches, acquired church property, and then asked the local bishops to supply them with ministers. As many trustees had given generously for the acquisition of church property, their organisations became fairly independent and self-confident bodies, as Beal observes: "Since they had contributed money for the construction and maintenance of the church and held legal title to the property, these trustees assumed responsibility for the financial administration of the mission and sometimes asserted the right to nominate and dismiss its rector".[35] Beal states that the trustee system can be understood as a typical American evolution of the European patronage system. Whilst according to the old European system a usually aristocratic patron had the right to appoint and remove the parish priest, in the American and more egalitarian model, the lay trustees claimed the right to participate in the ministers' appointment. Therefore, although one can trace the origins of trusteeism back to European feudalism, Beal interprets it as a typically American concept of lay participation, corresponding with "the republican temper of the times".[36] He sees it as an expression of the American mentality, combining an egalitarian understanding of participation with the principle of merit, endowing with responsibilities and rights particularly those parish members who supported the parish most.

However, trusteeism became the subject of disagreements between some bishops and the trustees. In the course of these disputes, the bishops managed to gain widespread control over ecclesiastical property and its administration. After 1884 and following the Third Plenary Council of Baltimore, they broadly succeeded in taking control over the appointment of lay trustees whose vote thenceforth regularly had a mere consultative function.[37] Yet whilst the bishops had managed to curb the laity's rights of participation to a considerable degree with regard to financial issues and the administration of ecclesiastical goods, they were unable to completely reverse lay participation. Anthropologist Michael Angrosino, for instance, observed how fervently American Catholics embraced the increase in lay participation after the Second Vatican Council. In the United States, the concept of *shared responsibility*

[34] See Beal (1996), pp. 50–51.

[35] Ibid., p. 50.

[36] Ibid.

[37] See ibid., p. 51.

entrusting laypeople with manifold responsibilities in the liturgies, parish organisation, and church leadership formerly reserved to the clergy gained prominence, as he notes. Similarly to Beal, Angrosino explains this development as a particular expression of American mentality, and draws a parallel between the political socialisation of Americans and their expectations with regard to the church. As the American political culture had evolved around checks and balances and public participation in the exercise and control of power, “it was only to be expected that they [the American Catholics, addition by the author] would seize the opportunity to exert such active ministry within the church when the possibility was opened for them”.[38] Angrosino adds: “If we can think of an indigenized American church in terms of American culture, it would be one with a high degree of lay institutional direction and an emphasis on decentralization of authority”.[39]

European political cultures and mentalities are different. However, one can observe similar developments in many European countries, too. German Catholics are similarly used to democratic standards of decision making and therefore frequently demand them in church as well. And they react negatively to attempts to curb their participation. Similarly to American Catholics, who are “sensitive to the apparent infringement on their rights by the Vatican” and “often chafe at Roman ‘interference’ and the insensitivity of the hierarchy to issues such as birth control, sexual morality, and women in the ministry”,[40] many German Catholics oppose attempts to restrict their autonomy and participation in ecclesiastical decision making. In many liberal Catholic circles in Germany, there is not much left of what Angrosino sees in his fellow American Catholics, namely that active Catholics nevertheless “profess a sincere loyalty toward and respect for the Vatican”.[41] Instead, many German Catholics tend to *other* the Apostolic See. They refer to Vatican officials as “those in Rome”, whose decisions are undeserving of closer attention. Ignoring centralist commands and cultivating an alternative perception of Catholicism has increasingly become part of many Catholics identity. This antipathy seems to be mutual. Even Pope Francis, in whom at the beginning of his pontificate many German Catholics had placed their hopes for improved lay participation, seemed to reproach the Germans and their demands for more participation when remarking:

> At times, I feel tremendous sadness when I see a community that has good will, but takes the wrong path because it thinks that the Church is built up in meetings, as if it were a political party: the majority, the minority, what does this one think, that one, the other.... ‘This is like a Synod, the synodal path that we must take’. I ask myself: where is the Holy Spirit there? Where is prayer? Where is communitarian love? Where is the Eucharist? Without these four coordinates, the Church becomes a human society, a political party—majority, minority—changes are made as if it were a company, according to majority or minority... But the Holy Spirit is not there.[42]

---

[38] Angrosino (1994), p. 826.

[39] Ibid.

[40] Ibid.

[41] Ibid.

[42] Francis (2020b).

Whether Francis in fact meant the Synodal Path is uncertain but likely. However, he makes clear what he thinks of decision making by majority, of implementing democratic procedures in church, and of substantive political representation of those to whom decisions pertain: They are not ecclesial, because they lack the Spirit. They turn the church into "a beautiful humanitarian charitable organization, good, good … even an ecclesial party … But it is not the Church. … There might be a beautiful friendship club, good, with good intentions, but not the Church, not synodality".[43] By thus devaluing democratic aspirations and discouraging more lay participation in church, Francis has contributed to deepening the rift between many German Catholics and the Apostolic See. It is therefore not surprising that global canon law, as the results of the latter's lawmaking, currently occupies a precarious position within German Catholicism.

2.9 Summary

This chapter has gathered observations on the state of global canon law by collecting recent case studies where global law has taken a contested stance between the Apostolic See and the local churches. These include conflicts over procedural standards in ecclesiastical adjudication; differing views on the operation of centralised and decentralised legislation; differing legal policies and practices between the Apostolic See and local churches; dissimilar interpretations of the law and how it should be applied; diverse strategies employed to integrate local concerns into the global framework; disagreement about the extent to which lay participation is desirable in a synodal church and about who is responsible for decision making. These examples of conflicts between the Apostolic See and the local churches exemplify the diversity of challenges in intercultural legal communication. The following chapters will provide an in-depth analysis of the reasons for these tensions.

[43] Ibid.

Chapter 3
The Cultural Universe of the Law

The aforementioned observations describe individual cases. One might therefore dismiss them as incidental findings. Yet they are more than mere coincidences. This is because many of them derive from Neo-Scholastic legal doctrine. This gives rise to manifold tensions in the local churches on various levels, ranging from different understandings of what is law to different views of how to interpret and apply it. The following chapter explores this source of conflict in more detail. Section 3.1 refers to Catholic natural law as an example of why Roman Catholicism, in its Neo-Scholastic tradition, struggles to engage with culture meaningfully. Catholic natural law arguments tend to prioritise the universal at the expense of the cultural. Consequently, current canon law tends to universalise its claims, marginalising the cultural and, with it, the diversity of the local churches, the theological value of their plurality, and its relevance for the law. This study refers to natural law as one supernatural source of canon law, setting aside a broader discussion of other sources of law. This focus is helpful because, particularly within the Catholic natural law tradition, one can see how the concept of a prepositive foundation of law promotes the notion of a supercultural and transcultural meaning of legal rules. While not all canon law is grounded in natural law—not even most of it—the connection of the legal order to its underlying supernatural foundation invites the marginalisation of the cultural dimension of legal rules. In any case, this chapter does not claim that this is necessarily an issue with natural law theories. In fact, some theories reinterpret natural law arguments as deeply cultural. According to this perspective, natural law can be considered both part of divine law and embedded in culture. This supports the argument that laws can have supernatural origins yet still be human artefacts and cultural products that can be analysed using the analytical tools of "law as culture". To clarify the consequences of this understanding of all legal rules as cultural phenomena, this chapter defines *culture* in Sect. 3.2. It then explains why it makes sense to speak of *legal cultures* when studying diverse ecclesial contexts that encounter global canon law in Sect. 3.3.

J. Hahn, *The Cultures of Canon Law*, Law and Religion in a Global Context 6,
https://doi.org/10.1007/978-3-032-14812-4_3

3.1 Between Nature and Culture

The nineteenth century had a major impact on church doctrine and law with regard to key issues of church structuring. It brought about a monarchic reinterpretation of the pope's and the bishop's office, established the idea that only the ordained can govern the church with the power of jurisdiction, and broadly excluded laypeople from ecclesiastical decision making. The hierarchical structure of the church today rests on the doctrinal and legal pathmaking of the nineteenth century. Its strategic decisions shaped contemporary canon law. Much of the law regulating power and jurisdiction, church leadership, offices and functions is influenced by these decisions. However, with its Neo-Scholastic reinterpretation of the law, the impact of the nineteenth century was more profound than merely affecting single rules of the law. Neo-Scholastic legal theory tended to interpret canon law as a supercultural and ahistorical reality. Against the relativism put forward by modern scholarly debates on legal positivism, which understand the law to result from mere human decisions, the magisterium emphasised the connection of the law with prepositive justice, thus intrinsically linking canon law with the transcendent reality of supercultural and ahistorical divine law. Judith Gruber examines this shift in theory with regard to ecclesiology. She observes that in the nineteenth century the magisterium developed an "antimodernist conception of theology"[1] and of ecclesiology as ecclesiastical identity politics. It perceived the church itself as well as its doctrine as being grounded in revelation as supernatural and, in consequence, ahistorical phenomena. From that point onwards, only supernatural and ahistorical sources could contribute to establishing the identity of the church and its teaching, as she explains. At the same time, this elevation of the church to eye level with its supercultural foundation resulted in a devaluation of history, the world, its contingency and particularity. As second-order phenomena, both human reality and history were marginalised regarding their theological value. As contingent sources, they were thenceforth considered unfit to contribute to building Catholic identity. The magisterium instead started focusing on universality. Yet, particularity disappeared neither in fact nor in theory, as Gruber perceives. It rather became the subject of *othering*. Within ecclesiastical identity politics, it became the antipode of universality and has served since to demarcate the universal from the contingent, historical, and cultural. With serious consequences for ecclesiology, as Gruber maintains: "In the attempt to define its identity without including its contingency, the pre-conciliar church continued to be confronted with historical and cultural particularity as its disturbing and silenced other—a deficit that haunts and threatens to undermine its ecclesiological construction".[2]

---

[1] Gruber (2018), p. 91.

[2] Ibid.

3.1.1 *Divine Sources*

What Gruber observes with regard to ecclesiology has major repercussions in the law—quite unsurprising if one understands canon law as applied ecclesiology.[3] Following the shift in ecclesiology towards the supernatural and ahistorical foundation of the church, Catholic jurisprudence, since the nineteenth century, has invested effort in emphasising the supernatural and ahistorical sources of the law. This led to a major focus on divine law and, with it, on the relevance of the divine will as a reason of law conveyed through revelation and nature. Catholic legal theory perceives these two sources, revelation and nature, as sources of divine law. It understands norms derived out of scripture—the revealed word of God—as laws of revelation. Adding to these are norms derived from tradition, as Catholicism also regards tradition as a font of theological insight. Hence, theological insight into God's will for God's church as revealed in scripture or tradition forms the basis of the law of revelation. The same quality of being a source of divine law applies to nature. However, nature is treated differently in the classification of divine law, namely as an independent rationale of divine law next to revelation. The Catholic tradition uses the term *natural law* to refer to those norms which human reason can derive out of nature as God's creation. According to Catholic teaching, knowing the naturally right is independent from revelation. It is open to all human beings who can perceive that what is right according to nature by studying natural things with the help of reason. Canonical legal theory therefore identifies nature and revelation as two subcategories of divine law (*ius divinum, sive naturale sive positivum*). One might criticise this simplification for several reasons.[4] For the purpose of the argument made in this book, it is important to note that the classification is based on the idea that both normative reasons, revelation and nature, derive from God. God is both the one who revealed Godself to humankind and the creator who endowed humanity with reason to derive norms from natural things. In consequence, the official teaching understands the norms derived out of revelation and nature as manifestations of God's will. However, they differ with regard to the subjects to whom they pertain: Divine law as revealed through revelation binds all Christians as those to whom God gave the revelation; divine law as discernible with the help of reason binds all human beings as those to whom God gave reason.

3.1.2 *Acultural Origins*

This idea that natural law binds all human beings, irrespective of their connection with the Christian faith, places natural law at the core of Catholic moral and legal universalism. According to Catholic teaching, norms such as the human rights

[3] For this concept, see Doe (1992), p. 336; Ombres (2016), p. 137.

[4] Which the author of this book has done elsewhere, see Hahn (2019), pp. 21–23.

which claim to bind human beings in all places and at all times are expressions of God's will for humanity, irrespective of whether human beings are aware of God as the origin of these norms. As humans are endowed by God with reason, they are capable of perceiving God's will in nature by using their reason. From a Catholic point of view, natural law is therefore identical with what the Enlightenment called the *law of reason*. Whilst Catholic natural law and the Enlightenment's law of reason have diverged from each other over the course of the history of both theories, both are guided by the idea of reason deriving norms by critically studying the normative implications of nature.

As the law of reason, natural law is at the core of Neo-Scholasticism's universalism. Under Neo-Scholasticism, natural law theory even regained some of the former glory which it had lost, to some extent, to the Enlightenment's law of reason and the modern human rights debate. For a short period of history, even in the twentieth century, the church was again successful in promoting natural law as universal law, even in the political sphere; the mid-twentieth century post-war period saw a natural law revival in Europe, for instance.[5] However, Catholic natural law, in the long run, proved to be conflictive in many modern-day plural societies, precisely due to its tendency to refer to ahistorical and supertemporal origins. By emphasising God's universal and supertemporal will for God's creation as conveyed through nature, natural law arguments draw heavily on ahistoricity and aculturality, which in turn makes them difficult answers to temporal needs, historical circumstances, and cultural challenges. Critical voices consequently accuse natural law and its universal claims of endorsing a blindness for the historical, the cultural, and the contingent, as natural law theorist David Novak notes: "Perhaps the greatest vulnerability of natural law theory, both in the ancient and modern times, is its seeming oblivion to and disrespect of cultural diversity, especially in normative matters".[6] Michael Angrosino makes a similar observation that natural law approaches tend to ignore the diversity of cultures due to their assumption that universal concepts when reified must inevitably lead to *one* reification. He maintains: "The very fact that there are different cultures, rather than the single human way of life that might be expected if culture were strictly an element of natural law, demonstrates that culture is a human rather than a divine creation".[7] Whilst this study agrees with him that natural law, particularly in its Neo-Scholastic reinterpretation, tends to focus on the one universal reality and to ignore the multiple human expressions of that reality, it wants to argue that divine and human creations are not mutually exclusive. Undoubtedly, cultures are human artefacts. However, as thinkers such as David Novak remind his readers, this does not mean they cannot be understood as manifestations of the divine.

---

[5] For the German post-war period meticulously described by Foljanty (2013).

The Anglo-Saxon natural law tradition has taken a different path. Here, natural law arguments still play a more important role than in continental European debates, and "New Natural Law" is a minority theory, but one of scholarly relevance and political impact.

[6] Novak (1998), p. 188.

[7] Angrosino (1994), p. 828.

3.1.3 Cultural Artefacts

Legal theorists like Novak therefore seek ways to reconcile the divine origin of law with its quality as a human artefact.[8] Whilst Novak argues in favour of natural law, he at the same time also expresses the need to understand the norms deriving from God's universal will, once they become concrete in history and cultures, as historical and cultural rules: "Natural law is taken as what is to be universal. But from where does one begin to constitute this universe?"[9] This constitutive point is an essential cultural standpoint. Whilst one might think of fundamental principles underlying norms as acultural and supertemporal, one cannot perceive concrete norms in isolation from their cultural and historical embedding. Novak therefore criticises the view held by many natural law scholars that discovering natural norms requires one to distance oneself from one's cultural standpoint: "Universal thinking by very particularly formed persons seems to be an imaginative attempt to constitute a world that would be the case if I were not part of the singular culture in which I now have been living concretely".[10] This idea that norms can be protected from cultural corruption by taking on a supercultural position when formulating them is essentially impossible, as human thinkers are essentially impregnated by culture, so that "[o]ur imagination can tentatively abstract us from our own cultures from time to time, but we cannot transcend them by some nonculturally conceived Archimedean fulcrum in order to either escape them, destroy them, or re-create them".[11] In consequence, one cannot even conceive of Platonic or Aristotelian natural law properly without considering their context of origin in ancient Greece, as Novak maintains. A norm, moral or legal, which one ascribes to natural law, is always a cultural product.

Novak encapsulates this finding in the elementary proposition: "Natural law is a cultural construct".[12] However, as a religious thinker, he links the essential historicity of natural law with God's acting as a creator. As a result of God's creation, natural law is something created and, accordingly, something determined by time: "Like all creation natural law is made in time".[13] In more general terms, John Huels remarks: "There is no such thing as a law—or philosophy, theology, or language—that does not reflect the culture which gives rise to it".[14] One can interpret his careful wording—speaking of the *reflection* of culture in law, language, or science, instead of speaking of their cultural *construction*—as a hesitance to adopt constructivist terminology, perhaps because many scholars tend to associate constructivism with arbitrariness. In this light, when conceiving of natural law as culturally constructed,

---

[8] With regard to canon law see Hahn (2019).

[9] Novak (1998), p. 188.

[10] Ibid., p. 189.

[11] Ibid.

[12] Ibid., p. 188.

[13] Novak (2014), p. 6.

[14] Huels (1987), p. 262.

it is tempting to misread this as the claim to understand natural law as a random phenomenon. To avoid giving this impression, one may differentiate between ontology and epistemology, as Novak suggests: "The 'construction' here is of the approach to the reality; it is not the reality itself that is constructed".[15] Many natural law theorists would agree that natural law is based on a prepositive fundament which is supercultural and supertemporal. Yet, when transforming these supercultural and supertemporal principles into concrete norms, they necessarily take on a cultural and historical shape. In a similar vein, systematic theologian Karl Rahner relates to divine law in general. He speaks of its "Wesensidentität in Gestaltwandel",[16] emphasising that, from a theological perspective, divine law can be regarded as having an identity with regard to its essence while changing its concrete shape in different times and cultures.

3.1.4 A Universal Horizon

If one assumes that the universal only becomes real in culture and time, one must explain how the universal relates to the cultural or temporal. David Novak makes a suggestion. He proposes reversing the perspective. Instead of focusing on the universal and asking how it might be articulated adequately in culture and time, he recommends starting where individuals currently stand as members of a particular culture in a certain historical context: "Instead of an attempt to find some universal phenomenon to ground natural law, it seems more authentic and more useful to see it as the constitution of a universal horizon by a thinker in a particular culture for his or her own culture".[17] Novak explains his reverse perspective by comparing it to a telescope with which one might scan the wider horizon: "It is like making a telescope, assuming there is something 'out there' to be discovered, but something unlike any object that could be seen by the naked eye. The object to be discovered must be believed to exist, even if there is no other way to see it except through the telescope".[18] In his model, respective cultures and times serve as contexts from which human beings direct their telescope towards the universal horizon. The key point of Novak's image is that all telescopes from their various standpoints focus on the same horizon. Hence, whilst all rules including those which human beings take as an expression of the naturally right are cultural and historically contingent, one may take them as rules directed at universal natural law. In a similar vein, the International Theological Commission—a papal expert commission assigned with the task of advising the pope and the Congregation for the Doctrine of the Faith on matters theological—stated in its considerations regarding "Faith and Inculturation"

---

[15] Novak (1998), p. 190.

[16] Rahner (1962), p. 252.

[17] Novak (1998), pp. 189–190.

[18] Ibid., p. 190.

that "[c]ultural pluralism cannot therefore be interpreted as the juxtaposition of a closed universe, but as participation in a unison of realities all directed toward the universal values of humanity".[19]

However, there are manifold and even contradictory rules facing that horizon. Thus, there is cause to doubt if these different rules are truly facing the *same* horizon. David Novak finds comfort in an extension of his telescope metaphor. He argues that it presents a reliable connection between the cultural standpoint and the universal horizon: "Quantum theory argues that such 'telescopes' themselves are inseparable from the objects they have in view. That is the most useful analogue for natural law theory".[20] If one assumes that human artefacts, such as norms and rules, have the capacity to face a universal horizon, then it is also plausible to assume that they can be directed by that horizon. Novak therefore believes it to be possible for human beings to perceive the naturally right and to capture at least some of it in human rules, even though individuals should never be too sure if they have got it right. Hence, when this study refers to ecclesiastical rules as cultural constructs, this does not imply a judgement on their origins. Depending on their beliefs, some thinkers may or may not consider these rules to represent divine law.

So far, this chapter has merely put forward two arguments: First, it has attempted to demonstrate that, since the nineteenth century, an antimodernist strand of ecclesiastical jurisprudence has devalued the cultural and the temporal, tending to view the church and its law as transcultural and supercultural entities. Second, it has argued that this interpretation is deceptive because all legal rules are essentially cultural, regardless of whether or not one believes in their supercultural roots. All rules are intrinsically interwoven with the culture from which they originate. The following section therefore explores the meaning of *culture* and the concept of *legal culture*, in order to provide a socio-legal framework for analysing conflicts between global canon law and the local churches.

3.2 Talking About Culture

Identifying law as a cultural construct requires a closer look at the concept of culture as it is used in legal contexts. In church, there is a somewhat ambiguous understanding of culture in the present debates. This ambiguity derives to no small degree from conciliar teaching. In its Pastoral Constitution *Gaudium et Spes*—which defined the status and role of the church in modern-day societies—the Second Vatican Council adopted an ambiguous approach to culture. This stance has been perpetuated in current teaching and legislation; this book will refer to the way in which canon law deals with culture more profoundly in Sect. 6.1. The council's

[19] International Theological Commission (1988), sect. 1 no. 7.

[20] Novak (1998), p. 190.

definition shifts between interpreting culture in a normative sense, as humanity's calling to greater cultural achievements, and in a descriptive sense, insofar as it acknowledges the existence of manifold cultures all over the globe. Bernard Lonergan points out that this tension reappears in academic theology, which frequently relies on two different notions of culture, a "classicist" or normative and an empirical notion of the term. The normative meaning of culture, which has dominated the use of the term in church for two millennia, draws on the idea that culture exists in a "universal and permanent" singular, "to its norms and ideals might aspire the uncultured".[21] Lonergan explains this traditional perception of culture to denote

> the opposite of barbarism. It was a matter of acquiring and assimilating the tastes and skills, the ideals, virtues, and ideas, that were pressed upon one in a good home and through a curriculum of the liberal arts. It stressed not facts but values. It could not but claim to be universalist. Its classics were immortal works of art, its philosophy was the perennial philosophy, its laws and structures were the deposit of the wisdom and the prudence of mankind. Classicist education was a matter of models to be imitated, of ideal characters to be emulated, of eternal verities and universally valid laws. It sought to produce not the mere specialist but the *uomo universale* that could turn his hand to anything and do it brilliantly.[22]

The empirical meaning of culture, on the other hand, understands culture as "the set of meanings and values that informs a way of life".[23] As such it can be long-lasting or highly transient—either way, it is a contingent phenomenon. And it essentially exists in the plural, as Lonergan notes: "A culture is a set of meanings and values informing a common way of life, and there are as many cultures as there are distinct sets of such meanings and values".[24] Depending on the way the term is used in theology, one ends up dealing with a different focus, as he maintains: "When the classicist notion of culture prevails, theology is conceived as a permanent achievement, and then one discourses on its nature. When culture is conceived empirically, theology is known to be an ongoing process, and then one writes on its method".[25] In calling his book *Method in Theology* and by opening it with precisely this statement, one can easily determine which perception of culture Lonergan prefers for theology.

3.2.1 Cultivated Nature

The council, for its part, was not as decided as Lonergan. Conciliar texts tend to shift from the normative to the empirical meaning of culture and back, as Marc de Mûelenaere observes: "The Council does not consistently use the word culture …

[21] Lonergan (1972), p. XI.

[22] Ibid., p. 301.

[23] Ibid., p. XI.

[24] Ibid., p. 301.

[25] Ibid., p. XI.

and frequently modifies it by the use of various adjectives, e.g., *modern* culture, *mass* culture, *new* culture, *higher* culture, etc."[26] He also realises that the council generates a normative notion of culture by contrasting general culture with *higher* culture, meaning those developments achieved through education. A closer look at the definition given in *Gaudium et Spes* helps to see his point. The document initially defines culture by demarcating it from nature. It describes culture as the "cultivation of the goods and values of nature",[27] and thus as a normative endeavour to subdue nature to human refinement. According to the council, culture as cultivated nature is the truly human response to nature. It is humanity's calling to perfect human nature, in a physical, spiritual, and social sense, as the document proposes:

> The word 'culture' in its general sense indicates everything whereby man develops and perfects his many bodily and spiritual qualities; he strives by his knowledge and his labour, to bring the world itself under his control. He renders social life more human both in the family and the civic community, through improvement of customs and institutions. Throughout the course of time he expresses, communicates, and conserves in his works, great spiritual experiences and desires, that they might be of advantage to the progress of many, even of the whole human family.[28]

Gaudium et Spes then acknowledges that, due to the essential historical and social dimension of human attempts to refine nature, cultures exist in the plural: "Thence it follows that human culture has necessarily a historical and social aspect and the word 'culture' also often assumes a sociological and ethnological sense".[29] This acknowledgement of the existence of many different cultures around the world is a common view in the social sciences. Bernard Lonergan concordantly states that the church developed this empirical notion of culture only just recently, as a consequence of receiving the findings of the empirical humanities.[30]

Gaudium et Spes goes on to perceive: "Different styles of life and multiple scales of values arise from the diverse manner of using things, of labouring, of expressing oneself, of practicing religion, of forming customs, of establishing laws and juridic institutions, of cultivating the sciences, the arts and beauty".[31] This normative dimension of humanity perfecting nature through culture also carries some legal connotations. The idea of culture as a force for bringing the world under humanity's control, the view of culture as shaping civic communities, and the notion of culture as improving customs and institutions suggest that humans succeed in their cultivation of natural realities inter alia by drawing on rules and institutions of a legal nature. In consequence, one might conceive of the law as an instrument for subjecting nature to human refinement. And yet again, the council's reference to the various ways of cultivating nature alludes to the fact that law can take different forms

[26] De Mûelenaere (1985b), p. 32 fn. 5.

[27] Second Vatican Council (1965c), no. 53. Acta Apostolicae Sedis (1966), p. 1075.

[28] Ibid.

[29] Ibid.

[30] See Lonergan (1972), p. 301.

[31] Second Vatican Council (1965c), no. 53. Acta Apostolicae Sedis (1966), p. 1075.

when serving humankind in this respect. This points to the existence of multiple legal cultures. *Gaudium et Spes* seems to acknowledge them when referring to "the diverse manner ... of establishing laws and juridic institutions".

3.2.2 Systems of Meaning

This book also speaks of *cultures* in the plural, and likewise of plural *legal cultures*. Nevertheless, its understanding of cultures and legal cultures differs from that which one might derive from conciliar teaching. In line with many scholars of the humanities, it relies on ethnologist Clifford Geertz's conception of culture—albeit with some caveats, as Geertz's approach has its pitfalls. Anthropologists such as Lila Abu-Lughod have pointed to the problem of referring to culture and also cultures in the plural, as this approach to mapping out reality essentially entails "diametrically opposed processes of self-construction through opposition to others—processes that begin from different sides of a power divide".[32] There is no way to avoid the power asymmetries that come with differentiating one culture from others as an antagonistic way of approaching reality via generalisation and hierarchisation. Consequently, Abu-Lughod criticises that "'culture' operates in anthropological discourse to enforce separations that inevitably carry a sense of hierarchy".[33] This has to be taken into account. But what are the alternatives, for instance if one wants to capture some of the conflicts that arise from encounters between global canon law and the local churches? Since these culture clashes are characterised by a power divide and by hierarchisation, the colonising undertone of culture is not entirely misplaced. Unlike Abu-Lughod, this book therefore chooses to use the term, but precisely with her warning in mind that it displays "the tendency towards essentialism" and "tends to freeze differences".[34] It consequently remains important to point out its disposition towards essentialism as well as the asymmetrical notions that the term carries.

It nevertheless seems possible to reference Geertz, precisely because his understanding of culture is concerned with preventing essentialisms, reacting to three common misconceptions of culture which he identified as the following: first, a reified or objectified concept of culture which perceives it as "a self-contained 'superorganic' reality with forces and purposes of its own"; second, a reduced concept of culture which suggests "that it consists in the brute pattern of behavioural events we observe in fact to occur in some identifiable community"; third, the idea that "culture [is located, addition by Clifford Geertz himself] in the minds and hearts of men".[35] Against these misconceptions, Geertz proposed a semiotic or interpretive

---

[32] Abu-Lughod (2006), p. 467.

[33] Ibid., p. 466.

[34] Ibid., p. 471.

[35] Geertz (1973a), p. 11.

understanding of culture which focuses on signs which convey their specific meaning to their interpreters within a specific context. He writes: "Believing, with Max Weber, that man is an animal suspended in webs of significance he himself has spun, I take culture to be those webs, and the analysis of it to be therefore not an experimental science in search of law but an interpretive one in search of meaning".[36] Culture, as he defines it, is a system of meaning which helps to attribute meaning to signs. It is "the fabric of meaning",[37] to which interpreters relate their experiences—the signs with which they find themselves confronted—to decipher their meaning. This derivation of meaning from signs is the process in which individuals refer to a system of meaning to "define their world, express their feelings, and make their judgements".[38] Geertz therefore maintains: "Culture, here, is not cults and customs, but the structures of meaning through which men give shape to their experience".[39] As a fabric of meaning, it is a "framework of beliefs, expressive symbols, and values".[40] It serves as the "context"[41] in which individuals attribute meaning to signs.

Theology has learned much from his approach to culture. This becomes apparent when recollecting Bernard Lonergan's empirical approach to culture, which he defines as "the set of meanings and values that informs a way of life".[42] And likewise when reading how liturgical scholar Anscar Chupungco refers to "cultural pattern" as

> the typical mode of thinking, speaking, and expressing oneself through rites, symbols, and art forms. It affects society's values and ideology, social and family traditions, socioeconomic life, and political system. Cultural pattern cuts across everything that constitutes the life of a society. It is a people's prescribed system of reflecting on, verbalizing, and ritualizing the values, traditions, and experiences of life.[43]

3.2.3 *Thick Descriptions*

It is difficult for outsiders to decipher the meanings which members of a group attach to signs. Nonetheless, Geertz believes there is a chance to communicate about meaning, even to cultural outsiders. This is because signs "can be

[36] Ibid., p. 5.

[37] Geertz (1973c), p. 145.

[38] Ibid., 144–145.

[39] Geertz (1973d), p. 312.

[40] Geertz (1973c), pp. 144–145.

[41] Ibid.

In accordance with Geertz's definition of culture as *context*, theologians such as Stephen Bevans prefer to speak of *context* instead of *culture* to avoid the ambiguity connected with culture, particularly in church, see Bevans (2002, 2018).

[42] Lonergan (1972), p. XI.

[43] Chupungco (1992), p. 35.

intelligibly—that is, thickly—described".[44] Thick description—as Geertz's method of doing ethnography—became most prominent through his work. It suggests that scholars can most effectively learn about a culture with the help of members of that culture, which allow outsiders to adopt their perspective: "The culture of a people is an ensemble of texts, themselves ensembles, which the anthropologist strains to read over the shoulders of those to whom they properly belong".[45] *Texts*, as used in this context, refer to various ensembles of signs which serve as carriers of meaning. They consist of words or ensembles of words, events, or persons. Geertz freely admits that reading these texts over the shoulders of individuals to whom they belong is open to misreadings of all kinds. Yet he sees his method as being without alternative, particularly in the light of other approaches to studying culture. These all fall prey to various misinterpretations of culture, such as understanding it as "a thing of shreds and patches"[46] which scholars must only collect and add to come to a full picture, or of perceiving culture as "a seamless web"[47] which allows for clear depictions and general conclusions. Yet there is no "heroic 'holistic' assault upon 'the basic configurations of the culture,' an overarching 'order of orders' from which more limited configurations can be seen as mere deductions",[48] as Geertz sees it. In refuting seamless-web approaches he counters ethnological and anthropological theories which attempt to find universals common to all cultures. In contrast to these rather supercultural or transcultural views of culture, he proposes thick description as a research strategy which asks how individual members of cultures interpret the signs they encounter. Their experience defies clear definitions. And there is also no direct correspondence between culture and sign in the sense that a culture directly inserts a meaning into a specific sign. Instead, one can only study signs when thickly described by taking into account the multifaceted and often contradictory layers of meaning which overlap. To illustrate this view of culture beyond additive or holistic concepts, Geertz suggests using the image of an octopus:

> The appropriate image, if one must have images, of cultural organization, is neither the spider web nor the pile of sand. It is rather more the octopus, whose tentacles are in large part separately integrated, neurally quite poorly connected with one another and with what in the octopus passes for a brain, and yet who nonetheless manages both to get around and to preserve himself, for a while anyway, as a viable if somewhat ungainly entity.[49]

Although one could debate Geertz's misconception about the intelligence of octopuses, his image helps to understand culture as a joint which connects meaning to form a system of meaning. This system is less conclusive and less centralistically governed than one might assume. However, despite its fragility, which defies essentialist approaches, culture does form some kind of an entity, at least for a certain

[44] Geertz (1973a), p. 14.

[45] Geertz (1973f), p. 452.

[46] Geertz (1973e), p. 407.

[47] Ibid.

[48] Ibid., p. 408.

[49] Ibid., pp. 407–408.

period of time. It is contingent, but nevertheless not entirely random. Because of this, it is possible to study culture. While it is difficult to scrutinise the octopus closely and entirely, as Geertz acknowledges, he sees no alternative to approaching culture, as every method that seeks to avoid the messiness of studying it means missing culture altogether: "There are a number of ways to escape this—turning culture into folklore and collecting it, turning it into traits and counting it, turning it into institutions and classifying it, turning it into structures and toying with it. But they are escapes".[50] Instead, it is the fragile webs of meaning that must be scrutinised in order to understand cultures. This involves identifying the markers of culture: "significant symbols, clusters of significant symbols, and clusters of clusters of significant symbols—the material vehicles of perception, emotion, and understanding—and the statement of the underlying regularities of human experience implicit in their formation".[51] In examining them, one might even succeed in arriving at a bigger picture of what characterises a specific culture and in developing a theory of culture, as Geertz carefully suggests:

> A workable theory of culture is to be achieved, if it is to be achieved, by building up from directly observable modes of thought, first to determinate families of them and then to more variable, less tightly coherent, but nonetheless ordered 'octopoid' systems of them, confluences of partial integrations, partial incongruencies, and partial independencies.[52]

3.3 Law as Culture

This study suggests following Geertz in his perception of culture as a system of meaning. It also proposes applying his concept of culture to examining the meaning of law. Following Geertz, perceiving law as a cultural phenomenon is to observe that it derives its meaning from culture as a web of significance in which it is embedded. Laws are ensembles of texts; as such they are part of the ensemble of texts which Geertz calls culture. Hence, social phenomena, such as rules, institutions, and practices, derive their meaning as *legal* rules, institutions, and practices from being part of an ensemble of texts acknowledged as law.

According to sociologist Niklas Luhmann, a meaning is *legal* when individuals define and process social reality by drawing on the binary codification of *legal* and *illegal*.[53] Whenever individuals or groups find sense in describing communications as legal or illegal, these communications are a part of the law as a subsystem of society, or in Geertzian terms, part of legal culture. Cultures as systems of meaning allow human beings to explain some of their experiences by offering them legal explanations. Cultures that form structures of legal meaning can be called legal

[50] Geertz (1973a), p. 29.
[51] Geertz (1973e), p. 408.
[52] Ibid.
[53] See Luhmann (2004), pp. 98–99.

cultures. As members of legal cultures, individuals or groups create meaning by defining their world as a legal reality, by raising legal claims, by making legal judgements—"guilty"/"not guilty"—and by identifying themselves and others as legal subjects.

3.3.1 Signs and Meanings

Following a semiotic or interpretive concept of culture, as proposed by Geertz, one can identify the law as an important part of cultural programmes, the term he uses to describe directive cultural mechanisms which govern behaviour. Two ideas help to clarify their connection:

> The first of these is that culture is best seen not as complexes of concrete behavior patterns—customs, usages, traditions, habit clusters—as has, by and large, been the case up to now, but as a set of control mechanisms—plans, recipes, rules, instructions (what computer engineers call 'programs')—for the governing of behavior. The second idea is that man is precisely the animal most desperately dependent upon such extragenetic, outside-the-skin control mechanisms, such cultural programs, for ordering his behavior.[54]

Hence, Geertz refuses to comprehend culture in a traditional sense as clustered patterns of behaviour. Instead, he proposes viewing it as programmes directing behaviour. Taking this definition of culture, he closely connects cultures with legal rules and other norms directing behaviour within groups. This is a similar understanding which Luhmann proposed to explain the functioning of the law. He emphasised the role of law in generating culture, stating: "The law is one of the many areas in which social communication not only takes place, but communicates extensively about itself. This creates, to some degree epigenetically, cultural assets, which are consistently in use and being replicated, reproduced, and modified".[55] Law, according to Luhmann, is therefore a producer of culture or, in Geertzian terminology, a producer of meaning. The law attributes signs with legal meaning and weaves them together into systems of meaning.

It is therefore plausible that one understands more of a culture when one studies its law. In this respect it is also of help to receive Robert Schreiter's reading of Geertz. Schreiter pointed to the procedural aspects of culture which support the production of meaning, one thought which he found to be less prominent in Geertz's original approach. Schreiter's interest in focusing more on the procedural implications of Geertz's definition of culture is that he used it to examine the function of a living tradition for the church. As Schreiter explores the conditions under which local theologies develop in the local churches, he ponders how the Christian

[54] Geertz (1973b), p. 44.

[55] Original quote: "Das Recht ist einer der vielen Bereiche, in denen gesellschaftliche Kommunikation nicht nur abläuft, sondern extensiv über sich selbst kommuniziert. Dabei entsteht, epigenetisch gewissermaßen, Kulturgut, das ständig in Gebrauch genommen, repliziert, reproduziert und abgewandelt wird", Luhmann (1986), p. 11.

tradition can express itself within a local culture. In this context, he describes the impact of tradition on culture as providing values, signs, and rules that support the creation of meaning: "It [tradition, addition by the author] provides basic messages (values) and codes (rules), which relate (signs) those messages to data in the environment. Together they create meaning".[56] Schreiter defines messages as the "basic meanings conveyed by a culture".[57] In broadening Geertz's view, which is primarily concentrated on signs as carriers of meaning to include codes and rules, he points to the "structures that make intelligibility possible".[58] Codes, as Schreiter defines them, are "the 'grammar' of culture texts. They encompass the rules of action of a culture, of what is done and what is not to be done".[59] And not least of how things are done, as he also emphasises. Whilst codes are not of primary interest to Geertz, who mainly considered signs as conveyers of meaning, they are particularly interesting for scholars studying the law. If one perceives the law as a system which evolves around texts carrying rules of action of what is to be done and how it is to be done, then studying cultures involves studying their legal codes. And, conversely, one has to consider culture to understand rules as cultural artefacts. Scholar of comparative law Pierre Legrand explains: "A rule is necessarily an incorporative cultural form. As an accretion of cultural elements, it is supported by impressive historical and ideological formations. A rule does not have any empirical existence that can be significantly detached from the world of meanings that characterizes a legal culture; the part is an expression and a synthesis of the whole: it resonates".[60]

This book, for its part, does not merely want to focus on the codes but also wants to gain a better understanding of the signs as carriers of meaning. Schreiter points to this possibility by noting that codes, by defining the rules of action of what to do and how to do it, in fact also reveal much about the signs as "they [the codes, addition by the author] not only define the range of activity of the sign, but can also tell us something of the basic message".[61] He elucidates this with the example of the codes of celebrating the Eucharist, before and after the reform of the liturgy. Whilst the Tridentine code of celebrating the Eucharist advised the priest to celebrate it with his back facing the congregation, modern liturgical codes advise the priests to celebrate the mass while facing the congregation. Yet changing the code as the "basic rules for the exercise of the sign function",[62] as he observes, also meant changing the meaning of the Eucharist itself. He describes the celebrant's change of direction as a shift in meaning from understanding the Eucharist as a sacrifice, to perceiving it more as a communal meal. This change, in turn, had further implications for other codes, for example how to distribute the Eucharist. It resulted in

---

[56] Schreiter (1985), p. 107.

[57] Ibid., p. 68.

[58] Ibid., p. 54.

[59] Ibid., p. 67.

[60] Legrand (1997), p. 116.

[61] Schreiter (1985), p. 67.

[62] Ibid.

further changes to codes, such as allowing laypeople to distribute the Eucharist or allowing the distributors to place the host into the recipients' hands instead of into their mouth. This example shows that signs and codes are mutually intertwined and exert a constant influence on each other. In cultures where the law serves as one influential code of action, as in the Roman Catholic Church, it is therefore evident why studying the law is not only examining one major grammar of ecclesiastical signs, but also enables scholars to understand the signs somewhat better.

3.3.2 Cultural Identifiers

Culture as a delicate tissue woven out of values, signs, and rules constitutes meaning, and it supports the construction of identity, as Schreiter states: "The proper interaction and working of these three dimensions makes for that fragile creation, identity".[63] The cultures in which human beings live provide them with various cultural identifiers—values, signs, and rules connected with nationality, race, history, language, religion, sex, and gender—that can become part of their individual self-perception or the collective identity of groups. Judith Gruber therefore calls cultures "hybrid and therefore heterogeneous identity constellations".[64] They provide the context from which identities are "performatively constituted in discursive processes",[65] which differentiate between the *self* and the *other*. To understand this process, Gruber reminds her readers that the construction of identity is not the defining and outcasting of the other for the sake of discovering the self, but is instead the integration of the excluded other into the image of the self: "Cultural identity is produced performatively through the discriminatory practices of cultural identification and therefore, their excluded others remain an irrevocable part of their own identity: every culture embodies the other-in-its-self".[66] Hence, in every cultural identity, the "other is present as the excluded, it is present as absence—an absence that remains constitutive for every cultural identity".[67] This finding suggests that, just as the other remains part of one's cultural identity, cultures cannot be understood as separate and clearly demarcated from each other. Instead, they must be conceived as essentially connected, as Gruber observes. This has a consequence for cultural identity itself, as she discerns that "cultural identity is always intercultural".[68]

Law is culture, and as such can contribute to constructing cultural identity. In fact, it is a meaningful identifier in many contemporary contexts. Political scholar

[63] Ibid., p. 107.

[64] Gruber (2018), p. 70.

[65] Ibid.

[66] Ibid.

[67] Ibid.

[68] Ibid., p. 71.

J. Peter Burgess has explained this influence of law on identity issues by identifying the law *with* identity:

> Identity is law. Identity, the most powerful and most tyrannical idea of Western civilization is the essence of law, the law of identity: A = B, Jacques = Albanian, Arnold = sociologist. If an individual is to be who/what s/he is, a law of identity is immediately—even preceding the thought of identity—in place. Understanding anything as anything, (this is a pencil, that is a Belgian) is submitting to the law of identity. The notion of collectivity is based on a law of belonging. If there is a collectivity, there is a rule, a law of who/what belongs and does not belong. ('Only Norwegians, that is individuals with properties x, y, z, are admissible in the Norwegian collectivity').[69]

If one understands legal identity in its essence to be about belonging, then it becomes clear why the law is a powerful cultural identifier, if not *the* cultural identifier, as Burgess would argue.

Robert Schreiter makes a similar observation when musing about the problem of where to start to decipher a culture. He suggests starting with those texts that are most likely to provide information about the identity of a culture's members and social change in that culture. He proposes starting with communal celebrations insofar as celebrations tell scholars much about cultural identity "both in terms of who belongs to the group and in terms of how the world is to be perceived".[70] Yet he then quickly turns to those texts which convey how cultures react to change as well as to threats posed to cultural identity. As typical examples of this kind, he identifies texts which one might call juridical texts, as he maintains: "The sign systems used in divination, in courts of law, in settling arguments, in dealing with strangers all give some idea of the codes that govern social change".[71] With regard to the aim of this book, one can take Schreiter's observation as a suggestion that "reading" the Catholic liturgies and the sacraments—as texts that constitute the celebratory dimension of the church—and "reading" canon law—as texts that constitute the legal dimension of the church—can teach one most about the church. While studying the liturgy and the sacraments helps to decode ecclesiastical cultures particularly with regard to how they perceive Catholic identity, studying the law might be key to understanding how the church reacts to change and to the threats posed to Catholic identities. Here, in the law, one finds many of the boundary markers of a culture, as illustrated by Schreiter's explanations of codes of behaviour as boundary markers which enable individuals and groups to define belonging: "Who may marry whom, boundaries in economic relations (what constitutes honesty and fraud), what is considered wrongdoing (e.g., killing an enemy is virtue, killing someone from the clan is a crime)".[72] J. Peter Burgess describes similarly the function of the law as that of demarcating the boundaries between social groups or other collective entities: "Any assembly is organized by a rule. The rule is what permits us to speak of, indeed to think of assembly. A good Bordeaux is inconceivable without the law

[69] Burgess (1997).

[70] Schreiter (1985), p. 62.

[71] Ibid.

[72] Ibid., p. 66.

which organizes the world according to good Bordeaux [and, addition by the author] not-good Bordeaux".[73] Whilst not all codes or rules which serve as boundary markers are legal codes or rules, as Burgess's example of Bordeaux reveals, the law is one major producer of cultural codes and rules which help to identify the boundaries of a culture. This in mind, it becomes clear why studying canon law enables scholars to analyse markers which signify the boundaries of the church. Schreiter even seems to suggest that analysing the liturgy and the law might provide a deeper understanding of ecclesiastical cultures than reading their doctrinal sources or spiritual texts. Religious texts with their "holistic concerns",[74] as he finds, are often too complex for outsiders and easily allow for misinterpretation. He therefore finds it preferable to start with those texts which can be decoded more easily, such as legal texts. Hence, investigating the law serves as a valuable starting point for approaching ecclesiastical cultures.

3.3.3 Identity Formation

Yet the cultural identifiers provided by the law are not merely helpful for outsiders, as they can identify them as markers of a culture; they also serve as markers of belonging to individuals identifying with a culture. Members can embrace them in processes of identity formation. This does not solely mean that they derive a legal identity from the law—in the sense of being registered as legal subjects of a certain legal order. Rather, it means that the law offers individuals a variety of markers and legal roles that they can integrate into their self-image. Similar to experiences which human beings have as part of social groups—as citizens of a nation state, members of an ethnic group, a social class, a certain generation, or as individuals with a particular gender—they can also derive self-constitutive features from being members of a legal community. Here, they experience themselves as persons with rights or duties, as obliged or entitled to a certain thing or action, as competent of performing a certain action, or as worthy of punishment following illegal behaviour. They define themselves and others in terms of legal roles—"the accused"—and thereby create legal subjectivity. As legal subjects of modern nation states, many individuals internalise principles such as gender equality and equal rights. Consequently, equality becomes more than just a principle they hold dear; it becomes part of their identity and worldview. Legal philosopher Ronald Dworkin described this power of the law to constitute its own subjects in his book *Law's Empire* as the capacity of the law to define human beings: "It makes us what we are: citizens and employees and doctors and spouses and people who own things. … We are subjects of law's empire".[75] This creation of legal subjectivity is in Geertzian terms the creation of a role which

[73] Burgess (1997).

[74] Schreiter (1985), p. 63.

[75] Dworkin (1998), p. VII.

derives its meaning from legal programmes. By ascribing legal subjectivity to individuals they are invited to identify with their roles, thus contributing to the emergence of identity from the law.

These legal markers which individuals incorporate into their identity can lead to conflicts involving incompatible claims, as illustrated by the example of gender equality. When being a legal subject with equal rights forms part of an individual's identity, this self-perception may come into conflict with identity markers offered by different cultures that do not embrace gender equality. However, it is precisely this confrontation that helps them to build their identity. As identity formation involves defining the other and integrating it into the image of the self as the excluded other, incompatible claims play a vital role in this process. While some claims become part of the self, others becomes part of the self as the excluded other from which individuals wish to distance themselves. As an example might show, canon law provides many of these markers which can influence the development of Catholic identities. As mentioned in Sect. 2.8, many Catholics socialised in liberal democracies find it difficult to accept the legal framework of the church and its non-transparent and non-participatory procedures. These tensions also affect how they develop their identity. For instance, disregarding the codes and rules presented by the Apostolic See and developing alternative identity markers of Catholicism has become an integral part of the Catholic identity of many liberal Germans. Their identity is constituted in discursive practices which differentiate between the liberal self and the Roman other. This other remains part of the self of many Catholics as the excluded other from which they wish to distance themselves. With Judith Gruber one can therefore assume that Catholic identities are essentially intercultural. They integrate several views of Catholicism, some of them affirmed as part of the self, some of them excluded as part of the *other-in-the-self*.[76]

Thus, the different legal experiences which Catholics bring to the table are an influential part of their intercultural identity formation. Catholics are members of at least two legal cultures, if not more. They are subject to both state law and canon law. Additionally, most belong to groups that develop their own sub-state law, such as associations, sports clubs, and universities. Hence, identity building with regard to legal experiences is evidently intercultural, in the sense described by Gruber. It is the fragile construction of a self-perception in light of different and even contradictory legal values, signs, and rules achieved by identifying some of these as part of the self and others as part of the other that is integrated into one's self-perception as the other-in-the-self. Many Catholics who were raised in a liberal environment integrate secular views on law and democratic values, as well as a positive attitude towards individual rights into their self-perception. At the same time, many also accommodate experiences with canon law, such as its focus on duties rather than rights. It is not entirely clear which experiences they integrate into their sense of self and which they categorise as the excluded other. Usually, individuals tend to identify with values, signs, and rules with which they are more familiar. As might be

[76] As Gruber (2018), p. 70, notes, "every culture embodies the other-in-its-self".

expected, more Catholics are familiar with state law than with canon law. In any case, this study does not explore the various ways in which canon law influences Catholic identities. Rather, it aims to demonstrate that law, as a significant provider of cultural markers, has a substantial impact on identity formation.

3.3.4 The Weasel Trap

It has become evident that law is a powerful cultural identifier, offering individuals a variety of codes, rules, markers, and roles through which they can create meaning, define their sense of belonging, and form their identity. Nevertheless, explaining how these processes relate to the webs of meaning collected under the heading legal culture is challenging. Sociologies of the law use the term "legal culture" frequently. However, they fill the term with often ambiguous meanings. Sociologist of law Erhard Blankenburg therefore once critically referred to legal culture as a weasel word, as the expression tends to appear whenever the discourse becomes slightly vague.[77] Just as weasels manage to suck out the content of eggs without breaking the shell, "legal culture" pretends to be a substantial concept, yet without truly contributing to understanding the law to any greater degree. According to Blankenburg, sociologists tend to use the term in three senses: it either denotes social expectations and attitudes with regard to the law and legal institutions; or it serves as a heading under which to collect distinct theoretical and professional views of the law and its interpretation, such as legal positivism, natural law, textualism, originalism, or living constitutionalism; or it is used to differentiate the law from other social subsystems, such as politics, often with the purpose of claiming the autonomy of the law. Whilst Blankenburg finds all of these meanings relevant, he proposes a fourfold classification to come to a clearer concept of legal culture. In his view, one can conceive of legal culture as a structure woven from norms, legal institutions, and legal practices, as well as attitudes and expectations with regard to the law, its norms, institutions, and practices.

Clifford Geertz might have embraced some aspects of Blankenburg's classification, such as understanding legal culture as a web of significance which gives legal meaning to norms, institutions, and practices. Yet he would probably have had some doubts concerning the clear and systematic layers which Blankenburg identifies as constituting legal culture. Geertz's proposal to compare culture with an octopus points to the difficulties of systematising legal culture in the way proposed by Blankenburg. In Geertz's view, the connection between cultural signs and their legal meaning seems less clear. While the picture of the octopus suggests that legal signs are obviously connected with legal meaning, it is problematic to assume that these signs bring about their legal meaning in a structured way. The image of the octopus rather suggests that the derivation of legal meaning from signs proceeds in

[77] See Blankenburg (1988), pp. 292–293.

independent moves and in an unpredictable way. This makes investigating cultural phenomena difficult, as mentioned above; however, as Geertz tells his readers, there is no way of escaping these difficulties—except escapism. As stated above, he considers all strategies employed to make studying culture easier to be escapes, including the strategies for "turning culture into folklore and collecting it, turning it into traits and counting it, turning it into institutions and classifying it, turning it into structures and toying with it".[78] Blankenburg's approach of systematising legal culture by analysing the layers of norms, institutions, practices, expectations, and attitudes seems to describe those escapes which Geertz is seeking to avoid.

From the perspective of canon law, it is tempting to identify the institutional and the structural levels of the law as an approach to its legal cultures. As shown above, the conciliar view of culture seems to recommend this view by describing cultures inter alia by referring to the "diverse manner … of establishing laws and juridic institutions".[79] However, these diverse manners do not represent legal cultures, following Geertz's criticism. To avoid examining the legal cultures of the church as if they were industrial production lines transporting legal meaning to local Catholics, mere hypostases of the one universal idea of canon law, one must comprehend them more as octopoid creatures, hard to grasp and difficult to define. Part of what makes them difficult to describe is that the formation of legal cultures works in a similar way to the creation of identity, as intercultural processes. As discussed, the creation of identity is intercultural, integrating some cultural elements into the self, while integrating others to become part of the self as the excluded other. The formation of legal cultures as systems of legal meaning works similarly. Some signs receive a legal meaning to become meaningful elements of a legal culture, whilst others are integrated into the culture as excluded others which fail to be meaningful within the culture. Hence, legal cultures as webs of legal meaning develop by including certain signs as meaningful and by including others as excluded meaningless signs.

3.3.5 Hybrid Systems

One can study this phenomenon more closely by examining hybrid legal systems. In the debate on legal transfer, the term usually denotes mixed jurisdictions such as Scotland or South Africa where a legal system is formed from different legal traditions such as civil law, common law, religious law, or customary law. However, in a broader sense, one can apply the term to all kinds of laws, as legal systems exchange legal signs on a regular basis and are therefore constantly challenged to process signs from an alien origin. This is apparent in the countries of the European Union where national law is in a permanent state of exchange with the law of the union, including the entering of foreign legal signs into the national jurisdictions. The

[78] Geertz (1973a), p. 29.

[79] Second Vatican Council (1965c), no. 53. Acta Apostolicae Sedis (1966), p. 1075.

entering signs find a home in their new contexts when they receive a new meaning and become part of the receiving systems' culture. Sometimes they are found to make no sense in their new home, becoming part of the receiving systems' culture as the excluded other which fails to resonate with local webs of meaning. These operations occur to a greater or lesser extent in every legal system, including canon law. Global canon law is a system of signs and rules of a civil law, continental European, and urban origin, which enters the local churches. Here, the alien signs and rules come into contact with a variety of local signs that generate local meaning: local legal rules, practices, interpretative methodologies, legal practitioners with a certain approach to the law, and legal subjects with a particular mentality. This local culture is not simply the context into which the global rules are to be imbedded. Rather, these rules are rules only *within* the receiving legal culture. Pierre Legrand once spoke of the "ruleness of the rule"[80] as being essentially connected with the meaning of a rule, as meaning can only derive from the legal culture as a system of meaning. Hence, it is the legal culture which makes a rule a rule by attributing it with meaning or by attributing to it the meaning of being meaningless and of being part of the ensemble of signs which fail to make sense in that culture.

One might also explain this phenomenon in theological terms. Wolfgang Beinert, for instance, reminds his readers that being Christian is an endeavour which is always embedded in a specific culture: "The environment does not belong to the context, but already to the text of a lived Christian life".[81] Applying his thought to the law, the local culture is not just a context for Roman canon law after it has entered the local church, but the ensemble of signs with legal meaning into which the entering rule is integrated, either as a legal sign with meaning or as an othered sign which fails to make sense. Consequently, one can understand the local churches as hybrid legal systems. They are webs of meaning where global rules meet with local rules, views of the law, approaches to legal interpretation, and diverse agents. This hybridity of ecclesiastical systems is particularly evident in the local churches with a common law background. However, one can also detect hybrid elements in all other local churches. Speaking of legal cultures in church therefore essentially requires the use of the plural. There is not one single ecclesiastical legal culture made in Rome and transported into the local churches. Instead, there are a multitude of local webs of meaning woven from signs which carry legal meaning in a particular context—and also from signs which fail to be meaningful in that context, but remain a part of legal cultures as the excluded other.

That legal cultures are hybrid structures does not imply that one cannot study ecclesiastical legal folklore, institutions, or structures without falling prey to some form of Geertzian escapism. On the contrary, these phenomena might serve as entry points for approaching ecclesiastical legal cultures, as they are part of what Geertz calls in his definition of culture "an ensemble of texts, themselves ensembles, which the anthropologist strains to read over the shoulders of those to whom they properly

[80] Legrand (1997), p. 117.

[81] Beinert (1997), p. 345.

belong".[82] In order to examine legal cultures, one has to decipher their meaning as conveyed by their "texts" as those ensembles of signs which convey legal meaning. Legal texts are diverse. As mentioned, they consist of words, gestures, events, or persons. An extensive approach to legal cultures therefore requires the deciphering of complex texts, as Robert Schreiter explains: "The task of description and analysis is to 'read' the text, that is, locate its signs, the codes that place the signs in dynamic interaction, and the messages that are conveyed".[83] Hence, when examining ecclesiastical legal cultures, it is essential to study the ensembles of texts collected under the head "canon law" and to interpret them over the shoulders of those to whom they belong—the legislator, legal practitioners, legal subjects, and scholars. Just as Geertz researched the Balinese cockfight to approach Balinese culture, one can explore Roman Catholic canon law as an ensemble of texts, legal norms, institutions, roles, folklore, attitudes to the law, and expectations of the law to come to an understanding of ecclesiastical legal cultures. However, these norms, institutions, roles, attitudes are neither identical with legal culture nor unite to become a legal culture. It is rather the meaning attributed to them which makes for a legal culture as a system of meaning. Thus, canonical institutions, the constitutional structures of the church, and ecclesiastical legal practices are not "culture". Yet they are markers of culture insofar as they convey legal meaning and contribute to structures of legal meaning. Merely studying these legal beliefs, values, and principles, signs and symbols, codes and rules does not in itself uncover their meaning. To do so it is also essential, as Geertz reminds his readers, to look over the shoulders of those to whom these texts belong. Hence, one has to research legal beliefs, values, and principles, signs and symbols, codes and rules over the shoulders of the members of the diverse local churches: of laypeople and clerics, parish members, office holders, and academics. It is their views of the ensembles of texts and of the ensembles of ensembles of texts which help scholars to detect legal meaning. Collecting their views is therefore key if one seeks to engage in the study of Catholic legal cultures.

3.4 Summary

This chapter has outlined the challenge of determining the place of canon law between universality and cultural reality. Currently, the law sits uneasily between the universal and the cultural. This is because, since the nineteenth century, an anti-modernist strand of jurisprudence has emphasised the universal at the expense of the cultural. This tension is particularly evident in Catholic natural law. This example illustrates why canon law tends to universalise its claims, thereby marginalising culture and the diversity of the local churches. However, the case of natural law also shows that there are alternatives to the marginalisation of culture. Some natural law

[82] Geertz (1973f), p. 452.

[83] Schreiter (1985), p. 61.

theories propose a non-exclusive view of nature and culture. Adopting this perspective reveals that all legal rules are cultural artefacts. In order to provide an analytical framework for studying law as culture and the tensions deriving from cross-cultural encounters, this chapter has also discussed this book's use of the term *culture* and clarified its Geertzian approach to *legal culture*.

Chapter 4
Incarnating the Christian Message

As an inherent part of systems of meaning, law is essentially cultural. It only makes sense within the webs of significance from which it derives its meaning. This finding includes those laws which religious individuals believe derive from God as a supercultural source of law. Even divine law—as an ensemble of texts to which a community attributes the meaning that it expresses what is right according to God's will—only makes sense when it is embedded in a culture as a web of significance from which it derives this meaning. This in mind, it is apparent why natural law is cultural law. Natural law—as an ensemble of texts to which a community attributes the meaning that it articulates what is right according to nature—derives this meaning from cultures which provide for this meaning. Robert Schreiter uses the term natural law in precisely this sense when speaking about phenomena that are self-evident to members of a certain group: "They are simply 'commonsense,' 'natural law,' 'the way things are.'"[1] Schreiter, thus defines natural law as those cultural signs which for the members of a certain group carry a manifest meaning. These observations can be applied to all laws which claim to have a universal meaning. Norms may indeed claim universal validity while being deeply cultural, as it is only from a cultural standpoint that one can discover their meaning, including their universal meaning; this is where David Novak's telescope metaphor once again comes to mind. Following approaches which understand all realities as essentially cultural, it is therefore misleading to set universality against culturality. Quite the opposite, culture is the framework in which the universal manifests itself and from which it obtains its meaning.

The Second Vatican Council echoed this idea, but somewhat in reverse. The council in its ecclesiology presents a hylemorphic concept of what the church is, by assuming the existence of a supertemporal and supercultural substance which takes on concrete historical and cultural accidents. The Pastoral Constitution *Gaudium et Spes* notes that the church, due to its universality, is not bound to a certain culture

[1] Schreiter (1985), p. 56.

J. Hahn, *The Cultures of Canon Law*, Law and Religion in a Global Context 6,
https://doi.org/10.1007/978-3-032-14812-4_4

and "is not bound exclusively and indissolubly to any race or nation, any particular way of life or any customary way of life recent or ancient".[2] Yet due to its supercultural character, it can become concrete in each and every culture. The constitution states that "since in virtue of her mission and nature she is bound to no particular form of human culture, nor to any political, economic or social system, the Church by her very universality can be a very close bond between diverse human communities and nations".[3] The church as "sent to all peoples of every time and place"[4] has the mission to embrace all peoples and cultures: "Faithful to her own tradition and at the same time conscious of her universal mission, she can enter into communion with the various civilizations, to their enrichment and the enrichment of the Church herself".[5] Whilst the Church of Christ is universal, according to doctrine, the church in its earthly representations is not. In its concrete manifestations, it is a cultural phenomenon which takes shape within the local churches.

The theory unfolded in Sect. 3.1 of this book regarding how the universal realises itself within the cultural enables a critical stance towards this concept that there is a universal essence from which to mould the local churches. Using David Novak's words, the conciliar ecclesiology does not understand the Church of Christ as serving as a "universal horizon"[6] for the local churches to which they direct their telescopes, but rather as a universal source from which to derive the local churches. Hence, it presents a top-down view which implies that the local churches derive from the universal church, whereas following Novak one can develop a bottom-up approach to detect the common universal church from one's own local ecclesial standpoint. What both attempts share is that they maintain a connection between the universal and the cultural. The cultural is the way in which the universal realises itself. However, the question remains open as to *how* one perceives this process in which the universal becomes a particular reality. For ecclesiology, this requires clarification how the Church of Christ manifests itself in the local churches.

This chapter examines this relationship between the universal and the particular in three steps. Section 4.1 studies how the church has addressed this dynamic throughout its history, with a focus on mission theology and missiological concepts reflecting how the church has conceptualised mediation between universal faith and particular cultures in mission contexts. The concept currently favoured by the Apostolic See is that of *inculturation*. However, it can be interpreted in various ways. The three main types of inculturation strategies—dynamic equivalence, creative assimilation, and organic progression—are discussed in Sect. 4.2. Each has its own merits and demerits with regard to enabling the preservation of local cultural identity and safeguarding the ecclesial tradition. Further complexity arises from conservative, neoconservative, liberal, and radical interpretations of these

[2] Second Vatican Council (1965c), no. 58. Acta Apostolicae Sedis (1966), p. 1079.

[3] Ibid., no. 42. Acta Apostolicae Sedis (1966), p. 1061.

[4] Ibid., no. 58. Acta Apostolicae Sedis (1966), p. 1079.

[5] Ibid.

[6] Novak (1998), p. 190.

strategies, which differ in that they place more emphasis on protecting either the ecclesial tradition or the local identity. Section 4.3 then seeks to shed more light on the current official church politics of inculturation. It examines the mostly neoconservative policies realised in official intercultural theology and missiology. The aim is to map out the Apostolic See's inculturation frameworks, which also guide global legislation and the inculturation of canon law in the local churches—a subject that is discussed in greater detail in Chap. 5.

4.1 Missiological Concepts

The challenge of determining how the universal church realises itself in concrete times and circumstances has accompanied the church since its earliest days, when early mission theology thought about ways of conveying the Christian faith to non-believers. Different beliefs of how best to convey the Christian message to non-Christians, as Michael Angrosino notes, have prevailed throughout the history of Christianity, ranging from imposition to translation to adaptation:

> When Christianity was first spread beyond Europe, Rome attempted a strategy of *imposition*, the enforced use of unmodified Roman forms. This attempt gave way to *translation*, the preservation of Roman forms encoded in the local vernaculars. At present the church is trying *adaptation*, the tailoring of Roman forms to local tastes and expectations. The idealized culmination of this process occurs when Roman forms become incarnate in new cultural settings.[7]

It is revealing how fervently Angrosino points to the Roman-ness of the Christian message to be revealed in other cultures. He does not speak of a universal faith and how it might take on a concrete shape in different circumstances; instead, he studies the phenomenon that the universal Christian faith, when communicated across the globe, has already taken on a specific local form. Just as natural law is always cultural, as one cannot perceive the natural apart from culture and time, the Catholic faith is always a cultural phenomenon when referred to from a cultural standpoint. Hence, when speaking about how to convey the universal truth of the faith to non-believers, believers are speaking about conveying what they understand to be a universal truth but one which is already expressed in a certain historical and cultural form. With regard to Catholicism, one might be tempted to miss this, as the Roman Catholic Church tends to communicate its message in a uniform doctrine and demands a relatively uniform praxis. However, this doctrine and praxis is based on particular ideas, traditions, and practices. Hence, the doctrinal and ritual uniformity of the Catholic world is less a consequence of the universality of the Christian message and more of its uniform manifestation in Roman ideas, traditions, and practices. In consequence, when discussing how the universal church can express its faith in concrete times and circumstances, one not only has to think about how a

[7] Angrosino (1994), pp. 824–825.

universal value might become real in history and under different circumstances, but also how a universal idea, which *was* realised in history and under very specific circumstances and has developed a tradition from that encounter, can communicate exactly that to others and encourage them to become part of that tradition without denying their own history and culture. Hence, the church faces the challenge of how to convey itself to others as a universal message in a concrete cultural shape without supressing the concrete cultures of others and while allowing others to connect their own traditions with the Christian message.

4.1.1 Accommodating Christianity

The church's struggle how to convey this message has been a challenge since its earliest days. However, this challenge became even greater in the Catholic missions after 1492 when the church began to communicate the Gospel extensively beyond European borders. Classical missiology found that communicating Christianity to non-Europeans provided considerably more effort than did traditional teaching and preaching, as it required the missionaries to take into account the plural cultures they encountered. Judith Gruber describes this discovery as a learning process which brought about new views of mission. Whilst mission initially allied closely with colonialism and cultural imperialism and their unidirectional approach of imposing established concepts on others, missionaries quickly began to find that they could not override the cultural pluralities with which they found themselves confronted, and also could not ignore the culturality of their own faith, as Gruber explains:

> In mission activity, the European export of Christianity encountered cultural plurality and diversity, and thus the understanding of the universality of the Gospel became problematic. Missionary border experiences, which made cultural alterity visible and tangible, clearly demonstrated the culturality of European Christianity. The confrontation with cultural plurality made it impossible to present this type of Christianity as universal and to transmit it to other cultures without further ado.[8]

Mission now faced the problem of how to convey the Christian message to groups which were profoundly different to the European societies in which Christianity had flourished. To allow for this, it particularly relied on the concept of *accommodation*. In early versions of this approach, the focus was on the missionaries as the agents who "adapted themselves to the objects of mission".[9] The Jesuit accommodation model, developed to support evangelisation in East Asia, particularly in China and Japan, may have played a special role in this respect. It involved adapting the Christian message and the missionary practices to align with local cultural

[8] Gruber (2018), p. 20.

[9] Ibid., p. 21.

expectations. The missionaries learnt the local languages, accepted local customs, and adopted local intellectual traditions such as Confucianism. They were open to embracing Asian cultures not only out of respect for other cultures or for strategic reasons but also because of their theological insight that Christianity is based on incarnation and therefore requires the faith to express itself within a specific culture. As sociologist José Casanova notes that

> the Jesuits … became convinced that in order to take roots in Japan Christianity itself would have to become Japanese, in the same way as Christianity, originally Hebrew, had to become truly Greek and Latin. If primitive Christianity could undergo such a fundamental translation and accommodation to Greek and to Roman culture, there was no reason why it could not become also Japanese, Chinese, etc. Christianity could only become truly universal and global by becoming freed from its European cultural habitus and accommodating the particular habitus of each culture.[10]

Although this strategy was widely successful, it also sparked controversy with other missionary orders, ultimately resulting in the suppression of the missions. In China, they were replaced by colonial mission strategies. In Japan, the Tokugawa state's anti-Christian policies led to the widespread elimination of Catholicism from Japanese culture.

As a second type of Catholic encounters with non-Western cultures, Casanova understands the political conquest and colonisation of the "New World", subjugating the colonised peoples to European politics and Christianity. He identifies this hegemonic type of mission as given in the colonising of the Americas, as well as of the Philippines, by the Iberian colonisers.[11] Later on, also in these contexts, the approach to mission became more reciprocal, paying more attention to the receptive processes of non-believers and new Christians, as well as to the insights gained from accommodating the faith in new contexts with regard to the faith itself. As a result, mission started to focus more on discernible elements of its operation such as accommodation, assimilation, and transformation.

4.1.2 Christian Essentialisms

Yet even though mission theology developed a differentiated view of accommodation, as Gruber emphasises, it did not solve one fundamental problem deriving from its theoretical foundation in ancient Aristotelian hylemorphism. Scholasticism had once transported substance and accident metaphysics into Western metaphysics and ontology, from which it was then received into mission theology to explain the relationship between faith and culture. As invariant substance, accommodation approaches identified key elements of Christian life such as doctrine with the quintessence of Catholic faith and morals. They were regarded as being the

[10] Casanova (2019), pp. 25–26.

[11] See Gruber (2018), p. 20.

supercultural, supertemporal, and immutable "essence of Christianity".[12] Successful mission, accordingly, required the non-Christians to receive the supercultural Christian truth without changing it. As this truth was regarded as being free from cultural contamination, Catholic faith and morals themselves were not subjected to cultural accommodation, as Gruber explains. Therefore, accommodation models understood the communication of doctrine more as a practical or a methodological challenge than as a hermeneutical or theological problem.[13] They were primarily addressing the challenge of how to communicate the doctrine in other languages without changing its meaning. Adding to these essential elements of Christianity, mission theology identified more accidental layers of a changeable nature, which, different from the substantial elements, did allow for cultural accommodation: "'Peripheral' matters in the area of liturgy, religious customs, or church architecture, for example, were considered accidental and could thus be adjusted to other cultures".[14]

This concept had various shortcomings, which Gruber discusses in detail.[15] From today's point of view and in light of critical cultural theories, its demerits derive particularly from a simplified view of Christianity and culture. This includes various limitations: a simplistic conception of Christianity as composed of substantial and accidental realities—a binarisation of social realities which "goes contrary to the complexity of cultural sign systems that develop meaning in the difference and interdependence of their symbols"[16]; the questionable idea of differentiating between Christian elements which defy accommodation and those which allow for it; an ahistorical and acultural view of truth; the fallacy of identifying European beliefs as universal faith; the dubious claim that it is possible to protect and control an invariable meaning when transplanting faith or morals into other cultural settings; as well as the instrumental idea of transplanting meaning in the first place. Accommodation models therefore did not outlast the twentieth century. Gruber describes their decline after the council:

> By the 1960s and 1970s, the missiological project had thus come under massive attack. The theological paradigm shifts of that time began to dismantle the neo-scholastic presuppositions of its theological framework; the paternalistic approach it took to the so-called 'objects of mission' and its monolithic ideal for the world church began to sit uneasily with a world shifting towards decolonization.[17]

Former missiology was replaced by intercultural theology. *Church planting*—as the idea of transferring the unchangeable Christian truth into a non-Christian culture while allowing the accidents of Christianity to take on some local flavour—gave

[12] Ibid., p. 22.

[13] See ibid., pp. 12, 21.

[14] Ibid., p. 21.

[15] See ibid., pp. 21–25.

[16] Ibid., p. 22.

[17] Ibid., p. 25.

way to more holistic approaches to how the Christian faith might find a home in a new environment.

4.1.3 Translation Approaches

As Gruber emphasises, the merit of intercultural theologies was that they understood communicating the faith in different contexts as a theological challenge, not merely a methodological one.[18] They were therefore particularly interested in understanding how different contexts inform theology. This involved recognising local cultures as *loci theologici* and relativising the Roman culture as the only embodiment of the church.[19] In their attempt to discover how signs can be interpreted and understood across cultural borders, intercultural theologies developed an intercultural hermeneutics. Some also adopted a normative stance, for example by supporting postcolonialism.[20] One ground-breaking contribution to intercultural theology was Robert Schreiter's book *Constructing Local Theologies*, which discussed various concepts of how cultures can embrace the Christian faith to accomplish their own local theologies. For the post-conciliar time, Schreiter identifies three major approaches to establishing local theologies, namely translation, adaptation, and contextual concepts, with each providing a different solution to the problem.

The approaches which Schreiter collects under the head *translation* apprehend the development of a local theology as a two-step activity: "In the first step, one frees the Christian message as much as possible from its previous cultural accretions. In doing so, the data of revelation are allowed to stand freely and be prepared for the second step of the procedure, namely, translation into a new situation".[21] The key concern of this concept is to uncover as much of the universal idea as possible by freeing it from its former cultural impregnation, with the purpose of relocating it in another culture. Schreiter describes this method by alluding to the image of a kernel and its husk, noting that "the basic Christian revelation is the kernel; the previous cultural settings in which it has been incarnated constitute the husk. The kernel has to be hulled time and again, as it were, to allow it to be translated into new cultural contexts".[22]

This idea of wrapping the supercultural Christian message in a variety of cultural contexts has received criticism. Schreiter inter alia criticises it for its superficial approach to cultural meaning, as translation often tends to turn to concepts in

---

[18] See ibid., pp. 42–45.

[19] See ibid., pp. 34, 42, 47.

[20] See ibid., p. 60.

[21] Schreiter (1985), p. 7.

Again, as mentioned in the introduction, it is important to note that the term *translation* is used differently in scholarly debates. For a study arguing in favour of a differentiated view of translation as used in legal discourse, see Bray (2020).

[22] Ibid.

different cultures which seem to carry a comparable meaning at first sight, without ensuring that this meaning truly concords with the message one wants to convey: "More attention is given to the surface patterns of a culture than to its deeper meanings or to the interconnections between different cultural patterns. ... The translation model assumes that there is a direct equivalent in the local culture for the cultural pattern coming from another church setting".[23] He calls this simplistic approach—of expecting different cultures to provide for synonymous meanings connected with different signs which allow for an easy exchange of signs to express an identical meaning—a "positivist understanding of culture".[24]

However, the difficulties connected with translation go deeper. They intersect with the problem that the image of the kernel and husk alludes to a hylemorphic approach. This brings with it all the challenges mentioned with regard to accommodation, even though translation presents hylemorphic thought in a more refined way compared to traditional accommodation concepts. Instead of segmenting Christianity into the immutable substance of Christian faith and morals and culturally adaptable accidents, such as liturgical rituals, religious customs, or church architecture, translation focuses on the substantial and accidental qualities of the Christian message itself. It identifies the kernel as a doctrinal substance covered by various interchangeable cultural husks. Catholic doctrine appears to be a reality composed of an essential kernel and additional variable elements. Hence, following a kernel and husk approach, doctrinal truths are always wrapped in cultural accidents. One can detect this idea in Pope John XXIII's speech given when he opened the Second Vatican Council: "The deposit of the faith itself, or the truths, which are contained in our venerable doctrine is namely one thing, and another thing the way in which they are expressed, but with the same sense and the same meaning".[25] Bernhard Lonergan critically commented on this view by noting "that the diversity of peoples, cultures, social arrangements can involve only a difference in the dress in which doctrines are expressed, but cannot involve any diversity in church doctrine itself".[26] Contextual theologian Stephen Bevans concordantly observes: "The values and thought forms of culture and the structures of social change are understood not so much as good in themselves, but as convenient vehicles for this essential, unchanging deposit of truth".[27] Hence, in this Neo-Scholastic version of perceiving concrete Christian realities in terms of substance and accidents, translation serves less to contrast the church with the world or the Christian truth with non-Christian cultures, and more to explain the hylemorphic conception of the church, its faith, and its norms themselves.

---

[23] Ibid., p. 8.

[24] Ibid.

[25] Original quote: "Est enim aliud ipsum depositum Fidei, seu veritates, quae veneranda doctrina nostra continentur, aliud modus, quo eaedem enuntiantur, eodem tamen sensu eademque sententia", John XXIII (1962b). Acta Apostolicae Sedis (1962), p. 792.

[26] Lonergan (1972), p. 302.

[27] Bevans (2002), p. 37.

4.1.4 Ontological Dualisms

Yet, while the hylemorphic differentiation is useful for explaining how the universal manifests itself in different times and cultures, it is not unproblematic. This is because the idea of things being composed of substance and accidents is a typical Western description of reality.[28] Karl Rahner also raises this criticism when describing the connection between divine law and human norms.[29] Many scholars connect their doubts that hylemorphic explanations of reality do not adequately translate into non-Western ontologies with linguist Benjamin Lee Whorf's famous findings on the different structure of languages and their influence on the perception of reality. Whorf's studies on the characteristics of the Hopi language have directed attention to the fact that many languages do not possess the typical European combination of mass nouns, which describe a substance without a definite outline such as *water*, *fruit*, or *grass*, with container nouns which provide those substances with an outline, like *glass* ("of water"), *piece* ("of fruit"), or *patch* ("of grass"). Whorf called this linguistic characteristic the "duality of formless item and form",[30] which is typically European. This European combination of formless item and form is not a random phenomenon of European thought, but deeply intertwined with Western reasoning, due to the impact of Aristotelian ontology on the European history of ideas.[31] European thought, including Catholic theology, is deeply impregnated by this dualism. However, it is rather alien to thinkers from non-European contexts. Hence, whilst hylemorphism might be well-suited in Western settings to explain particular concretions of universal ideas, it is not a universal approach to ontology that is plausible in all cultures or local churches.

The problem, however, is not merely that hylemorphism does not translate easily into non-Western philosophy. A more profound challenge, which Rahner alludes to, connects with hylemorphic epistemology and ontology. The epistemological pitfall of hylemorphism, when narrowed down to a kernel and husk configuration, lies in identifying the invariant substance, whilst there is no way of perceiving invariant realities apart from their cultural concretion. Ontologically, Rahner points at the problem of identity between the supercultural and the cultural. If the divine will or supercultural principles are understood as essential essences which manifest themselves differently in diverse cultures and times, it is unclear how to conceive of them as being essentially identical while taking on different historical and cultural shapes.[32] As substances and accidents are not identical, there is no way to claim that the cultural is a true manifestation of the universal when analysed in the light of hylemorphism. Rahner's approach therefore disfavours an interpretation of historical and cultural realities as accidental layers laid around an unchangeable kernel

[28] E.g. Schreiter (1985), p. 77.

[29] See Rahner (1962), p. 252.

[30] Whorf (1956), p. 142.

[31] This observation is made inter alia by Schreiter (1985), p. 77; Huels (1987), pp. 261–262.

[32] See Rahner (1962), p. 253.

("eine akzidentielle Schicht um eine unverändert bleibende Natur herum").[33] Instead, he argues in favour of interpreting the historical realities expressing the universal *as* the concrete history *of* the universal. This view also solves the mentioned epistemological problem, as it explains why one can study the universal only in its historical realisations.

In a similar vein as Rahner, Robert Schreiter criticises the kernel and husk approach for its assumption that a universal message develops "in some privileged, supracultural sphere".[34] This assumption, as he finds, ignores the fact that a universal idea is necessarily embodied in culture: "A closer examination would show that kernel and cultural husk are given together, even in the Bible, and they come to have a profound effect on each other over a period of time".[35] Schreiter—in explaining why the embedding of the Christian message into a specific cultural or historical context is an essential quality of Christian truth—refers to incarnation theology. As the Catholic Creed regards Christ to be true God and true man at the same time, a kernel and husk approach does not give adequate credit to the human nature of Christ. Schreiter therefore considers the magisterium's tendency to marginalise culture and history to be a theological problem, when noting with regard to tradition: "The church tradition's form and its formulation are considered as being somehow supracultural. But forms and formulations are always born in some cultural context … To forget this does the tradition a disfavour by disincarnating it".[36] Hence, in the light of the incarnation analogy, the idea of kernel and husk—with its inclination to hyper-substantiate the kernel and to marginalise the accidental husks—is theologically questionable. It tends to identify an essence of the church and of Christian faith by focusing on a supercultural kernel, as Stephen Bevans observes that "translation is not a model for daring and creative ways to state the message; it is conceived much more as a way of being faithful to an essential content".[37] And it has a propensity to marginalise culture and history, thus missing the essential culturality and historicity of the church and its faith. Judith Gruber points to both problems, asking: "How can we identify the culture-transcending 'essence' of Christianity without falling back into essentialist and substantialist thinking?"[38] To avoid the fallacies deriving from essentialist and substantialist approaches, it seems necessary to escape traditional binarisations and hierarchisations, as she proposes, saying that "the 'principle of the incarnation' does not allow Christian theology to understand dogma and history, nature and grace, faith and reason as mutually exclusive entities. Rather, when reflecting on the historical Christ event as the revelation of God's history, it has to take into account the place *in* which the revelation occurs".[39] In

[33] Ibid., p. 259.
[34] Schreiter (1985), p. 8.
[35] Ibid.
[36] Ibid., p. 77.
[37] Bevans (2002), p. 37.
[38] Gruber (2018), p. 11.
[39] Ibid., p. 92.

consequence, Gruber sees particularity not as the antipode to universality to demarcate the universal from the contingent and historical, but as the very way in which the universal becomes concrete: "Particularity is not a deficit in the revelation of universality but its very condition".[40] Schreiter therefore suggests finding a new image to explain the connection between universal truth and culture which does not allow for their easy segmentation: "Rather than the kernel-and-husk image of an incarnate Christianity, which allows for a ready hulling to reveal the kernel of divine revelation, perhaps the image of an onion would be more appropriate: each successive layer is intimately bound to the next".[41] Stephen Bevans relates to this image of the onion by adding that "rather than looking for a kernel to wrap in a new husk, the theologian should be looking for God's presence at every layer of the onion and point that out in terms of the older and wider tradition".[42]

4.1.5 Adaptation Approaches

Due to this and similar criticism, many theologians have relinquished translation models as unsuitable for providing the church with a feasible theory to explain how the local churches embrace the Christian faith by developing local theologies. Some have turned to adaptation as an alternative. There are several adaptation approaches. In some, representatives of traditional European churches or representatives of local churches with a classical European education in philosophy and theology adopt a typical Western philosophy, such as Thomism, which, in the West, serves as a theoretical basis for theology. From evaluating it in the light of non-Western concepts, they derive their own philosophical theories based on local traditions.[43] This local philosophy then serves as a foundation for a local theology, in a similar way to which systems of thought such as Aristotelian metaphysics or Thomism have served European theology.

Schreiter finds this method more open to local thought than translation approaches. However, he criticises the idea of building a theology on a well-defined philosophical fundament as being in itself strikingly Western and a Scholastic notion from the Middle Ages. While its age does not necessarily make it a bad idea, it is fair to say that the imposition of a fixed philosophical system onto theology has not served Western theology consistently well. As a result, theologians grapple with traditional concepts that have proved a burden to the development of Catholic doctrine, such as Augustine's view of sexuality. With regard to the law, Ladislas Orsy alludes to the Aristotelian ontology as one decisive factor preventing current canon

---

[40] Ibid.

[41] Ibid.

[42] Bevans (2002), p. 44.

[43] See Schreiter (1985), pp. 9–10.

law from developing. He calls it a "Philosophy holding the law captive",[44] along with other classical Western philosophies such as Plato's hierarchical conception of society, Aquinas's concept of the law, and late Scholasticism's view of the soul. Hence, there is reason to be sceptical of whether the core concern of adaptation, namely selecting a philosophical foundation of theology or legal theory as a basis for establishing a local approach is a recommendable strategy.

Other adaptation models work differently. There are approaches which start with a humbler basis, as they do not rebuild a whole philosophical system to create the foundation for a local theology, but rather perceive the local growth of faith as a slow and independent development from the seed of the Gospel message planted in a community. These approaches follow the idea that biblical texts can provoke bottom-up theological responses from a group, which develop into local theologies. This idea has a biblical ancestry, as the New Testament describes the growth of Christian communities as an act of receiving the Gospel (see Acts 2:37–42; 1 Corinthians 11:23 and 15:1). When the early Christians were encouraged by the Apostles' preaching and teaching, they took up this stimulus to develop their own theology, building communities around their local theology.[45] Schreiter, for his part, finds this model rather idealistic. There were hardly any local churches where the seed of the Gospel had a fair chance to grow independently, as the Gospel message was usually accompanied by manifold Western concepts and artefacts for expressing that message, from Latin hymns to fully predefined Western rites. So the chances that the Gospel unfolds a pure theological dynamic are rather low. Schreiter himself is obviously fascinated by the idea of allowing the Gospel to trigger the development of local theologies, but he also considers it somewhat innocent: "This model represents an ideal that is almost always skewed by human circumstances. It assumes that the Holy Spirit works in a community in ways basically disengaged from normal human events. It has a stronger theology of unfettered grace than of human sin".[46]

4.1.6 *Contextual Theologies*

Missiology, when endeavouring to cut its Neo-Scholastic strings, largely turned to contextual theologies in the second half of the twentieth century. Contextual approaches modify the perspective taken by the adaptation approach to some degree. Whereas adaptation takes the faith as a starting point for considering how a local theology might adequately express it, contextual approaches concentrate on the local culture and ask how the Christian message can relate to it. Robert Schreiter explains:

---

[44] Orsy (1996b), p. 12.

[45] E.g. Beinert (1991), pp. 23–24.

[46] Schreiter (1985), p. 12.

> Their particular strength lies in beginning with the questions that the people themselves have—not those posed immediately by other Christian churches or those necessary for a systematic understanding of faith. In other words they try to initiate a dialogue with Christian tradition whereby that tradition can address questions genuinely posed by the local circumstances, rather than only those questions that the Christian tradition has treated in the past.[47]

Contextual approaches address these questions in several ways. Schreiter roughly differentiates between contextual theologies as ethnographies of a nascent theology, with a strong focus on local identities, or as liberation theologies focusing on local needs and challenges, for instance by focusing on social problems such as oppression or violence to which the local theologies might respond. Starting from local idiosyncrasies, contextual theologies develop a local view of what being a Christian and having a particular identity or responding to the social questions of a particular society might mean. In doing so, ethnographic approaches (or anthropological approaches, as Stephen Bevans prefers to call them)[48] tend to focus on continuity and the preservation of cultural identity when responding to the Gospel. One such example is *indigenisation* with its focus on recreating Catholic practices such as the liturgies by relying on indigenous traditions and by using indigenous artefacts. Liberation theologies, on the contrary, focus more on change as initiated by the Gospel message. Hence, they develop in close connection with the particular social and political circumstances. These circumstances influence the evolving local theologies to a significant degree, a factor which might become challenging, as Schreiter notes, for instance if contextual approaches idealise the local culture, trivialise its social problems, or ignore that some practices are incompatible with the Gospel. Furthermore, what he also sees as a shortcoming of contextual theologies is that they often remain in an embryonic state.

According to Schreiter, contextual theologies primarily focus on local idiosyncrasies and approach the Christian faith from this perspective. Other scholars, however, have proposed a more balanced relationship. For instance, Judith Gruber emphasises that contextual models are not about reversing the perspective of adaptation by placing culture over the universal Christian message, but rather consider both the universal faith and the local culture in order to ask how both communicate with each other: "Contextual theologies aim to make their contextuality and the universal claim of the Christian message two equal starting points of theological reflection. They thus address the tension between universality and particularity, between unity and plurality, between the normativity and contingency of the Christian message".[49] Thus, contextual approaches support a mutual dialogue between the universal and the local—a view of contextuality received by the Catholic concept of *inculturation*. Whilst Protestant theology has widely continued to speak of contextual theology, inculturation has become the dominant term in the

[47] Ibid., pp. 13–14.

[48] See Bevans (2002), p. 55; Bevans (2018), pp. 12–15.

[49] Gruber (2018), p. 30.

Catholic debates on communicating the faith since the late 1970s.[50] It understands the encounter between Christianity and non-Christian cultures as a mutual enrichment which affects the culture receiving the Christian message as well as the message itself. While the term inculturation is close to *acculturation* as used by the social sciences to describe cultural changes in which individuals or groups adapt to another culture—by segregation, integration, assimilation, or marginalisation—the meaning of inculturation differs from acculturation precisely with respect to the idea of mutual learning, as Michael Angrosino explains:

> [I]nculturation refers to encounters whose outcome is a convergence that does not replace either of the cultures from which it arose. Both parties to the inculturative exchange undergo internal transformation, but neither loses its autonomous identity. Acculturation may be accidental, but inculturation occurs when a dominant culture attempts to make itself accessible to a subdominant one without losing its own particular character.[51]

Whilst the term inculturation enjoys prominence in the Catholic debates today, it is not free from criticism. For instance, not all scholars embrace the shift from contextualisation to inculturation. Stephen Bevans argues in favour of abiding with contextualisation to avoid the narrowness of inculturation as well as of indigenisation.[52] He favours contextualisation, as this term includes social, political, and economic dimensions of relevance for contextual theologies, connotations which Bevans does not find in inculturation or indigenisation.

Another point of criticism expressed by Robert Schreiter is that inculturation seems to be "a dilettantish kind of neologism"[53] as compared to the established acculturation terminology of the social sciences. Anscar Chupungco similarly calls inculturation and related ecclesiastical neologisms slightly odd jargons: "They belong to the peculiar terminology used on different occasions by anthropologists and borrowed gratefully by theologians, missiologists, and liturgists. To the uninitiated most of them are outlandish, if not linguistically barbarous".[54] One might indeed discuss the usefulness of these terminological choices for theology. In this sense, Michael Angrosino finds it awkward from an anthropological point of view that the church does not make greater use of the concepts developed by the social sciences: "The point is that a global institution with vast potential for touching the lives of millions could benefit from a more open dialogue with anthropology rather than relying on its own formulation of the culture concept".[55]

[50] For a short overview over the history of the term see Chupungco (1992), pp. 25–26.

[51] Angrosino (1994), p. 825.

[52] See Bevans (2002), pp. 26–27; Bevans (2018), pp. 32–33.

[53] Schreiter (1985), p. 5.

[54] Chupungco (1992), p. 13.

[55] Angrosino (1994), p. 830.

4.1.7 Inculturation as Incarnation

This book is particularly concerned with this conceptual dimension of culture cultivated in the church's official inculturation politics. It therefore seems important to note that ecclesiastical terminology often borrows some meaning from concepts used in other areas of study, such as the social sciences, whilst using linguistic peculiarities to introduce alternative meanings into the terms.[56] Hence, one can expect the term inculturation to carry some ecclesiastical idiosyncrasies which acculturation does not contain. And one can expect these idiosyncrasies as contained in inculturation to impact the very perception of culture in church. This assumption—that inculturation borrows only parts of its meaning from acculturation to introduce into the term its own ecclesiastical view of culture—makes it necessary to examine the particular meaning of inculturation and how it deviates from the terminology of the social sciences somewhat more closely.

Schreiter qualifies inculturation as a mixed concept: "A combination of the theological principle of incarnation with the social-science concept of acculturation (adapting oneself to a culture)".[57] His explanation refers to the finding that Catholic documents often couple the term inculturation with *incarnation*. This connection has its roots in the Second Vatican Council and its Decree *Ad Gentes* on the mission of the church. The decree describes conveying the faith to non-Christians as implanting the church in their cultures, a process analogous to the incarnate Christ who took on the social praxis of his culture and time: "The church, in order to be able to offer all of them the mystery of salvation and the life brought by God, must implant itself into these groups for the same motive which led Christ to bind himself, in virtue of his incarnation, to certain social and cultural conditions of those human beings among whom he dwelt".[58] Following *Ad Gentes*, official documents since the council have tended to rely on the image of the incarnation to elucidate the connection between the universal message of faith and the concrete expressions of that faith in the local churches. The International Theological Commission, in their 1988 considerations on faith and inculturation, expounded this analogy to some extent. The document explains the necessity of inculturating the faith by pointing at Christ's incarnation as an act of God becoming human and therefore essentially becoming a cultural being: "It is because he became man that God has also assumed, in a certain way, a race, a country and a time".[59] As Christ essentially had to become involved with human culture to fulfil God's plan of salvation for humankind, communicating the Christian message depends on the inculturation of the Gospel becoming real for humanity, as the commission records: "Christ would not be one with us in the reality

[56] For instance, canonists Norbert Lüdecke and Georg Bier devoted their attention to the introduction of the adjective "true" as a marker of inserting a specific ecclesiastical meaning into common terms, as in "true equality" (see canon 208 CIC/1983), see Lüdecke and Bier (2012), pp. 57–75.

[57] Schreiter (1985), p. 5.

[58] Second Vatican Council (1965b), no. 10. Acta Apostolicae Sedis (1966), p. 959.

[59] International Theological Commission (1988), sect. 2 no. 18.

of our concrete humanity if he did not affect us as well in the diversity and the complementarity of our cultures".[60] Past popes have likewise accentuated the connection between inculturation and incarnation in several papal exhortations following special assemblies of the Synod of Bishops for certain continents.[61] Pope John Paul II, for instance, refers to the analogy of inculturation and incarnation to determine several aspects of why and how the Gospel might become part of local culture in his 2001 Post-synodal Apostolic Exhortation *Ecclesia in Oceania*. The pope clarifies that he does not understand Christ's incarnation merely as an image for the inculturation of the faith, but as the very fundament upon which inculturation rests: "Authentic inculturation of the Christian faith is grounded in the mystery of the Incarnation".[62] From this foundation derives the possibility as well as the need to inculturate the Gospel into all cultures: "The Word made flesh is foreign to no culture and must be preached to all cultures".[63]

However, inculturating the faith seems to differ from Christ's incarnation insofar as it is a "gradual way in which the Gospel is incarnated in the various cultures".[64] Some papal documents also emphasise inculturation as being a selective process, as the Christian message does not enter the whole receiving culture but rather those parts suited to incarnate the faith. In his 1995 document *Ecclesia in Africa* John Paul II writes: "Just as in the incarnation Christ assumed human nature in everything but sin, analogously through inculturation the Christian message assimilates the values of the society to which it is proclaimed, rejecting whatever is marked by sin".[65] In a similar vein, Benedict XVI in his 2011 Post-synodal Apostolic Exhortation *Africae Munus* referred to "a dichotomy between certain traditional practices of African cultures and the specific demands of Christ's message. In her concern for relevance and credibility, the Church needs to carry out a thorough discernment in order to identify those aspects of the culture which represent an obstacle to the incarnation of Gospel values, as well as those aspects which promote them".[66]

The papal documents, in any case, also emphasise that inculturation as the incarnation of the Christian faith in the diverse cultures touches upon the message itself. In *Ecclesia in Oceania* John Paul II notes: "Inculturation, the 'incarnation' of the Gospel in the various cultures, affects the very way in which the Gospel is preached, understood and lived. The Church teaches the unchanging truth of God, addressed to the history and the culture of a particular people. Therefore, in each culture the

[60] Ibid., sect. 2 no. 20.

[61] See John Paul II (1999a). Acta Apostolicae Sedis (1999), pp. 737–815; John Paul II (1999b). Acta Apostolicae Sedis (2000), pp. 449–528; John Paul II (2001). Acta Apostolicae Sedis (2002), pp. 361–428; John Paul II (2003). Acta Apostolicae Sedis (2003), pp. 649–719; Benedict XVI (2011). Acta Apostolicae Sedis (2012), pp. 239–314.

[62] John Paul II (2001), no. 16. Acta Apostolicae Sedis (2002), p. 383.

[63] Ibid.

[64] Ibid.

[65] John Paul II (1995), no. 87. Acta Apostolicae Sedis (1996), p. 55.

[66] Benedict XVI (2011), no. 36. Acta Apostolicae Sedis (2012), pp. 257–258.

Christian faith will be lived in a unique way".[67] Here again one encounters the idea that the Christian truth is a supercultural and immutable reality. This truth then, once embodied in a particular local church, takes on diverse local shapes.

4.2 Methods of Inculturation

Hence, official texts closely link inculturation with incarnation. However, it is still unclear how this translates into mission and evangelisation as concepts of communicating the Christian message to individuals and groups from different local contexts. In his article "The Culture Concept and the Mission of the Roman Catholic Church" in which he studies the Catholic approach of inculturation from an anthropological perspective, Michael Angrosino observes that the concept of inculturation as applied in the church embraces different methods of communicating the Gospel in various cultural settings:

> Experiments with inculturation have ranged all the way from the replacement of Euro-American missionaries by local clergy who celebrate the Roman ritual in a more or less intact form to the approval of full liturgies in Zaire and the Philippines. In most cases only a few culturally significant symbols are tinkered with. However, in Latin American communities there has been a suggestion that inculturation means fundamental change in church structure, in keeping with alternative political and economic realities.[68]

All of these methods are collected under the head inculturation, which makes it necessary to structure the debates in some way. Many contextual theologians apply a threefold classification. They differentiate between the approaches of dynamic equivalence, creative assimilation, and organic progression.[69]

4.2.1 Differing Strategies

Dynamic equivalence, as Angrosino elucidates, "involves the replacement of an element of the Roman form with something in the local culture that has equal meaning or value".[70] He gives the example of different signs which serve to exchange a greeting of peace during the mass, depending on local customs. In the United States, as he mentions, most Catholics perceive a handshake or a hug as the adequate sign, also depending on the specific character of the local community, whilst Catholics in Zaire might choose a ritual washing from one common bowl as a sign of peace in their community. Anscar Chupungco, from whom Angrosino apparently draws his

[67] John Paul II (2001), no. 16. Acta Apostolicae Sedis (2002), p. 383.

[68] Angrosino (1994), p. 826.

[69] E.g. Chupungco (1992), pp. 37–51.

[70] Angrosino (1994), p. 825.

insight, decodes the meaning of the communal washing: "It is a graphic and expressive declaration of forgiveness, a concrete way of saying, 'I wash away everything I have against you'".[71] Chupungco also gives another example from the Filipino mass rubric, which—different from the Roman rubric—prescribes that the celebrant has to take communion *after* the assembly has received it:

> To eat last is not only a sign of urbanity and social grace. Above all it represents service. Thus the host eats after the guests, because the host is expected to serve and move around. Parents take their meal after the children out of solicitude. At home a person forfeits or at least weakens his or her role as leader by taking food ahead of the others. In short, taking Communion last is, in the Filipino cultural context, an affirmation of the role of the priest as the president of the assembly.[72]

Chupungco's example provides food for thought on several levels. For instance, it is interesting to note that from a different cultural point of view, such as that of German liberal Catholicism, some of the comparisons mentioned by Chupungco are controversial. Individuals with a liberal German background might feel uneasy about comparing the assembly to children and the celebrant to a caring parent because they consider this to be a paternalistic image. Some might also feel uncomfortable with the imagery of guest and host, as it tends to either equate the congregation with consumers and patrons or depict the congregation as passive recipients facing an active celebrant. Hence, it might be insightful to discuss in greater depth why Catholics from different backgrounds favour or disfavour certain imagery. However, this study also wants to mention a surprising similarity between Chupungco's considerations and a German view of the matter. Despite many cultural differences, there are obviously similar concerns which move Christians in both contexts. The Filipino practice reflects the controversy in German parishes over when priests should take communion. Many parishioners find it rude for priests to take communion before other members of the congregation have done so. In Germany, different from the Filipino custom, hosts, parents, or leaders are not expected to eat last. However, eating first is also not an option. Instead hosts, parents, or leaders must eat together with all the others at the table. Whilst hosts are to take the first bite of a meal to indicate to their guests that the meal has started, Germans tend to view it as impolite if individuals start eating before all others are ready to eat. So they tend to understand eating "in front" of others who have not yet received their share as a social faux pas, as behaviour which is at best inconsiderate and at worst deeply selfish. Consequently, for many Germans, a priest taking the time to consume the host while the assembly waits for communion to be distributed is a sign of clericalism, elitism, and egoism. Therefore they prefer the celebrant to consume the host *after* the assembly, too. Hence, the motifs of Filipino and German Catholics might differ, yet the concerns are similar. They challenge the respective local churches to find culturally adequate forms in which the priests can express their leadership in the liturgies without displaying domination or ignorance. Dynamic equivalence—as a

[71] Chupungco (1992), p. 41.

[72] Ibid.; see also pp. 170–171.

method of replacing inadequate signs with culturally adequate alternatives—helps to prevent these kinds of cultural conflicts.

A second method of inculturation is creative assimilation, which takes up local concerns or customs and integrates them into Christian routines. Chupungco mentions examples of local marriage rituals being integrated into the Catholic marriage rites or traditional elements of initiation being integrated into Catholic baptism.[73] Angrosino observes that choosing to celebrate Christmas on the day in which pagan traditions celebrated the winter solstice was one early example of creatively assimilating local festive customs into the Christian ritual calendar.[74] Modern equivalents include the integration of secular holidays into the Christian calendar. For the United States, Angrosino mentions the custom of liturgically celebrating Memorial Day and Thanksgiving "in order to give a spiritual dimension to the secular, political acts of remembering and giving thanks".[75] He also mentions Martin Luther King Day which many Catholic communities use for prayers against racism or liturgies celebrating unity and human siblinghood.

A third method of inculturation is organic progression. It takes up the impulses given by the Second Vatican Council and its constitution on the liturgy, which were left in an initial state by the council, to complement and realise these conciliar ideas. By way of example, Angrosino mentions the rite of initiation of adults as a ritual which introduces adult catechumens into the communities. Throughout church history, public forms of initiation had been widely abandoned due to the Western praxis of infant baptism. However, the council encouraged the reinstitution of a public rite.[76] This initiative resulted in numerous rites dependent on cultural customs, as Angrosino expounds by referring to the example of the United States and South Korea:

> In the United States, adult initiation consists of instructional lectures, group sharing, and a series of public rites; it brings together a varied group of 'inquirers' who go through the process together and perform the rites in the presence of the entire parish congregation. This process seems particularly well attuned to modern American culture, with its zest for support groups and public self-revelation. In Korea, by contrast, norms of dignity militate against the sharing of intimate revelations with strangers. Adult initiation in Korea, therefore, involves the family circle but not the congregation at large.[77]

Hence, as Angrosino observes, the local churches approach adult initiation in various ways, according to their cultural preferences. Organic progression allows for these differentiated solutions to developing a common initiative in culturally adequate ways.

---

[73] See ibid., pp. 46–47.

[74] See Angrosino (1994), p. 825.

[75] Ibid., p. 826.

[76] See Second Vatican Council (1963), nos. 64–66. Acta Apostolicae Sedis (1964), pp. 117–118.

[77] Angrosino (1994), p. 826.

4.2.2 Identity and Change

Inculturation, thus, has served the church over the past decades as a theoretical umbrella for various methods of reconciling universal faith and local cultures. However, similar to other concepts of incarnating the universal in concrete particular settings, inculturation poses several difficulties of its own. One major theoretical shortcoming of inculturation theories lies in their assumption that inculturation is providing a home for the universal Gospel message in a particular context while afflicting neither the message nor the receiving culture to any greater degree. This blind spot becomes clear by pondering one image which Anscar Chupungco uses for explaining inculturation with regard to the liturgy: "Inculturation … is like lighting a candle simultaneously at both ends. One end is what the typical editions and the official documents propose. The other end is what culture is able to offer".[78] Whilst Chupungco's use of the expression "burn the candle at both ends" is idiosyncratic, his analogy is helpful for pointing at one major issue connected with the concept of inculturation. As inculturation is an attempt to reconcile universal faith and local cultures by motivating mutual development while at the same time allowing both to preserve their original identity, one may wonder how both ends of the candle can burn *and* preserve their identity simultaneously. What if burning both ends of the candle causes it to melt away quickly?

Michael Angrosino voices similar criticism with inculturation theories. He challenges their assumption that the inculturation of the Christian message into the local cultures leaves the Christian message and the receiving cultures widely unchanged. He refers to the Zaire Use as the local Zairean variant of the Roman Rite to note: "The inculturated liturgy, for example, is said to have created a common ground in Zaire, although neither the basic message of Catholicism nor the 'heart' of Zairian culture (however that may be defined) is said to have been changed".[79] Angrosino, for his part, doubts whether mutual exchange without essential change is realistic:

> It is doubtful that any anthropologist would agree that a culture could remain unchanged in the wake of its encounter with a large, external system of beliefs and behaviors that purport to represent a higher moral authority. It is also doubtful that this larger system can remain unchanged, since culture is not a thin veneer of interchangeable symbols that can be taken on or cast off without affecting internal realities.[80]

As a result, one should expect the local culture to be deeply affected by encountering the Christian message, particularly as this message is embedded in a complex belief system and, in the past, was imposed on many local cultures with pressure or force; Angrosino compares the church in inculturation contexts with international development agencies insofar as both represent political and economic power and not merely moral authority, even though the church tends to disguise its power as

[78] Chupungco (1992), p. 64.

[79] Angrosino (1994), p. 827.

[80] Ibid.

moral authority.[81] And one can likewise expect the encounter with culture to influence the Christian message itself. Conveying a message in different signs, as Angrosino indicates, is a sure way of changing its meaning. He gives the example of the East African practice of covering the tabernacle with a leopard skin. This use of this East African symbol of chieftainship to articulate Christ's kingship has a profound impact on the conception of Christ's kingship. As the concept of East African chieftainship differs from that of Near Eastern or Western kingship, East African Catholics derive a different idea of kingship from the leopard skin than Catholics of the Global North might get when thinking of Christ as king: "[T]he chieftainship symbolized by leopard skin, deeply rooted in the values and expectations of African people, is a profoundly different concept of royalty from that implied when Westerners talk about 'Christ the King'".[82]

This analysis points to the hylemorphic dilemma in inculturation concepts, as previously discussed in relation to accommodation and translation approaches. Karl Rahner's concept of "Wesensidentität in Gestaltwandel",[83] whereby divine law is considered to have an identity with regard to its essence while changing its concrete shape in different contexts, raises the question of how the Christian message can be incorporated into the various local churches. The risk of losing the identity of the Christian message by giving it a true home all over the globe meets the risk of preserving the identity of the original message at all costs. The latter risks keeping the message alien to many individuals due to the disconnect between Christian symbols and local systems of meaning. There are various ways in which inculturation theories can respond to the finding that exchange without profound change on both sides is dubious. The scholarly debates identify four types of policies for balancing the tensions between change and identity: conservative, neoconservative, liberal, and radical approaches.[84] These require closer study to understand how they differ in their emphasis on either protecting the universal faith, including its traditional cultural expressions, or protecting the local identity, and, in turn, allowing for more or less alteration with regard to the traditional expressions of the Christian message. Studying these different policies reveals that inculturation concepts usually tend to burn the candle more from one end *or* from the other, to reuse Anscar Chupungco's image, whilst it is difficult to find a balance so that the candle burns down equally from both ends.

---

[81] See ibid., p. 829.

[82] Ibid., p. 827.

[83] Rahner (1962), p. 252.

[84] E.g. Mannion (1990), pp. 310–312.

4.2.3 Protecting Tradition

One can identify as conservative all those policies which prioritise the protection of immutable doctrine from cultural corruption. As a result, conservatives are also protective of established manifestations of that immutable doctrine, such as of the traditional liturgies and other classical forms of living the faith. Liturgical scholar M. Francis Mannion refers by way of example to Marcel Lefebvre and the Fraternity of Pius X and their refusal to accept parts of conciliar teaching and, in consequence, also to accept the reformed liturgical rites as manifestations of reformed doctrine.[85] With regard to allowing new elements to enter the Catholic usage, conservatives frequently allow for signs of minor importance to be locally accommodated if this does not endanger the integrity of traditional praxis. Michael Angrosino notes: "Conservatives will admit some indigenous artistic elements in peripheral roles, but their principal concern is the integrity of the Latin rite".[86]

One might conclude from this that conservatives tend to undervalue local identity over the integrity of the established rites. However, this view is slightly simplistic, as closer study helps to reveal. In fact, one might instead come to find that conservatives tend to derive their identity from tradition and therefore fight for the preservation of the traditional rites precisely because they want to preserve their identity. An observation made by Angrosino elucidates this connection. He notes that inculturation theories frequently rely on the assumption that local Christians tend to favour local approaches to expressing the Christian message over foreign and imported approaches. However, as he discerns, this is not always the case. He alludes inter alia to the increasing popularity of the Tridentine liturgy among many US-American Catholics. Angrosino assumes that those Catholics who prefer the Latin mass over the modern vernacular liturgies are individuals "who feel that Catholicism is only valid when celebrated in Latin. Such people have never accepted the vernacular mass, even though it is easier to understand and relate to everyday life".[87] By saying this, he questions the propositions of inculturation theories, namely that local Christians essentially prefer those rituals which they can relate easily to their own experience. While this might be true for many individuals, others might be drawn to foreign-language liturgies precisely because they are unfamiliar and mysterious. Angrosino also mentions the example of Asian or African churches where inculturation theories tend to hold similar misconceptions: "Inculturationists assume that people in Africa or Asia will automatically reject the Roman forms, although experience suggests that those forms might seem more desirable because they are the 'real thing' even when they are not totally comprehensible".[88] In a similar vein, Stephen Bevans remarks with regard to Filipino communities that not all signs representing inculturated faith might seem appropriate to local Christians: "It

[85] See ibid., p. 310.

[86] Angrosino (1994), p. 829.

[87] Ibid., p. 827.

[88] Ibid.

might be more genuinely Filipino, for instance, to substitute palm wine and rice cakes for bread and wine at the Eucharist, but whether the people will actually feel comfortable with such a substitution might be very much in doubt".[89] These observations are plausible if one avoids establishing a dichotomy between the integrity of tradition versus expressions of local identity, instead considering the aforementioned cases as examples of identities based on the integrity of the tradition. Christians, thus, do not necessarily derive their Christian identity from being *local* Christians, but can also draw on other sources of identity formation, including foreign traditions. Judith Gruber, in this vein, emphasises that missiology has learnt from cultural studies that "the encounter between two cultural sign systems has been considered to be a highly productive place of identification that cannot be completely controlled in the negotiations for meaning".[90]

Scholars usually discuss these issues with regard to the liturgy. This is because the struggle to preserve the integrity of the liturgical tradition is often at the centre of conservative policies aimed at preserving identity. However, conservativism is not only expressed in the preference for the Tridentine Rite, but has major repercussions in ecclesiology, as M. Francis Mannion observes. With regard to ecclesiological issues, it tends to protect a view of the church as *societas perfecta* and define church members' adherence to this society as essential for their salvation.[91] Michael Angrosino describes the conservative ecclesiological agenda as follows:

> They uphold a society whose culture represents a nearly complete integration of religion and social life. Liturgical and catechetical innovations are to be avoided because they can disrupt the link between the church (seen as the model of the perfect society) and believers. The church, in effect, has an existence apart from its believers, and people are perfected insofar as they permit themselves to experience the ministry of the church. The church, therefore, derives spiritual as well as political and economic power from its position as the unchallenged authority on the question of what constitutes the perfect society. To allow more than a cautious smattering of liturgical innovations is to call into question the authoritative perfection of the church and, hence, to jeopardize the salvation of all souls.[92]

As a result, allowing the Christian message to fully merge with other cultures is not an option for conservative thinkers. Whenever Christianity blends in with plural cultures, it is suspected of relativism. As it is truth that saves, salvation is potentially at risk whenever the church endangers its immutable doctrine and its supercultural identity by drawing too close to culture, or, to be precise, to cultures different from those in which conservatives see the truth embedded.

Neoconservative policies mirror conservative approaches insofar as they understand the protection of the ecclesiastical tradition to be key. They are critical of modern liberal values and individualist beliefs and understand them as posing a danger to the Catholic faith. However, they attempt to reconcile their protective attitude with some cultural mediation, because they recognise that the church must

---

89 Bevans (2002), p. 26.

90 Gruber (2018), p. 22.

91 See Mannion (1990), p. 310.

92 Angrosino (1994), p. 829.

communicate its message in a culturally appropriate manner if it is to be received locally. Mannion therefore differentiates between neoconservative and conservative policies by acknowledging in the former "a more sophisticated appreciation of change and development within the tradition".[93] Neoconservative approaches frequently apply a hermeneutic of continuity to explain how change is possible without separating the church from its tradition.[94] Hence, one can identify neoconservative agendas as mediating between conservative and liberal policies, as Angrosino notes: "Like the conservatives, the neoconservatives see the church as the model of the perfect society; like the liberals, however, they recognize that people in the modem world must be sensitively drawn back to that model of perfection, not coerced into it".[95] Whenever this succeeds and individuals embrace the traditional faith, neoconservatives attribute to the church and its message the power to purify its new context, such as liberal societies.[96]

4.2.4 Embracing Transformation

In contrast to conservative approaches, liberal policies seek to spread the Gospel message in new contexts, in particular, by adaptation. They understand the church and local societies, their political systems, and social dynamics more as agents at eye level. According to the liberal view, culture is an essential factor which the church must deal with if it is to communicate its message. Liberalism thus supports dialogue to bring about local expressions of the Christian faith. Mannion describes liberal policies as follows: "It seeks to overcome the rupture between Christian tradition and the modern world and tends to be optimistic about the congruence between the gospel and culture. It is enthusiastic about cultural pluralism, interreligious dialogue and the emergence of a world church incarnated in diverse cultures".[97] In the eyes of liberals, an authentic dialogue requires culture to be taken seriously as the church members' reality and the context of inculturation. Angrosino explains:

> Like the conservatives, the liberals implicitly view the church and the people as distinct units of analysis. The crucial difference, however, is that the liberals see them as units having roughly equivalent moral authority. This approach is based on a pluralistic vision of society, the essence of which is that religion and social life are no longer automatically intertwined. People can find satisfaction in many other forms and institutions, and there is no automatic belief that perfection is the unique province of a single institutional church. In order for that church to be relevant, therefore, it must go out to meet people where they are.[98]

---

[93] Mannion (1990), p. 312.

[94] See ibid.

[95] Angrosino (1994), p. 830.

[96] See Mannion (1990), p. 312.

[97] Ibid., p. 311.

[98] Angrosino (1994), p. 829.

While conservative policies tend to overlook the value of plural cultures for protecting the universal truth, liberal policies address the issue of reconciling the Gospel with culture, while still maintaining a clear distinction between the two, as Angrosino maintains: "Even the most liberal inculturationist must at some point believe that immutable truth is at stake; otherwise there would be no need to 'incarnate the gospel' in the first place".[99] Liberal thinkers are therefore continuously tasked with the challenge of mediating between Gospel and local reality. They bring them together with inculturation, while keeping them separate as distinct entities. Hence, they remain sensitive to tensions whenever inculturation gets difficult.

Radical policies, which are at work in many liberation or feminist theologies, analyse the need for reform on both sides, the Gospel message and the local cultures. They employ a general "hermeneutic of suspicion",[100] as Mannion maintains, with regard to the Christian tradition and the local customs. Hence, they criticise the Catholic tradition for its promotion of sexism and racism, while at the same time criticising modern societies for cultivating hyper-individualism and consumerism. Some radical policies even have an apocalyptic and millenarian tendency, as Mannion notes. They accept religious pluralism as such and not only as an expression of the universal Christian message. Angrosino holds:

> Radicals are committed to true religious pluralism, not merely to a diversity of cultural expressions of something held to be an essential truth. … The radical approach is a broadly based rejection of tradition, as tainted by centuries of bias. It supports instead what might be called the popular religion in which the church is the people, who are held to have a greater moral authority than any formalized institution or hierarchy ever could.[101]

4.3 Official Policies of Inculturation

For the purposes of this study, it is not particularly relevant to discuss the strengths and weaknesses of the various strategies for balancing identity and change in inculturation, as it is not its task to evaluate inculturation itself. Its primary concern is to assess the current status of global canon law in relation to the tensions between legislation and the local reception of global rules. These tensions are largely the result of official inculturation policies. The next section therefore analyses the current position of the Apostolic See with regard to inculturation. Chapter 5 will then apply these findings to the law to ask how the Apostolic See's inculturation policies are reflected in current legislation and processes of legal reception.

---

[99] Ibid.

[100] Mannion (1990), p. 311.

[101] Angrosino (1994), p. 830.

4.3.1 Neoconservative Policies

Michael Angrosino finds that, at present, the Apostolic See frequently relies on neoconservative policies of inculturation. Following a neoconservative agenda, the official politics of inculturation tend to focus on the protection of the ecclesiastical tradition while allowing for some cultural mediation as a way of helping the local reception of the universal faith. This is rather unsurprising, as Robert Schreiter notes. He alludes to the general tendency of those in charge to rely on more conservative policies. In intercultural communication, individuals in leadership positions regularly turn to more traditional approaches such as translation as these are more speaker-oriented and therefore better suited to preserving the integrity of the tradition, including their own role as leaders. On the contrary, members of a group who wish to protect their group and preserve its cohesion and identity tend to prefer hearer-oriented approaches, if only, as Schreiter remarks, "if their own identity as leaders is not at stake".[102] With regard to the church, he maintains:

> One sees this pattern recurring in the Roman Catholic Church since the changes wrought by Vatican Council II. Leadership in Rome and in parts of the episcopal magisterium will often stress speaker-oriented models for transmitting the gospel message, even to the point of preferring neo-scholastic formulations. They will be concerned about uniformity of teaching and practice (minimal loss of information in transmission) in discussions of pluralism.[103]

Schreiter contrasts this approach with more hearer-oriented models: "Leadership in the theological magisterium, in parts of the episcopal magisterium, and local pastors will often stress hearer-oriented models for transmitting the gospel message. They will be concerned about whether traditional formulations are intelligible, or even alienating to a people".[104]

Yet since translation is the most effective way of ensuring that doctrine and practice, once inculturated, closely resemble the original Roman model, the Apostolic See, following the council, has tended to favour translation whenever core elements of the Christian faith and practice have been at stake. Translation, consequently, served as the paradigm for guiding the liturgical reform after the Second Vatican Council to translate the Roman liturgies into local rites. Many scholars have disputed this choice of strategy because of its evident limitations in allowing local views and customs to influence the rites. James Provost, for instance, called translation a "centralized strategy"[105] and criticised it for its tendency to curb reform in favour of protecting traditional views. He found it a "particularly discouraging effect" during the liturgical reform that "Vatican officials regularly warned and excoriated those who were going 'too far', while those who resisted the reforms (and even claimed they were invalid) seemed to be accommodated".[106] In particular,

[102] Schreiter (1985), p. 60.

[103] Ibid.

[104] Ibid.

[105] Provost (1996), p. 120.

[106] Ibid.

he mentioned how the Vatican dealt with the group around Marcel Lefebvre and the establishment of the Commission *Ecclesia Dei*, which undermined local bishops who were in favour of reform by supporting local groups who resisted it. As a consequence, the translation approach of the Apostolic See quickly began to draw criticism from among those who shared a more hearer-oriented perspective towards inculturation. Michael Angrosino provides a classification of the critical aspects which connect with the Apostolic See's policies. His observations deserve further study in the following, as they help to define more precisely the limits of the present policy, particularly its reliance on top-down communication, its resistance to change, its focus on aesthetics, and its tendency to be blind to the issue of power involved in inculturation.

4.3.2 Top-Down Decisions

Neoconservative policies understand inculturation as giving the universal faith a more local touch, albeit without truly affecting the message itself. They are "calling people to the truth and only use[s] cultural forms to induce people to heed that calling".[107] This view reflects the way in which Vatican officials describe inculturation as a top-down process, as Angrosino finds: "There is an underlying assumption that inculturation is something that the Vatican, out of a sense of *noblesse oblige*, is in a position to grant".[108] The Apostolic See therefore tends to reduce inculturation to one-way routes and to centralistically controlled operations which allow for some cultural variation, mainly with regard to the liturgy, to encourage the local Catholics to identify with the church, its universal message, and its uniform praxis. From this point of view, inculturation primarily serves a strategic purpose, namely to motivate the local reception of the Catholic tradition. Whenever the local Christians embrace the tradition, it is regarded as capable of purifying the local societies. One can discover this typical neoconservative thinking, for instance, in Pope John Paul II's 1995 Post-synodal Exhortation *Ecclesia in Africa*: "An inculturation wisely carried out purifies and elevates the cultures of the various peoples".[109] It is no coincidence that the document emphasised this specific notion of inculturation as an instrument of cultural purification, as Angrosino remarks. He also sees this as the result of concrete conflicts between the Apostolic See and the African churches. One major disagreement was linked with the 1994 Synod of African Bishops. In this case, the bishops had planned to discuss inculturation in depth during the synod: "They prepared to argue for a form of inculturation that went far beyond the aesthetics of liturgy and touched on issues of social organization (including norms of marriage) and

---

[107] Angrosino (1994), p. 830.

[108] Ibid.

[109] John Paul II (1995), no. 87. Acta Apostolicae Sedis (1996), p. 55.

hierarchical structure (including the role of women)".[110] The synod had originally been scheduled to take place in Africa. But due to the growing tensions between the African bishops and the Vatican, it was then relocated to Rome, putting it "under the watchful eyes of the Vatican",[111] as Angrosino comments. In 1994, theologian and journalist Peter Hebblethwaite commented on the decision to move the synod to Rome by noting that this fully "changes the nature of the event. It makes it a Roman synod about Africa rather than a genuinely African synod. The preparatory document actually speaks of 'that continent,' as if it were someplace else".[112] With regard to the preparatory document, he remarked: "The problems of Africa are seen from the Vatican's point of view rather than Africa's. It is a top-down document. Principles stated by the magisterium are the starting point, and African experience is cut to size and shape in their Procrustean bed".[113] The synod's decisions reflect that view. The underlying tone of the decisions, as Angrosino finds, does not express the freedom of the local churches to allow their own expressions of the faith to flourish; instead, it makes heavy use of the argument that the inculturation of the Gospel is an instrument to purify the local cultures. Later, John Paul II similarly noted in his 2001 Post-synodal Apostolic Exhortation *Ecclesia in Oceania* that "certain cultural values must be transformed and purified, if they are to find a place in a genuinely Christian culture".[114] According to a centralistic view of authority, it is the Apostolic See which decides which elements of a culture seem suitable for purification and elevation, as Norbert Lüdecke explains:

> It is up to the universal ecclesiastical authority to decide what the authentic cultural values worth preserving are (see canon 747 §2), concretely: what is genuinely Asian or African and may be purified and elevated by a prudent inculturation of the faith (see EcclAfr 59. 85). It is the authority who carries the washing pan with which to sift nuggets compatible with the faith out of the sand of their original cultures.[115]

4.3.3 Preserving Continuity

Neoconservative policies allow for local variations with the purpose of leading all Catholics to the universal message and to consistent manifestations of it. Their key aim is a uniform praxis. Yet they tolerate diversity inasmuch as it serves the unity of

---

[110] Angrosino (1994), p. 831.

[111] Ibid.

[112] Hebblethwaite (1994), p. 8.

[113] Ibid.

[114] John Paul II (2001), no. 16. Acta Apostolicae Sedis (2002), p. 382.

[115] Original quote: "Was authentische und erhaltenswerte kulturelle Werte sind, konkret: Was genuin asiatisch oder afrikanisch ist und durch eine kluge Inkulturation des Glaubens gereinigt und erhoben werden kann (vgl. EcclAfr 59. 85), entscheidet die universalkirchliche Autorität (vgl. c. 747 § 2). Sie hält das Goldsieb, mit dem die glaubenskompatiblen Nuggets aus dem Sand der Ursprungskulturen gewaschen werden", Lüdecke (2011), pp. 56–57.

tradition and relative uniformity of praxis. Thus, while neoconservative policies are less rigid in preserving the universal truth and the Roman expressions of that truth than conservative approaches and more open to cultural variations, they nevertheless represent strategies for defending tradition against overwhelming pluralism. Bernard Lonergan observes: "The classicist is no pluralist. He knows that circumstances alter cases but he is far more deeply convinced that circumstances are somehow accidental and that, beyond them, there is some substance or kernel or root that fits in with classicist assumptions of stability, fixity, immutability".[116] In this sense, the Apostolic See advocates for a hermeneutic of continuity, which seeks to present tradition as both unwavering and developing. Along these lines, Pope Benedict XVI described the history of the church as that of an institution which "increases in time and develops, yet always remaining the same, the one subject of the journeying People of God".[117] The pope counters this hermeneutic of continuity with a "hermeneutic of discontinuity" or "hermeneutic of rupture", with its tendency to relativise the truth through compromise and adaptability to trends and mass media. In a similar vein, John Paul II noted in *Ecclesia in Africa* that inculturation "includes the whole of Christian existence", yet "without of course compromising what is of divine right and the great discipline of the Church, confirmed in the course of centuries by remarkable fruits of virtue and heroism".[118] In this light, inculturation appears as a possible danger to doctrine and discipline if it breaks with tradition, allowing a hermeneutic of rupture to rule. Hence, while Christian existence has to articulate itself in a plurality of local expressions of the faith, the church must take care to ensure that those local idiosyncrasies conform with the tradition. Whilst plurality is essential, it also poses a threat to the continuity of tradition. Stephen Bevans comments: "In Roman Catholic theology, pluralism is a fact, but it is also a fact that pluralism is often viewed with suspicion and caution".[119]

This is primarily due to the fact that pluralism raises concerns about cultural relativism. Many papal and curial documents issued over the past years speak highly of culture and the need for the faith to find local reception, while at the same time warning against the danger of relativism posed by too great an involvement with culture. One most prominent example of this thought is the homily which Joseph Ratzinger gave in the Mass "Pro Eligendo Romano Pontifice" shortly before being elected to become the next pope. Here, the future pope spoke of a "dictatorship of relativism" as an attitude "that does not recognize anything as definitive and whose ultimate goal consists solely of one's own ego and desires".[120] He contrasted the relativist attitude with "a clear faith based on the Creed of the Church". While adherence to definite doctrine might be called "fundamentalism" by many, it is the solid ground on which the only true faith stands, as Ratzinger emphasised. It

---

[116] Lonergan (1972), p. 301.

[117] Benedict XVI (2005). Acta Apostolicae Sedis (2006), p. 46.

[118] John Paul II (1995), no. 78. Acta Apostolicae Sedis (1996), p. 51.

[119] Bevans (2002), p. 22.

[120] Ratzinger (2005). Acta Apostolicae Sedis (2005), p. 687.

therefore deserves protection from the relativist tendencies common in modern individualist cultures. As a result, care must be taken when dealing with inculturation to prevent cultures corrupting the Christian message. In this vein, John Paul II, in *Ecclesia in Africa*, accentuated two criteria for inculturation: first, compatibility of the cultural elements with the Christian message; second, that cultural elements do not inhibit communion with the universal church. Adding to this, as the pope stated, is the need to avoid syncretism: "Inculturation is a difficult and delicate task, since it raises the question of the Church's fidelity to the Gospel and the Apostolic Tradition amidst the constant evolution of cultures".[121]

4.3.4 Focus on Aesthetics

One further feature of current inculturation policies of the Apostolic See is that they often seem to focus exclusively on the liturgy. This suggests that inculturation only requires a small degree of ritual variation to meet local customs. Peter Hebblethwaite, in his 1994 coverage of the Synod of African Bishops in Rome, sensed that the African bishops and the Vatican had a different view of inculturation, when he observed: "One suspects that for the Vatican it [inculturation, addition by the author] means rather tinkering with the liturgy, permitting drums and a little genteel dancing at the Gloria and the offertory procession".[122] This limited focus on culture as a system of ritual meaning obviously affects not only the Apostolic See's concept of culture but also has implications for how church officials tend to understand the liturgy. Michael Angrosino connects this observation with a criticism of a narrow view on ritual and a resistance to receiving the findings of ritual theory: "The Roman Catholic church uses a version of the culture concept in its contemporary evangelization strategy that relies overmuch on the aesthetics of ritual"[123] and "on the interpretive meaning of symbols".[124] Due to this restricted reading of culture as expressed in ritual and a narrow "view of culture as divorced from social action",[125] the Apostolic See tends to miss a dimension of inculturation, as he finds. The method of allowing selective local elements to enter the Catholic praxis tends to ignore the broader system of meaning in which these elements are embedded in a particular group: "Inculturation tends to divorce ritual from its social context".[126] Angrosino gives the example of marriage rites. Whilst liturgical inculturation, in many local churches, is at pains to integrate local customs into the respective local rites, it often ignores the cultural embedding of these customs, thereby creating tensions between

[121] John Paul II (1995), no. 62. Acta Apostolicae Sedis (1996), p. 39.

[122] Hebblethwaite (1994), p. 8.

[123] Angrosino (1994), p. 830.

[124] Ibid., p. 828.

[125] Ibid., p. 830.

[126] Ibid., p. 827.

the Catholic view of marriage and the local social view of it, which burdens the liturgies:

> Thus, while the Vatican is quite open to inculturating the liturgy of a wedding ceremony, being sensitive to various customs regarding veiling the bride, it may not be able to inculturate the social structure of marriage. Polygyny, for example, is culturally valid in some places but can have no place in Catholic marriage. But there are practices, such as matrilateral cross-cousin marriage, that fall into a greyer area. Questions about birth control and abortion, so obvious a part of marriage, are matters that exhibit considerable cross-cultural diversity. It makes little sense to have a properly inculturated ritual while condemning the social reality that the ritual is meant to celebrate. However, the church implies that ritual may be culturally varied, whereas social action is subject to unvarying teachings.[127]

Hence, when rites take up selective elements from local customs to integrate them into the liturgies, they often do so by dismissing the original meaning of the customs that derive from local systems of meaning. This can lead to several problems. For instance, the inculturated customs can remain isolated within the Catholic rites. In this case, they can eventually lose their original meaning, maybe even becoming part of the Catholic liturgies as conventional elements without any specific meaning. In other cases, these borrowed ritual elements continue to convey their original message to the congregation. In these cases they can continue to be disruptive elements in the Catholic liturgies, creating cracks in the surface of Catholic meaning through which permeate alternative views of life, marriage, and the social. One can also conceive of cases where local customs integrated into the Catholic rites remain connected with their original meaning and carry conflictive elements into the liturgies, even opposing Catholic doctrine. In the case of marriage liturgies, one should not be tempted to shrug off these issues as singular problems of churches where polygyny or cross-cousin marriage are socially accepted. To many Catholics from the Global North it is still a cherished practice that, in the wedding procession, the bride's father leads his daughter down the aisle. This custom revives the old Germanic practice of fathers releasing their daughters from their paternal power to hand them over to their soon-to-be husbands as their new masters. As a sign that devalues the autonomy of women and renders them objects of male guidance, this custom is not fit to be part of Catholic ceremonies, as it opposes the spouses' equal dignity as part of Catholic teaching and their equality in marital rights and duties.[128] The Roman *Rite of Marriage*, accordingly, does not include the tradition. The Missal simply states: "The procession to the altar then takes place in the customary manner".[129] Yet this open expression "in the customary manner" allows for the paternalistic custom to re-enter the Christian ceremony. Many dioceses try to avoid this by regulating that the bride and groom have to enter the church together or that, when accompanied by their families in the procession, they should be attended by

---

[127] Ibid.

[128] See Second Vatican Council (1965c), no. 49. Acta Apostolicae Sedis (1966), p. 1070; canon 1135 CIC/1983.

[129] The Roman Missal: The Order of Celebrating Matrimony, no. 46. In: Second Typical Edition (2016), p. 9.

both of their parents. However, resistance is strong, rendering it difficult to root out this practice. We can therefore still find it in many Catholic ceremonies, despite it drawing a problematic sign and its debatable meaning into the marriage liturgies.

4.3.5 Power Blindness

The temptation to perceive signs in a mere aesthetic light instead of studying their social meaning might derive from the more general view of liturgies as being detached from their social background, a view which Angrosino detects in neoconservative ideas of inculturation. He notices this rift between Catholic liturgies and their social surroundings in the Apostolic See's failure to recognise that rituals are always power plays. Whilst the Apostolic See tends to emphasise the liturgical signs and their capacity to represent a Catholic meaning, it also tends to focus "not enough on the social forces that dispose people to act on the message imparted by those symbols".[130] This results in a top-down view of inculturation which ignores, as Angrosino maintains, that inculturation involves a complex agency and "that, in a diverse multicultural world, inculturation can be achieved only by negotiation among players with varying access to political, economic, and social power".[131] By disregarding the power struggle connected with inculturation, church officials, as he perceives, tend to neglect local factors granting or obstructing access to power, such as class, race, or gender, which act as "conditioners of power".[132] As these factors do not play an open role in the liturgies, they tend to be downplayed in inculturation contexts.

Upon closer study, in any case, Angrosino seems less convinced that this ignorance of social issues is a mishap. Instead he suggests that many Vatican officials are aware of the connection between ritual and power, but apparently do not wish to address it within their policies of inculturation. Angrosino supports his view by recalling that the Apostolic See has suppressed local initiatives which forged a close link between liturgical inculturation and social issues, for instance by curbing Brazilian liturgical projects which reached out to poor, indigenous, and black Christians: "This move indicates that the church understands that ritual has the capacity to link participants with sources of power in the wider society but does not favor the use of ritual for such a purpose".[133] Instead of activating the potential for reform connected with inculturation, the Apostolic See's policy seems to reverse the perspective and to hope that the inculturated faith will tacitly cure social problems. Angrosino maintains: "The church is in the position of assuming that if people are involved in properly inculturated liturgies, then they will be able to use their spiritual

[130] Angrosino (1994), p. 828.
[131] Ibid., p. 830.
[132] Ibid., p. 828.
[133] Ibid., p. 829.

empowerment to ennoble the culture around them".[134] He is sceptical of this approach, as anthropological study indicates "that such ennoblement of culture can occur only if the Gospel message is inculturated at the level of the social disciplines, in equal measure with idealized ritual".[135]

4.4 Summary

Throughout its history, the church has continuously mediated between the universality of the Christian message and its cultural representations with some unease, producing various missiological models about how to incarnate the universal Christian truth within diverse contexts. This chapter has discussed concepts developed over the last decades of how the Christian message can become part of local contexts, from early twentieth-century missiological concepts to contemporary contextual theologies. Since the Second Vatican Council, the Apostolic See has relied on a neoconservative variety of *inculturation*, which promises continuity of ecclesiastical doctrine, tradition, and rites, and the protection of their supercultural message while allowing for careful translations and adaptations to be made to implement them on the local level. This policy is not without its problems. It relies mostly on top-down communication, is resistance to change, has a focus on aesthetics, and tends to be blind to the issue of power involved in cross-cultural exchange. The next chapter will discuss the consequences of this particular approach for the inculturation of canon law.

[134] Ibid., pp. 828–829.

[135] Ibid., p. 829.

Chapter 5
Inculturating Canon Law

The observation that the Christian message requires inculturation to have an effect on the local churches brings up the question of what role global canon law plays in inculturation, as a *matter* of inculturation, on the one hand, and as an instrument or *vehicle* for transporting meaning within the church and between the local churches, on the other. The following two chapters shed some light on how the church, at present, deals with the law in light of the inculturation paradigm in these two respects. Before Chap. 6 devotes attention to how the law handles cultural diversity, Chap. 5 will examine how the church treats its law as a subject of inculturation. This relates to two procedural aspects of legal practice: to global *lawmaking* as well as to the *reception* of this law in the local churches. These two perspectives are two sides of one dynamic. They represent what Boaventura de Sousa Santos identified as the two sides of globalisation, namely *globalised localism* as the globalisation of a local artefact or phenomenon with the aim of making a global impact, and *localised globalism* as "the specific impact of transnational practices and imperatives on local conditions that are thereby altered [and, addition by the author] restructured in order to respond to transnational imperatives".[1]

The first issue in need of discussion is whether canon law is indeed subject to inculturation, as suggested above. This seems debateable if one defines inculturation as processes in which the church conveys a *universal* message in concrete contexts. Positive laws are never universal but always historical and cultural rules. As analysed in Sect. 3.1, Catholic doctrine assumes that some legal rules have roots in God's will. Nevertheless, despite the supercultural foundation of some canons, global canon law is a body of positive rules and therefore a deeply cultural artefact, as can be drawn from David Novak's considerations on natural law.[2] However, as Novak illustrated with the help of his telescope metaphor, the culturality of legal rules does not render them random phenomena. If they are considered concrete

[1] De Sousa Santos (2020), p. 215.

[2] See Novak (1998), p. 188.

J. Hahn, *The Cultures of Canon Law*, Law and Religion in a Global Context 6,
https://doi.org/10.1007/978-3-032-14812-4_5

manifestations of God's will, they can be viewed as both heavenly and earthly, just like the church.[3] Based on this finding, it is plausible to argue that the law as a cultural artefact can be an object of inculturation as the process of giving a universal idea a new home in a concrete local context. There is not much difference in the need to inculturate doctrine, the liturgy, or the law in that respect. They are all essentially cultural, even though parts of them may be recognised as being cultural expressions of universal ideas. Hence, one may argue that they require inculturation to articulate this idea in different contexts. Pope John Paul II noted concordantly in his 1995 Post-synodal Exhortation *Ecclesia in Africa*, that inculturation is "a process that includes the whole of Christian existence—theology, liturgy, customs, structures".[4] It is notable that the pope does not mention the law explicitly,[5] but somehow refers to it implicitly by speaking of customs and structures. Ladislas Orsy has taken up this thought to argue how law is part of the essential ecclesiastical structures which constitute church life and requires inculturation to fulfil its theological purpose:

> Now the good news is proclaimed not with words only but with the whole life of the church, including its structure and operations. As the words cannot effectively convey the content of the gospel unless they are taken from, and inserted into, an existing culture, so the structures and norms of the church cannot effectively witness the freedom that God's grace brought to the world unless they blend with local cultures.[6]

This finding that inculturation is not the insertion of universal ideas into concrete contexts but the transmission of cultural artefacts—with and without universal roots—to individuals or groups living in different contexts draws attention to every communicative act between one church and another. These acts are operations in which a deeply inculturated message is passed on from one local church to another. At present, the magisterium communicates a doctrine based on the monotheistic tradition of the Hebrew Bible and Greek metaphysics to churches all over the globe. It encourages Christians throughout the world to find meaning in the Roman liturgies. Catholics worldwide are bound by law issued by the Apostolic See, in a legal tradition reaching back to Roman law. Speaking of inculturation thus refers to those critical processes in which a profoundly inculturated message attempts to receive meaning in a different context.

---

[3] See Second Vatican Council (1964), no. 8. Acta Apostolicae Sedis (1965), pp. 11–12.

[4] John Paul II (1995), no. 78. Acta Apostolicae Sedis (1996), p. 51.

[5] It is generally striking that none of the papal post-synodal exhortations on inculturation explicitly refer to the law and to the challenge of inculturating global canon law into the local churches. Similarly, other official documents fail to mention canon law as an object of inculturation, e.g. Pontifical Council for Culture (1999).

[6] Orsy (1996a), p. 22.

5.1 Lawmaking for a Global Church

When studying Roman Catholic legislation, one major focus is on the Code of Canon Law. The Code is the key piece of legislation with a frame-like function providing all Catholic churches of the Latin rite with a skeleton of legal rules to be fleshed out by decentralised legislation. Accompanying the Code are numerous papal laws which add to global canon law. These are usually given in the form of Apostolic Constitutions or *Motu Proprios*—with which the pope directly responds to an urgent need for regulation which he addresses *motu proprio*, on his own initiative. Norms issued by dicasteries of the Roman Curia receive the force of law with papal approbation. Contract law such as concordats between the Apostolic See and the states also add to the body of ecclesiastical rules. These different sources of canon law also differ with regard to how they come into being. The processes vary with regard to their complexity—the period of time needed, the stages taken, and the agents involved in lawmaking. They are more complex with regard to major pieces of legislation, such as the reform of the whole Code before 1983 or of parts of the Code, as in the 2021 reform of the Code's penal law.[7] These complex reforms consisted of multiple and time-consuming phases of expert revision, official global consultation, and papal promulgation, which involved a myriad of Vatican and other ecclesiastical agents and kept them busy for decades or, in the case of penal law, for a decade. Single papal laws are often less complex pieces of legislation. Lawmaking regularly involves merely the pope's or a dicastery's initiative, some curial officials tasked with the preparation of the draft law over a couple of months, a rather informal consultation of some experts, and papal promulgation or approbation. So it is somehow deceptive to speak of ecclesiastical legislation in the singular. There is no uniform process of ecclesiastical lawmaking for the global church. Neither is there supposed to be one, as the pope as the supreme legislator of the church is free to decide how to make his laws. Whilst canon law commands that laws require promulgation to enter into being (see canons 7, 8 CIC/1983), it does not regulate the stages of lawmaking to be taken *before* promulgation. Hence, in each case of papal legislation, the pope is free to decide which steps to take to ready his laws for promulgation.

5.1.1 Past Legal Reforms

Hence, one cannot study a standard procedure of lawmaking as there is none. Nevertheless, one can examine past processes to derive from them how the Apostolic See has dealt with law as a subject of inculturation on a legislative level so far. By way of example this book will briefly outline the course of action which brought about the reformed Code of 1983 to examine how this key piece of legislation dealt

[7] See Francis (2021a). Acta Apostolicae Sedis (2021), pp. 534–537; 537–555.

with global law as a matter of inculturation. As indicated, the reform works before 1983 consisted of three major stages. First, the pope endowed several working groups and the Commission for the Revision of the Code with the operative work of revising the norms of the old 1917 Code and of composing drafts of single legal matters and later of the whole revised Code. Second, a global consultation process followed the revision and re-composition of the Code. It invited the dicasteries of the Roman Curia, the bishops' conferences all over the globe, the Union of Superiors General of the religious orders, and ecclesiastical universities and faculties to share their critical opinion on the draft of the Code; a similar procedure applied in the 2021 reform of the Code's penal law, including the same addressees who were invited to consult on the draft law. These agents critically discussed the commission's draft of the Code. Many of them handed in their suggestions for improvement. Their comments often considered the particular perspectives of the local churches by pointing to particular needs and also to difficulties deriving from the proposed norms for the local churches. These interventions led to some further discussion in the commission and also to further revisions of the law. The third step in the reform process consisted of the pope's final redaction, advised by a small group of Vatican consultants. The process ended with the pope's promulgation of the Code, just as it did 2021 with the promulgation of the reformed penal law.

5.1.2 Prioritising Continuity

Studying the steps which led to the current Code of Canon Law reveals typical neo-conservative views of inculturation. For instance, it is apparent that the reform process before 1983—as well as the 2021 reform of canonical penal law—applied a hermeneutic of continuity with regard to the development of the law. Whilst the 1983 reform broke with some traditions of the 1917 Code, it did so without causing much rupture. By organising the drafting of the new law not as a radical reinvention of the Code, but as a *revision* of the 1917 norms, the reform was guided by the idea of continuity, even though some legal matters underwent major change. Ecclesiastical marriage law is a typical example. The revised law of the 1983 Code with its personalist conciliar terminology of marriage revolving around a concept of marriage as a covenant designed to serve the good of the spouses (see canon 1055 §1 CIC/1983) suggests that the legal matter of marriage has undergone a full reinvention. But it actually also presents a striking continuity with the old law, presenting the 1917 contractualist approach to marriage as a contract *sui generis* in pastorally more agreeable terms. The same continuity guided the 2021 reform of the Code's penal law. While the reform of the sixth book of the Code, published in June 2021, was presented to the public as a massive improvement, it is in fact only a modest development of the old law. After 10 years of study, the reform commission had come up with some minor adjustments to the penal matter. It did reform the law on the sexual abuse of minors by clerics. However, it failed to address most other issues of penal law which have been the object of criticism for a long time.

One example can be of help to see this point: With regard to the former law on sexual delicts committed by clerics one major point of criticism was that the old law treated these offenses not as delicts violating the integrity of the victims, but as breaches of the clerics' vow to celibacy. Hence, the focus of the old law was not on the victims but on the clerics and their duty to lead a celibate life. This focus had long been criticised for supporting a distorted view of sexual violence. One suggestion for reform therefore was to remove sexual delicts from the list of clerical offenses against celibacy and to insert them into the section of the Code dealing with offenses against human life and freedom. In the 2021 reform of penal law, the sexual abuse of minors was indeed revised in the recommended way. It was removed from the list of sex offenses of former canon 1395 §2 CIC/1983 and given its own place in a new canon 1398 CIC/1983. This canon is now part of the so-called *offenses against human life, dignity, and liberty* (canons 1397–1398 CIC/1983). This classification is an acknowledgment that sexual abuse is an offense that violates the victims' dignity and liberty. Against this backdrop, it is all the more striking that sexual violence against adults was not added to this particular section of the Code's penal law. Whenever a cleric "by force, threats, or abuse of his authority commits an offense against the sixth commandment of the Decalogue or forces someone to perform or submit to sexual acts" (canon 1395 §3 CIC/1983), these offenses still fall under the section on *offenses against special obligations* and are regarded as worthy of punishment merely insofar as they violate the clerical obligation to lead a celibate life. So the reformed penal law represents rape and sexual assault as punishable primarily because these offenses are incompatible with a celibate lifestyle, and, consequently, mainly as disciplinary issues. Hence, the reformers altered the qualification of sexual abuse of minors following considerable external pressure, but left all other sexual offenses against adults untouched. It is impossible to understand this decision as an editorial mishap. Instead, one must assume that the reform was guided by an agenda with a focus on preserving continuity by not allowing for too much change. This study will not comment on the misogynist tendency of this decision which failed to improve the law for the mostly female adult victims of clerical sex offenses and abuse of power, as the author has discussed elsewhere.[8] For the purposes of this book, which is interested in understanding the policy behind Vatican lawmaking, one can derive from this observation that the 2021 reform was driven by a neoconservative agenda, protecting the law against all changes which did not seem urgently needed, even at the cost of producing inconsistency.

[8] See Hahn (2022b).

5.1.3 Centralised Lawmaking

Lawmaking in both cases, the reform of the whole Code before 1983 and the 2021 reform of penal law, was designed as a centralised endeavour to produce a uniform body of rules that serves as an expression of the unity of the church; in this sense, James Provost regarded the reform of the Code as having been guided by a "centralized strategy".[9] This is most evident with regard to the pope's key role in lawmaking. The reform of the Code culminated in the pope's promulgation of the law. Historically, this is somewhat surprising insofar as papal codification, as Provost remarks, was only introduced with the 1917 Code. Since it was a relatively new approach serving "as an expression of the papal primacy as defined at Vatican I",[10] one might have expected that the post-conciliar legal reform would have chosen a different model. Yet, as Provost observes: "Despite suggestions to the contrary, it was decided after the Council to continue this strategy of codification".[11] The Apostolic See's control over the reform process helped to ensure the uniformity of the result as well as its coherence with ecclesiastical tradition. The Secretariat of the Commission for the Revision of the Code as an agency of the Apostolic See was in charge of conducting the reform tasks. The pope's final redaction of the law, which he undertook advised by a small group of Vatican consultants, also symbolically represented the Apostolic See as the centre of global canonical legislation.

In any case, it seemed that the legislator was eager to avoid the impression of a culture-blind top-down imposition of the law onto the local churches. The process ensured some diversity by engaging representatives of the local churches in drafting the law.[12] The working groups consisted of canonists and church officials with canonical expertise from all over the globe. The Commission for the Revision of the Code entrusted with the main operative work consisted of cardinals of the Roman Curia but also of bishops and cardinals from all continents. The *Relatio ad novissimum Schema* of 1981, which lists the commission members at that time, includes the names of cardinals and bishops from Africa, from Addis Ababa, Algiers, Antananarivo, Dakar, Darussalam, Jos, Kenge, Nairobi, Ouagadougou, as well as the Catholic Coptic Patriarch; from Australia, an auxiliary bishop of Melbourne and the cardinal of Sydney; from the North American continent, cardinals and bishops from Chicago, Cincinnati, Montréal, Philadelphia, Quebec, and Toronto; from the South American continent, cardinals and bishops from Bogota, Lima, Mexico City, Parnaíba, Quito, Rio de Janeiro, San José de Costa Rica, Santiago de Chile, Santiago de Cuba, Teresina, and Valencia en Venezuela; from Asia, from Bombay, Butuan City, Cebu, Chuncheon, Colombo, Ernakulam-Angamaly, Kiayi, Nagasaki, and Seoul; and from Europe, from Albi, Armagh, Barcelona, Brussels, Cologne,

---

9 Provost (1996), p. 121.

10 Ibid., p. 120.

11 Ibid.

12 See John Paul II (1983). Acta Apostolicae Sedis (1983), pp. VIII–IX; Preface to the Code of Canon Law (1983). Acta Apostolicae Sedis (1983), pp. XXVIII–XXIX.

Cordoba, Florence, Genoa, Helsinki, Lisbon, Madrid, Milan, Munich-Freising, Paris, Turin, Utrecht, Vác, Vienna, Warsaw, and Westminster.[13] The consultation process also contributed to giving the local churches a voice. It asked not only the dicasteries of the Roman Curia to give their critical opinion on the draft of the Code—and likewise on the draft of the 2021 revision of penal law—but also all bishops' conferences, the Union of Superiors General of the religious orders, and ecclesiastical universities and faculties.

5.1.4 Voluntary Transplants

The law shaped by the mentioned bodies and promulgated by the pope became law for the global church. One may explain this process best in terms developed by legal scholar Alan Watson in his famous book *Legal Transplants*. In his book, Watson describes the various ways in which legal rules, institutions, concepts, and structures are transplanted from one legal system into another. These acts of transplantation might take on different forms, as he acknowledges. They sometimes affect single rules borrowed by one system. In other cases, a whole bundle of foreign laws is imposed on another group. The methods of transplantation also vary, as Watson mentions, as "receptions and transplants come in all shapes and sizes … imposed reception, solicited impositions, penetration, infiltration, crypto-reception, inoculation and so on".[14] Although he primarily considers secular legal systems, his approach can also be used to classify transplants of religious law. To transfer canonical rules from their origin at the Apostolic See into the local churches is what Watson would likely call "[v]oluntary major transplants—that is when either an entire legal system or a large portion of it is moved to a new sphere".[15] However, the scenarios which he describes when speaking about major transplants are somewhat different. He considers major transplantations to be taking place when groups move into uninhabited territories and carry their law to these places; when they move into new territories where other groups already reside, and confront these groups with their law; and when groups freely borrow foreign law and integrate it into their systems. The transplantation of canon law into the local churches is best compared with Watson's second scenario, where a group moves into a foreign territory and confronts those living there with new rules and institutions. However, as will be discussed in the upcoming section on reception, the expectation is that the receiving church freely takes on global legislation, an idea which is best reflected in Watson's third scenario. Global lawmaking in the church can therefore be most accurately described as a mixed system of transplantation. It practises a top-down transfer of

[13] See Pontifical Commission for the Revision of the Code of Canon Law (1981), pp. 5–8.

[14] Watson (1993), p. 30.

[15] Ibid., p. 29.

global laws into the local churches, but also expects the local churches to voluntarily receive that law. Watson's terms *imposed reception* or *solicited imposition* which reflect the tension between external pressure and voluntary appropriation are well suited to describe this dynamic.

5.1.5 Episcopal Cooperation

The law itself exerts some pressure to encourage its reception in the local churches by obliging the diocesan bishops to enforce it, regulating: "Since he must protect the unity of the universal church, a bishop is bound to promote the common discipline of the whole church and therefore to urge the observance of all ecclesiastical laws" (canon 392 §1 CIC/1983). The bishops' duty is to protect the unity of the church by supporting a uniform discipline, which includes enforcing papal laws in their local churches. Viewed in the light of this rule, bishops appear less as independent leaders of their local churches and more as papal "administration officials"—an insult voiced by German Reich Chancellor Otto von Bismarck after the First Vatican Council.[16] It is tempting to draw a parallel between this centripetal strategy of securing uniform law and the policy which currently ensures the global reach of international law, following an observation made by Antony Anghie. He finds that international law has revitalised many colonial and imperialist motifs after 9/11 such as its "civilising mission"[17] to protect the world from terrorism: "This has resulted in the formulation of a new form of imperialism that asserts itself in the name of 'national security', as self-defence".[18] We can reinterpret the function of global canon law in a similar light, as the church's self-defence against disgregation. By mobilising global canon law, centralised legislation "civilises" the local churches to preserve the unity of the whole church. Hence, the rather imperialist way of proceeding is part of a neoconservative strategy for protecting church unity by controlling the local units with the help of the decentralised leaders, namely the diocesan bishops who act as the papacy's extended arm to enforce global rules.

Nevertheless, in certain cases in which bishops find a global law to be inadequate for their churches, this expectation can cause conflicts. Diocesan bishops may then make use of their so-called right of remonstration to counter centralist pressure to enforce the law. This right did not enter the Code of Canon Law; it is nevertheless regarded as a valid instrument which has derived from canonical tradition. As a traditional remedy for conflicts between global legislation and the local churches, the right of remonstration entitles diocesan bishops to request the legislator's abrogation of a global law which is detrimental to their local church to prevent its entering into force in this local church. Thus, a remonstration against a global law targets

[16] See von Bismarck (1872), no. 304 p. 2.

[17] Anghie (2006), p. 750.

[18] Ibid.

the validity of the respective law in a local church. If remonstration is successful, the contested law does not become valid law in that respective church. The act of remonstrating itself has a suspensive effect, so that the law does not come into effect in the local churches until the legislator has decided the case. Yet, it is up to the pope as the supreme legislator to decide whether he consents to the abrogation of a global rule or rejects it. If the supreme legislator does not endorse a remonstration, the remonstrating bishop is obliged to enforce the contested law in his local church.

5.2 Receiving Global Laws Locally

Global laws are generated in Rome. They become valid laws upon being promulgated by the supreme legislator. Nonetheless, they gain their effectiveness for the global church only upon being received in the local churches. James Provost notes concordantly: "Technically, laws come into existence when they are promulgated. In life, however, even a promulgated law can remain a dead letter until it is put into practice by those for whom it is intended".[19] Laws are effective merely when they influence the legal reality of a group by affecting the behaviour of its members. Global laws have an impact on the life of the local churches when they change their legal praxis and influence local conduct. As discussed in Sect. 4.1, the major issue regarding reception which concerned Christianity from its earliest days was how to encourage the reception of the faith among non-Christians. In a similar vein as Robert Schreiter has analysed under what conditions contact with the Gospel stimulates reception which takes shape in a local theology, one can ask if and under what conditions global legislation sparks reception among local individuals and groups, as it kindles the development of a local practice and the growth of local rules and institutions which add flesh to the global legal skeleton.

5.2.1 Appropriating Goods

One can best describe the dynamic of transmission and reception between the Roman origin and the local receivers of a law as an act of communication or of exchanging a good, as suggested by systematic theologian Wolfgang Beinert. He speaks of reception in terms borrowed from communication theory, by alluding to the senders or transmitters of a message and to the receivers of that message. Occasionally, he also relies on the language of trade relations when he speaks of reception as a process in which a sender transfers a good to a receiver who appropriates it so that "the intended good is conveyed from the transmitter's own domain to

[19] Provost (1996), p. 121.

the recipient".[20] The act of receiving that good, as Beinert describes it, consists of "the appropriation of an alien good, of the good which is being received, into the domain of the receiver".[21] Similarly, the jurisprudential debates on legal transfer describe practices in which a law is transmitted from one domain to another in an equally mercantile language, suggesting the frugality of these actions. They frequently use the term *export* to describe the transmission of a law from one order to another. And they use the term *import* to describe the reception of these laws in the receiving order.[22] This terminology implies dynamic intercultural processes where different systems interact to exchange cultural goods, such as legal rules, which benefit both of them, stimulating legal development.

Alan Watson, who describes legal transplants as the frequent and common "borrowing and transmissibility of rules from one society or system to another",[23] draws a further analogy in comparing legal transplants with organ transplants: "A successful legal transplant—like that of a human organ—will grow in its new body, and become part of that body just as the rule or institution would have continued to develop in its parent system".[24] His image is suited to depict the reception of laws as an organic act. It is the growth of a local practice from a new rule which makes that rule an integral part of the receiving system. The image is also suitable as it expresses the possibility that transplanted laws, similarly to organs, might be rejected by the receiving system; legal scholar and sociologist Gunther Teubner once used the image of legal transplants as being "rejected by an immune reaction"[25] of the receiving system. In a similar vein, Wolfgang Beinert's statement—that reception is about appropriation and not about the imposition of an alien good onto a particular community—alludes to the finding that it requires the receivers' acceptance of that good. The receivers can be forced to receive it, or they can decide to do so of their own accord. However, if they refuse to take on the alien good, no reception takes place. Robert Schreiter expounds the same thought for the exchange of theologies. Receiving the Christian message, as he finds, is more than merely tolerating a foreign concept of Christian thinking and living, but is the growth of a distinct local response to the faith. Schreiter therefore opts to understand reception as a series of steps which allow the Christian message to grow into an independent local theology.[26]

---

[20] Beinert (1997), p. 321.

[21] Ibid.

[22] For overviews over the various expressions used in comparative law and the legal pluralism debate to describe these phenomena see Örücü (2002), pp. 205–223; Foljanty (2015), pp. 4–5.

[23] Watson (1993), p. 19.

[24] Ibid., p. 27.

[25] Teubner (1998), p. 12.

[26] See Schreiter (1985), p. 11.

5.2.2 *Growth of Local Practices*

Similarly to Schreiter's discussion with regard to the Gospel message, one can understand other ecclesiastical goods, such as the liturgies or the law, as goods which require more than toleration if they are to gain effectiveness in the local churches. True reception requires individuals and groups who embrace the Roman liturgies to initiate the development of local liturgical practices. Likewise, reception of global laws requires the local legal practitioners and legal subjects to appropriate the law by allowing it to impact the local praxis and to stimulate the development of local rules and institutions to bring the rules to life. Reception, thus, more generally speaking, describes an alien impulse to foster the generation of local practices. This makes reception an act which consists of various steps. Receiving a good is, first, an act of intellectual evaluation, as Wolfgang Beinert explains. The reception of the faith, as he notes, frequently starts off with individuals critically assessing the offered good. In a similar vein, Ladislas Orsy perceives with regard to the law that the local legal subjects commence their reception of global rules by critically scrutinising them. He ties in this practical step of Christians assessing the offered legal good with a theological idea, as he sees their capacity to make wise decisions as rooted in their supernatural sense of faith. As Christians share a supernatural capacity to assess which decisions are beneficial for the faith, Orsy finds it plausible to assume that they also have the capacity to evaluate which laws are good for their church, so that "by this sense of faith, God's people can penetrate the law by accurate insights and apply them correctly to life. When this happens, the law is received in the community".[27] Orsy's explanation that reception is, first, the rational scrutiny of the law, and, second, the application of the law to life, alludes to the fact that reception requires the received good to become practical in the receiving community. Reception is in its core a hands-on activity, as Beinert finds. The faith is received when expressed in liturgies and worship, when individuals live according to it, forming their personal spirituality or basing their individual or collective practices on it.[28] Global law is received when it impacts the social reality of local Catholics, because it is reflected in local legislation, adjudication, and administration and brings about new local rules, customs, and institutions.

5.2.3 *Diverse Interests*

The finding that reception is an intellectual and a practical endeavour reveals its complexity. The Archbishop of Pamplona, Fernando Sebastian Aguilar, described reception in the closing session of the colloquium "Reception and Communion

[27] Orsy (1992), p. 88; see also Orsy (1984), pp. 69–70; Orsy (1995), pp. 516–517.

[28] See Beinert (1991), p. 43.

among Churches"[29] as a composite process involving manifold stages and various agents. He discerned that within ecclesiastical reception, steps of "initial volitive consent, intellectual reception, theological interpretation, practical application and juridical translation of the doctrine or decision of authority, are distinct aspects and moments, each with its own exigencies, phases, and protagonists".[30] His words indicate that the local churches are complex social fields, a finding which was also elaborated by theologian Jean Joncheray. As social fields, they are relatively autonomous—semi-autonomous—and function according to their proper rules, whilst at the same time being connected with other social fields and their religious, economic, political, and cultural agents.[31] Within social fields, there are manifold agents at work who fulfil different functions. As Joncheray maintains, here one finds "instances of reproduction and conservation, agents of transmission, agents which produce innovations, whether they be avant garde or already on the way to being legitimated, different segments of the public which forge alliances, be it with the instances of conservation or with those proposing innovations or changes".[32] The reception of alien goods into social fields requires intricate interactions between those agents. In the local churches, reception requires agents of transmission to receive the good from transmitters from outside the field and introduce it into their churches. With regard to receiving global legislation one can think of the diocesan bishops or other authorities who preside over a local church as agents of transmission whose duty it is "to promote the common discipline of the whole church and therefore to urge the observance of all ecclesiastical laws" (canon 392 §1 CIC/1983). However, reception of the laws also requires agents of innovation. With regard to receiving foreign law, one might think of the diocesan bishops once more who, as the decentralised legislators, respond to legal transplants by producing legal innovations (see canon 391 CIC/1983). Whenever they use global law as an impulse for decentralised legislation and develop laws to fill in the global legal frame, they are receiving those laws. Comparative legal scholar Esin Örücü captures this innovative dimension of reception by remarking: "Times of reception are also times for domestic creativity".[33]

Agents of legal innovation, in any case, whenever they develop something new, have to convince the agents of reproduction and conservation to likewise accept those legal changes brought about by the reception of alien rules. This includes persuading these agents, such as the courts and administrative bodies, to act against their conservative and protective nature and to change the legal fundament on which they have based their decisions so far to adapt to the new law. Ecclesiastical tribunals and administration are agents of reproduction and conservation. Their duty is to apply the law in a reliable and predictable way. This makes them naturally

[29] Pontifical University of Salamanca, 8–14 April 1996, papers published in *The Jurist* (1997).

[30] Aguilar (1997), p. 447.

[31] On the concept of semi-autonomous social fields, e.g. Moore (1973).

[32] Joncheray (1997), pp. 349–350.

[33] Örücü (2002), p. 216.

resistant to change. Hence, a successful reception of a new law in a local church requires not merely the agents of transmission and innovation to accept the law, it also requires the cooperation of those agents whose common duty it is to conserve and reproduce the traditions of a social field. Global canon law, thus, is received by ecclesiastical tribunals and administrative bodies when these agents take up the new law and base their decisions on it, thereby applying the law to those single cases which they have to decide.

5.2.4 Community Reaction

Joncheray also notes that reception requires "different segments of the public which forge alliances, be it with the instances of conservation or with those proposing innovations or changes".[34] With regard to reception in the local churches, this alludes to the role of the community and their share in taking on a foreign good. Thus, the reception of global laws involves the local legal subjects. Most interestingly, as Alan Watson notices, transplanting a rule is frequently fairly uncomplicated when it comes to the local communities. Even in those cases in which transplantation is carried out with external pressure, groups tend to embrace alien rules rather willingly. Whilst professional agents, particularly those with a conservative function, tend to oppose new rules for a while, legal communities tolerate them fairly well, particularly in those cases in which new rules do not affect individual group members to any greater degree. Watson states: "The truth of the matter seems to be that many legal rules make little impact on individuals, and that very often it is important that there be a rule; but what rule actually is adopted is of restricted significance for general human happiness".[35] Whilst it is therefore often not too difficult to convince local communities, their response is of some relevance for successful reception. For a law to be effectively received, it is essential that the community, or at least those members of it to whom a new law relates, receive the law by adopting it. This reception is given when legal subjects adjust their behaviour so that it concords with the new rule. This predicates, first of all, that the subjects know of the new law. And it requires, second, that they decide to abide by it, a decision which might be motivated by force or also by their own initiative. Both requirements, knowledge of the law and a rudimentary acceptance of it, do not usually come about automatically, as Joncheray perceives. They often require instruments to foster public reception, such a public debates, votes, and surveys.[36]

Abiding by the new rules is one typical way in which groups receive laws. However, a more intense way of embracing new rules is to make them the foundation of new customs. Theologian Jean Tillard states: "Custom is a major expression

---

[34] Joncheray (1997), pp. 349–350.

[35] Watson (1993), p. 96.

[36] See Joncheray (1997), pp. 357–359.

of this entry [of the law, addition by the author] into the concrete reality of the local church".[37] John Huels similarly defines customs as living law: "The customs of a country, an ethnic group, a diocese, a parish, a religious institute, etc. represent the lived practices of Christian communities".[38] By integrating a global rule into local practices, custom reconciles law and life, as Huels notes, calling custom "a key mechanism for the inculturation of canon law" and "a principal way in which a universal law can be adapted in diverse cultures".[39] He therefore acknowledges custom as "an important force for promoting a healthy diversity in the world-wide, Latin church".[40] The generation of customs as a specific form of reception might even result in the development of customary law responding to global laws. Groups that generate customary law are agents of legal innovation, similar to legislators, yet they are more of what Joncheray calls *avant garde*, as they contribute to the development of decentralised law more in an experimental fashion, often pushing the boundaries of canon law to a greater extent than official legislation. It is particularly those local customs which conform to canon law (*secundum legem*) or go beyond the law and add decentralised rules to it (*praeter legem*) that serve as ways of receiving global laws. Those *secundum legem* and *praeter legem* customs receive the global legal frame by fleshing it out in a way which makes sense in a specific context and which concords with local legal usage.

5.2.5 Rejecting Legal Rules

So far this study has discussed how the local community can receive the law by abiding by it or by giving flesh to the global legal frame. What it has not addressed so far is that legal transfer allows not only for the appropriation of an alien rule, but is also an opportunity to reject it. This includes the possibility that global canon law is not received when it is transmitted into a local church and fails to become effective law there. Saying this does not only imply an occasional non-compliance with global canon law. This is a fairly normal reaction that happens to all laws and does not affect their general effectiveness. However, non-compliance can have a fundamental impact when it manifests as total rejection. As laws require reception to become effective means of organising a community, a group's complete refusal to receive them prevents the law from becoming a living reality.

It is important to note that canonical tradition does not treat non-reception as a mere malfunction of reception, but understands it as an instrument to prevent conflicting laws impacting a community. This strategic use of non-reception goes back to the times of the early church. John Huels relates to the biblical traces of

[37] Tillard (1996), p. 33.

[38] Huels (1996), p. 24.

[39] Ibid.

[40] Ibid., p. 22.

non-reception by referring to the Council of Jerusalem (see Acts 15:1–35; Galatians 2:1–10), which dealt with the Gentile Christians' difficulties in observing Jewish law.[41] The question of whether the Gentiles needed to be circumcised according to Jewish law before becoming Christians was a source of trouble in the early Gentile communities. After a controversy at the Council of Jerusalem, the Apostles decided to relieve the Gentile Christians of this obligation, as it would be wise to "not trouble those Gentiles who are turning to God" (Acts 15:19) and not make their decision to become Christians a more difficult one by obliging them to follow Jewish laws. According to Huels, this consideration of both cultural contexts, Jewish and Gentile, from which the early Christians originated, is a key idea in the church's dealing with cultural conflicts. It resulted in a compromise acceptable to Christians from both backgrounds for the sake of avoiding particular hardship to one group. Hence, the community agreed to give up a regulation that was particularly burdensome to one part to avoid endangering that group's solidarity. In that sense, the Council of Jerusalem can serve as a biblical example of how non-reception of a law might protect a local church and its members from the detrimental impact of overburdening law.[42]

Over the course of church history, ecclesiastical jurisprudence then developed a theory expounding the consequences of non-reception, the doctrine of *receptio legis*. According to *receptio legis*, law essentially requires reception to come into being and to remain in existence.[43] Hence, the law must have some effects on the legal community for it to become and remain valid law, be it that some individuals abide by it or that an authority sanctions a breach of the law. In those cases where this impact is completely missing, one can speak of a complete non-reception of a law. Those laws which fully lack any impact on the legal community from the outset are regarded as lacking their validity right from the start; those laws which have been observed for some time are regarded as losing their validity when their desuetude becomes manifest, even when they are not formally repealed. Canonists often refer to the example of the Apostolic Constitution *Veterum Sapientia* on the Promotion of the Study of Latin when explaining the invalidating effect of non-

[41] See Huels (1987), p. 250 fn. 4.

[42] For an alternative reading of this decision see Coughlin (2012), p. 20. Coughlin does not interpret the council's decision as an example of non-reception but of relativising a deeply cultural law due to the universality of Christianity. As Christianity is universal, it promptly began to transcend cultural borders. Therefore it quickly became "necessary to develop law that transcended the boundaries of culture, race, nationality, and other circumstances" (20). One might in any case discuss whether the council's decision is rightly understood as a phenomenon of the church universalising its law. Instead one can argue that the law remained as particular as it was before, but with a new focus on a different context. Christianity was quick in connecting its law with hegemonic cultures, such as the Roman view of the law. As a result, the Apostles' compromise to let go off the Jewish laws on circumcision can be seen less as a step towards universalising Christian law than as a step towards developing it to accord more with Gentile-Christian cultural backgrounds.

[43] On the historical roots of *receptio legis* and on the canonical controversies of whether non-reception actually prevents a law from coming into being or rather inhibits its effectiveness, e.g. Coriden (1982), pp. 289–290; Coriden (1990), pp. 58–82.

reception.[44] Pope John XXIII promulgated this law in 1962 to increase the use of Latin in theological education. The constitution advised all lecturers of theology to teach the main theological disciplines in Latin and to use Latin textbooks for their instruction. The constitution even ordered the gradual replacement of any lecturers who could not adjust to Latin teaching. Canonist Bertram Griffin laconically remarked with respect to the effects of that papal law: "A few professors tried this for about a week and then gave up".[45] The Catholic universities and theological faculties never made any efforts to enforce the law or replace those who did not adhere to it. So *Veterum Sapientia* became one example of a papal law that was not received by its addressees, as it was ignored by nearly all theological scholars and had next to no effect on theological training. Those scholars who were used to teach in Latin continued to do so; those who had never used Latin in their classes before did not take up that practice. One can therefore consider the law to have been fully ineffective and assume that it never entered into force.

The example of *Veterum Sapientia* is somewhat amusing. When citing this example in class, theology students frequently sigh with relief after hearing that their teachers are not obliged to continue the class in Latin. However, the idea of non-reception is of some theological significance. In relation to ecclesiastical doctrine, non-reception can be an expression of the faithful's sense of faith. Analogically, in relation to the law, non-reception can be a manifestation of what one might call the faithful's *sense of law*, as a sense for practical elements serving the faith. Ladislas Orsy has alluded to this connection, as mentioned. He finds that Christians are imbued with the capacity to identify laws which are meaningful for their faith, identifying a "power (*dynamis* in biblical speech) in the Christian community to create good laws".[46] For him, it is evident that if Christians have a particular sense for what is right with regard to their faith, it is implausible to assume that this spirit is inactive when it comes to rules supporting their faith. Hence, the reception of a law can be an expression of Catholics sensing the meaningfulness of that law for their community, while non-reception might suggest that they anticipate a negative impact on their faith and communal life. Systematic theologian John J. Burkhard observes correspondingly that "there are many situations in the church today, especially when the church is considered as a world church, that defy our ability to spell out the implications of a non-reception of a teaching of the magisterium in terms of its truth or falsity. In some situations the appropriate question is not 'Is it objectively true?' but 'Is it life-giving?'"[47] This criterion might also be applied to the law. While some laws develop a life of their own after reception, some fail to be meaningful. In this light, reception can be interpreted as the process in which a community, driven by the Spirit, affirms the validity of a law for them. Non-reception, on the contrary, can be interpreted as dissent worked by the Spirit, rejecting the law as meaningful

[44] See John XXIII (1962a). Acta Apostolicae Sedis (1962), pp. 129–135.

[45] Griffin (1984), p. 25.

[46] Orsy (1992), p. 116.

[47] Burkhard (2016), p. 141.

for the group. Wolfgang Beinert has incorporated the idea that rejecting a command can sometimes be an effective way to protect the church into a simple story, emphasising that

> it could be that pride is not the cause of disobedience, but the fact that someone has better insights into an issue might be. A rather dramatic example can illustrate this point. When it was discovered that spinach contains iron and that iron is good for the human body, generations of mothers wanted to feed their children spinach. Despite the opposition of their children, the mothers knew what was good and nutritional. But with time science discovered that the children's opposition was quite reasonable; spinach did indeed contain iron, but in a form that could damage the delicate bodies of children. Thus disobedience can at times protect life.[48]

One might find Beinert's comparison appealing or a little simplistic. Either way, he is certainly right to observe that in some cases, rejecting a good, such as a law, can protect a community. This is particularly evident if one accepts that dissent, in a similar way to consent, can be a manifestation of the Spirit at work in local communities. It is for this reason that the ecclesiastical authorities should take the non-reception of laws seriously, as Bertram Griffin notes: "Non-reception of law is not disobedience. It is a reasonable act of the community approved by the legislator and an important way in the canonical system of adjusting law to reality".[49] Unlike "rebellious disobedience or disregard for rightful authority", non-reception, as canonist James Coriden says, is an expression "of virtue, not vice".[50] Ladislas Orsy similarly connects non-reception with decisions of conscience.[51] Hence, the non-reception of global laws in the local churches sends an important message to the supreme legislator: namely, that these laws might not be the kind of rules that the legal subjects require or deserve.

5.2.6 Command and Obedience

Leaving theory behind and studying the law itself reveals, in any case, that there is little mention in the law of the power of reception and even less of non-reception. Legal sources rather tend to view reception as a matter of command and obedience with regard to both doctrinal and disciplinary issues. This alternative view is supported by ecclesiastical doctrine. An example of the magisterium's view of the relation between the church authorities and those governed by them is Pope Pius X's 1906 Encyclical *Vehementer Nos* which explains

> that the Church is essentially an unequal society, that is, a society comprising two categories of persons, the pastors and the flock, those who occupy a rank in the different degrees of the hierarchy and the multitude of the faithful. So distinct are these categories that with

[48] Beinert (1997), p. 323.

[49] Griffin (1984), p. 25.

[50] Coriden (1990), p. 76.

[51] See Orsy (1995), p. 518.

> the pastoral body only rests the necessary right and authority for promoting the end of the society and directing all its members towards that end; the one duty of the multitude is to allow themselves to be led, and, like a docile flock, to follow the pastors.[52]

This tradition is reflected in the law, which does not give much consideration to the opinion of the "flock". Consequently, receiving legal rules, as reflected in the law itself, has been restricted to a simple act of ratification.[53] Canon 209 §2 CIC/1983 obliges all Catholics to diligently "fulfil the duties which they owe to the universal Church and the particular church to which they belong according to the prescripts of the law". According to canon 212 §1 CIC/1983 Catholics must "follow with Christian obedience those things which the sacred pastors, inasmuch as they represent Christ, declare as teachers of the faith or establish as rulers of the church". As the law belongs to those matters which ecclesiastical legislators "establish as rulers of the church", Catholics are obliged to abide by the law obediently as part of their Christian duties. Their legitimate response to a legal command is therefore considerably restrained as it includes merely their obedience. The law provides for a faint reciprocal dynamic though, by regulating that Catholics "are free to make known to the pastors of the church their needs, especially spiritual ones, and their desires" (canon 212 §2 CIC/1983). They may also communicate "their opinion on matters which pertain to the good of the church" to church authorities and even to the Catholic public, in those cases in which they have a particular expertise and "without prejudice to the integrity of faith and morals, with reverence towards their pastors, and attentive to common advantage and the dignity of persons" (canon 212 §3 CIC/1983). Hence, with various caveats, Catholics may approach the authorities to raise legal concerns. It is entirely up to the authorities whether they address these concerns.

Hence, with regard to the issue of reception, the law supports the binary operation of *command and obedience* by obliging Catholics to abide by the law. Catholics burdened by a law may communicate this to the authorities, discreetly and politely. This right of Catholics to reveal their needs to the authorities and to give their opinion when opportune does not include a right of non-reception of those rules which might be harmful for their church. Thus, current canon law does not draw too many practical consequences from the doctrinal resource provided by *receptio legis*. Whilst *receptio legis* emphasises the essential relevance of the community for a law to come into being and to remain effective, legislation has so far abstained from paying practical attention to this. It is no coincidence that canonists frequently cite *Veterum Sapientia* as an example of a non-received law—in want of a better example. It reveals that the Apostolic See acknowledges the invalidating effect of non-reception only in rare cases and only retrospectively. Canonists may now agree that *Veterum Sapientia* has failed to become a valid law, sixty years after its promulgation and based on sixty years of proof of its total ineffectiveness. Challenging contemporary legislation is an entirely different matter. James Coriden alludes to

---

[52] Pius X (1906), no. 8. Acta Sanctae Sedis (1906), pp. 8–9.

[53] See Orsy (1983), p. 114 fn. 22.

reasons for this attitude. He inter alia sees a strong notion of voluntarism in canonical jurisprudence as being responsible for its focus on the legislator and its tendency to ignore the community and its relevance for the emergence of law.[54] This neoconservative view has fostered a narrow reading of the doctrine of *receptio legis*, which attributes the invalidating effect of non-reception to a low number of strikingly evident cases. By assigning to non-reception its invalidating effect only in cases where total non-reception is manifest, legislation is ignoring the manifold cases in which laws are not fully, but partially ignored. As a consequence, even the total rejection of a law in a local church does not qualify as invalidating the law with regard to that church if there is some compliance with the law in other churches. Likewise, the rejection of a law by the majority of Catholics all over the globe does not provide a reason to conceive of that law as invalid if a minority of Catholics abide by it.

Paradoxically, this restricted view of non-reception is supported by connecting *receptio legis* with the faithful's sense of faith. According to church doctrine, the faithful's sense of faith reaffirms the truth of a doctrine when "the entire body of the faithful, … from the bishops down to the last of the lay faithful … show universal agreement in matters of faith and morals".[55] In a similar vein, as mentioned above, legal reception can be understood as articulating the faithful's sense of law, as a sense for practical elements serving their faith. And one can likewise understand non-reception as an expression of the faithful's dissent, conveying their sense for the detrimental effect of a law to their church and their faith. However, by coupling *receptio legis* with the theory of the sense of faith, ecclesiastical jurisprudence restricts the invalidating effects of non-reception to those cases where the *entire* body of the church, including all of its members, agrees to disagree. Only absolute dissent prevents a law from coming into being. Predominant dissent, on the contrary, is not attributed with this effect, even if the dissent is shared by an overwhelming majority of Catholics. In a normative light, one can discuss how convincing this understanding is. In a descriptive light, however, one can see that *receptio legis* in its current form is supportive of a neoconservative policy that widely suppresses non-reception to protect a uniform law in the global church.

5.2.7 *Contra Legem* Customs

One example for establishing local laws which express the spirit of particular communities is the growth of legal customs into customary law. This is one way of developing laws which "are safeguarding the local soul of the people and its history",[56] as Jean Tillard finds. As canon law excludes the growth of customs into

[54] See Coriden (1990), p. 82.

[55] Second Vatican Council (1964), no. 12. Acta Apostolicae Sedis (1965), p. 16.

[56] Tillard (1996), p. 33.

customary law only in cases where customary law would conflict with divine law (see canon 24 §1 CIC/1983), customs can become customary law not only when conforming to canon law or going beyond the law but also in cases where customs are contrary to the law. Those *contra legem* customs can grow into customary law that collides with global rules, allowing local churches to oppose global legislation by confronting it with divergent decentralised rules. With Tillard's classification in mind, one can perceive customs which conform to global law or go beyond the law as customs which safeguard the spirit of local groups by fleshing out the global frame in a way which makes sense in a specific context. Customs which collide with global laws, on the contrary, can protect the local churches by replacing harmful global rules with adequate local laws. However, as already mentioned in the introduction, global legislation has set several provisions which decrease the chances of customary law prevailing over global law. When the Code came into force in 1983, it abrogated all customary laws contrary to the Code (see canon 5 §1 CIC/1983). Only centenary or immemorial customs received protection. Adding to this, legislation set a high bar to prevent new customary laws from redeveloping in the future by disallowing the revival of any reprobated customs (see canon 5 §1 CIC/1983). The emergence of customary law is also limited by canon 23 CIC/1983 which establishes that only customs approved by the legislator can obtain the force of law. This approval does not need to be given expressly. Often approval is given tacitly by a legislator tolerating a certain custom without reprobating it. Nevertheless, in such cases of tacit consent, global law sets extensive periods of time for customs to receive the force of law to make sure that this does not happen easily. Canon 26 CIC/1983 regulates:

> Unless the competent legislator has specifically approved it, a custom contrary to canon law now in force or one beyond a canonical law obtains the force of law only if it has been legitimately observed for thirty continuous and complete years. Only a centenary or immemorial custom, however, can prevail against a canonical law which contains a clause prohibiting future customs.

By regularly requiring observance for thirty continuous years before acquiring the force of law, the current standard is high for a *contra legem* custom (as well as for a *praeter legem* custom) to become customary law. This kind of formalism used to determine when a custom has become law is found in many legal systems. Yet, in church, it appears to be used strategically to prevent the emergence of decentralised rules that could undermine the uniformity of global legal practice. In the reform of the Code before 1983, the reformers' draft suggested reducing the period from forty years in the old Code to twenty years. However, this proposed reduction was extended again in the last stage of the reform to thirty years, a rollback "striking one as petty",[57] as canonist and legal scholar Richard Potz remarks. He classifies this as a deliberate de facto prevention of customary law: "Given the dynamism of our society, which is so marked by the multiplicity of communications, a 30-year-term is almost equivalent to a deliberate block".[58] This makes it particularly

[57] Potz (1986), p. 21.

[58] Ibid.

challenging for customary law to develop in churches under the scrutiny of the Apostolic See. As one reviewer of this book rightly remarked, "where the Vatican is watching more closely, customs are more difficult to become law". These restrictive regulations suppress a greater diversification of the Catholic legal landscape in favour of more legal uniformity. Adding to this, this policy discourages the local reception of global law.

5.3 Summary

This chapter has focused on global canon law as a subject of inculturation, in relation to global lawmaking and the reception of these laws in the local churches. Lawmaking is organised in a centralised way with little involvement of decentralised agents. Relying on the inculturation approach of translation, the transfer of law into the local churches is mostly structured as the monodirectional transplantation of global legislation. Decentralised authorities, such as diocesan bishops, are obliged to enforce these transplanted rules locally. With remonstration, they only have a weak instrument at their disposal to protect their churches from the harmful effects of such rules. Reception is imposed, leaving local agents with limited means of preventing global rules from taking effect in the local churches. Although canonical jurisprudence upholds the doctrine of *receptio legis*, which attributes a vital role to the receiving community for the law to become and remain valid, this idea is not reflected in current legal practice. Instead, the law obliges Catholics to embrace global legislation, following the concept of command and obedience. The local generation of customs contrary to the law is limited, so there are few options for establishing alternative local regulations. These factors make the inculturation of canon law a challenging task.

Chapter 6
Legal Responses to Cultural Diversity

The previous chapter of this book explored how the church treats global canon law as a subject of inculturation in processes of lawmaking and the reception of the law. This chapter devotes some attention to how global canon law itself responds to the cultural diversity which it encounters in the local churches. Three issues deserve further enquiry, as they illustrate how the way in which the law addresses cultural matters reflects the tension between global legislation and the local churches. Section 6.1 investigates how global legislation responds to culture by examining the canons of the Code of Canon Law which mention culture. This analysis reveals an ambiguous use of the term and exposes a terminological vagueness which helps to understand why culture in general has a difficult position with regard to the law. Section 6.2 discusses the way in which global legislation incorporates cultural idiosyncrasies and local circumstances into the law by taking account of particular challenges of local churches, such as priest shortage. Section 6.3 reviews the instruments of legal flexibility which current canon law provides to respond to conflicts emerging from collisions between global rules and local cultures.

6.1 Culture in the Code of Canon Law

In his article on how the Code of Canon Law deals with culture, Marc de Mûelenaere reports that the Code mentions *culture* only four times and *cultural* only two times, in canons 248, 787 §1, 807, 821, 1136, and 1283 no. 2 CIC/1983.[1] While the mentions of culture scattered throughout the Code cover a variety of legal matters, a closer look reveals that in five of the six canons the context in which culture is mentioned is an educational one. These canons refer to culture when regulating the formation of clerics and missionaries, the education of children, and studies at

[1] See de Mûelenaere (1985b), p. 45 fn. 70.

J. Hahn, *The Cultures of Canon Law*, Law and Religion in a Global Context 6,
https://doi.org/10.1007/978-3-032-14812-4_6

Catholic universities or higher institutes of religious sciences. This is surprising in light of the previous finding recorded in Chap. 4 of this book, that the Apostolic See when referring to culture in doctrinal documents frequently connects it with the liturgy. The law, in contrast, ties culture closely to education; canon 1283 no. 2 CIC/1983 is the only exception, as it relates to cultural goods with regard to asset management in the administration of ecclesiastical goods. De Mûelenaere criticises this "paucity of references to cultures, and their apparent emphasis on the link with education"[2] as a serious limitation of the Code's view of culture.

Whilst he is right with his criticism, one has to acknowledge that the canons, even though they couple culture almost exclusively with education, use the term with different meanings; the following section develops a rough classification to show the ambiguous use of the term in the Code. The variety of meanings include culture as a descriptive term describing a certain cultural imprinting of a society or a subculture; as a normative term, referring to cultural achievements as valuable resources of society and the church; as an instrument of conveying meaning, such as the Gospel, across cultural borders; and, not least, as a learning topic which allows learners either to understand foreign values or beliefs or to become more *cultivated* or educated within their own contexts. One might discover even more meanings in these canons, making culture a good example of the problematic ambiguity common in ecclesiastical legal rules.[3]

6.1.1 Christian Subcultures

A first mention of culture appears in canon 821 CIC/1983, which encourages the establishment of higher institutes for religious sciences supporting the study of theology "and other subjects pertaining to Christian culture". Here, in connection with theology as a term embracing academic disciplines studying structures of believing, belonging, and behaving from a religious standpoint, culture seems to denote a certain segment of cultural studies, namely those disciplines which study Christianity with the help of cultural analysis. Hence, the canon seems to address both strands of studies in religion, those which apply an *ad intra* perspective arguing from the point of view of believers of the Catholic faith and those who study the church *ad extra* arguing from the point of external observers, such as scholars of religious studies. In Geertzian terms one can say that the definition of culture as used in this connection with *Christian culture* refers to systems or subsystems of meaning highly impregnated by Christianity; the term seems to carry a mostly descriptive meaning. These Christian systems or subsystems of meaning allow for detailed cultural study, for instance by ethnology or anthropology.

---

[2] Ibid.

[3] On this problem, see Hahn (2024).

6.1.2 Concept of Value

Another meaning of culture surfaces in canon 807 CIC/1983. The canon asserts the right of the church to run universities which "contribute to a higher human culture, the fuller development of the human person, and the fulfilment of the teaching function of the church". The norm refers to the term culture to denote social achievements. In connection with the adjective *higher* ("*altiorem*"), the expression evokes associations connected with high culture, relating to artistic and intellectual works but also to the idea of using education to develop and refine the society's educated classes. By using the comparative form "higher" in connection with culture, the legislator introduces Catholic universities as contributors to high culture, which one might read as not only producing more of the fine arts and intellectual excellence but also a greater number of individuals belonging to the educated classes. Hence, one might read "higher human culture" to demarcate Catholic education from low class education. Speaking of "higher", in any case, also shows that the legislator relies on a gradable idea of culture. Culture, thus, is not simply a fact, as in the Geertzian approach, but an achievement to which greater accomplishments might be added. It is a concept of value. In canon 807 CIC/1983, culture as this valuable resource is coupled with individual personal development and the ecclesiastical purpose to use higher academic education as an environment of ecclesiastical teaching. The canon consequently attributes three purposes to higher academic education as a value and good serving the individual, the human community, and the church.

The mention of cultural goods in canon 1283 no. 2 CIC/1983 has a similar connotation. The embedding of this canon is different, which makes the reference to culture as a concept of value slightly different, too. In any case, both norms, canons 807 and 1283 no. 2 CIC/1983, share an understanding of culture as a value. Whilst canon 807 CIC/1983, in the context of education, refers to the immaterial value of higher education, canon 1283 CIC/1983, in regulating what administrators of ecclesiastical goods have to prepare for when commencing their duty, refers to the material value of cultural goods which the administrators have to list in their inventory of immovable property and moveable items of value.

6.1.3 Instrumental Views

Canon 248 CIC/1983 regulates that priest candidates are to receive a solid doctrinal instruction "together with a general culture which is appropriate to the needs of place and time". This rather awkward wording couples doctrine and culture as two fields of knowledge promoted in theological education. The intention is to provide priest candidates with both doctrinal expertise and cultural training to allow for their successful pastoral mission. The canon goes on to explain the purpose of this regulation: "As a result, with their own faith founded on and nourished by this teaching, they ought to be able properly to proclaim the Gospel to the people of their own time, in a fashion suited to the manner of the people's thinking". This approach of employing cultural skills as means of spreading the Christian message accords with a neoconservative policy which tends to use inculturation strategically in favour of supporting the reception of ecclesiastical doctrine. The canon, with its dichotomy of theological education as "doctrinal instruction" and "culture", echoes the hylemorphic approach to realities as composed of supercultural and supertemporal substances and concrete cultural accidents, as mentioned in Sect. 4.1. In referring to doctrinal instruction, the norm alludes to the training of priest candidates required to understand the universal Christian message. It refers to culture to point to accidental qualities of how to pass on that message in a way which is understandable to individuals in their concrete circumstances. In Clifford Geertz's terms one could state that those approaching priesthood are expected to learn to express the Christian signs and symbols in a way in which they resonate in culture as a system of meaning so that individuals from that culture can attribute meaning to them.

In a similar vein, canon 787 §1 CIC/1983 takes up the need for cultural and intercultural competence for the proclamation of the faith when regulating that missionaries have to engage in a sensitive dialogue with non-believers in order to allow them to come to faith. Missionaries are called to initiate this dialogue with non-believers "in a manner adapted to their own way and culture". The norm couples culture with the Latin term *ingenium*, "ingenuity". Canonists all over the globe struggle to translate this term adequately. Whilst some English translations read "temperament", others translate it as "native character". The official German translation of the Code uses "*Eigenart*" hinting at the unique way in which a dialogue might prove to be suited for communication across cultural borders. The norm goes on to reveal the purpose of "taking their [the non-believers', addition by the author] native character and culture into account", which is to open ways to the non-believers "enabling them to understand the message of the Gospel". Canon 787 §2 CIC/1983 then goes on to advise missionaries to teach the doctrinal truth to those non-believers who react to the Christian message affirmatively and therefore seem fit to receive baptism. Here again, one encounters the hylemorphic dualism of the supercultural truth of the faith and the accidental cultural ways of communicating it. As the norm directs missionaries to teach the truth of the faith to non-believers, once they have been successful in establishing dialogue with them, the truth seems to be of substantial quality, whilst a culturally sensitive proclamation of the Gospel seems to be of merely accidental quality—so that it remains doubtful if it was revealing the Christian truth "properly" in the first place. By making sure that truth is told, once culture has led the missionaries to success, truth seems to prevail over culture in a gradual manner resembling the kernel and husk approach. In this sense, both norms, canons 248 and 787 §1 CIC/1983, refer to culture as a strategic instrument for spreading the real thing, the universal truth as articulated in Christian doctrine.

6.1.4 Fields of Knowledge

As mentioned, in coupling doctrine and culture as elements of theological education, canon 248 CIC/1983 presents culture as a field of knowledge and therefore as a topic which one can learn. In a similar vein, canon 1136 CIC/1983 advises parents to care for their children's cultural upbringing. The canon establishes the duty and right of parents to ensure "the physical, social, cultural, moral, and religious education of their offspring". Just as children require physical training, social learning, moral guidance, and religious practice, they are to receive a cultural education—whatever that implies. Cultural education, as used in the context of cultural politics, usually refers to educating children to reflect upon their own culture and the culture of others, thus gaining some intercultural knowledge, and also to reflect on the general relevance of culture in social contexts. However, the term also applies to education in the arts, denoting processes of cultural learning with regard to aesthetic learning and creativity and the interpretation and production of cultural assets. One cannot be sure what the canon means precisely by cultural education. But it evidently wants to ensure that whatever cultural leaning implies, it lies first and foremost in the parental scope of responsibility.

6.1.5 Legal Cultures

Studying the Code of Canon Law reveals that canonical legislation embraces different meanings of the term culture. In a more critical vein, one might note that it is not committed to clear terminology, which is a rather widespread problem in canon law language.[4] One can explain shifts in meaning with regard to culture as hereditary, as canon law inherited its ambiguous reference to culture from conciliar teaching. However, this ambiguity in legal norms is particularly problematic, as law with its demand of legal certainty requires clarity more essentially than doctrine.

The unclear use of language in the law also has repercussions in scholarship, as it gives rise to an equivocal use of the term culture in scholarly contributions to canon law. Here, were reencounter the same shifts from culture(s) in a descriptive sense[5] to culture in a normative sense as humanity's calling to greater refinement and social achievements. Canonists also use the term legal culture(s) ambiguously, shifting between a descriptive and normative meaning. Two collected volumes of German canonists can serve as examples. In 2006, Ilona Riedel-Spangenberger edited the volume *Rechtskultur in der Diözese* [*Legal Culture in the Diocese*][6]; in 2020, three canonists honoured fellow scholar Wilhelm Rees with a *festschrift*

[4] See Hahn (2023), particularly pp. 86–101.

[5] For contributions referring to culture descriptively, e.g. Sobański (1986), pp. 3–15; Huels (1987), pp. 249–293; Robitaille (1999), pp. 125–138; Bier (2009), p. 205.

[6] See Riedel-Spangenberger (2006).

Rechtskultur und Rechtspflege in der Kirche [*Legal Culture and Administration of Justice in the Church*].[7] Both volumes refer to legal culture in their title in the singular and explain their choice by alluding to legal culture as a normative term. Riedel-Spangenberger applies it to refer to the merits of good law, such as solving conflict, giving peace, providing for justice, protecting rights, and granting legal certainty. She therefore speaks of legal culture as a "value"[8] which should guide the development of diocesan law. The editors of the 2020 collection explain their choice of title by referring to Wilhelm Rees's work as a canonist who is engaged in improving the law of the church, bringing it more in line with justice as its ideal.[9] Reading the articles collected in both books, one can find that the authors now and then loosely take up the term legal culture to explain the inclusion of their contributions into the respective collections. However, they frequently do this without explaining their use of the terms culture or legal culture to any greater degree. The use of the terms is therefore rather arbitrary, reflected in shifts from singular to plural and from descriptive to normative meaning. This is, unsurprisingly, perfectly in line with the legislator's ambiguous reference to culture in the Code.

6.2 Considering Local Circumstances

In addition to terminological studies, shedding more light on how global legislation responds to culture and the cultural diversity of the local churches must also include how the law considers the local churches and their cultural background. One approach to perceiving more clearly how the law responds to culture is to study legislation with regard to its responsiveness to local demands. In this vein, canonist Francis Morrisey attests the Code of 1983 a greater concern for cultural issues in comparison to the Code of 1917. He names several reasons which support his observation. Besides alluding to norms such as canons 787 or 1136 CIC/1983 which explicitly refer to culture, as discussed above, he also makes reference to canons 396 §2, 423 §1, and 1076 CIC/1983 as norms which relate to local customs.[10] Closer study reveals, however, that these canons reprobate former privileges or customs contrary to the norms of the Code. Canon 396 §2 CIC/1983 entitles the bishops to freely choose their clerical companions on a visitation, reprobating all contrary privileges or customs limiting the bishops' free choice. According to canon 423 §1 CIC/1983, the college of consultors has to elect a single diocesan administrator after a diocesan see has become vacant, while any contrary custom to select several administrators is reprobated. Canon 1076 CIC/1983 reprobates customs which

[7] See Ohly, Haering, and Müller (2020).

[8] Original quote: "Zur kirchlichen Rechtskultur, soll sie als Wert anerkannt sein…", Riedel-Spangenberger (2006), p. 10.

[9] See Ohly, Haering, and Müller (2020), p. 5.

[10] See Morrisey (1986), p. 36.

introduce new impediments to marriage or are contrary to existing impediments. Hence, one can find that these canons as mentioned by Morrisey as proof of the Code's concern for culture are in fact norms which suppress local customs in favour of uniform global rules. This is certainly a way of articulating concern for culture, though not the approach that one might have expected. The legislator's concern for culture, as these canons show, frequently manifests itself as the concern to protect his global laws *from* culture and from practices diverging from global regulation.

6.2.1 Regional Idiosyncrasies

Morrisey also observes that other parts of the 1983 Code grant more local freedom, for instance by authorising decentralised authorities, such as the diocesan bishops or bishops' conferences, to fill in the frame provided by global legislation with local laws. He discovers this greater openness to decentralised regulations particularly in contexts pertaining to the organisation of the local churches, the administration of the sacraments and the liturgies, and the ministers' formation. In a similar vein, José Dammert Bellido alludes to several norms as examples where global legislation allows decentralised authorities "to adapt the common legislation to regional situations".[11] He recognises this in norms such as canon 1120 CIC/1983 authorising the bishops' conferences to generate rites of marriage "in keeping with the usages of places and peoples which are adapted to the Christian spirit". He also mentions canon 242 §1 CIC/1983 which issues programmes of priestly formation to accord "to the pastoral needs of each region or province". Dammert Bellido also detects some sensitivity to local idiosyncrasies in canon 22 CIC/1983 which refers to local secular laws and their relevance for canon law in those cases where canon law pertains to secular law. A concrete example of such a regulation is canon 1290 CIC/1983 which directs local authorities to take the respective local contract law as a basis for entering contracts in church. Another example is canon 1286 CIC/1983 which advises administrators of ecclesiastical goods to observe secular labour laws when employing personnel. This openness towards letting secular rules influence local ecclesiastical law, according to Dammert Bellido, expresses the legislator's concern to harmonise the application of global canon law with local legal usage.

[11] Dammert Bellido (1986), p. 111.

6.2.2 Particular Requirements

Many changes to global canon law initiated by the reform of the Code of Canon Law before 1983 were inspired by the difficulties which local churches encountered in applying the old law. Particularly their troublesome experiences of organising pastoral ministry on the basis of the old Code served as the grounds for reforming global legislation in many respects. It was to no small degree the struggles experienced by the so-called mission countries in providing for pastoral ministry in large regions with a low number of clergy which stimulated reform. Dammert Bellido, himself a bishop of an Andean diocese, alludes to several norms where the new Code responded to challenges experienced in Latin America.[12] A classic example is canon 517 §2 CIC/1983 which, inspired by the situation in missionary churches, authorises the diocesan bishop in churches with a shortage of priests to appoint deacons or laypeople with the exercise of pastoral care in parishes.[13] The possibility of assigning lay missionaries and catechists in missionary contexts answers to the same need (see canons 784, 785 CIC/1983). A similar background applies to canons which permit laypeople to engage in the administration of the sacraments and sacramentals when clerics are scarce. Canon 861 §2 CIC/1983 allows for laypeople to administer baptisms when ordinary ministers are impeded. Dammert Bellido mentions that this regulation stems from a favour first granted orally by Pope Paul VI to the Diocese of Cajamarca, then extended to include the whole of Peru. It was then "included in the present Code, because it was working well",[14] as he comments. According to the current Code, laypeople may also distribute communion when ordinary ministers, such as bishops, priests, and deacons, are unavailable (see canons 230 §3, 910 §2 CIC/1983). Whilst the old law did not provide for the option of laypeople distributing communion, the Apostolic See, in 1927, granted the Mexican Church the faculty to permit lay men to administer communion to the sick and authorised a similar practice in Russia in 1930, as John Huels recalls.[15] These and subsequent developments paved the way for introducing laypeople as extraordinary ministers of communion to canon law in 1973[16] and finally to the Code of 1983. Today, bishops may also delegate laypeople to assist at marriages when there is a lack of priests and deacons (see canon 1112 §1 CIC/1983). Pastors may permit laypeople to preach, in accordance with the bishops' conferences' provisions, if this seems necessary or desirable in particular cases (see canon 766 CIC/1983). Huels alludes to the origin of this regulation which lay in an indult granted by the Congregation for the Clergy for Germany, which established an exemption from the

---

[12] See ibid., p. 113.

[13] On this and other examples where the missionary law of the church influenced universal ecclesiastical legislation by paving the way for new global regulations see Pulte (2006).

[14] Dammert Bellido (1986), p. 113.

[15] See Huels (1996), pp. 27–28.

[16] See Congregation for the Discipline of the Sacraments (1973), no. 1. Acta Apostolicae Sedis (1973), pp. 265–266.

strict prohibition of lay preaching contained in canon 1342 §2 CIC/1917 when priests and deacons were unavailable.[17] What started as a favour for some dioceses later became part of the law for the global church. One can take these norms as examples where the legislator learnt from challenges in particular local churches. Yet, one should nevertheless discuss the problematic restriction of accepting the pastoral and liturgical service of laypeople only in situations of clerical shortage. Instead of generally establishing more lay participation in governing the church, in the teaching function of the church, and in the administration of sacraments and sacramentals, the law authorises the local authorities to allow for lay service only in cases of acute need. One can call this strategy a *rule-and-exception policy*. It enables the legislator to establish a clergy-centred law, while, with the help of exemption clauses, authorising local authorities to deviate from this rule in cases of clergy shortage.

6.2.3 Local Interpretations

Cultural concerns play a significant role when global laws are applied in the local churches. They are particularly relevant in interpretation as the process of attributing norms with meaning when applying them to particular cases. Canonists refer to the role of culture for interpretation in a twofold sense: either as the interpreters' essential cultural standpoint or as their responsibility to consider cultural idiosyncrasies when interpreting legal rules. In the first sense, John Huels refers to interpretation as a task which interpreters necessarily perform from their own cultural point of view. In his article "Interpreting Canon Law in Diverse Cultures" he states accordingly: "If the insights of anthropology, theology, comparative law, and other disciplines are to be taken seriously, then we must recognize that the interpretation of canon law always takes place within a culture and is affected by culture, because human beings cannot act apart from culture".[18] Their cultural point of view is not a perspective which interpreters take on voluntarily when scrutinising the law, but a rather intuitive view which individuals adopt at an early age based on their legal experiences. Pierre Legrand writes:

> Each English child, for example, is a common-law-lawyer-in-being long before she even contemplates going to law school. Inevitably, therefore, a significant part of the very real emotional and intellectual investment that presides over the formulation of the meaning of a rule lies beneath consciousness because the act of interpretation is embedded, in a way that the interpreter is often unable to appreciate empirically, in a language and in a tradition, in sum, in a whole cultural ambience.[19]

---

[17] See Congregation for the Clergy (1973). Archiv für katholisches Kirchenrecht (1973), pp. 480–482.

[18] Huels (1987), p. 290.

[19] Legrand (1997), pp. 114–115.

The interpreters' cultural standpoints are indispensable for how they perceive the law. John Beal alludes to the example of nineteenth-century American bishops who, as bishops of churches regarded by state law as entities of private law, developed a certain business-like leadership style. The economic lens through which the bishops started to conceive of their role as leaders became, as he states, a particular cultural standpoint from which they also started to perceive the law. This style "became the lens through which canon law was interpreted and implemented in the United States. It was a governance style truly made in the USA".[20]

As individuals attribute signs with meaning which they derive from their culture as their system of meaning, interpretation makes essential reference to culture. In consequence, interpretations of laws are cultural processes and are, therefore, diverse by necessity, as Huels maintains: "Interpretations of canon law should not, and cannot, be uniform. Since interpretation is a human act and human beings are psychologically and culturally diverse, we should always expect a variety of interpretations, the more so as the background and culture of the interpreters are various".[21] Huels, who seems to observe that canon law, with its focus on the uniformity of the law, also seems to encourage a uniformity of interpretation, finds it necessary to remind his readers that these plural interpretations are no mishaps but the regular consequence of cultural diversity. He therefore encourages canonists and legal practitioners to embrace plural interpretations: "Plurality of canonical interpretation is not something to be lamented or eradicated, but should be seen as the norm and the ideal in a 'world Church' made up of local churches".[22] By presenting plurality as a value, he transcends his descriptive observation on essential cultural standpoints and adopts a normative position which endorses the diversity of canonical interpretations. James Coriden takes a similar stance in his prominent article "Rules for Interpreters". He primarily refers to the second sense in which canon law has to consider culture with regard to interpretation, as he advises interpreters to reflect on their respective community when interpreting laws. In his list of interpretation rules, he includes the rule: "Consider your people".[23] This consideration can be essential, not merely for the community but also for the law. Esin Örücü makes a similar suggestion by proposing to understand the processes which legal scholars with reference to Alan Watson usually call transplantations of law as legal *transpositions*. In using the analogy of musical transpositions, she voices the idea that laws entering a new context require cultural tuning in order "to suit the particular socio-legal culture and needs of the recipient."[24] If laws fail to adjust to their new environment, they may become ineffective. One instrument which can provide for that cultural tuning is interpretation. When interpreting the laws for their communities, the interpreters, as Coriden emphasises, are encouraged to consider their commu-

[20] Beal (1996), pp. 55–56.

[21] Huels (1987), p. 290.

[22] Ibid.

[23] Coriden (1982), p. 286.

[24] Örücü (2002), p. 207.

nity's requirements. They have to take into account their community's character, whether it is a province, diocese, or a specific religious community, its size, the nature of the members' relationship with each other, the mentality, the level of formality of communication, the members' level of education, economic conditions and political situation, and the political pressure on the group and inside the group.[25] When studying the body of global canon law one can detect canons in which the legislator seems to encourage such a diversity of interpretations as some norms are particularly open to divergent interpretations depending on one's cultural standpoint. Francis Morrisey, in this vein, points at the manifold general concepts introduced into canonical norms, such as the "good of the spouses", "partnership of the whole life", or "irrevocable covenant", as examples of expressions used in marriage law. He understands these terms to serve as containers to be filled with culturally adequate interpretations. These "general terms to describe fundamental attitudes",[26] as he sees it, allow for a thoroughly cultural reception of general rules.

6.2.4 Autonomous Meaning

Adding to the assumption that legislation supports a cultural appropriation of laws in the local churches through interpretation is the observation that canon law does not endow ecclesiastical tribunals with the power to create precedents.[27] As there is no doctrine of *stare decisis* in church, judicial rulings do not unfold a precedential effect on the lower tribunals. As a result, judicial interpretations only bind those bound by a particular sentence. The tribunals' interpretations as given in form of judicial sentences, and likewise interpretations given by ecclesiastical administration in form of administrative acts do not have the force of law. They merely bind those individuals or groups to whom they pertain and only affect the concrete cases for which they were issued, as the Code states explicitly (see canon 16 §3 CIC/1983). Each local tribunal or administrative body is therefore free to interpret the law differently. Even Roman tribunals, such as the Roman Rota, the verdicts of which have some exemplary function for the lower tribunals, do not oblige the lower tribunals to adapt to their interpretations.[28] Hence, "Consider your people",[29] James Coriden's phrase which indicates that there is an authorised *you* in charge of interpreting the law for a certain group of people, clearly has these ecclesiastical authorities as official interpreters in mind. By advising interpreters to consider their legal subjects, he indicates that interpreting a global law in the local churches is a function performed

---

[25] See Coriden (1982), p. 286.

[26] Morrisey (1986), p. 36.

[27] For a contribution which analyses in what way this difference distinguishes Roman Catholic adjudication from adjudication of the Church of England see Doe (1994), pp. 205–215.

[28] See Griffin (1984), p. 22.

[29] Coriden (1982), p. 286.

by local officials who have to derive a meaning from global rules when applying them in the service of a particular church. As they are not bound by legal precedents, these officials are free to discover this meaning independently, while being morally obliged to keep the local legal subjects in mind when making use of their interpretive freedom, as Coriden's rule emphasises.

That courts are not subject to precedent decisions but only to the law itself when rendering their interpretations is a classic civil law approach to dealing with interpretations given by courts or administrative bodies. Canon law is clearly civil law with regard to the limited contribution of ecclesiastical adjudication to developing the law. This might create some conflicts in hybrid legal systems of churches at home in common law countries, which see the role of the courts in the development of the law differently. One can nevertheless recognise the lack of a precedential development in canon law as being one of the legislator's important decisions with regard to a culture-sensitive interpretation of law, as it allows the local tribunals to develop and cultivate their own interpretations of canonical norms. However, there is also reason to doubt whether legislation wants to provide the tribunals with abundant freedom in interpreting global rules. These doubts derive from the fact that the legislator took pains to restrain the interpretive freedom enjoyed by the local appliers of law, which is also traditionally a characteristic of civil law, by establishing strict rules of interpretation within the law itself, in canons 6, 17, and 18 CIC/1983. These rules are discussed one by one briefly in the following to demonstrate how they provide official interpretation with a centralised dynamic which points to the Apostolic See—not merely as the origin of the laws to be interpreted but also as the authentic source of their meaning.

6.2.5 Authentic Interpretation

The canons on interpretation commence with a rule on authentic interpretation, that is the official interpretation of laws in the name of the church by competent ecclesiastical authorities. Canon 16 §1 CIC/1983 emphasises that authentic interpretation is restricted to the legislator himself and to those institutions endowed by him with the power of authentic interpretation. The legislator endowed the Dicastery for Legislative Texts with the authority to issue authentic interpretations to officially clarify doubts of legal meaning.[30] The dicastery is competent to issue official interpretations which determine the meaning of ambiguous or unclear rules with a binding force, as their exegesis becomes legally binding. Canon law, thus, demonstrates a unique closeness between legislation and the interpretation of laws by establishing that authentic interpretations can take on the form of law (see canon 16 §2 CIC/1983). As they bind the legal subjects in the same way as the legal rules to which they relate, authentic interpretations in form of law require promulgation in the same

[30] See Francis (2022), art. 176. Acta Apostolicae Sedis (2022), p. 435.

way required for laws themselves (see canon 7 CIC/1983). This method of developing canon law by issuing interpretations in the form of law is virtually unknown in most legal systems. Secular legislators enact the law, but they frequently have no control over its meaning. Deriving meaning from laws is usually a task which the courts and administrative bodies perform independently when interpreting the law in the course of its application. While most secular systems thus ensure a decentralist development of legal meaning, the Apostolic See tends to centralise both the development of laws and their meaning, thus supporting a consistent and uniform development of the law. The pope is not merely *dominus canonum*, the lord of his laws, but also the lord of the meaning of his laws.

This centralised dynamic, which points to the Apostolic See whenever a law is unclear, has a longstanding history. Its origin can be traced back to the ancient Roman pontiffs' authority to authentically interpret the Twelve Tables.[31] In the more recent history of the church, the Council of Trent and its stance on authentic interpretation established the Apostolic See as the main agent in all legal matters of the Catholic Church. This was the result of Pope Pius IV's decision to reserve the interpretation of conciliar legislation to the Congregation of the Council. In his 1564 Bull *Benedictus Deus* which affirmed the council's decisions, the pope installed the Congregation of the Council as the only legitimate interpreter of conciliar legislation, laying the foundation for the Roman Curia to act as the nucleus of legal interpretations in church. Pius IV disallowed any private or official interpretations of the council's documents, threatening lawbreakers with interdicts and automatic excommunications. It is instructive to read parts of the bull at some length to understand the cultural mindset in which rules such as canon 16 §1 CIC/1983 have their roots. The text regulates that

> in order to avoid the perversion and confusion which might arise, if each one were permitted, as he might think fit, to publish his own commentaries and interpretations on the decrees of the council; We, by apostolic authority, forbid all persons, as well ecclesiastics, of what order, condition, and rank soever they may be, as laymen, with what honour and power soever invested; prelates to wit, under pain of being interdicted from entering the church, and all others, whosoever they be, under pain of excommunication incurred by the fact, that they presume, without our authority, to publish, in any form, any commentaries, glosses, annotations, scholia, or any kind of interpretation soever touching the decrees of the said council; or to settle anything in regard thereof, under any plea soever, even under pretext of greater corroboration of the decrees, or the execution thereof, or under any other colourable pretext soever.[32]

Pius IV's main argument for centralising the interpretation of conciliar legislation was to avoid confusion among Catholics which might be brought about by a variety of interpretations. Precluding divergent interpretations which might perplex church members, the pope aimed at clarity by endowing merely one single interpreter with the task of issuing official interpretations and by criminalising all others who

[31] See Watson (1995), pp. 471–472.

[32] Pius IV (1564). In: Canons and Decrees of the Council of Trent (1851), pp. 271–272.

published their own readings of conciliar texts. Those in any doubt as to the meaning of conciliar decisions were not free to derive this meaning from the text themselves. Instead they had to turn to Rome to gain clarity, as the pope commanded:

> But if anything therein shall seem to any one to have been expressed and ordained obscurely, and it shall, on that account, appear to stand in need of an interpretation or decision, let him go up to the place which the Lord hath chosen; to wit, to the Apostolic See, the mistress of all the faithful, whose authority the holy synod also has so reverently acknowledged. For if any difficulties and controversies shall arise touching the said decrees, We reserve them to be by us explained and decided, even as the holy synod has itself in like manner decreed; being prepared, as that [synod] has justly expressed its confidence in regard of us, to provide for the necessities of all the provinces, in such manner as shall seem to us most convenient; decreeing that whatsoever may be attempted to the contrary touching these matters, whether wittingly or unwittingly, by any one, by what authority soever, is, notwithstanding, null and void.[33]

The pope emphasised the authority of the Apostolic See to explain and decide all matters legal which require clarification. Adding to the penal sanction to which the pope subjected all those who issued their own interpretations was his declaration that all decisions based on illegal interpretations were null, even those based unintentionally on subjective readings which do not fully concur with the Roman opinion. With this combination of penal sanction and the threat of invalidity of acts based on private interpretations, the pope took two significant steps towards Catholic thought control. All Catholics, thus, received the robust advice to let the Apostolic See do the thinking and stick to observing its commands.

Pius IV, in his bull, then went on to issue a complex system of how the Roman interpretations of conciliar legislation had to be made public, so that the legal subjects had a fair chance of getting to know them:

> And to the end that these things may come to the knowledge of all men, and that no one may be able to use the excuse of ignorance; We will and ordain, that in the Vatican Basilica of the prince of the apostles, and in the Lateran church, at the time when the people is wont to assemble there in order to be present at the solemnization of masses, these letters be publicly read in a clear tone by certain officers of our court; and that after they have been read, they be affixed to the doors of those churches, and also to the gates of the Apostolic Chancery, and to the usual place in the Campo di Fiore; and be left there for some time, to be read by, and to come to the knowledge of all men. But when they shall be removed thence, copies being, according to custom, left in those same places, they shall be committed to the press in our noble city, that so they may more conveniently be made known throughout the provinces and kingdoms of the Christian name. And we command and decree, that without any doubt, faith be given to copies thereof, which are written or subscribed by the hand of a public notary, and guaranteed by the seal and signature of some person constituted in ecclesiastical dignity.[34]

Certainly, it would be unrealistic to assume that these complex regulations were scrupulously observed throughout the Catholic world over the course of the following centuries. However, one should not underestimate their impact on the

[33] Ibid., p. 272.

[34] Ibid., pp. 272–273.

understanding of interpretation in church. They point to the Apostolic See as the instance where doctrinal and disciplinary rules come into being and receive their meaning through official interpretation. Pius IV's ruling established the Apostolic See as the instance to which all legal practitioners have to turn to derive not merely the laws but also the meaning of these laws. Different from Pius IV and his Bull *Benedictus Deus*, appliers of law today are no longer punished for rendering their own interpretations. Instead, their interpretation, in line with modern interpretation theory, is regarded as an essential step in applying the law. There is no adjudication or administration without interpretation, as canon 16 §3 CIC/1983 emphasises when speaking of "interpretation in the form of a judicial sentence or of an administrative act". Yet whilst the independent interpretation of rules by the tribunals and administrative bodies is no longer in question, it is not entirely free. Appliers of law, when in doubt about legal meaning, are expected to turn to the Apostolic See if they do not want to risk their decisions being overturned due to a nonconformity with the official reading of laws.

6.2.6 Rules of Interpretation

The Code of Canon Law, in canons 6, 17, and 18 CIC/1983, also contains several regulations which provide the appliers of law with an official methodology of interpretation. Most legal orders restrict the official interpretation by the courts and administrative bodies to some extent; British and US-American interpreters of law for instance follow the *canons of construction*. However, these canons are not part of the law itself. This is different in church where the canons on interpretation are legal rules. They restrict locally diverse methods of interpretation and try to enforce a uniform understanding of the law. This can be seen as a neoconservative policy aimed at avoiding broad differentiation in interpretation.

The key rule on interpretation is canon 17 CIC/1983: "Ecclesiastical laws are to be understood according to the proper meaning of the words considered in their text and context. If the meaning remains doubtful or obscure, there must be recourse to parallel places, if there be any, to the purpose and circumstances of the law, and to the mind of the legislator". The fundamental rule as proposed by this canon is a canonical version of the plain meaning rule as a grammatical-logical approach to interpretation. Interpreters have to analyse the text and context of laws to extract from them the proper meaning of legal terms. To this fundamental rule of grammatical and logical interpretation, canon 17 CIC/1983 adds subsidiary rules: analogical interpretation looking into parallel norms to derive from them the meaning of terms used in a rule; teleological interpretation exploring the purposes and ends at which a law aims and their relevance for the meaning of a rule; historical interpretation reminding the interpreters of a law's origin and development and their significance for legal meaning; and considering the *mind of the legislator* in search of meaning, that is the legislator's fundamental values and principles which influenced legislation. We can consider this last-mentioned approach as an ecclesiastical version of intentionalism. The expression *mens legislatoris* is misleading to some degree,[35] as the "mind" of the legislator is not about the individual reasoning and personal beliefs which motivated a certain legislation but about the legislator's ideology in general and with respect to the law—his fundamental values, beliefs, and concerns as laid down in the law and in other official statements. Canon 6 §2 CIC/1983 supplements canon 17 CIC/1983 by obliging interpreters to consider former law when interpreting present rules in the light of tradition: "Insofar as they repeat former law, the canons of this Code must be assessed also in accord with canonical tradition". A further rule of interpretation—the ecclesiastical version of the rule of lenity—is found in canon 18 CIC/1983: "Laws which establish a penalty, restrict the free exercise of rights, or contain an exception from the law are subject to strict interpretation".

By binding the interpreters of canonical laws worldwide to canons 6, 17, and 18 CIC/1983, legislation suppresses not merely plural interpretations but also confines the establishment of local methodologies of interpretation. There are two reasons why this constraint poses a challenge to a culturally sensitive interpretation of canon law by its local appliers. First, the canonical methodology of interpretation follows a typically continental methodology. By supporting grammatical, contextual, historical, and teleological methods of interpretation, canon law invokes the canons of interpretation, which legal scholar Friedrich Carl von Savigny developed in the nineteenth century.[36] These canons became influential not only for German interpretation theory but also for many European legal traditions. By adopting this methodology, modern canon law reproduces the interpretation theory of late nineteenth- and early twentieth-century secular civil law. Applying these rules might therefore not merely be challenging for legal practitioners from common law traditions but also for civil lawyers to whom the classical scheme of von Savigny seems partly outdated.

Second, the canonical rules on interpretation also pose a challenge to a culturally sensitive interpretation of the law because they support a centralised dynamic which binds interpreters to the Apostolic See's reading of norms. Grammatical interpretation and logical interpretation analysing "the proper meaning of the words" attempt to detect the typical meaning of terms as connected with them in official ecclesiastical terminology. Many words as used in current legislation carry a meaning attributed to them by ecclesiastical doctrine and the legal tradition of the church as two fields fundamentally influenced by the Apostolic See. The same applies to

[35] James Coriden rightly points out that there is not much clarity in canonical theory of what the *mind of the legislator* actually is. Whilst most authors interpret it as an expression of legislative voluntarism, Coriden interprets *mens legislatoris* as the principle to listen to the *sensus Ecclesiae* when interpreting canon law, letting the "mind of the church" become influential on interpretation, see Coriden (1982), pp. 299–300. That is an interpretation of the expression which is theologically more convincing than interpreting the rule as an intentionalist rule. However, following the basic rule of *propria verborum significatio* when interpreting rules on interpretation, there is no linguistic ground which supports interpreting *mens legislatoris* as *mens Ecclesiae*. Instead, it suggests interpreting the *mind of the legislator* as a rule which is concerned with the *legislator's* intention, in the sense of interpretive intentionalism.

[36] See von Savigny (1840), pp. 213–216.

analogical interpretation of understanding norms by studying other norms in the Code or in other ecclesiastical documents which correspond to the unclear passage and help to clarify ambiguous terms. Discovering meaning by studying parallel places involves drawing on papal texts and Vatican documents to understand the law. Asking what a norm was designed for and what good is to be achieved by its observation, as teleological interpretation does, points strongly at those purposes and goods attached to the law by the legislator and by the Roman authorities. Similarly, the circumstances of the law—that is the historical context of its formation, the historical reasons that moved the legislator to create a law, and its development—help in discovering, first of all, the meaning which centralised legislation associated with a law when creating it. Historical interpretation is supplemented by canon 6 §2 CIC/1983, which obliges the interpreters to consider the canonical tradition when interpreting canons that repeat former law. Whilst James Coriden observed—by quoting principles such as "that which affects everyone should be approved by everyone" ("*Quod omnes tangit debet ab omnibus approbari*")—that the canonical tradition is broader than those of its strands which have been cultivated by centralised interpretation,[37] one has to note that only those strands of tradition which found the approval of the Apostolic See ultimately became successful. An example might help to illustrate this. Whilst one might conceive of a more participatory interpretation of laws regulating the relationship between the bishops and their subjects by interpreting them in the light of the principle *Quod omnes tangit*, the tradition of employing the principle to increase participatory elements in the dioceses did not prevail in church. Hence, the rule of interpretation to turn to canonical tradition is rather a rule obliging interpreters to rely on the Apostolic See's interpretation of what is canonical tradition. Tradition is less about the plural historical options for deciding a case. It is more about *who* is to decide what the official tradition is. Canonical tradition is invented tradition.[38] It is the canonical history reimagined by the Apostolic See to support current centralised interpretation. The rule of historical interpretation in canon 17 CIC/1983 does not therefore promote a search for meaning in counterfactual legal history. It does not follow a theoretical *what if*—what could a law mean if the Apostolic See had decided to interpret *Quod omnes tangit* in a more participatory light?—but is bound to follow the authorities in their decision about what constitutes ecclesiastical tradition. In a similar vein, the *mind of the legislator*, the ecclesiastical version of intentionalism, directs interpreters to interpret laws in line with the worldview of the Apostolic See.

---

[37] See Coriden (1982), p. 303.

[38] On the concept of invented tradition, see Hobsbawm and Ranger (1983).

6.2.7 Strategic Ambiguity

By standardising interpretation and guiding interpreters towards the legal meaning as determined by the Apostolic See, current canon law aims at preventing conflicts deriving from different interpretations of the law. While the tribunals are not bound by the doctrine of *stare decisis* and are therefore free to interpret the law in a culturally sensitive way, they are legally bound by the canonical rules of interpretation, which guide their derivation of meaning from the legal texts. In the light of these findings, one may ask what to make of Francis Morrisey's observation, mentioned earlier on, that canon law encourages a culturally sensitive interpretation of legal rules. Morrisey proposed this in particular by referring to the manifold open terms and expressions that are used in the Code, which, as he found, allow for diverse interpretations, reflecting the interpreters' cultural point of view.[39] According to Morrisey, the law encourages interpreters to fill open concepts, such as the good of the spouses, partnership of the whole life, or irrevocable covenant, with culturally adequate interpretations. The canonical rules of interpretation in mind, one may ask if this is actually an option. Examining Morrissey's examples in light of the canonical methodology suggests otherwise. His examples inter alia allude to canon 1055 §1 CIC/1983, the first canon of the Code's marriage law: "The matrimonial covenant, by which a man and a woman establish between themselves a partnership of the whole of life and which is ordered by its nature to the good of the spouses and the procreation and education of offspring, has been raised by Christ the Lord to the dignity of a sacrament between the baptised". Here, concepts such as the good of the spouses and partnership of the whole life seem qualified for a culturally sensitive interpretation. However, closer study reveals that there is not much flexibility in interpreting these terms. For instance, if one subjects partnership of the whole life ("*consortium totius vitae*") to a proper interpretation according to canon 17 CIC/1983, one has to start by applying the rule of textual interpretation. Indeed, textualism might encourage collecting various concepts of lifelong partnerships from various cultural points of view. From a liberal European perspective on marriage, one can conceive of interpretations of lifetime partnership which include two persons of the same sex with a lifelong commitment. Maybe an African interpreter from a country where polygyny is an accepted social practice might want to include polygynous marriages where the spouses form a family in which they provide for each other for life. However, as canon 17 CIC/1983 is quick to note, the proper meaning of terms is that which is taken from text *and context*. Studying the context of canon 1055 §1 CIC/1983 shows that it presents a clear idea of which unions may be considered as canonical partnerships of the whole life, as canon 1057 §2 CIC/1983 defines marriage as a lifelong heterosexual union of one man and one woman. If one digs deeper into the origins of the expression, one comes up with the same result. "Partnership of the whole life" is a legal expression with roots in ancient Roman law. In the Roman emperor Justinian's

[39] See Morrisey (1986), p. 36.

compilation of juristic writings and definitions of his time, the Digest, the expression is to be found in the first quote under the title dealing with the marriage ceremony which reads: "Marriage is the union of a man and a woman, a partnership for the whole life involving divine as well as human law".[40] Thus, in contrast to what one might assume at first glance, *consortium totius vitae* does not invite interpreters to introduce their own readings of which lifelong concepts they consider adequate interpretations from their cultural point of view. On the contrary, canon 1055 §1 CIC/1983 uses a vague or rather opaque expression to introduce precisely the official doctrinal view of what constitutes marriage. In this sense, canonist Patrick Connolly refers to the fact that terms such as partnership of the whole life are open to interpretation due to their indeterminacy. However, it is not private interpretation which they encourage. Instead they remain flexible to make it easier for legislation and official doctrine to develop their concepts:

> The phrase *consortium totius vitae* has not been defined by canon law, as indeed it had not been by Roman law, since there is a certain wisdom in not giving a precise definition of a legal term, so that a concept's meaning is not completely fixed, something which would prevent any unfolding of the idea. By leaving the notion of *consortium* undelineated, its essential elements can then be ascertained by canonical doctrine and jurisprudence.[41]

Consequently, the Code is not full of indeterminate terms and general concepts because it wants to encourage a culturally diverse interpretation. On the contrary, the law uses ambiguity and indeterminacy to enable the ecclesiastical authorities and, above all, the Apostolic See to determine and develop the meaning of legal rules according to canonical doctrine and jurisprudence. Following Connolly, one may assume that many expressions are kept deliberately vague to help centralised authorities bind the local interpreters to their continually changing interpretations.

6.2.8 *Exclusive Legalese*

Connected with this observation is another phenomenon worth discussing, namely that the meaning of legal norms is to be derived from Latin terms and expressions. The official language of ecclesiastical legislation is Latin. Most papal laws are promulgated in Latin, although Italian, as the administrative language of the Roman Curia, is gaining in importance for legislation too. Yet the authentic text of the Code of Canon Law is still the Latin text alone.[42] Under the 1917 Code this claim was supported by legislation actively suppressing translations of the Code into vernacular languages[43] to avoid spoiling the original text—a reminder of Pope Pius IV and

[40] Justinian (530–33), Digest 23.2.1. In: The Digest of Justinian (1998), p. 199.

[41] Connolly (2023), p. 244.

[42] See Secretariat of State (1983). Communicationes (1983), p. 41.

[43] The official Vatican edition of the Code of 1917, in front of its preface, noted the explicit prohibition to reprint or translate the Code: "Nemini liceat, sine venia Sanctae Sedis hunc Codicem denuo

his Bull *Benedictus Deus*. This policy was changed for the 1983 Code, as the Apostolic See now authorises vernacular translations. Following the promulgation of the 1983 Code, many bishops' conferences issued translations so that the text is now available in most of the world languages. However, the vernacular translations only serve as working aids to help with deciphering the Latin rules, while the Latin original remains the authentic text of the Code which binds appliers of law when interpreting the norms. Due to this decision, the legislator has more control over the content of the law and its meaning. Any potential dissonances and ambiguities in legal terminology caused by translations are kept to a minimum. One can therefore interpret the decision to rely on dead Latin as a neoconservative policy that supports uniform interpretations around the world.

This decision in favour of Latin seems to enjoy most canonists' endorsement. While there are many critical voices on single aspects of legal terminology, there is barely any criticism of using Latin as the main language of canon law. Canonist Klaus Mörsdorf, for instance, when republishing his 1937 book on the language of the 1917 Code in 1967, did not challenge the use of Latin. He acknowledged that secular law would rightly attempt to improve vernacular language use to become more comprehensible; yet canon law, due to it being composed in dead Latin, could not follow this example. Mörsdorf did not discuss this as a problem, probably as canon law mostly pertained to the *leading church*, as he found, thus primarily addressing clerics with a theological education and, therefore, some knowledge of Latin.[44] Surprisingly, in any case, not much seems to have changed since the 1960s. In an article which provides an overview of the history of Canon Law Latin and the advantages of its use, canonist Stephan Haering argues in favour of Latin as it symbolises the unity of the church and its law, privileges none of the modern languages, indicates differences vis-à-vis secular law, and expresses the continuity of the canonical tradition.[45] These arguments in favour of Latin are supportive of neoconservative concerns. Haering, for instance, emphasises the merit of having one uniform authentic language of the law as a symbol of the unity of the church. That it is currently Latin that takes on this role and not one of the common world languages, such as English or Spanish, privileges no particular local churches over others, as he maintains. As Latin is a dead language, and therefore not spoken in any of the churches, no church has an advantage over any other in understanding the law. It is an intriguing idea to assess the equal linguistic disadvantages of all as assisting egalitarianism. However, what this approach fails to acknowledge is that clerics are more familiar with Latin than most other Catholics, because Latin is still present in clerical formation (see canon 249 CIC/1983). By privileging clerics educated in Rome and versed in Canon Law Latin, this language choice also reinforces the centralised position of the Apostolic See over decentralised agents. So one might argue that by promoting Latin, legislation in fact places a certain clerical culture above all

imprimere aut in aliam linguam vertere".

[44] See Mörsdorf (1967), p. 18.

[45] See Haering (2003), p. 244.

others. This suggests that the laity's comprehension of the law is of lesser relevance compared to that of the clergy. This is not unsurprising in the light of a neoconservative policy of reception, as mentioned in Sect. 5.2.6, which has reduced reception to a binary operation of command and obedience. Since Catholics are expected to abide by the law rather than discuss it, they only need to understand the commands given by the authorities in the vernacular languages.

In a similar vein, one can also understand the distinction claim as a neoconservative argument. It is unclear why Latin, as a symbol of distinction which differentiates canon law from secular legal orders, has a particular value. However, this does make sense if the aim is to establish and maintain a particular canonical culture. In this context, Latin as a unique marker of canon law helps to typify this culture as a specific system of meaning which allows individuals to develop a particular canonical identity. As relying on a dead language implies that comprehending the law requires expert knowledge, the use of Latin endorses the building of expert identities by those capable of deciphering the secret language that others do not understand. That members of this circle are mostly clerical, many of them educated in Rome, reinforces the centralist agenda. Haering's last argument, that the use of Latin honours the canonical tradition with its roots in ancient Roman law of late antiquity, also supports neoconservative policies. By emphasising this tradition with the help of Latin, the legislator refers not only to the historical roots of his laws but also to the continuous tradition of canon law since the days of its origin, thereby encouraging a traditional view of the law. As mentioned, tradition with regard to interpretation is not about selecting a meaning from diverse historical interpretations. It is about who is authorised to decide what the official tradition is. As this debate is merely open to those who speak Latin Legalese, the circle of those who can influence what the tradition of the church is and, consequently, which meaning is traditionally attached to a legal rule, is rather exclusive.

6.3 Responses to Legal Conflicts

The previous section has shown that global legislation does not pay much attention to cultural issues or the local adaptation of global rules, for instance by encouraging culturally sensitive interpretation. The following section examines how the law responds to cases in which global laws prove to be incompatible with cultural values and concerns. Analysing how the law deals with circumstances in which global rules and local requirements fail to align allows a more detailed assessment of how current legislation reacts to cultural diversity. Canon law deals with all sorts of collisions deriving from confrontations between law and reality by making use of so-called instruments of legal flexibility. These deal with conflicts deriving from the application of laws in singular situations. The global rules are generally in force. However, local authorities such as the diocesan bishops may apply them equitably, for instance by dispensing their legal subjects from following the law in distinct cases of conflict. In some cases, the legal subjects may also free themselves from burdens put upon them by the law by practising epiky when they find a law to grossly fail in responding to their personal situation. The following section discusses these different instruments to establish the way in which they also contribute to preventing or resolving cultural clashes.

6.3.1 Equity and Economy

According to canonical jurisprudence, equity is an applier of law's official response to finding a law in force but unjust in addressing a specific situation. The term equity as used in this context does not refer to a body of laws in the Anglo-American sense of the term. Instead, it denotes a principle of fairness utilised in legal application which attempts to ease hardship deriving from the law in a specific situation where a rule fails to respond adequately to a particular case. Thomas Aquinas believed that the appliers of law are required to act equitably where positive law contradicts natural law.[46] This problem inevitably arises because general rules cannot relate to each single case appropriately. A human legislator can merely consider the usual circumstances but cannot provide rules considering all possible situations. As a consequence, general rules can collide with individual fairness and the common good on unique occasions.[47] In church, where the appliers of law face the challenge of enforcing a uniform body of global rules in the local churches, these rules frequently fail to answer adequately to the local needs or cultural concerns. If this creates a particular hardship in that church, it may be justified to apply the rules equitably. Following Aquinas, in such cases, it is wrong to adhere to the letter of the law and right to act according to its spirit by practising equity. This can lead the appliers of law to different responses, depending on the appropriate way of preserving individual fairness or the common good. It might guide them to apply a law mercifully, for instance by reducing a punishment. In a similar way, the principle of economy, which is particularly influential in the Eastern churches, authorises the appliers of law to find a compromise, preventing hardship in a specific situation, as James Coriden explains: "Economy is the concession by legitimate pastors of a certain kind of compromise which, safeguarding both dogma and divine law, involves a mitigated rather than strict application of norms for the sake of the salvation of the faithful".[48] Yet equity can, even more radically, advise the appliers of law not to follow the law at all, preventing its application to a specific case. Coriden mentions several examples where he finds circumstances demand the non-application of rules: "Common sense has something to say about urging the rules for fast and abstinence during a famine, or initiating a fundraising drive during an economic depression, or imposing formal and elaborate procedures in a small community of

---

[46] See Thomas Aquinas (1265–73), STh II–II, q. 60 art. 5. In: Editio Leonina (1897), pp. 31–32.

[47] See ibid., q. 120 art. 1. In: Editio Leonina (1897), p. 468.

[48] Coriden (1982), p. 286.

simple people, or pressing the obligation of Sunday Mass attendance where there is an acute shortage of celebrants".[49] The recent history in mind, one might also assess the Prefect of the Congregation for Divine Worship's directive instructing the bishops' conferences to urge all Catholics to follow their Sunday obligation and resume their physical mass attendance in the midst of a global pandemic as an example in which the circumstances would have been better served through an equitable handling of the law.[50]

6.3.2 Ubiquitous Dispensation

One of the key instruments in the Western tradition of applying the law equitably is dispensation. The Code defines dispensation as "the relaxation of a merely ecclesiastical law in a particular case" (canon 85 CIC/1983). When "a just and reasonable cause" (canon 90 §1 CIC/1983) demands lifting the burden of the law, ecclesiastical authorities may allow for this in single cases. The competent authority has to evaluate whether granting a dispensation is just and reasonable by "taking into account the circumstances of the case and the gravity of the law from which dispensation is given" (canon 90 §1 CIC/1983). Over the course of the history of canon law dispensation has become *the* instrument used to respond to specific circumstances where the application of laws creates fundamental conflicts. Dispensation, one might say, has become the universal remedy to cure unfairness or injustice which general rules inflict upon individual subjects or particular groups. In the 1983 reform of the Code, as already stated in the introduction, the legislator made the use of dispensation even more flexible by removing the old restriction in canon 81 CIC/1917 that diocesan bishops could regularly dispense their legal subjects from general laws only after a higher authority had granted them the power to do so. After the Second Vatican Council had changed the old approach of concession to an approach of reservation,[51] the 1983 reform of the Code extended the bishops' rights so that they may now dispense their legal subjects from most global laws, with the exception of procedural and penal laws and those the dispensation of which is expressly reserved to the Apostolic See or another authority (see canon 87 §1 CIC/1983). The bishops, for instance, may dispense their subjects from all disciplinary laws issued by the supreme legislator or other authorities, whenever they deem dispensation just and reasonable to protect their legal subjects' well-being (see canons 87 §1, 88 CIC/1983). Hence, in cases in which a law endangers the local Catholics' welfare, the bishops can turn to dispensation to protect their subjects from harmful law. Shortly after the introduction of the new Code, Peruvian bishop José Dammert

[49] Ibid., p. 287.

[50] See Prefect of the Congregation for Divine Worship (2020), pp. 7–8.

[51] See Second Vatican Council (1965a), no. 8b. Acta Apostolicae Sedis (1966), p. 676.

Bellido commented on this greater flexibility by noting: "This innovation will make the pastoral mission of Third World bishops considerably easier".[52]

One might critically remark that dispensation also makes the legislator's life considerably easier. Without the local authorities' ability to resolve conflicts arising from inadequate legislation, many global regulations would come under enormous pressure. Thus, dispensation can be seen as a mechanism that enables global law-making to impose a uniform body of general rules on the local churches. It is the glue that holds this body of laws together. This can be illustrated with an example. According to ecclesiastical marriage law, a marriage between a Catholic and an unbaptised individual is invalid (see canon 1086 §1 CIC/1983). However, the law allows for dispensation from this impediment under certain conditions as regulated in canons 1125 and 1126 CIC/1983. In many churches of the Global North, such as in Germany, which are seeing an increasing number of marriages between Catholics and non-baptised individuals, dispensation from the impediment of *disparity of cult* has become a regular practice. Whilst the couples must provide reasons why they ask for dispensation, a reason accepted by the diocesan curias as a just and reasonable cause is that the couples express their determination to marry, making it clear that they will live together regardless of the church's blessing. So the general rule impedes interreligious marriages, while legal practice grants dispensation from this impediment in (nearly) all cases. In contexts where interfaith marriages are common and dispensation is granted in almost all cases, one might ask why these marriages are impeded in the first place. Yet, studying the phenomenon more profoundly reveals that this paradox of having a rule which impedes an action, while practically permitting the very same action, allows for a differentiated symbol politics. This politics communicates two messages. One is that the official doctrine favours marriages between baptised spouses. Allowing interfaith marriages in general would imply that they are of equal value to Christian unions. Therefore, the law impedes them and allows them only in singular cases and with the couple's promise to fulfil certain stipulations. This enables the Apostolic See to express its low appraisal of interfaith marriages without hindering Catholics from entering them. Hence, dispensation is a tool that allows doctrine to maintain its standards while reconciling them with demands that deviate from those standards. Closer scrutiny reveals, however, that this routine seems to respond less to pastoral concerns with regard to the legal subjects, and more to concerns pertaining to the law. By inhibiting an action and allowing it at the same time, dispensation protects the law from greater pressure to change. Conflictive laws may continue to exist without being challenged to any greater degree, because dispensation effectively reduces the pressure on the legislator to improve his rules.

But there is another layer of symbolic meaning inherent in dispensation. This is that the legal subjects have to trust in the church authorities. Dispensation places the legal subjects at the discretion of the authorities who decide whether to grant it. While dispensation requires "a just and reasonable cause" and its evaluation "taking

[52] Dammert Bellido (1986), p. 111.

into account the circumstances of the case and the gravity of the law from which dispensation is given" (canon 90 §1 CIC/1983), it is in the hands of the ecclesiastical authorities to decide whether or not the particular circumstances provide a just reason which justifies setting the law aside. As dispensation is a favour, it makes the legal subjects dependent on their authorities and their willingness to ease the hardship of the law in a particular case. Whilst changing the law would attribute the legal subjects with rights to enforce, for instance the right to enter interfaith marriages, dispensation is a way of symbolising that the legal subjects are constantly dependent on their authorities' goodwill. This makes dispensation an effective means of centralising power in church, revealing, once again, the centralised policy of current legislation.

6.3.3 Autonomous Epiky

Despite this focus on the authorities, ecclesiastical subjects can also reject global laws autonomously where abiding by a rule might otherwise lead to an unjust or unfair outcome. This decision can be based on epiky, the individual virtue of assessing a situation, which can justify breaking the rule for reasons of conscience. Epiky empowers the individual to do the right thing in situations of conflict between the positive law and the naturally just. Subjects bound by a rule may refer to epiky if they can argue that the legislator, if he had known the circumstances of their specific case, would have regulated differently. For Aristotle, epiky is part of the law itself, not part of positive law but an integral correction of positive law. According to Aristotle, individuals have to emend the law sometimes, for the reason "that all law is universal, but about some things it is not possible to make a universal statement which shall be correct. In those cases, then, in which it is necessary to speak universally, but not possible to do so correctly, the law takes the usual case, though it is not ignorant of the possibility of error".[53] This lack of precision of laws is grounded in the nature of laws. And there is nothing which human beings can do about it, except allowing for epiky "to correct the omission"[54] based on a careful evaluation of how legislators would have decided if they were in their legal subjects' position. Aristotle describes this act of practising epiky as an act of working out "what the legislator himself would have said had he been present, and would have put into his law if he had known".[55]

It is reasonable to assume that Catholics rarely break the law by explicitly invoking the principle of epiky. The narrow view of reception as command and obedience promoted by the Apostolic See since the nineteenth century has not supported decisions of conscience in relation to the law. In fact, there is reason to doubt whether

[53] Aristotle (350 BCE), Book 5 Chap. 14. In: The Nicomachean Ethics (1966), p. 133.

[54] Ibid.

[55] Ibid.

Catholics are aware of this option. While noncompliance with the law is common, only a few Catholics will reinterpret their decision to break a law as epiky. However, many refusals to abide by the law may be unintentionally based on similar considerations. When legal subjects follow their conscience and allow it to triumph over rules they consider unjust, their decision may reflect epiky. An example might help to illustrate this. In many German parishes it has become standard practice for laypeople to preach the homily during mass. This practice deliberately rejects canon 767 §1 CIC/1983 reserving the homily to priests and deacons. For many Catholics this is a matter of conscience. They find that the legislator, were he to assess the German situation correctly—with a good number of well-educated lay theologians and a growing lack of priests—should and would have allowed for lay homilies, a practice which was even allowed under certain circumstances for some time after the Synod of Würzburg,[56] before the 1983 Code entered into force. For many parishioners, ignoring the restriction set up by the Code is therefore a matter of conscience allowing the just to rule over the legally correct.

6.4 Summary

This chapter has examined how global legislation responds to the diversity of the local churches by scrutinising the legal rules that address cultural issues. An analysis of the canons of the Code of Canon Law that mention culture reveals terminological ambiguity and conceptual vagueness, avoiding a definition of culture or a clarification of its significance for the church and its law. This uncertainty is reflected in the strategies employed by legislation to address cultural idiosyncrasies and the specific challenges faced by the local churches. Local needs are mostly safeguarded through a rule-and-exception policy which allows decentralised authorities to depart from a global rule if it poses a significant problem for their church. Cultural issues also come into play when applying the law. Although the absence of a doctrine of *stare decisis* enables ecclesiastical tribunals and administration to interpret legal rules without being bound by precedents, they must apply the canonical rules of interpretation and adhere to a standardised methodology guiding interpreters towards legal meaning as determined by the Apostolic See. Instruments of legal flexibility enable appliers of law to respond to clashes between centralised regulations and local demands. These instruments serve to ease hardship deriving from legal rules in particular situations. However, they also prevent the reform of culturally insensitive laws by offering an immediate alternative to actual legal change.

---

[56] See Congregation for the Clergy (1973). Archiv für katholisches Kirchenrecht (1973), pp. 480–482.

Chapter 7
Local Responses to Legal Transplants

The previous two chapters of this book examined how ecclesiastical legislature deals with global canon law as a subject of inculturation in lawmaking and the reception of the law, and how the law itself responds to the cultural diversity of the local churches. Their findings confirm the observation taken from other studies on inculturation that the Apostolic See's current politics of inculturation is ambiguous, also with regard to the law. If one identifies the council and its shifting between descriptive and normative meanings of culture as one source of this ambiguity, it seems unsurprising that canon law has so far failed to relate itself fully to the diversity of the local churches. However, this is not merely the result of terminological ambiguity. It is evidently also strategically motivated. As with other key elements of ecclesiastical life, such as the doctrine of faith, Catholic moral teaching, and the liturgy, the Apostolic See also promotes a neoconservative policy with respect to inculturation regarding the law. As the authorities are concerned that an official message loses its original meaning when finding its home in new contexts, they tend to rely on the inculturation concept of translation as a speaker-oriented standard, as Robert Schreiter explained.[1] Accordingly, the liturgical reform after the Second Vatican Council was guided by translation. And the inculturation of global canon law in the local churches follows a similar paradigm. Because translation is suitable for protecting a uniform law and its uniform meaning, John Huels even assesses it to be the most suitable concept for the law. Adaptation and contextual approaches do not deal easily with global canon law, as both are less open to taking on an alien body of rules. Rather, they aim at developing their own local equivalents. Translation, on the contrary, takes legal texts as set and tries to implement them as comprehensively as it can, as Huels discerns: "The goal of the translation approach is to facilitate the accommodation of these texts and traditions in alien cultures. It assumes that a universal canon law is a reality that must somehow be dealt with in diverse

[1] See Schreiter (1985), p. 60.

J. Hahn, *The Cultures of Canon Law*, Law and Religion in a Global Context 6,
https://doi.org/10.1007/978-3-032-14812-4_7

cultural settings."[2] This allows legislation to communicate new rules to the local churches without losing much of their original meaning. The legal norms are translated, if only superficially, to serve as norms guiding behaviour in the local churches in approximately the same way as intended by the legislator.

The following section will probe somewhat deeper into the analysis by asking if the inculturation of canon law with the help of the standard of translation pays enough attention to the diversity that the law encounters in the local churches. Studying the local responses to the transplanted rules can help to answer this question. They become visible through two related enquiries: whether the current inculturation policy with regard to the law is sufficient with respect to the *law*, ensuring its widespread effectiveness in the local churches; and whether it does justice to the *churches*, allowing the local Catholics to profit from global law as a support for their communities. Both dynamics are mutually intertwined, as legal scholar Jan Smits indicates with regard to legal transfer: "Successful export of law can only take place if the importing country is prepared not only to perceive the exporter's rules as useful, but is also willing to implement them."[3] His remark contains several findings that require further consideration. It covers the idea that alien law is successfully transplanted only in those cases in which it is effectively implemented in its new home; that implementation is closely connected with acceptance; and that acceptance, to no small degree, depends on the local assessment of whether the alien law is useful for the receiving community. Based on these observations, Section 7.1 examines centralised lawmaking in closer detail, while Section 7.2 looks at the process of imposed reception in the local churches. This analysis aims to compile the broad range of responses from local Catholics to global rules, including negative responses to the law, such as indifference or rejection. At the same time, even laws that irritate the receiving community can eventually find acceptance if they are reconstructed by the receiving group in a way that attributes them with local meaning. Section 7.3 examines these struggles for meaning, discussing how and under what conditions contentious legal transplants can acquire a new meaning in the local churches.

7.1 Solicited Imposition

As mentioned, canonical lawmaking and reception of these laws display a tension between external pressure and voluntary appropriation, which can be best described by applying Alan Watson's terminology of *solicited imposition* and *imposed reception*.[4] Catholic legislation for the global church is at present the result of the Apostolic See's lawmaking, which is then transported from Rome into the local

[2] Huels (1987), p. 287.

[3] Smits (2003), p. 558.

[4] See Watson (1993), p. 30.

churches to be received there. As a centralistically organised top-down endeavour to provide the global church with a uniform legal frame, one can perceive global lawmaking to be guided by a neoconservative agenda, protecting the continuity of the canonical tradition against disruption and the unity of the church and its law against the pluralising effects of more decentralised legislation. The following considerations examine how this policy is reflected in local responses to global legislation.

7.1.1 Lack of Transparency

At present, no rules exist to make the stages of global lawmaking transparent to the Catholic public. The publication of new laws usually comes as a surprise to those whom they concern. The 2021 reform of canonical penal law is an example of this. Whilst the general public was aware of the ongoing revision process, which began in 2007, hardly anybody was aware of the progress of the procedures, what changes the bodies of reform were discussing, and when to expect publication. Whilst most canonists knew somebody who knew somebody rumoured to be part of the expert body preparing the drafts of the new law, hardly anybody was well informed. This shows that ecclesiastical lawmaking proceeds rather secretively, even when it comes to bigger projects that take a long time. The legislative results then suddenly arrive in the legal community as surprises. This is even more the case with single papal laws, which often take the legal community completely by surprise—sometimes with a rumour that spreads among canonists a couple of days before publication. When Pope Francis, for instance, abrogated his predecessor's regulations on the old Latin Tridentine liturgy in 2021 with the promulgation of the papal law *Traditionis Custodes*,[5] this legal change sent shockwaves through some traditional Catholic circles, as they had not seen it coming. Another example—a much-discussed case of surprise legislation among canonists—is the disappearance of the *Lex Ecclesiae Fundamentalis*, the project of establishing a fundamental law of the church, which was abandoned without prior notice during the course of the 1983 reform of the Code. The *Lex Ecclesiae Fundamentalis* was planned as a constitutional law for the global Catholic Church, superordinated to the Code of the Latin Church and the Code of the Oriental Churches. Several drafts were produced during the reform work. Yet in the last stage of the process, most of its norms were inserted into the final draft of the Latin Code, the 1982 Schema, and later into the Oriental Code, without pursuing the plan to establish a separate constitutional document. Even today, little is known about the reason for this unexpected change.

Similarly little is known about the final papal redaction of the 1983 Code. "As one hears time and again in Roman circles", noted canonist Winfried Aymans in the German bishops' introduction to the new Code in 1983, "the pope himself together with a small study group intensively studied and discussed the whole Schema; with

[5] See Francis (2021b). Acta Apostolicae Sedis (2021), pp. 793–796.

matters that were not yet ready for a decision, a small circle of leading cardinals was supposedly entrusted with their re-examination."[6] No reasons were given for the decisions to re-examine some matters, even though these papal adaptations have to be evaluated as papal interventions against the comprehensive groundwork of the commission. One example of a papal intervention during the final stage of the reform, which was intensively discussed by canonists, is the disappearance of the norms on an ecclesiastical administrative procedure. They had simply vanished from the law when the pope promulgated the 1983 Code.

Surprise legislation, in any case, challenges the legal subjects' acceptance of the law from a sociological point of view. It is helpful to study Niklas Luhmann's observations on the conditions under which laws stand a chance of finding acceptance to see this point. According to Luhmann, transparent procedures in general serve individuals and groups as buffers that help them to absorb the shock effect of social change. Their merit is to present developments as decisions and, thus, as purposeful progress. Consequently, as Luhmann notes: "A decision does not fall upon the individual as an unexpectable surprise, as luck or bad luck, which one can only expect helplessly without having a chance to prepare for it, but as the result of decision making which one can prepare for by witnessing it and acting according to it."[7] Luhmann, therefore, finds expectability to be one key criterion that provides procedures, including lawmaking, with legitimacy. Transparent operations are described as "an existential complement of positivising the law. They minimise and absorb the moment of shock which is connected with the decision."[8] They hold out the promise of security without seeming to be arbitrary:

> In light of an uncertain future and an overload of an immense complexity of options of variable law, procedures help to create security, und to allow for a significant, expressive, meaningful, and dutiful behaviour in the present time. In this way, those affected can experience the present time as meaningful and can act according to it, even though they live up to an uncertain future.[9]

[6] Original quote: "Wie man aus römische Kreisen immer wieder hören kann, hat der Papst selbst zusammen mit einer kleinen Arbeitsgruppe dieses Gesamtschema gründlich studiert und diskutiert; noch nicht entscheidungsreife Frage sollen einem kleinen Kreis führender Kardinäle zur nochmaligen Überprüfung anvertraut worden sein", Aymans (1983), pp. 9–10.

[7] Original quote: "Die Entscheidung fällt nicht als eine unerwartbare Überraschung auf ihn zu, als Glück oder Unglück, dem man ratlos entgegensieht, ohne sich darauf einstellen zu können, sondern als Ergebnis eines Entscheidungsprozesses, in dem man sich miterlebend und mithandelnd auf sie vorbereiten kann", Luhmann (1969), p. 232.

[8] Original quote: "ein existentielles Komplement der Positivierung des Rechts. Sie verkleinern und entschärfen das Moment der Überraschung, das mit der Entscheidung verbunden ist", Luhmann (1969), p. 232.

[9] Original quote: "Verfahren verhelfen dazu, angesichts einer ungewissen Zukunft und vornehmlich angesichts einer Überforderung durch eine unübersehbare Komplexität von Möglichkeiten des variablen Rechts gegenwärtige Sicherheit zu schaffen und ein darstellendes, expressives, sinnerfülltes, verpflichtendes Verhalten in der Gegenwart zu ermöglichen. So kann der Betroffene in einer laufend aktuellen Gegenwart sinnvoll miterleben und mithandeln, obwohl er auf eine ungewisse Zukunft zulebt", Luhmann (1969), p. 232.

Hence, transparency motivates legal subjects to accept the law, even if it is the result of an evidently contingent decision. In any case, as Luhmann also notes, the need for transparency can vary depending on the nature of the affected legal matter. Although changes to rights and obligations must be communicated clearly in advance, rules referred to by Luhmann as *trivial law* rarely affect most legal subjects[10]; therefore, it does no harm if little is known about their changes. As one reviewer of this book remarked, procedural rules often only affect legal subjects to a minor degree. Therefore, limited knowledge of changes to these rules does not affect acceptance to any greater extent. However, when studying ecclesiastical legislation, it becomes clear that surprise legislation occurs regardless of the nature of the matter under consideration. It affects widely unknown procedural rules or laws of little practical significance to most legal subjects, but also rights and duties that are important to some groups, as demonstrated by the examples of *Traditionis Custodes* and the rules on ecclesiastical administrative procedures. For this reason, ecclesiastical lawmaking can struggle to gain acceptance. As it follows no clear procedural rules and is non-transparent, it does not take any provisions to absorb the shock effects of legal development by preparing the legal subjects for new rules. In church, legislative decisions frequently hit legal subjects unexpectedly, by luck or bad luck. As a result of secret operations, global legislation does not help many church members to deal with a complex present or an uncertain future. It does not promise security. And often it does not endow Catholics with options for behaviour that is meaningful for their life or their faith. That global canon law, at present, has problems finding recognition among its legal subjects is, in its core, already established in the non-transparent lawmaking from which it derives.

7.1.2 Non-Participation

According to Luhmann, transparency of lawmaking is one criterion that fosters the acceptance of laws. Another criterion is participation. According to Luhmann, legal subjects embrace most contingent decisions if they have had a fair chance to influence the decision making and impact its outcome. This criterion challenges global canon law as much as its lack of transparency. Even though global law affects the local churches all over the globe, decentralised stakeholders are frequently underrepresented in global lawmaking or, as in the case of single papal laws for the global church, are completely unrepresented. No rules exist to ensure the participation of local stakeholders in lawmaking. There are no systemic features that help to represent the specific interests of the local churches in global lawmaking.

One can see this when studying the process that resulted in the reformed Code of 1983. As mentioned in Sect. 5.1.1, the reform bodies consisted of representatives of local churches from all over the globe. However, when studying the exact

[10] See Luhmann (2014), p. 196.

composition of the reform bodies, one can discover several limitations with regard to their diversity. In the introduction to the then-new Code, published by the German Bishops' Conference in 1983, Winfried Aymans noted a regional disproportion, particularly with regard to the working groups and the commission of the reform, emphasising that the main reform work was largely carried out by European and US-American canonists.[11] The reform commission itself was heavily influenced by representatives of the Apostolic See. It included the prefects of the Congregation for the Doctrine of the Faith and of the Congregation for the Bishops, the heads of the Congregations for the Clergy, for Divine Worship and the Discipline of the Sacraments, for the Oriental Churches, for the Evangelisation of Peoples, for Catholic Education, and the Causes of Saints, along with the Cardinal Secretary of State, the Cardinal-Camerlengo, the Cardinal Librarian, and the Prefect of the Prefecture for the Economic Affairs of the Holy See.[12] Whilst these cardinals, prefects, and other church officials working in Rome came from various local churches, the majority of them, back in the 1980s, had an Italian or at least a European background. Ladislas Orsy, therefore, considers the Code to be strongly influenced by the Italian legal culture.[13] Adding to this, many episcopal members of the commission from the local churches had received some Roman formation during their theological studies. One can see this when studying the *vitae* of the four cardinals from German-speaking countries who were members of the commission in 1981. Cardinals König and Höffner as well as the German Curial Cardinal Schröffer had spent part of their studies in Rome and were ordained there. Ironically, only the Archbishop of Munich and Freising, Cardinal Ratzinger, who for many Catholics later became synonymous with *the* Apostolic See and a Roman view of the church, had not been educated in Rome. With regard to the African bishops in the commission, legal scholar Steven Bwana noticed the same phenomenon, observing that "those representatives had been 'mented' in Rome or Europe."[14] His remark also implies that the worldwide practice of sending priest candidates to Rome to study at Roman universities—especially those who seem apt to become higher clergy in the future—results in their "Roman" formation, making it likely that they develop a centralist perspective on matters of doctrine, discipline, and law. John Huels points to the same issue, which he perceives to be a general problem of church governance. He suspects that granting a Roman education to the candidates for higher office decreases their sensitivity for their home churches, as he implies by asking: "Can … the locally born clergy, religious, lay leaders, theologians, and canonists communicate effectively with their people if, during their formative years, they are taken out of their culture and are resocialized in religious houses, seminaries, and universities in the First World?"[15] Huels devotes particular attention to priest candidates from

[11] See Aymans (1983), p. 9.

[12] See Pontifical Commission for the Revision of the Code of Canon Law (1981), pp. 5–7.

[13] See Orsy (1983), p. 122 fn. 28.

[14] Bwana (1986), p. 104.

[15] Huels (1987), p. 257; see also Schreiter (1985), p. 39.

the Global South, but his analysis is equally true for the aspirants to higher office of the Global North, who, after their undergraduate studies, are also frequently sent to Rome for their postgraduate studies and are often ordained there. If one assumes that these Romanised clergy share the centralist view of the church and its law, one has to receive the multicultural composition of the reform commission in a different light. In this light, it seems that the commission was less an encounter of differing views from various churches and more an assembly of church officials from around the world—with a Roman view of the law.

The consultation process on the current Code, as noted in Sect. 5.1.1, provided the local churches with a critical voice by addressing not merely the dicasteries of the Roman Curia but also all bishops' conferences, the Union of Superiors General of the religious orders, and ecclesiastical universities and faculties from all over the world. Hence, the consultation process encouraged decentralised agents to comment on the drafts from their particular perspective. One can assume that it delivered helpful suggestions. One shortcoming was that only a small number of diocesan bishops returned their opinion.[16] Adding to this shortcoming was that we do not know how the commission handled these comments and what influence they had on further revisions of the draft law. It is, in fact, unclear what significance the global input had on the shape of the current Code of Canon Law and, similarly, on the development of the 2021 revision of penal law. While one can assume that it had some relevance, the extent to which the suggestions from the local churches changed the draft laws is unknown. In James Provost's view, the consultation process therefore did not prevent the reform work on the Code from being a highly centralist endeavour.[17]

So studying global lawmaking relating to the Code illustrates why its results, despite attempts to integrate decentralised perspectives, can be considered Roman laws. Global canon law is made in Rome, shaped by centralist agents, supervised by canonical experts and bishops mostly educated in Rome, and promulgated by the Roman pontiff. While global voices, at least in major pieces of reform, are encouraged to share their views in a consultation process, it is unclear what significance their contributions have. The Roman impact on the formation of the law is maximal, and the impact of the world church is limited to granting the unity of the process and its outcome. A similar verdict can be rendered with regard to other ecclesiastical laws for the global church. Most agents involved in creating papal laws or laws prepared by Vatican dicasteries with papal approval are Vatican officials as well as bishops and experts educated in Rome. A *Motu Proprio* or an Apostolic Constitution does not even regularly envisage a global consultation. Especially in the form of a *Motu Proprio*, papal legislation is the pope's direct reaction to a need for regulation, which he addresses on his own initiative without being bound by any formal rule of participation. Neither is it standard to allow other agents to participate in acts of papal lawmaking in which the pope adopts a curial regulation as a papal law by

[16] See Provost (1996), p. 121.

[17] See ibid.

approving the text. Hence, global canon law is largely a centralist product; it is exported from Rome into the Catholic world. Coming back to Luhmann's considerations, it is therefore apparent why it has difficulties gaining the legal subjects' acceptance. In light of this finding, Ladislas Orsy poses several questions, saying that "the faithful at large are not expected (not allowed) to play any role in the shaping of the legal life of the church. Understandably, a community that has the Spirit and (dare we say?) is bursting with divine energy senses an anomaly. Is it surprising if they become alienated from the law?"[18]

7.1.3 Excluding Language

Pope John Paul II stated in his 1986 address to Aboriginal Peoples and Torres Strait Islanders in Alice Springs: "The Gospel of our Lord Jesus Christ speaks all languages."[19] The law of the church does not. That translation, as an approach of inculturation, is not supposed to touch the law substantially finds literal expression in the fact that the authentic text of the Code of Canon Law is merely the Latin version. Translating a rule into another language essentially attributes it with a new meaning, as John Huels notes, "Translation is always interpretation; in translating a text, we create another."[20] Vernacular translations of the Code are therefore restricted to serve legal subjects and practitioners as working aids, without becoming an authentic source of law.

Thus, Canon Law Latin is an exclusive language, drawing a symbolic line between those who understand and those who do not. This line divides Latinised European from non-European cultures, a hierarchical elite from the ordinary church members, clerics from laypeople, and the educated from the non-educated. As a symbolic marker of distinction, it contributes to the establishment of a canonical professional elite, on whose support depend those who are unable to decipher the Latin original. By shunning the majority of Catholics from the official legal discourses, the use of dead Latin promotes legal communication in the form of command and obedience. In this light, it is revealing to read Antony Anghie's considerations about creating colonial patterns in law based on language usage. He studies how international law became a truly global phenomenon with the support of colonialism, which introduced to it a "dynamic of difference".[21] This "distinction between the civilised and the uncivilised" equipped international law with the aim "to bring the uncivilized/aberrant/violent/backward/oppressed into the realm of civilisation, the universal order governed by (European) international law."[22] By

[18] Orsy (1996b), pp. 16–17.

[19] John Paul II (1986), no. 12. Acta Apostolicae Sedis (1987), p. 977.

[20] Huels (1987), p. 252.

[21] Anghie (2006), p. 742.

[22] Ibid.

cultivating these dichotomies, the law has been able to continue its "civilising mission"[23] until the present day. As mentioned when speaking about canonical legislation and reception as solicited imposition and imposed reception, in Alan Watson's terms,[24] canon law with its ambition to serve the church as a global order shares with international law this temptation to rely on a dynamic of difference. Attention is therefore needed whenever it reproduces dichotomies, for example with reference to linguistic matters. The use of Latin produces a symbolic difference between the global Latinised elite, who understand canonical Legalese, and the local Catholics, who do not. In ecclesiastical adjudication, for example, the language divide accentuates the distinction between the professional Roman tribunals and the local tribunals, which are frequently criticised for failing to adhere to ecclesiastical procedural rules and communicate effectively with Roman authorities.[25] These differences not only allude to the fact that the use of Latin makes it difficult for many Catholics, including many canonists, to decipher and deal with authentic legal texts, but they also point to the more fundamental problem that the use of Latin in law tends to reproduce hierarchical distinctions to justify its ongoing civilising mission in the local churches.

7.1.4 Rule and Exception

As major transplants, calling to mind Alan Watson's theory once again, global laws are transferred to the local churches in a top-down manner. The expectation is that the local community receives them voluntarily. Watson's terms solicited imposition and imposed reception, which reflect the tension between external pressure and voluntary elements, describe this dichotomy. Yet this approach has practical limits in cases in which the decentralised agents of transmission, such as the diocesan bishops, find the law inadequate and hesitate to receive it. As mentioned in Chap. 6, the current Code provides some instruments to mediate these conflicts. However, as has also become clear, these instruments have a limited range, as shown by the example of enabling the bishops to allow for more lay participation in pastoral and liturgical functions. Instead of generally authorising more lay participation in governing the church, in the teaching function of the church, and in the administration of sacraments and sacramentals, legislation provides a rule-and-exception system which allows the authorities to include laypeople, but only when ordinary ministers are unavailable. This protects the traditional clergy-centred structuring of ecclesiastical ministry while similarly enabling the local authorities to depart from this standard in cases of clergy shortage. One can find this rule-and-exception approach to

[23] Ibid.

[24] See Watson (1993), p. 30.

[25] E.g. yearly reporting duties to the Apostolic Signatura are in place to control the local tribunals' work, see Apostolic Signatura (2016).

be a typical neoconservative policy. It preserves a traditional and uniform body of clergy-centred regulations while using exemption clauses to release the pressure on the local appliers of law as well as on the law itself in cases of urgent need.

7.1.5 Limits of Remonstration

Thus, rule and exception protects culturally insensitive laws from contestation, as long as exemption clauses permit the local authorities to address a contested issue. It is important to note though, that most laws do not contain exemption clauses. If the local authorities still conceive of them as being detrimental to their churches, they can be tempted to refuse reception. As was mentioned in Sect. 5.1.5, canonical tradition has anticipated this problem. It provides the diocesan bishops and others who preside over local Catholic communities with the right to remonstrate laws harmful to their community. However, as was also mentioned, it is up to the pope as the supreme legislator to decide whether he consents to abrogation or directs the local authorities to enforce the contested law in their church. This limited authority of the bishops requires critical examination for several reasons. First, one can criticise it for historical reasons. Wolfgang Beinert noticed that for the first few centuries of church history, the bishops enjoyed considerable freedom in deciding whether a papal decree was compatible with the customs of their church, by freely assessing the benefit of a directive for local communities.[26] Beinert substantiated his observation by referring to Augustine's reference to Ambrose, who followed the Roman laws on fasting when staying in Rome, but did not follow them when residing in Milan.[27] Over the course of church history, though, the papacy has curbed this flexible way of dealing with centralist instructions, culminating in the First Vatican Council and its focus on the pope as the centralist guarantor of Catholic unity. The obligation that diocesan bishops receive and enforce papal laws in their dioceses (see canon 392 §1 CIC/1983) connects with this idea, as does restricting the bishops' power to fight global laws detrimental to their local churches.

A second reason why one can view the local authorities' limited power critically is an ecclesiological one. Local churches are true realisations of the Church of Christ.[28] As such, they participate in the universal church. This universal church is not identical with the Apostolic See. In fact, the local churches have an ecclesiological relevance that the Apostolic See does not. Yet the pope and the Apostolic See serve the universal church. They do so in a number of ways including lawmaking supporting the unity of the universal church by endowing it with a uniform legal frame. Global laws, thus, can legitimately bind the local churches insofar as they protect the unity of the universal church. Hence, the uniform body of global rules

---

[26] See Beinert (1991), p. 26.

[27] See Augustine (396), Chap. 14.32. In Migne (1865), p. 151.

[28] See Second Vatican Council (1964), nos. 23, 26. Acta Apostolicae Sedis (1965), pp. 27–29, 31–32.

binding the local churches is legitimised by the fact that it assists the unity of the universal church. Consequently in cases in which legal uniformity is not grounded in the legitimising reason of attending to the unity of the church, but becomes a source of *disunity* in a local church, it seems hardly justified to subject the local churches to uniform laws and to enforce these against the protest by the local authorities. More fundamentally one may ask if unity essentially requires a solid body of uniform rules. Robert Schreiter alludes to a similar finding when he observes: "Unity is not the same as uniformity."[29] Yet the two are connected. Schreiter explains this by referring to semiotics as the study of signs and the way in which they convey meaning. He points to the fact that it is difficult to communicate an identical meaning by using an abundant variety of signs. Delivering a message in a reliable way requires at least some correspondence between the signs that serve to convey its meaning. He therefore asks: "How many varieties of church order can be had before the churches can no longer work together or communicate with one another?"[30] Uniformity, at least to some extent, serves unity. However, as Schreiter's words also reveal, uniformity is not identical with unity. A message can be conveyed by various signs—and has to be depending on its cultural context. As the universal church is *one church*, one might find that a uniform body of legal rules is an appropriate approach for expressing this unity. However, ecclesiologically, one should bear in mind that the universal church is one church composed of *many churches*. Their diversity is not a mishap but is constitutive of the universal church as a unity out of plurality. If this plurality is of ecclesiological value, it is difficult to justify the tendency of global canon law to suppress legal diversity for the sake of unity.

A third question that one might level at the limitations of the local authorities' power is due to practical reasons, namely that these authorities usually know better about local legal needs and can assess better than distant Vatican officials which laws might have a detrimental effect on their local churches. It also seems rather impractical to enforce a law in a church against the local authority's protest. Compelling the authorities to enforce a law in their church despite their remonstration can damage the relationship between the local authority and the Apostolic See, but it can also undermine the law and its chance of getting the authority's support with regard to its enforcement. An example might help by way of illustration. In 1989, the Congregation for the Doctrine of the Faith issued new regulations on the profession of faith and the oath of fidelity, which Catholics who assume key ecclesiastical offices mentioned in canon 833 CIC/1983 have to take.[31] The German bishops remonstrated by raising legal and pastoral concerns.[32] They also expressed their

---

[29] Schreiter (1985), p. 102.

[30] Ibid.

[31] See Congregation for the Doctrine of the Faith (1989). Acta Apostolicae Sedis (1989), pp. 105–106; republication: Acta Apostolicae Sedis (1998), pp. 542–544.

[32] See Schmitz and Rhode (2011), pp. 131–132 fn. 238.

protest by subsequently remaining hesitant to publish a German translation of the formulas. The congregation finally published its own German translation nine years later, in 1998, as the bishops obviously made no move to proceed with the issue themselves. This translation then seems to have found the German bishops' grudging acceptance, as they then, one by one, published the text in their diocesan law gazettes. By 2000, the congregation had evidently managed to break the bishops' resistance. Whilst not much is known—neither of the concrete form of the bishops' objection, nor of the congregational handling of their remonstration, nor of the instruments with which the congregation defeated the bishops' resistance—it is evident that their remonstration did not achieve the desired result. The Roman command to commit key ecclesiastical officeholders to a wide-ranging oath of fidelity prevailed. However, local practice reveals subversive resistance, as many bishops fail to enforce the oath of fidelity when endowing individuals with offices mentioned in canon 833 CIC/1983. This results in an ambiguous situation, which one can assess as being somewhat typical for canon law. Whilst global rules triumph and are technically valid all over the globe, many Catholics, including authorities, fail to abide by them or enforce them within their jurisdiction. One can therefore find the diocesan bishops' limited authority to fight laws of which they disapprove to be problematic also for the reason that it produces paradoxical situations in which even bishops undermine the law of an institution which they represent.

7.1.6 Suppressing Customs

Another example of a strategy that global legislature uses to inhibit resistance to centralist rules is the suppression of local customs that challenge global laws. Customs, as discussed in Sect. 5.2.7, can help communities to create their own living law. As a bottom-up law, customary law can aptly respond to legal needs. And it can work as a counter-force against global laws imposed upon the local churches in a top-down manner. However, the legislator set a high bar for the emergence of customary law. Richard Potz, as already mentioned, perceives this decision as "a deliberate block"[33] by the legislator which actively prevents the emergence of new customary law. In a similar vein, Ladislas Orsy criticises the legislator for widely preventing customary laws from replacing canonical laws.[34] In light of the concern to preserve the unity of global law, it is understandable that canon law accentuates the authorities' contribution as being essential for customs to obtain the force of law and sets a high hurdle particularly for the development of *contra legem* customs. These provisions, however, impede local communities from developing norms responding to their needs. Orsy therefore finds "a latent irony"[35] in the fact that the

---

[33] Potz (1986), p. 21.

[34] See Orsy (1984), pp. 67–68; Orsy (1992), p. 116.

[35] Orsy (1992), p. 116; see also Orsy (1996b), p. 16.

legislator praises customs as "the best interpreter of laws" (canon 27 CIC/1983) where they support conformity with his law, yet strives to avoid the emergence of customary law in conflict with global rules.

7.2 Imposed Reception

As mentioned in Chap. 5, Boaventura de Sousa Santos characterises processes of globalisation, including those of the law, as consisting of two dynamics: globalised localism and localised globalism. With legal transfers between national or transnational systems in mind, he notes that "the international division of the production of globalism assumes the following pattern: the core countries specialize in globalized localisms, while upon the peripheral countries is imposed the choice of localized globalisms."[36] His thoughts resemble observations which one might also make in church, where centralised legislation confronts the local churches with the globalised localism of Roman law, as "a cultural process whereby a hegemonic local culture cannibalizes and digests other subordinated cultures",[37] as de Sousa Santos outlines, while the local churches respond to it with localised globalisms, allowing or disallowing the imported rules to stimulate the local production of rules and practices responding to that law. This dimension of localised globalism is what jurisprudence calls *reception*. In applying Alan Watson's terminology of solicited imposition and imposed reception to describe global lawmaking and the reception of its results in the local churches,[38] this book suggests that critical study is required not only of top-down lawmaking but also of the bottom-up responses of the local churches. Watson's terminology expresses the tension between the element of external force or pressure to which legislation subjects the receiving community and the independent local activities connected with reception. By focusing more on the effects of this dynamic on the side of the receiving community, the following section will discuss the diversity of local responses to canon law. All churches face the challenge of how to deal with laws that prove to be difficult to inculturate due to differing views of legal matters or due to circumstances that do not meet the situation considered in the law. One might therefore ask whether it is reasonable to expect the law to achieve a level of inculturation that allows local Catholicism to profit from it. Aylward Shorter is rather sceptical. He regards the inculturation of canon law as more difficult than that of the liturgy: "Inculturation in the field of liturgy is a comparatively simple prospect, even if it has not been fully implemented, compared to inculturation in such fields as that of marriage, family life or the practice of healing and medicine. A universal Church Law cannot ever hope to do justice to the diverse

[36] De Sousa Santos (2020), p. 215.

[37] Ibid., p. 327.

[38] See Watson (1993), p. 30.

cultural realities in the entire world."[39] The following section will identify the types of challenges deriving from the imposed reception of global canon law in the local churches and how local agents address them.

7.2.1 *Reception as Incarnation*

As set out in Sect. 4.1.7, ecclesiastical doctrine explains inculturation with the help of the incarnation analogy as a theological image of how universal ideas become real in concrete times and social settings. It understands reception as those processes that embrace universal ideas when they enter a particular context. Fernando Sebastian Aguilar defines reception in this light as follows:

> Reception can be a constitutive structure of Christianity, in so far as revelation is positive, is realized in history as a gift of a personal God, who in his liberty directed his word to us through the prophets until he gave us his Son incarnate. To receive him is the first reaction of people, once they discover God speaking and acting. We do not invent revelation, but receive it; we do not create the incarnation, we welcome it; but it is God who first speaks to us as friends, who invites us into his company and welcomes us.[40]

Applying this idea to human reception creates an analogy between God giving Godself to humanity and communities welcoming a doctrine, a liturgical ritual, or a legal rule by embracing it. However, there are at least two dangers connected with comparing human reception with the incarnation. First, the analogy is blind to the problem that humans receiving other goods are not faced with the task of embracing a universal idea as such, but a human and thus deeply cultural expression of that idea. Hence, using the incarnation metaphor to describe the local churches receiving global canon law tends to obscure the fact that this is not about the reception of universal law but about receiving a human artefact, even if this artefact can be understood in part as the cultural realisation of a universal idea. Hence, comparing legal reception with the incarnation tends to absolutise a certain human expression of law, to prioritise it over others, and to compel others to accept that expression instead of developing their own. Judith Gruber alludes to this problem in relation to the reception of the Gospel when remarking that "the metaphor of inculturation suggests a static one-dimensionality in the relation between Gospel and culture that allows the Gospel to be viewed as an extracultural entity. Thus, the danger of equating it with Western culture remains and the culturalistic annexation of the universal Christian message is encouraged."[41]

A second difficulty connected with comparing reception with the incarnation is that this image does not sufficiently take into account the reciprocal dynamic of reception. The incarnation metaphor focuses on Christ's entry into earthly

[39] Shorter (1988), p. 70.

[40] Aguilar (1997), p. 446.

[41] Gruber (2018), p. 47.

existence. The reaction of the receiving culture is secondary. Gruber correspondingly voices criticism that incarnation tends to focus on the identity of a message instead of on the receiving cultures. She therefore suggests favouring pneumatological and creation approaches over Christological approaches when explaining inculturation: "While incarnational models thus focus on a fixed Christian identity in the inculturation process, pneumatological and creation theology models concentrate instead on cultural identity."[42] Reception, particularly if understood as communication, is more of a dialogue and a communal learning process. Hence, unlike the incarnation, it is not a one-way route from sender to receiver, such as God communicating Godself to humankind, but is a mutual exchange of ideas in which the receivers share their new interpretations with the original senders. They thus provide the senders with deepened insights into the nature of their message, which has an impact on the message itself. If reception is communication, then a message sent necessitates a response. Yet this response does not merely confirm the submitted ecclesiastical doctrine, Roman liturgies, or global laws. It also contributes to the development of the doctrine, the liturgical rites, and the legal rules, providing for a deepened insight into the truth of a doctrine or the meaning of the liturgies or the law. In this vein, Wolfgang Beinert maintains that transmission and reception have

> at least a two-fold character, unfolding in such a way that the roles can change as a matter of principle. This interchangeability is a well known part of the governing circle of communication theory. The sender can become the receiver, the receiver the transmitter. The good being received can change either fully or only in certain aspects. One can exchange topics, or deepen the current topic so as to come to a better understanding of it. This is the case in every true dialogue.[43]

In theory, the local churches should have a similar impact on the global church as the global church has on the local churches. The idea of reciprocity, which relates both to each other as learning systems, includes not only that the local churches welcome ideas of alien origin but also that the magisterium and legislature adopt local ideas and integrate them into ecclesiastical doctrine, the Roman liturgies, and global canon law. Gruber therefore argues in favour of exchanging inculturation with *interculturation* to overcome the unidirectional view of reception in church, suggesting that

> the morphological switch in the concept of interculturation reflects the theological and cultural studies reorientation that is at the heart of Intercultural Theology. The prefix 'inter' implies a plurality of cultures and their inextricable connections with each other. While inculturation views the relation of Gospel and culture as a linear, one-dimensional process in which the Gospel is placed in relation to a culture, interculturation highlights the mutual communication processes between cultures.[44]

For theology after the cultural turn, this implies, as she finds, that the church not only has to learn to live with difference but has to acknowledge it as essential, as

---

[42] Ibid., p. 33.

[43] Beinert (1997), p. 321.

[44] Gruber (2018), p. 47.

Christian identity is profoundly intercultural.[45] Christians relate to God from the perspective of their culture whilst knowing that others equally do so from their background. Christian identities are constituted by that experience of difference. A theology that understands this constitutive significance of cultural disparity necessarily finds difference epistemologically relevant, as Gruber maintains. For this reason, theology and interculturality are intrinsically intertwined.

7.2.2 Unidirectional Law Planting

In this light, the interculturality of canon law seems to be a defining feature rather than a flaw. And indeed, global legislation derives inspiration from the local churches, as shown in Sect. 6.2. Several regulations on parish organisation, the teaching function of the church, and the administration of the sacraments have their roots in local practices. However, legislation still lacks an institutional feedback channel to stabilise the reciprocity of mutual learning. Thus, reception is frequently reduced to a mechanism of accepting the law without much attention to reciprocal dynamics. Wolfgang Beinert discovers this limited view of reception to be a historical development of the past centuries. When the church gave itself the constitution of an absolute monarchy, it transformed reception into a top-down practice transmitting centralist commands into the local churches.[46] One can discover the same dynamic in Neo-Scholastic mission concepts, which remained in place until the mid-twentieth century.[47] As mentioned in Sect. 4.1, mission was understood as church planting, including the establishment of all institutions a new church required, such as the law. While ecclesiology and mission theology have changed, canon law still cultivates remnants of this idea. The 1983 Code, as mentioned in Sect. 5.1.2, is not a radical reinvention but an updated version of the 1917 Code. Thus, the ecclesiology of the perfect society is still visible in the background of the reformed law. As a result, concepts such as church planting and its top-down imposition of goods onto the local churches are still operative in the law. This is reflected in the way the Code interprets legislation and how laws are received in a framework that could be called *law planting*. This paradigm has several consequences. One is that it endorses the idea that laws can easily be transplanted into different contexts. It is remarkable that this idea has prevailed despite the longstanding tradition of doubting the feasibility of comprehensive transplantations. It is revealing to read what English jurist and politician William Blackstone noted as early as 1765 in his *Commentaries on the Laws of England* when discussing how to deal with English law in the British colonies. Whilst Blackstone did not question the export of law

[45] See Gruber (2013), p. 204.

[46] See Beinert (1997), pp. 329–330.

[47] See Gruber (2018), pp. 16–17.

once British feet touched legal *terra nullius*, he was nevertheless aware of the limits of transplanting law into new territories:

> [I]f an uninhabited country be discovered and planted by English subjects, all the English laws then in being, which are the birthright of every subject, are immediately there in force. But it must be understood with very many and very great restrictions. Such colonists carry with them only so much of the English law, as is applicable to their own situation and the condition of the infant colony; such, for instance, as the general rules of inheritance, and of protection from personal injuries. The artificial refinements and distinctions incident to the property of a great and commercial people, the laws of police and revenue (such especially as are enforced by penalties), the mode of maintenance for the established clergy, the jurisdiction of spiritual courts, and a multitude of other provisions, are neither necessary nor convenient for them, and therefore are not in force.[48]

Hence, Blackstone was clear about the limits of law planting, even though he found much sense in a common constitutional frame and a framework of basic rights and duties. Thus, he seemed aware of the fact that the full imposition of British law onto the colonies would not support the flourishing of British life all over the globe but rather inhibit it. There is much to learn from his thoughts on the limits of law planting.

With its unidirectional view of reception, the concept of law planting has as a further effect, as Judith Gruber elucidates, that it cultivates a binary view of reception. She observes with regard to the missiological concept of church planting: "This binary coding of the mission process into active giver and passive receiver, into Christian civilization and heathen savagery, left no room for reflection on the processes of mutual exchange and transformation in which the communication of the Gospel between two cultures occurred."[49] Similarly, reception as law planting is not a dialectic concept. It is a one-way route upon which Roman commands travel to the local churches to be received there by the local Catholics, following the binary dynamic of command and obedience. The legal debates reveal that this narrow understanding of active giver and passive receiver is a challenge for legal transfer in general. As legal scholar Lena Foljanty observes, these debates have often failed to pay attention to the receiving community. One could therefore even question the use of reception as a concept, as she notes: "The concept of reception no longer proves to be sufficient; it is too closely related to a research tradition that perceived legal transfer as a one-way street from Europe to the world, aiming at mapping and measuring influences, only to proudly point out the significance of European law as a model that has been well copied or unfortunately misunderstood."[50] Canon law proves to be a typical European law in this respect, with a tendency to focus on its export to the world and to miss the essential contribution of the receiving churches.

The observation that legal transfers are often understood as being unidirectional alludes to their traditional association with colonialism. History, and particularly colonial history, has shown that what is neutrally called "transfer" often has an

[48] Blackstone (1983), p. 107.

[49] Gruber (2018), p. 20.

[50] Foljanty (2015), p. 5.

imperialistic tilt. Critical legal studies, since the 1970s, in its critique of public international law, has drawn attention to the fact that legal transfers have often relied on asymmetrical relations between colonisers and colonised groups. Whenever groups were colonised by alien powers, this usually entailed the imposition of alien law onto the subjugated societies or communities. Even today, legal transfer often resembles an asymmetrical, top-down endeavour rather than a mutual exchange. With this phenomenon in mind, one can speak of colonialism with regard to the law in a twofold sense, as Sally Merry explained. In a narrow sense, it relates to the export of European politics, economy, and culture into African, Asian, Latin American, and Pacific countries over the course of colonial history. In a broader sense, colonialism "is a relation between two or more groups of unequal power in which one not only controls and rules the other but also endeavours to impose its cultural order onto the subordinate group(s)."[51] With regard to current transplants, Esin Örücü asserts that legal exchanges have still not become symmetrical and reciprocal, with the effect that

> although the present time is not a period of imposition, as we do not any more encounter colonial relationships, neither is it one of voluntary reception. The time is one of imposed reception, that is, voluntary activity of import under circumstances in which exporters hold all the cards. There is still a tendency to assess the whole process from the point of view of the exporter rather than that of the importer, though the interest of the importer is more effectively fought for now.[52]

In a similar vein, Boaventura de Sousa Santos characterises legal globalisation as the production of asymmetrical relations: "It reproduces the hierarchy of the world system and the asymmetries among core, peripheral and semiperipheral societies."[53] And Antony Anghie sees a permanent danger connected with global laws on their "civilising mission" to replicate colonial and imperialist structures, as "[i]t was only because of colonialism that international law became universal".[54] Without colonial strategies, as he proposes, international law could not have become a global success. Based on his proposition one might assume that all effective international systems tend to recreate these patterns. One can consequently also expect canon law, with its aspiration to serve the global church, to have a tendency to embark on a civilising mission by subjugating the plural churches under its unifying roof. Hence, it is plausible to presume that canon law, like all global law, has a preference for asymmetrical transfers of legal rules between two unequal agents and, thus, is inclined to create colonialist patterns. In fact, Steven Bwana emphasises that the church's top-down and one-way view of lawmaking and reception raises a couple of questions in light of the debate on legal colonialism.[55] Whilst exports of canon law into the local churches try to avoid appearing as hegemonic impositions of the law, they pay little

---

[51] Merry (1991), p. 894.

[52] Örücü (2002), p. 213.

[53] De Sousa Santos (2020), p. 213.

[54] Anghie (2006), p. 742.

[55] See Bwana (1986), p. 104.

attention to the actual importers. This is problematic because these imbalances between the Apostolic See and the local churches can have a negative impact on the local Catholics. They are also ecclesiologically questionable if they marginalise the local churches, even though these churches are genuine constituents of the Church of Christ. Furthermore, sociologically, they can discourage legal subjects from accepting the law.

7.2.3 Reconstructing Rules

The asymmetrical structure of law planting concords with the inculturation approach of translation. The legislator's reliance on translation goes hand in hand with a speaker-oriented view, which helps to preserve the integrity of the message by granting a "minimal loss of information in transmission",[56] as Robert Schreiter explains. With regard to legal transfer, this is realised in an exporter-oriented approach, which protects the uniformity of global laws through unidirectional transfers in which the exporters dominate the field. Yet supreme legislation is not merely concerned with protecting the uniformity of the rules when transplanting them but also with preserving their uniform *meaning* throughout their relocation. By binding the decentralised agents not only to the legal texts but also to their meaning as produced in centralised contexts, law planting wants to ensure that legal rules undergo their transfer largely unaltered. However, as stated in Sect. 4.1, this idea is somewhat of a fiction. John Huels explained this when referring to legislation's futile attempt to protect a uniform meaning of canon law by obliging the legal subjects to abide by the authentic Latin text of global rules, as "having one official language for a universal law does not ensure that the law will have universal applicability, nor that it will be interpreted identically everywhere."[57] He gives the example of different implications of the term *right* in US-American legal language in comparison to canonical *ius*, the discrepancy deriving from the non-differentiation of *ius* and *lex* in the English language, which expresses both meanings by using the term *law*. He similarly refers to the challenge that the South African Tswana people do not distinguish terminologically between *rights* and *duties* but rely on the term *tshwanelo* to denote both dimensions of legal claims and obligations. He concludes: "While the words can be accurately translated, the context in which they are used is essential for determining their actual meaning."[58] This alludes to a wider consequence, namely that even if terms translate accurately into another language, they can still be attributed with a different meaning. Huels gives the example of canon 218 CIC/1983: "Those engaged in the sacred disciplines have a just freedom of enquiry and of expressing their opinion prudently on those matters in which they possess

---

[56] Schreiter (1985), p. 60.

[57] Huels (1987), pp. 252–253.

[58] Ibid., p. 253.

expertise, while observing the submission due to the magisterium of the church". While the canon might be terminologically undisputed, as he finds, it gives rise to various interpretations, depending on the interpreter's standpoint. Quite naturally, as he contends, a theological scholar or a Vatican official tends to interpret this canon in their own way: "Such a law is likely to be restructured much differently by an American university professor who highly esteems academic freedom than by a Vatican official charged with protecting unity of faith and discipline."[59] Hence, global rules, when transferred into the local churches, do not necessarily preserve their original meaning. In fact, it is more likely that reception alters their meaning.

It is helpful to read Judith Gruber to integrate Huels's observations into the greater context of intercultural theology. She describes the shift in intercultural theology from understanding culture as text to conceiving of it as translation.[60] However, translation, in this context, is not the reestablishment of an identical meaning in another context, as the traditional approach suggested, but is understood as a transformation that conveys fragile meaning through changeable signs. Instead of perceiving cultures as fixed entities that engage with each other via the exchange of signs which convey certain meaning, she interprets exchange processes as fluid generations of brittle meaning: "Cultures are always translated; their identity cannot be traced back to a permanent, essentialist basis. Instead of finding their 'roots,' we can only inquire about the 'routes' along which momentary identity constellations have travelled to crystallize in compositions and translation."[61] Socio-legal scholars have been discussing similar issues since the 1970s in debates on legal pluralism and legal transfer. Alan Watson, when describing the act of transplanting legal rules, mentions that transplants in their new context frequently receive a new meaning: "Transplanting frequently, perhaps always, involves legal transformation. Even when the transplanted rule remains unchanged, its impact in a new social setting can be different. The insertion of an alien rule into another complex system can cause it to operate in a fresh way."[62] Transplants, when received in their new home, start to develop an independent existence. Watson finds that "a rule once transplanted is different in its new home."[63] This is because legal transplants relocate norms, but not their cultural background, as "it is rules …, institutions, legal concepts, and structures that are borrowed, not the 'spirit' of a legal system."[64] Lena Foljanty similarly speaks of a *cultural translation* of transported law, thus indicating that transferring laws is a complex process of giving and receiving which includes not merely the textual translation of legal rules, but also touches upon legal thought, traditions, the cultural and political context, the possibilities and restrictions of expressing a legal thought in a certain language, and the habitus of legal professionals: "All these

[59] Ibid., p. 254.

[60] See Gruber (2018), pp. 68–70.

[61] Ibid., p. 69.

[62] Watson (1993), p. 116.

[63] Watson (2000), p. 2.

[64] Ibid.

factors set up the framework in which law is practiced, and it is this framework that starts shifting the moment that it comes into contact with foreign law."[65] With this in mind, it seems impossible to understand translation as the transfer of a legal thought into another language which expresses the same meaning in that new language. Whilst Foljanty also relies on the term "translation" to describe legal transfer, she evidently attributes it with a different meaning compared to mission theology and intercultural theology. Translation, thus, does not denote the expression of the same meaning in another language, but always entails the emergence of a new meaning after transplantation.

Due to this finding that rules receive another meaning whenever they find a new home, one might ask what this reveals about the act of transplantation itself. One may indeed doubt whether transplanting legal rules is truly a transfer of laws. In this sense, some legal sociologists criticise the idea of legal rules transcending the borders of legal systems. Gunther Teubner, for instance, questioned whether the term "transplantation" is appropriate for describing the fact that legal norms transferred into another environment usually become "legal irritants" there and develop a new life detached from their old one. Whilst speaking of transplantation suggests that the transferred rule is identical before and after its introduction into a new context, one has to understand the transplant "as a fundamental irritation which triggers a whole series of new and unexpected events."[66] As they challenge the receiving legal order, integrating transplants, as Teubner finds, is not merely a process of adapting the rules to their new contexts. Instead, "they will unleash an evolutionary dynamic in which the external rule's meaning will be reconstructed and the internal context will undergo fundamental change."[67] Together with legal scholar Marie Theres Fögen, he therefore suggested perceiving legal transplantations as acts of *reconstructing* rules in another context.[68] This act of reconstruction attributes the rules with another meaning. Thus, legal transplants, if one wants to call them that, always undergo reinterpretation and resignification in the receiving legal culture. Pierre Legrand describes this inevitable change of meaning as a process whereby "a crucial element of the ruleness of the rule—its meaning—does not survive the journey from one legal system to another."[69] For Legrand it is therefore clear that legal transplants do not exist. As the meaning of a legal rule is an integral part of its "ruleness", the transplantation of a rule is not a transplantation of the very same rule but the creation of a different one:

> So, the transplant does not, in effect, happen: a key feature of the rule—its meaning—stays behind so that the rule that was 'there', in effect, is not itself displaced over 'here'. Assuming a common language, the position is as follows: there was one rule (inscribed words a + meaning x), and there is now a second rule elsewhere (inscribed words a + meaning y). It is

[65] Foljanty (2015), p. 7.

[66] Teubner (1998), p. 12.

[67] Ibid.

[68] See Fögen and Teubner (2005), p. 45.

[69] Legrand (1997), p. 117.

> not the same rule. … The borrowed form of words thus rapidly finds itself indigenized on account of the host culture's inherent integrative capacity.[70]

For global canon law, this observation raises the question of whether global rules, after being received in the local churches, are still the same rules. Following Legrand, it is more accurate to understand them as reconstructions of the original rule. Hence, successful global legislation and reception is the creation of rules—legal texts with a certain meaning—which, through transplantation, undergo reconstruction so that they result in new rules—the identical texts with *different* meanings—in the local churches.

7.2.4 Disruptive Encounters

In any case, this reconstruction may also not be successful. It can fail and result in a transplanted rule that has no local meaning. Gunther Teubner finds this outcome highly probable. He studies the failure of transplants by investigating transplants that become irritants in the receiving legal order. Teubner sees one difficulty of successful transplanting in the fact that the transplants resonate not only in the legal but also in the social realm. Legal institutions have a legal side and a social side—Teubner describes them as Janus-faced realities. Hence, transplants have repercussions in legal and social discourse, which influence each other. An effective transfer of a rule requires the rule to form a connection between the legal and the social discourse, thus becoming part of the receiving group's "binding arrangements". Yet this is unlikely to work, as Teubner assumes, since the transplant causes continuous disruption to the regeneration of existing binding arrangements. It might be easy to imagine a transplant being accepted within legal discourse: "On the legal side of the binding institution, the rule will be recontextualised in the new network of legal distinctions and it may still be recognisable as the original legal rule even if its legal interpretation changes."[71] But reception is more complicated in social discourse: "The legal impulse, if it is recognised as well, will create perturbations in the other social system and will trigger there some changes covered by the internal logics of this world of meaning. It will be reconstructed in the different language of the social system involved, reformulated in its codes and programmes".[72] This social reformulation of the transplant then triggers events on the legal side, as Teubner argues, as it interferes in the legal discourse. This mutual irritation of the legal and the social sphere can continue more or less indefinitely and prevent the transplant from becoming an effective rule in the receiving order. He perceives several ways in which legal systems react to this constant irritation. These range from outright rejection of the

[70] Ibid., p. 118.

[71] Teubner (1998), p. 28.

[72] Ibid.

transplant to "cool indifference",[73] as the receiving group ignores the transplant and turns it into a dead letter. What Teubner also anticipates is that the continuous disruption can damage the binding arrangements and disturb the connection between legal and social discourse. Alternatively, a group can preserve the connection by fundamentally altering the transplanted concept. In this case, the transplant will develop a life of its own, changing its meaning profoundly. Teubner therefore concludes that it is difficult to speak of legal transplants—and more appropriate to speak of legal *irritants*. Thus, in his view, transplantation typically fails to achieve its aims. Whilst it frequently aims at creating greater unity and uniformity of legal systems—Teubner has the European project of an "ever closer union" in mind—it often has the opposite effect. With regard to European legislation and its intention to harmonise European law, he finds that these processes rarely bring about "a convergence of the participating legal orders, but rather the creation of new cleavages in the interrelation of operationally closed social discourses."[74] Instead of creating more unity, they create constant irritation and resistance against the legal intrusions. "New dissonances from harmonisation!",[75] as he concludes.

If Teubner is right to assume that transplanted rules either irritate the receiving group or blend in by changing their meaning so that it accords with the local arrangements, it is plausible that similar responses occur in the local churches. The transplant might be rejected outright or coolly ignored, might damage the existing binding arrangements, or might find acceptance after having been modified in meaning to reconnect the legal and social discourses. Examples of outright rejection are rare, in any case. Due to ecclesiastical law planting by way of solicited imposition and imposed reception, global rules frequently defy outright rejection. As mentioned, the diocesan bishops have only limited possibilities for preventing global laws from coming into force in their local churches. Local authorities commonly fulfil their duty as agents of transmission and formally integrate these laws into their jurisdictions. However, whilst outright rejection is uncommon, legal transplants often meet with more tacit rejection. Bishops, for instance, refuse to enforce the alien rules within their churches. As referenced by way of example, some German bishops do not enforce the oath of fidelity when endowing individuals with offices mentioned in canon 833 CIC/1983. Generally speaking, they act as agents of transmission and tolerate the Roman directive, but fail to act as agents of innovation by bringing it to life, turning the transplant into mere law on paper. Similarly, agents of conservation, such as the ecclesiastical tribunals and administrative bodies, can decline to apply a law. Local Catholics can ignore it or abide merely by those laws they find supportive of their communities. These reactions describe forms of tacit rejection that transplants meet on a regular basis.

There are many cases though which are slightly more ambiguous. As a complete rejection of legal transplants is frequently not an option due to the asymmetrical

---

[73] Ibid.

[74] Ibid., p. 32.

[75] Ibid., p. 20.

power relations, law planting often results in the formation of hybrid legal systems which connect global rules and local praxis in some way but do not fully implement the transplants. These legal systems attempt to reconcile the transplanted laws and the local culture with each other formally, but without allowing the alien law to impact the social discourses to any greater degree. Gunther Teubner's theory of legal irritants and Robert Schreiter's considerations on syncretistic religious systems help to understand these hybrid arrangements. Schreiter studied the reception of religious signs transferred into another culture and the culture's reaction to the enforced entrance of these signs, which he called an "invasion".[76] Whenever Christianity enters non-Christian cultures, this often results in syncretism as the merging of two religious systems. Schreiter named several reasons why the entering elements fail to persuade so that parallel and even competing elements remain powerful within the receiving culture. These are discussed in the following—in dialogue with Teubner's theory of legal irritants—to better understand the local churches' responses to global legal transplants.

7.2.5 *Cool Indifference*

One reason for conflicts between sign systems, which Schreiter discovers, is that the newly introduced signs only superficially touch upon the receiving culture so that "the encounter with the invading culture is incomplete."[77] The entering signs do not relate to the signs that convey meaning in that culture, so it seems evident to the members of the receiving culture that these new signs cannot adequately address their concerns. As a result, "[t]he invading sign system remains 'foreign'; it does not effectively penetrate either the world-view or the group-boundary-formation process of the receiving culture. It is held at arm's length."[78] Schreiter's words offer an alternative description of the reaction to legal transplants which Gunther Teubner called "cool indifference".[79] The transplanted elements remain present in the receiving culture but become isolated in their new context without having a profound impact on social discourse. Many global rules thus enter the local churches formally, yet some of them do not find meaning there and are subsequently disregarded by local Catholics. While global canon law is valid law in the Peruvian Andes,[80] it only partly impacts the pastoral ministry in that region. For many African churches, Steven Bwana sees canon law in one line with other cultural imports which have not been fully accepted in African contexts: "The Continental system brought by the French and Portuguese proved alien to Africans. The Anglo-Saxon tradition was

[76] Schreiter (1985), pp. 155–156.

[77] Ibid., p. 155.

[78] Ibid.

[79] Teubner (1998), p. 28.

[80] See Dammert Bellido (1986), pp. 115–116.

and remains too complex to be admired by the majority of the people as promoting justice."[81] In a similar vein, as Bwana reckons, Roman Catholic canon law never gained a firm foothold in many African local churches. Many local Catholics adopted an indifferent attitude towards it in order to prevent the law from damaging the binding arrangements between the legal and social spheres. Scholar of comparative law and legal anthropology Salvatore Mancuso observes accordingly that "many institutions and organizations indicated in the Code of Canon Law are set up in certain ecclesial communities in Africa but remain unoperative [sic]."[82]

Another reason why cultures adhere to their old signs instead of embracing new ones, as Schreiter discerns, is because the new signs fail to respond convincingly to challenges posed in a particular context, so that "the local culture accepts the sign system of the invading culture, but believes that there are still problems that the invading culture's sign system does not adequately handle."[83] Old signs therefore remain in force to respond to the needs to which the new ones do not answer properly, because they "seem too abstract, too concerned with words, and not sufficiently able to meet the day-to-day needs".[84] This observation resonates with many Catholics' experiences with canon law. Historian Patricia Goler expressed similar thoughts in the 1970s, when analysing the relevance of the law in responding to the needs of black American Catholics. She connected the failure of the Catholic Church to combat racial segregation by its parish organisation and school policy with the failure of canon law to address black concerns, observing: "Up to this point the relationship between the Church and the black community has been marked by paternalism and irrelevance. Therefore, it should come as no surprise that in the black community, canon law is usually considered irrelevant."[85] Goler collected several examples of situations in which black Catholics encountered the limited use of the law:

> Most black Catholics have heard that there is someplace where people with money can go to get it fixed so they can get married again and remain in the Church. … Many times we have been told that we can't get rid of a particular pastor, or have a voice in the selection of the next Archbishop of Washington, or have a separate liturgical rite because 'it's against canon law.'[86]

As the law does not provide black Catholics with any support, they have widely learnt to ignore it, as Goler found. She concluded that "canon law or canon lawyers—they aren't real to the average black Catholic."[87] However, her analysis went further to note that even if black Catholics took the law for real, it would offer them little help. She gave the example of black Catholics approaching an ecclesiastical

[81] Bwana (1986), p. 104.

[82] Mancuso (2024), p. 80.

[83] Schreiter (1985), p. 156.

[84] Ibid.

[85] Goler (1972), p. 295.

[86] Ibid.

[87] Ibid.

tribunal in a marriage case, only to find that the tribunal staff had little knowledge of black communities and their understanding of marriage and family. Her description reflects Schreiter's considerations on alien cultural signs which formally enter a community but do not adequately handle the local challenges and therefore fail to be thoroughly received there. Studying the Code of Canon Law, other examples come to mind. As mentioned, José Dammert Bellido challenged the rules on ecclesiastical administration for their origin in European contexts, displaying a perception of dioceses as urban organisations with a professional apparatus of modern bureaucracy, a view of administration which did not connect with his experiences as an Andean bishop.[88] He also alluded to the obligation which the Code stipulates in canon 948 CIC/1983 to apply separate masses for single intentions, which he found an improbable task for overburdened Andean priests, rendering this a rule which makes no sense in the Andes. Instead, Andean priests would usually celebrate masses for shared intentions in conflict with the law, ignoring the law to adequately respond to the pastoral needs of rural communities.

Ecclesiastical jurisprudence, in any case, tends to ignore this ignorance. At least it fails to attribute any theoretical relevance to the ineffectiveness of the laws in many contexts. The doctrine of *receptio legis* provides the legal subjects with a tool to express dissent, invalidating laws that prove detrimental to their communities. However, the power of this instrument was relinquished in order to protect the unity of canon law. By attributing cool indifference towards the law an invalidating effect only in cases where the total non-reception of a law becomes evident—as in those manifest cases such as the Apostolic Constitution *Veterum Sapientia*—jurisprudence ignores the manifold cases in which laws are not fully rejected but widely ignored. This leads to peculiar results. Laws that the local Catholics meet with indifference remain valid laws, even though they fail to impact local church life. Bertram Griffin collected a bundle of examples from the 1917 Code which the US-American churches had widely ignored:

> Canon 356 demanded that every diocese hold a synod every ten years. This law was observed in the period immediately after the promulgation of the 1917 code, but the custom was finally abandoned. Canon 711 demands that a Confraternity of Christian Doctrine and a Confraternity of the Blessed Sacrament be established in every parish. In the American church the Confraternity of Christian Doctrine became widely rooted in Catholic life. I know of no parish where a Confraternity of the Blessed Sacrament exists. Canon 753 reminded pastors that they were to fast before an adult baptism. Pastors don't even know about this law. Canon 78 [sic, the correct canon is 788, remark by the author] of the 1917 code established the ordinary age of confirmation at seven years old, the same age as for First Communion. The American church accepted First Communion at the age of seven, but continued to delay confirmation until the end of grade school. Canons 1128 to 1132 have a legal process for 'separation from bed and board' rarely used in the American church. Canon 1236 refers to the sharing of the funeral stipend among several parishes which did not become customary in our country. Canon 1520 requires every diocese to have a finance council. This was not totally received by the American church.[89]

---

[88] See Dammert Bellido (1986), pp. 113–114.

[89] Griffin (1984), pp. 24–25.

Griffin's examples raise the question of what difference it made that all of these laws remained valid laws when they ultimately became law on paper without much meaning for American Catholics. Whilst acknowledging non-reception only in manifest cases protects the formal uniformity of the law, the law so protected becomes ineffective or even irritating within certain contexts.

7.2.6 *Competing Claims*

A further challenge that obstructs the reception of legal transplants in the local churches results from what Robert Schreiter calls *double belonging*. It hinders the reception of alien signs in receiving cultures, because "the invading sign system and the local sign system are seen as dealing with two different things."[90] He understands this problem as becoming particularly acute with respect to intercultural identities, giving the following example to elucidate it: "How can I venerate my ancestors by praying for them as Christians do, since my ancestors were Buddhist? Only the Buddhist rites provide proper veneration."[91] Theologian Michael Muonwe describes similar phenomena with regard to Nigeria, noting that "many Nigerian Christians see Christianity as not addressing their deep yearnings".[92] This poses the challenge of how to deal with the exclusivism of Catholicism in those cases in which an exclusivist view is incompatible with local identities. With regard to the law one encounters similar dilemmas, as double belonging in a legal sense is a typical consequence of legal pluralism. John Huels relates to the experience shared by many Catholics as subjects of different and sometimes competing legal systems:

> Individuals are usually exposed to several legal systems simultaneously and to the 'laws' and conventions of every group to which they belong. Sometimes the laws or norms of one group may conflict with those of another, and individuals must choose between competing loyalties, or else, if they are not free to choose, they are forced to observe a norm of the group which has the most power to enforce it.[93]

He goes on to substantiate his observation with an example taken from an African context:

> A missionary once lamented that after arduously preparing a sermon in an African language and driving a great distance to celebrate Sunday Mass, he found that the whole congregation had been ordered to appear elsewhere at a civic function organized by the local chief. The Church's law of the Sunday obligation, which has only moral sanctions to enforce it, could not match the 'law' of the chief who had quite tangible power of coercion.[94]

---

[90] Schreiter (1985), p. 156.

[91] Ibid.

[92] Hall and Muonwe (2017), p. 64.

[93] Huels (1987), pp. 277–278.

[94] Ibid., p. 278.

Huels's example reveals a special case of Teubner's cool indifference. It reconciles conflicting claims deriving from the transplanted and the local rule by creating a hierarchical scheme, subordinating the transplant to the local rule. Hence, the transplant is not per se rejected but is widely ignored, as only by doing this the group can fulfil the established social commitments.

Further examples come to mind, such as Catholics brought up in liberal and democratic societies dealing with competing legal claims with the help of indifference. Due to their socialisation as legal subjects of modern secular law, global canon law often fails to fulfil many Catholics' expectations of law due to its less liberal and non-democratic constitution. Whilst liberal state law grants freedom of speech, canon law restricts it (see canon 212 §3 CIC/1983). Whilst state law assures freedom of science, canon law confines it (see canon 218 CIC/1983). Whilst state law commits to the equality of women and men, canon law excludes women from ordination (see canon 1024 CIC/1983) and subsequently from obtaining ecclesiastical offices endowed with the power of orders or the power to govern the church (see canon 274 §1 CIC/1983). Certainly, neither state law nor canon law claims exclusivism with regard to legal belonging. Furthermore, as legal pluralism shows, it is rather normal for individuals to find themselves subject to different legal systems. Yet it can nevertheless be difficult to reconcile competing claims and to integrate irreconcilable expectations. Following Schreiter, this conflict commonly prompts individuals to find that the transplanted "sign system is alien, inferior, inadequate, or not to the point."[95] For contemporary Catholics socialised in liberal orders, the law they are less familiar with is frequently Roman Catholic canon law—and not the law of their states—which is why they tend to perceive canon law as more alien. Hence, they can be expected to usually reconcile conflicting claims by disregarding canon law in favour of the established binding arrangements of secular legal and social discourse.

7.2.7 *Inferior Intruders*

Robert Schreiter observes that there are also cases where signs forcefully enter a culture and are tolerated there precisely for being so powerful, yet continue to be seen as being symbolically inferior to established signs. Therefore, "it becomes a point of pride to keep the two sign systems separate, even while giving the necessary obeisance to the sign system of the invading culture."[96] His observation is helpful to explain the precarious stance of many legal transplants. While the new rules might enforce compliance, this does not necessarily indicate their acceptance. On the contrary, as Schreiter finds, enforced compliance with new signs might even attribute the original system with more meaning, contributing to its symbolic capital.

[95] Schreiter (1985), p. 157.

[96] Ibid., p. 156.

This analysis is also helpful to understand many Catholics' stance towards global canon law. While they cannot prevent its imposition onto their churches and a formal adherence to it, they can resist attributing these rules with profound meaning. In their stead, they cultivate alternative norms that serve as true sources of meaning. One can witness this phenomenon in many German parishes where parish structure, pastoral offices, and liturgical life seem to accord with global rules, whilst pastoral praxis differs to a notable extent. Here, we find laypeople preaching the homily in Sunday mass against the regulation of canon 767 §1 CIC/1983, or pastors who, even before *Fiducia Supplicans*, blessed homosexual couples in solemn liturgical rites, against the express prohibition of the Congregation for the Doctrine of the Faith.[97] While few bishops or parish priests openly resist global law, they often support alternative sign systems that provide local communities with different interpretations of Catholic practice. Many German Catholics regard these alternative normative frameworks, which allow for greater lay participation and embrace various forms of lifelong partnerships, as more credible than Roman rules.

Another example where competing rules weaken the acceptance of canon law is canonical marriage and family issues in many African communities. With regard to marriage, Steven Bwana outrightly states: "There is nothing in the Code which is more touchy for most Christians in Africa than marriage."[98] In a similar vein, Peter Hebblethwaite mentioned that marriage, for many African churches, "is a crucial instance of non-inculturation".[99] Many Catholics refuse to marry in canonical form, as they do not feel the canonical view of marriage represents their understanding of marriage as a gradual process ranging over several steps from betrothal to the birth of children.[100] This clash of marriage and family concepts has repercussions in several legal issues. Many scholars mention the opposition of African Catholics to the fact that sterility is no ground for the invalidity of marriages according to canon law (see canon 1084 §3 CIC/1983), as begetting children from a marriage is a crucial aspect for many couples and intimately connected with their concept of marriage.[101] John Huels adds the observation: "That a marriage be considered indissoluble before children are born is nonsensical for many of the world's peoples."[102] Due to this finding, many couples prefer to enter a traditional customary marriage, which

[97] See Congregation for the Doctrine of the Faith (2021a).

[98] Bwana (1986), p. 105; see also Busugutsala (1987), pp. 46–62; Mwaungulu (1996), p. 82; Orobator (1996), pp. 9–18.

[99] Hebblethwaite (1994), p. 8.

[100] Steven Bwana is careful to demand legal change but diplomatically alludes to the option of understanding marriages as consumed only after the birth of the first child, see Bwana (1986), p. 106. Without suggesting changing canon law accordingly, he paves the way for integrating that thought into an African rereading of canon law. Other scholars discuss the option of a *marriage by stages* or a marriage catechumenate, allowing couples to approach a sacramental marriage over a course of steps, including the begetting of their first children, e.g. Kisembo et al. (1977), pp. 25–28; de Mûelenaere (1985a), pp. 73–84; Orobator (1996), p. 15.

[101] See Kisembo et al. (1977), pp. 24–25; de Mûelenaere (1985a), pp. 93–99; Bwana (1986), p. 106; Orobator (1996), pp. 12–16.

[102] Huels (1987), p. 276.

they find more suitable for protecting their family values. Rephrased in Schreiter's terms, these couples find the values protected by canonical marriage, such as the indissolubility of the bond between the spouses, inferior to those preserved in traditional customary marriage with its focus on the begetting of children and the role of the wider family. Other couples enter a canonical marriage formally, without embracing the canonical concept, which often leads to invalid marriages. Hebblethwaite records: "The imposition of Roman canon law means that a very large number of marriages—the figure 80 percent has been cited—are technically invalid".[103] Anglican theologian Benezeri Kisembo and his Catholic colleagues Laurenti Magesa and Aylward Shorter made the same observation in their ecumenical study, *African Christian Marriage*.[104] Hence, legal transplants such as ecclesiastical marriage law fail to synchronise the legal and social discourses around marriage in many African churches so that they do not become part of the established binding arrangements. Decoupled from social discourse they remain rather isolated, while at the same time contributing to the symbolic capital of alternative normative frameworks.

7.2.8 Irreconcilable Values

Studying current canon law also reveals cases in which the transplantation of global rules disrupts the connection between legal and social discourse and obstructs the development of binding arrangements with regard to the transplants, thus preventing the receiving group from realising their needs. José Dammert Bellido mentions one example from his experience. Whilst he welcomed the fact that the 1983 Code gave rural bishops more opportunities to employ laypeople in pastoral ministry and the administration of certain sacraments, he believed the legal reform did not go far enough as it did not allow laypeople to administer the anointing of the sick in remote areas. For Dammert Bellido, restricting its administration to priests as ministers, as established by doctrine and law,[105] makes it an impossible sacrament to administer in remote areas where priests visit their various congregations only a couple of times over the course of the year. As a result, the anointing of the sick is "a non-existent sacrament in the Andes."[106] Hence, according to Dammert Bellido, the rule that only priests can administer the anointing of the sick to priests deprives many Andean Christians of sacramental consolation, disrupting the connection between the legal and the pastoral discourse.

Further examples come to mind. Robert Schreiter refers to the dilemma which the rule of canon 924 §3 CIC/1983—to use grape wine as a Eucharistic

[103] Hebblethwaite (1994), p. 8.

[104] See Kisembo et al. (1977), p. 22.

[105] See Catechism of the Catholic Church (1992), no. 1516; canon 1003 §1 CIC/1983.

[106] Dammert Bellido (1986), p. 116.

species—poses in countries where grape wine is uncommon or alcohol is forbidden, by asking: "How was one to celebrate the Eucharist in countries that were Muslim theocracies and forbade the production or importation of fermented beverages?"[107] Christians socialised in cultures in which wine is regarded as a forbidden substance, connected with immorality and excess, cannot readjust their social discourse to concord with canon 924 §3 CIC/1983. Instead the legal transplant will remain a constant irritant. Schreiter also alludes to the challenge of celebrating baptism among Maasai Christians in East Africa by following the rules on baptism, which essentially require the immersion in or pouring of water over the head of the individual to be baptised.[108] Many Maasai believe that pouring water on a woman's head is a curse that can result in the woman's infertility. It is impossible to imagine how Catholic baptismal law could stop being an irritant to the Maasai people and become part of binding arrangements in Maasai culture. Instead one can expect it to constantly disrupt the connection between the legal and the social. In a similar vein, Anscar Chupungco mentions that in many Southeast Asian cultures the laying on of hands on the head of an individual is a social taboo.[109] Touching another person's head as the most sacred part of the body is considered insulting. This is a challenge for the administration of confirmation and ordination, where the ministers impose their hands on the recipients as an essential element of the sacramental matter,[110] and for the anointing of the sick, which regularly includes the touching of the receiver's forehead.[111]

A similar disconnection between the legal and the social discourse applies to regulations such as obliging the clergy to live celibately (see canon 277 §1 CIC/1983). For many African clerics from backgrounds where being married and having children is of key importance and where living celibately is regarded as cursing one's parents,[112] a harmonisation of canonical rule and social expectations is not at hand. As the rule on celibacy violates many Africans' family values, it is impossible to achieve an equilibrium between legal and social discourse. This is also the case in some regions with regard to so-called levirate marriages, where men marry the wives of their deceased brothers to provide them and their deceased brothers with children, as John Huels observes. In contrast to perceptions prevalent in the Global North, "[t]he woman whom the surviving brother espouses is not considered *his* wife, but the wife of the deceased brother, and her children are not his children but those of their dead *pater*."[113] Consequently, it would be impossible to reconcile

---

[107] Schreiter (1985), p. 2.

[108] See Catechism of the Catholic Church (1992), no. 1239; canon 849 CIC/1983.

[109] See Chupungco (1992), p. 81.

[110] For confirmation see Catechism of the Catholic Church (1992), no. 1300; canon 880 §1 CIC/1983; for ordination see Catechism of the Catholic Church (1992), no. 1573; canon 1009 §2 CIC/1983.

[111] See Catechism of the Catholic Church (1992), nos. 1513, 1531; canon 998 CIC/1983.

[112] See Schreiter (1985), p. 2.

[113] Huels (1987), p. 266; see also de Mûelenaere (1985a), pp. 86–93.

this view with the common perception of marriage in the Global North, with potential conflicts for the parties whenever canon law comes into play. Huels asks:

> How does the missionary explain to a convert in this situation that canon law will not allow him to take a wife of his own because, according to our perception, he is already married when he knows he is not? How does the missionary convince the people that the levirate is immoral when in their culture it is not only morally good but is even noble and virtuous?[114]

Huels finds this conflict impossible to resolve without either compromising the family values of the local Christians or the ecclesiastical doctrine and law on marriage. Steven Bwana refers to a related issue, the role of polygamy as a social reality in some African communities, which he himself views critically.[115] Schreiter, for his part, criticises the one-sided view of the Global North to regard polygamy largely as an issue of male dominance over women and of sexual exploitation, whereas it might also be an instrument that provides for women and gives them some economic security, particularly in rural areas.[116] Canonical transplants of marriage law cut the tie between existing legal and social discourses on the issue of polygamy and can therefore damage existing binding arrangements to the detriment of those who currently derive some social security from the institution of polygamy.

As already mentioned, some scholars guess that about 80 per cent of marriages among African Christians do not conform to the church's view of marriage and are invalid from the legal point of view.[117] This has some further legal and social effects, as "many people are denied communion on those grounds",[118] as Peter Hebblethwaite noted in his 1994 coverage of the Synod of African Bishops in Rome. A typical Vatican response to this problem consists of suggesting couples undergo a marriage nullity procedure if their marriage fails. However, as Huels observes, this is not an option for many Catholics from cultures in which taking legal action and bringing disputes to the courts has a negative connotation: "Among many African cultures the object of customary justice is reconciliation, restoring harmony between individuals and clans through mediation and compromise, and ensuring that the reputation of neither disputant is irreparably harmed."[119] Legal action, on the contrary, is suspected of obstructing the parties' reconciliation by creating winners and losers, thus endangering social peace. As a result, many African Catholics would not consider a marriage annulment. Huels refuses to shrug off this finding as a unique cultural phenomenon among African Catholics. Instead, he places the burden upon legislature to rethink whether a concept that seems inadequate to many Catholics should be part of the law for the entire Catholic Church. He proposes a revision of the law in light of these conflicts by viewing them through a cross-cultural lens: "A cross-cultural approach to the interpretation and application of canon law would

---

[114] Huels (1987), p. 266.

[115] See Bwana (1986), p. 107.

[116] See Schreiter (1985), p. 2.

[117] E.g. Kisembo et al. (1977), p. 22.

[118] Hebblethwaite (1994), p. 8.

[119] Huels (1987), p. 275.

include the question of whether the annulment process is not fundamentally alienating and offensive to the sensibilities of peoples in cultures whose approach to the settling of disputes is wholly different from the contentious process of European and other legal systems."[120]

Huels adds one even deeper concern, as he sees cases where the law as such seems irreconcilable with local values. He mentions China, as Confucian traditions have little esteem for the law as a medium of organising social life: "In Confucianism, a ruler must govern by means of virtue rather than law; the moral uprightness of the ruler serves as the example for the proper behavior of the subjects."[121] The law, in contrast, is regarded as a subordinate instrument directing those who fail to adhere to their moral compass. For Catholics who share this idea of the law as a substitute for better instruments of social organisation, it can be difficult to accept canon law as the common framework for organising church life.

7.2.9 Altered Meaning

There are also examples where a transplanted rule becomes meaningful in its new context, but only through a radical change of its meaning—one of the ways Gunther Teubner identified in how communities deal with irritating transplants. Peter Hebblethwaite made such an observation in the context of the African Synod in 1994. He proposed that the shortage of priests in many African churches "has led to a situation described as 'eucharistic famine' in which a priest visits an out-station only once or twice a year".[122] He found that "for many people the Catholic church is becoming a word-based church rather than a eucharistic church. It has become a standard joke: 'The Catholic church turns people into Protestants.'"[123] This connects with Teubner's observation about how to overcome the irritation caused by a legal transplant, namely by fundamentally *altering* the meaning of the transplant so that it succeeds in reconnecting the legal and the social discourse. The official meaning of canon 900 §1 CIC/1983, which solely attributes priests with the capacity to administer the Eucharist, is that the Eucharist as the "fount and apex of the whole Christian life"[124] is celebrated validly by those with the capacity to act in the person of Christ the head. However, in churches with a scarcity of ministers, the rule can develop the meaning that the Eucharist is of lesser importance than the liturgy of the word, as infrequent celebrations of the Eucharist cannot support its social meaning as the fundamental constituent of Christian life. Hence, canon 900 CIC/1983 ceases to be an irritant by attributing the Eucharist with a new meaning.

---

[120] Ibid.

[121] Ibid., p. 274.

[122] Hebblethwaite (1994), p. 8.

[123] Ibid.

[124] Second Vatican Council (1964), no. 11. Acta Apostolicae Sedis (1965), p. 15.

Further examples might support this finding, such as the rule to celebrate the Eucharist using the Eucharistic species of wheat bread and grape wine,[125] which poses difficulties in some contexts. In cultures where the use of wheat bread is uncommon, the species can fail to symbolise real food and nourishment and, thus, can be unsuitable for conveying its sacramental meaning. The hosts are even sometimes considered magical objects,[126] as Robert Schreiter notes, due to their alien appearance for the celebrating community. John Huels alludes to the same example: "In many parts of the world, wheat bread or grape wine are exotic and can be difficult to obtain, and instead of being perceived as the food 'which earth has given' and the drink as 'the work of human hands,' they tend to be regarded by newly Christianized people as magical elements."[127] Here one can likewise observe that a reconnection between the legal and the social side of the transplant works by changing the meaning of the transplant from symbolic matter to magical object.

7.2.10 Lack of Meaning

That the law fails to adequately relate to the local realities in the above-mentioned cases is frequently due to its conflict with competing norms—be they legal, social, or moral—the claims of which convince the local Catholics more than the legal rules. That they find the competing claims more persuasive might be for various reasons, ranging from external pressure—such as in Huels's example of the local chief having more power over the local population than the missionary—over communal conviction, to personal belief in their greater value. Social beliefs are particularly influential for the acceptance or non-acceptance of legal transplants. Whenever canon law proves to be compatible with the receiving communities' viewpoints, it stands a good chance of finding approval as a reconstructed rule with a local meaning. Whenever it conflicts with the prevalent view of the law, acceptance is naturally low. These collisions can have several reasons. As discussed, they may be due to irreconcilable views of what constitutes law or the role of law in religious communities. Alternatively, they may be due to rules failing to adequately address local circumstances and needs. In many cases, lawmaking had European churches in mind when modelling rules for the global church. Canons on the organisation of parish ministry regulate communal life mainly for urban situations and developed rural areas. Norms on ecclesiastical administration and the bishop's curia expect wealthy dioceses with a professional workforce supporting the bishops' administration. Churches that do not provide for similar conditions find it difficult to receive these laws, reconstruct their meaning, and bring them to life. In some cases, the law even fails to make any sense in the local churches. This is the case when transplanted

[125] See Catechism of the Catholic Church (1992), no. 1412; canon 924 §§2 and 3 CIC/1983.

[126] See Schreiter (1985), p. 2.

[127] Huels (1987), p. 281.

rules are incompatible with local systems of meaning, either because they do not connect with local fabrics of meaning or because they connect with a meaning detrimental to their acceptance. In these cases the transplant creates cultural miscommunication, often disconnecting the legal and the social discourse.

Robert Schreiter elucidates this by referring to the example of celibacy. In the context where celibacy developed, it has been connected with an idea derived from Matthew 19:12, where Jesus links sexual abstinence with keeping oneself uncommitted to worldly things "for the sake of the kingdom of heaven". Hence, celibacy in traditional Western theology stands as a sign for men designating themselves to a specific service to the church to serve it with an undivided heart as the earthly anticipation of the kingdom of heaven. Canon 277 §1 CIC/1983 rules accordingly that "clerics are obliged to observe perfect and perpetual continence for the sake of the kingdom of heaven and therefore are bound to celibacy which is a special gift of God by which sacred ministers can adhere more easily to Christ with an undivided heart and are able to dedicate themselves more freely to the service of God and humanity". However, this connection between celibacy and the kingdom of heaven is dissolving in many churches, in both the Global North and South. Schreiter observes:

> Many members of local churches, including bishops, have communicated to central Roman Catholic authority their doubts about the relative value of this sign system in their culture, particularly when it seems to be a principal cause of the shortage of applicants for the priesthood, on the one hand, and a scandal to the church, on the other, because of the practice of concubinage. Hence a sign system long part of the discipline of the Western church is not only not communicating the message for which it was intended, but has become a countersign to the detriment of the local church.[128]

In addition, as Peter Hebblethwaite noted, because celibacy discourages candidates from entering the priesthood, it is also regarded by many Catholics as being co-responsible for depriving their local communities of the Eucharist: "Much of the eucharistic famine could end if married men were ordained as they are in other non-Latin rites. That was first suggested as early as 1534, before the Council of Trent. The papal nuncio, Marco Vigerio della Rovere, wrote to the cardinal secretary of state: 'In my view it is necessary to grant the priests of the Congo permission to marry, just as was done in the case of the Maronites in Syria and Lebanon under Pope Leo X (1513–21).'"[129] Today, many Catholics, clerics and laypeople alike, see celibacy mainly as a source of hardship. It has no meaningful repercussions in their social discourse and is rarely identified as a symbol of the kingdom of heaven. On the contrary, in the eyes of many Catholics, it fails to make any sense.

---

[128] Schreiter (1985), p. 98.

[129] Hebblethwaite (1994), p. 8.

7.2.11 Culture Clashes

These disparities between meanings of signs as used in the law and in social discourse can result not only in miscommunication but also in profound clashes whenever divergent sign systems collide over the meaning of particular signs. With regard to the examples mentioned this is particularly apparent in cases from sacramental law. The difference in meaning which signs carry in various cultures can make them incapablę of conveying their intended message, for instance when pouring water over the head of a person is supposed to be a blessing and is, on the contrary, received as a curse; when imposing the hands onto an individual is supposed to signify the receiving of the Spirit but is instead perceived as an insult; when wheat bread fails to signify food which earth has given and grape wine fails to signify the work of human hands and appear to be magical items instead; when grape wine is used to symbolise Christ's blood but is regarded as an illicit substance, connected with immorality and excess; when spouses exchange their consent as a sign of their irrevocable covenant, while they perceive the procedure as individualist and exclusivist, disregarding their social ties with their families; when celibacy is supposed to signify Christ' undivided love, but is perceived as a sign of disrespect for family values and suppressed sexual desires. Robert Schreiter elucidates that many of these miscommunications are not merely temporary arising when non-Christian cultures encounter Catholicism, but can be of a lasting nature. They often pertain to conflicts between the meaning of a sign as developed in traditional Western theology and a differing meaning of the same sign in other contexts. One cannot easily defeat these conflicts if these meanings *are* fundamentally different. As marriage is a family matter in many African cultures, Catholics from these backgrounds will continue to perceive it as such. If bread is not part of daily meals, it cannot become a symbol of everyday nourishment. If grape wine is not a regular drink, it cannot become a symbol of human craftsmanship and festive celebrations. If touching a person's head is an insult in regular situations, one cannot expect Southeast Asian Christians to attribute this sign with a fundamentally different meaning in church. For Anscar Chupungco, it is clear that a symbolic action which a culture regards as a social taboo is wholly inadequate for conveying a sacramental meaning to members of this culture and therefore requires replacement.[130] Since global canon law does not provide solutions for these conflicts, local appliers of law must currently decide for themselves how to deal with situations where the law does not reflect the moral values, normative beliefs, and social customs of Catholic communities.

[130] See Chupungco (1992), p. 81.

7.3 Struggles for Meaning

Thus far, this chapter has mainly dealt with the irritation that legal transplants can cause in receiving cultures. Gunther Teubner acknowledges, in any case, that there is a way for legal irritants to find a home in their new contexts. This occurs when the recipients attribute transplanted rules with a new meaning, resulting in a new rule that successfully reconnects the legal and the social discourse. With regard to global legislation in church, this occurs when canonical transplants enter the local churches to be reconstructed there, thereby giving them a local meaning.

7.3.1 Methodological Centralism

One key instrument for achieving this is interpretation. However, as the analysis of the canons of interpretation has revealed, legislation restricts the local interpreters' freedom to reconstruct the legal rules in a way that responds to local needs. In doing so, it also obstructs what successful legal transfers require, namely the reconstruction of a rule as a genuinely local rule with its own meaning. This complicates effective transplantation in three ways. First, the canonical rules of interpretation give legal interpretation a centralist orientation. In directing the interpreters to the Apostolic See, not merely as the origin of the rules, but also as the authentic source of their meaning, legislation seeks to suppress a greater variety of interpretations. Whilst Catholics no longer live in the times of Pius IV and his Bull *Benedictus Deus*, the legislator's stance on interpretation remains focused on protecting the uniformity of canon law, requiring interpreters to bind their interpretation closely to the meaning of the words as deriving from official ecclesiastical terminology, the legal tradition of the church, and the intention of the legislator. Second, by establishing the canons of interpretation as part of the law itself, legislation compels the interpreters to follow a centralised methodology. As previously mentioned, this methodology imitates the typical continental approach of the nineteenth century. This presents a challenge for interpreters from churches based in common law countries, whose hybrid legal cultures are particularly sensitive to methodological discrepancies. Nevertheless, as this approach to interpretation is also considered outdated by many civil law practitioners, interpreters with a secular civil law background may also struggle with ecclesiastical methodology. Third, by restricting the ecclesiastical methodology to a fixed canon of rules, global legislation not only confronts many interpreters with the challenge of applying an unfamiliar method but also prevents the development of alternative methodologies. This inhibits the emergence of local approaches for deriving a meaning from a rule that concords with the local view of the law and a meaningful way of interpreting it. Without these methodological restrictions, one might imagine, for example, that Latin American interpreters develop a rule based on the *option for the poor*, directing their interpretation in a way most favourable for the marginalised. One might think of Asian interpreters developing the *rule of peace*, directing their interpretation in a way supportive of protecting peace in the community. African interpreters might develop the *communal rule*, pointing their interpretations towards understanding the law in a way that supports communities. One could conceive of European interpreters developing a rule of interpretation *sensus fidelium*, which directs their interpretation in a way that is most sensitive to the church members' common opinion. And one might also imagine an interchange between these various methods encouraging mutual intercultural learning.

7.3.2 Continental Transplants

As mentioned, the current restrictions are particularly challenging for churches based in common law countries and may prevent successful legal transfers to these churches. Canonists such as Bertram Griffin have suggested that canon law as civil law might create particular tensions in churches from common law countries.[131] There is reason to assume that this is due, among other things, to different views of interpretation. Gunther Teubner is a valuable conversation partner from secular law to discuss why differences in the methodologies of civil and common law impede legal transfers. He dealt with the problem of exporting principles of civil law origin, such as *good faith*, *legitimate expectation*, or *proportionality*, into British law via European law. His research, as specific as it is, might also explain the tensions arising from the import of civil law principles and continental general clauses into common law cultures via canonical legislation. It is useful for elucidating why civil canon law—which makes extensive use of indeterminate terms, legal principles, and general clauses, such as *just cause*, *just penalty*, or *grave necessity*—faces difficulties when entering cultures impregnated by common law thought. The major tension resulting from these transfers, as Teubner finds, derives from different methodologies of interpretation. In his studies, he focused on *good faith* as an example. This principle of continental European civil law, and in particular of German contract law, emerged from Rhineland capitalism, where the contracting parties traditionally interacted autonomously but also depended on mutual trust. "Good faith" was used to express the idea that contract law is connected with social morality: "Whenever the application of strict formal contract rules led to morally unacceptable results, *bona fides* was invoked to counteract the formalism of contract law doctrine with a substantive social morality."[132] Today, under more pluralised conditions, the clause has become more of "making visible how contractual expectations depend upon a variety of non-contractual social expectations".[133] Thus, good faith restricts the priority of the contracting partners' consensus in cases in which

[131] See Griffin (1984), p. 22.

[132] Teubner (1998), p. 23.

[133] Ibid.

alternative social expectations, such as questions of conscience, religious prohibitions, civil and political rights, regulatory measures, or economic constraints, require the contracting parties to depart from the letter of the contract. Teubner notes: "Due to its high degree of indeterminacy, the general clause of good faith is particularly suited to link contracts selectively to their unstable social environments with constantly shifting and conflicting requirements."[134]

Typical indeterminate terms and general clauses as used in canon law, such as *just cause*, *just penalty*, or *grave necessity*, have a different background both historically and systematically. Nevertheless, in analogy to Teubner's example, they respond to comparable concerns. Much like the original use of good faith, they embody the idea that the law connects with social values and morality, particularly with the Catholic faith and morals. The abundant reference of canon law to a just cause, which justifies a certain action or inaction, introduces moral beliefs into the legal evaluation of whether a certain action or inaction seems appropriate. In the same way, "grave necessity" hands legal interpreters an open concept with which to evaluate a particular challenge in their contexts to justify a certain action or inaction, usually departing from the general rule. Hence, *gravis necessitas* is a typical phrase used in canonical rule-and-exception regulations which enables local authorities to depart from a general rule to address pressing challenges in emergency situations. As an indeterminate term, it allows for the local assessment of which cases should be considered emergencies in specific circumstances, taking into account local morals, values, and expectations. "Just penalty" enables the authorities to subject offenders to those sanctions which under the particular circumstances seem most apt to restore justice, better the offender, and repair the scandal (see canon 1311 §2 CIC/1983). Thus, as different as they are from those used in secular continental law, indeterminate terms, legal principles, and general clauses as used in canon law fulfil a similar function: to make the social reality and its normative evaluation part of a legal assessment.

This similarity makes it interesting for canon law to study how Teubner evaluates the transplantation of continental concepts into common law contexts. Having studied his example of good faith, he became sceptical as to whether its transplantation into British law might prove successful, due to differing views of legal interpretation. Teubner describes the continental reading of general clauses, such as good faith, as follows: "The specific way in which continental lawyers deal with such a 'general clause' is abstract, open-ended, principle-oriented, but at the same time strongly systematised and dogmatised."[135] Civil lawyers tend to develop "abstract and general 'conditional programmes'", but also "finely circumscribed doctrinal figures based upon good faith".[136] Their methodology is based on discretionary, principle-driven judicial reasoning. The common law approach, by contrast, is characterised by a high degree of formality and a focus on rules in decision making.

[134] Ibid.

[135] Ibid., p. 19.

[136] Ibid., p. 21.

Consequently, a continental understanding of good faith "is clearly at odds with the more rule-oriented, technical, concrete, but loosely systematised British style of legal reasoning, especially when it comes to the interpretation of statutes."[137] Hence, Teubner finds it likely that common lawyers will reject continental general clauses and legal principles or coolly ignore them as concepts that are too irritating to serve the local legal system. Yet when rejection or ignorance is not an option and common lawyers are required to apply continental concepts, Teubner believes that their different methodologies will profoundly alter the transplanted concepts. He suggests that even in cases in which common lawyers submit to the continental approach to develop a more principle-based style of reasoning, their interpretive results will be dissimilar. It is unlikely that common lawyers will develop "elaborate intermediate structures, dogmatic constructs, juridical theories and conceptual systematisation which is so close to the heart of German law"[138] and continental law in general. Instead, they will keep dogmatic systematisation and the construction of legal theories to a minimum, producing merely "loosely arranged arguments from broad principles and policies."[139] In fact, their main concern will be to "distinguish and elaborate different factual situations", "typify different 'relationships which are of common occurrence'", and engage in "close fact-oriented case analysis".[140] Thus, their different methodology will give rise to the development of "a judicial doctrine of good faith that is much more 'situational' in character."[141] This doctrine is different, and necessarily so, as Teubner maintains, due to the different circumstances in civil law and common law cultures. As clauses such as *good faith* are established to connect the law with its social environment, their interpretation essentially reflects that environment in a double sense. It reflects the social values, beliefs, and customs prevalent in the context in which the clause is applied but is also significantly shaped by the methodology used to derive its meaning. Teubner therefore states: "If, under European law, good faith is transferred from the Continent to British law if it is supposed to play also in the new context its role of linking contracts to a variety of different discourses, then it is bound to produce results at great variance with continental legal orders."[142] He concludes: "Good faith will reproduce in legal form larger differences of the national cultures involved, and it will do so, paradoxically, because it was meant to make their laws more uniform."[143]

[137] Ibid., p. 19.

[138] Ibid., p. 21.

[139] Ibid.

[140] Ibid.

[141] Ibid.

[142] Ibid., pp. 23–24.

[143] Ibid., p. 24.

7.3.3 Common Law Methodology

Applying Teubner's observations to canon law supports the assumption that its transfer into churches from common law countries might lead to similar irritations and also to equally different interpretive results deriving from different methodologies for interpreting the transplants. Geoffrey Robinson, with his home country Australia in mind, describes these differences. He focuses on the Apostolic See's view of the law as a continental tradition and its potential to conflict with common law interpretation: "It has been said that the Latin mind believes in a strict law with a liberal interpretation, while the Anglo-Saxon mind believes in a liberal law with a strict interpretation."[144] This is a generalised but helpful description. Among other things, it alludes to the problem of common lawyers interpreting global legislation, as "there are obvious dangers in a strict Latin law strictly interpreted by Anglo-Saxons."[145] Robinson mentions some examples. He inter alia alludes to Paul VI's 1964 legislation in which the pope reduced the time for the Eucharistic fast from three hours to one hour.[146] This decree, when published in the *Acta Apostolicae Sedis*, made explicit mention of alcoholic beverages. However, the first publication of the text as distributed in Australia did not, as Robinson recalls. This gave rise to discussions, as interpretation of the text differed depending on whether the interpreters relied on a common law or a Roman methodology of interpretation: "The good Anglo-Saxon interpretation said: the Pope speaks only of food and does not mention alcohol; therefore the law on this remains at three hours. The good Latin interpretation said: but how can you have a meal without a glass of *vino*?"[147] A further example Robinson mentions is the former regulation of canon 533 §1 no. 1 CIC/1917, according to which superiors of religious institutes of diocesan right required the local ordinary's consent to make investments. An institute that invested its money into diversified stocks on the stock market through a stockbroker faced the challenge of obtaining permission for *each* individual investment. Whilst the strict interpretation of the rule by canon lawyers with a common law background did not result in an easier way of dealing with this issue, Robinson found the Roman interpretation of the rule to offer a feasible workaround: "The Latin mind would have no difficulty in arranging a solution which respected the bishop's obligation of vigilance and yet allowed the nuns freely to operate their necessary business, e.g., by asking them to submit a report once a year."[148]

Whilst the Apostolic See's methodology tends to connect interpretation with instruments of legal flexibility to ease conflicts deriving from the literal interpretation of a rule, such as interpreting the law equitably, common lawyers tend to be hesitant in this respect. Their strict interpretation—or "a literalistic attitude towards

[144] Robinson (1983), p. 60.

[145] Ibid.

[146] See Paul VI (1964), p. 186.

[147] Robinson (1983), p. 61.

[148] Ibid., 60–61.

interpretation",[149] as John Huels describes Anglo-American interpretation—often results in mere binary options, as Robinson concludes: "The Anglo-Saxon mind can often feel that there are only two choices: to obey the very letter of the law or to break it."[150] Yet, this could be seen as misguided from a Roman point of view. Robinson finds that from a Roman perspective, common law methodology commits "two cardinal sins",[151] namely of taking the law literally so that it loses its value to serve the community, and of disregarding the law in a wider sense. This is because when including prepositive justice into the law one could perceive a literal abiding by the legal rules as unlawful. Robinson therefore ends his observation with some advice to his fellow canon lawyers with a common law background: "So my final word to you is this: whenever you chew over and seek to digest any part of the new Code, have a deep respect for law in your head and in your heart, but make sure you also have a glass of good Italian *vino* by your side."[152]

According to Roman thought, practising equity by interpreting the law in a way that avoids hardship on the legal subjects is not against the law but part of the law. It is the proper way to handle it. Hence, *liberal interpretation*, in Robinson's terms, is regarded as the suitable methodology to approach strict law. The examples mentioned in Sect. 6.3.1 that the appliers of law can find it unjust to enforce laws on fasting during a famine or the obligation of Sunday mass attendance during a global pandemic, show that there are situational challenges where the regular application of laws seems inappropriate. In such cases, an equitable decision to refrain from enforcing the law seems to be the adequate answer. However, the extensive use of equity may cause concern among common lawyers as well as civil lawyers. Following Robinson, the Apostolic See's view of the law can be described as *strict rules* with *liberal interpretation*, involving the frequent use of instruments such as equitable interpretation and dispensation. In contrast, the typical common law view is *liberal rules* with *strict interpretation*, while many civil law approaches, such as German law, are characterised by *strict rules* with *strict interpretation*. This last-mentioned approach likewise creates conflicts with the Apostolic See's view of the law, as discussed in more detail in the next section.

7.3.4 Shared Reservations

Bertram Griffin, as a canonist with a common law background, puts common lawyers' unease with a liberal handling of legal rules down to the fact that the ubiquitous praxis of dispensation in church is problematic in their eyes: "The very concept of dispensation is alien to the common law system. … In our American civil law,

---

[149] Huels (1987), p. 274.

[150] Robinson (1983), p. 60.

[151] Ibid., p. 61.

[152] Ibid.

dispensations, or relaxations of the law, do not occur. If the law is to be relaxed, the legislators themselves must change the law. Courts can, in some cases, grant exceptions, but the executive branch of civil government does not grant dispensations."[153] Griffin elucidates how alien dispensation is to American legal culture by recalling one of his own experiences:

> When I was a young priest, I served as moderator of a youth club which wanted to hold a dance on the night before a holy day of obligation when the young people were not obliged to attend school. Portland had a very rigorously enforced curfew, however, and the parents were anxious that I obtain some kind of 'dispensation.' I went to the local police, who were frankly horrified that a minister of the cloth would ask for permission to break a law. In canon law, however, the executive branch of Church government readily grants dispensations in accordance with law, and the power to dispense is widely delegated.[154]

The reaction of the Portland police resembles much of that of the German bishop to whom this book referred in Sect. 2.3. The bishop had attempted to legislate a major piece of diocesan reform and failed because the Apostolic See put a stop to his legislation. He did, however, manage to establish a viable workaround together with the curial official in charge, which, in the end, resulted in the same result that the bishop with his original legislation had intended. Yet he achieved this outcome by taking a different path, namely by relying on the curial official who organised all necessary dispensations from global law for the bishop to address the issue. While the bishop, in the end, got exactly what he had wished for, he was disconcerted by the proceeding. Different from his original plan, the new regulation was not based on his independent acting as a legislator but on Roman concession, thereby weakening his role as the legislator of his church while fostering the Apostolic See's power. This is ecclesiologically questionable but also critical from the perspective of jurisprudence. Ubiquitous dispensations weaken the law, as they undermine the general validity of the law. When rule-and-exception systems become *systems of exception*, they question the fundamental role of the rule. The bishop found this approach to be incompatible with his fellow Germans' understanding of the law. One can take this example as illustrative of the fact that many civil lawyers feel uneasy about combining a strict rule with broad discretion in its application. German civil lawyers, for their part, prefer a clear rule with a strict interpretation, as this allows for a maximum of legal certainty. Hence, one can assume that many legal cultures, of civil law and common law traditions alike, find the abundant reference to equity and dispensation as common in church to be challenging for several reasons: it calls into question the general validity of the law; it invites arbitrary decisions, undermining legal certainty, equality, and justice as principles connected with the rule of law; and it covers up inadequate legislation, thus impeding legal reform.

The main reason for civil and common lawyers' shared reservations about the flexibility instruments that Robinson classifies as *liberal interpretation* is that these mechanisms do not align with their understanding of the law. Legal rules might

---

[153] Griffin (1984), p. 23.

[154] Ibid.

derive from abstract statute law or case-related precedents; yet, despite these evident differences, they deserve a search for meaning that focuses on the rule itself and avoids bending it. In contrast, the extensive use of equity and dispensation is, to most common and civil lawyers alike, a relic of premodern law which compromises legal certainty by making the rule subject to the authorities' discretion. Law becomes *gutsherrliches Entscheiden*, as the bishop in the mentioned case criticised. It loses its abstract and general nature and is turned into an arbitrary decision with an absolutist flavour. Whilst one can agree that law does indeed consist of decision, as Niklas Luhmann suggested,[155] this decision itself, as modern individuals frequently find, requires legal control and has to be constrained by the rule of law to be considered as law. As the mentioned German bishop observed, Catholics socialised in constitutional states under the rule of law "want clear and reliable laws, not Roman concessions".

Certainly, not all bishops reject liberal interpretation as fervently as the bishop in the given case. Many bishops oppose the discretionary style of governance when applied by the Apostolic See to restrict their actions, and not so much when they govern their dioceses. Andean bishop José Dammert Bellido, shortly after the promulgation of the Code, praised the legislator for the reduction of the Code's penal law, as fewer rules allow for more "creative strength of the bishops; they must have the boldness recommended by Pope Paul VI and not be afraid of possible risks or fall into narrow scruples."[156] What he described as creative courage may appear to others as arbitrary decision making based on power rather than law. Therefore the abundant use of equity and dispensation in church may seem generous at first but problematic on closer inspection. Equitable solutions are unreliable. As much as they allow for the easing of hardship deriving from legal rules in particular situations, they make legal subjects dependent on the authority's mercy. As equity is an act of grace granted by the respective authorities and not a right which the legal subjects enjoy, extensive equity and dispensation undermine legal certainty, equality, and justice. This could explain some of the fundamental reservations about the Apostolic See's approach held by both common and civil lawyers.

7.3.5 Increased Concerns

Their unease may be intensified by the fact that equity and dispensation are currently being used extensively to prevent the global body of canon law from contestation. Grace that flows plentifully prevents pressure on the law, thus diminishing the legal subjects' demands for change. Without instruments granting the authorities flexibility to solve conflicts resulting from inadequate legislation, many legal matters would come under pressure. However, most legal scholars would subject laws

[155] See Luhmann (1970), pp. 190–195.

[156] Dammert Bellido (1986), p. 111.

that require far-reaching equity and dispensation to critical scrutiny, as these laws seem unable to adequately accommodate local needs and circumstances. As Bertram Griffin observed, it is the duty of the legislator to change the law whenever it fails to provide for adequate rules, not the appliers' duty to bend the rules so that they fit particular needs. Most civil lawyers would agree. Hence, despite their differing understandings of law, both common and civil lawyers believe that rules must be robust enough to withstand strict interpretation. If they do not, they may be inadequate and require reform. In this light, it appears that the widespread use of instruments of legal flexibility in the application of canon law is more about protecting the rules from demands for reform than protecting local Catholics from the negative consequences of their application. Certainly, rules cannot account for every situation.[157] However, one can doubt whether the adequate way to address this issue is by broadening the use of flexibility instruments.

The example of dispensation as a universal remedy for the shortcomings of global canon law in addressing plural cultures, mentioned in Sect. 6.3.2, comes to mind once again. For instance, extensive dispensations allow ecclesiastical marriage law to uphold rules such as canon 1086 §1 CIC/1983, which renders a marriage between a Catholic and an unbaptised individual invalid, even in societies where these marriages are the norm. Here, dispensation from the marriage impediment is granted in practically all cases. By establishing a rule to inhibit an action and using dispensation to enable it at the same time, this ambiguous practice protects the law from pressure to change. In these cases, dispensation is less about bringing relaxation to a specific situation in which the application of a rule would bring about harsh results. Rather, it is a means of applying and adapting the law to culturally diverse environments. This is problematic, as the law of the church, like the law of constitutional states, must provide its subjects with some stability. Legal certainty is a demand of justice. An exuberant reference to equity conflicts with justice. Accordingly, a rule that requires dispensation in almost every case to adapt to typical social situations does not require flexibility instruments. Rather, it requires critical analysis and revision.

Furthermore, using flexibility instruments all too readily to address situations in which a rule continuously makes no sense is not just a problem with regard to legal certainty. It also prevents engagement in the analysis of what would be required to restore its meaning. Thus, by swiftly turning to dispensations, church authorities avoid addressing the intricate issue of why rules become meaningless in certain situations and how communities could relate to these rules in a meaningful way. Avoiding these struggles for meaning, in any case, is not a way to make the law more meaningful but rather a way to exclude the legal subjects from processes of meaning-making. As successful transplants require the reconstruction of meaning in the receiving community, this praxis is an obstacle for the reception of global rules in the local churches, as it inhibits the local appropriation of the transplants by attributing them a new local meaning.

---

[157] See Huels (1987), p. 272.

7.4 Summary

Taking into account the local responses to global legislation, this chapter has discussed whether the church's current framework for the inculturation of global canon law in the local churches is sufficient with respect to the law and its effectiveness and with respect to the local churches and their needs. Lawmaking is both widely non-transparent and non-participatory. Its lack of diversity supports the creation of culturally insensitive rules. The law is implemented in the local churches through imposed reception. As a result, transplants of global law are often perceived as irritants in the local churches and met with different forms of non-acceptance, ranging from rejection to indifference. Yet even irritants can find acceptance when they undergo reconstruction in the receiving group, which attributes them with a local meaning. With regard to canon law, in any case, it is challenging that the local appropriation of transplanted rules is inhibited by various factors. One factor is that interpretation is limited by the canonical rules of interpretation, which prescribe to the interpreters a certain methodology of how to make sense of a rule. Another factor is that rules that do not make sense often become subject to dispensation, rather than being submitted to a deeper analysis of why they fail to make sense and how their meaning could be restored.

Chapter 8
Revising Global Legislation

The observation that current legislation transfers a body of culturally rather insensitive rules into the local churches in the form of asymmetrical law planting—or imposed reception or solicited imposition,[1] to use Alan Watson's terms—raises the question of how to deal with global canon law in a postcolonial light. Section 8.1 will submit the current law to postcolonial criticism. Based on its theoretical deconstruction, one may discuss whether a global body of ecclesiastical rules has a future. It has become clear throughout this book that there is a need to broaden the authority of decentralised over centralised lawmaking; some consequences of this finding will be set out in Sect. 8.2. However, what is not yet clear is whether a uniform body of global rules for the entire church is a legitimate option for global Catholicism, as discussed in Sect. 8.3.

8.1 Postcolonial Criticism

In deliberating how to deal with a law that is imbued with an imperialist past and recurrent colonialist patterns, canonists can learn from the ongoing debates among scholars of critical legal studies. Critical legal scholars typically recognise the colonial history of international legislation, such as public international law, and the tendency for these laws to perpetuate colonial structures in the present day. But they often disagree on how to deal with these findings. Some scholars take the colonial origin and neo-colonial imbalance of international law as a reason to challenge its existence. Others suggest accepting its existence but deem it necessary to debate its Western roots and its tendency to recreate hegemonic structures. Instead of rejecting public international law for being colonialist law, they understand it as being essential to reveal the power asymmetries behind the law and to deconstruct them by

[1] See Watson (1993), p. 30.

J. Hahn, *The Cultures of Canon Law*, Law and Religion in a Global Context 6,
https://doi.org/10.1007/978-3-032-14812-4_8

submitting the law to postcolonial criticism.[2] Whilst these scholars do not question the existence of public international law as such, they are demanding a fundamental reform of the law to overcome its colonialist relapses. Postcolonialism includes confronting the law with alternative views from the Global South to challenge the dominance of Western legal thought. In a similar vein, Judith Gruber argues that postcolonialism in theology is not about cutting off the Eurocentric roots of mainstream theological traditions but about deconstructing them by confronting them with alternative views and narratives.

8.1.1 Revealing Power Relations

With regard to whether or not global canon law has a future, similar considerations seem applicable. One can dismiss global canon law fundamentally due to its asymmetrical structuring. Or one can accept its existence whilst acknowledging its hegemonic nature and discuss potential ways of improving it. This necessitates subjecting the law to postcolonial criticism. Gruber sets the scene for such a scenario by explaining several aspects of a postcolonial criticism of theology, which likewise seem applicable to the law. First of all, she observes that postcolonialism reveals the hegemonic power relations between the parties involved. There is no "reason as purified from power relations".[3] Postcolonialism therefore cannot confront colonial reason with non-power but with challenging and reversing established power relations. For the law this requires the critical examination of the asymmetrical power relations which are re-established and re-institutionalised by global canon law. The law has contributed to establishing top-down power relations in church, codifying the power of the pope over the bishops, of clerics over laypeople, and of men over women. And it has supported the asymmetrical exercise of power, enabling Vatican officials to overrule local church representatives, officials from the Global North to decide over those from the Global South, and traditional churches to dominate newly Christianised communities. A first step to approaching the question of whether there can and should be a body of legal rules for global Catholicism is to acknowledge that the law has fundamentally contributed to establishing and re-establishing these asymmetries.

---

[2] E.g. Tamanaha (2017), p. 166; Goldmann (2019).
On the various approaches of dealing with hegemonic law, see Carty (1991), pp. 1–27.

[3] Gruber (2018), p. 60.

8.1.2 Deconstructing Universality

Gruber sees the second step of postcolonial criticism in addressing the epistemological foundation of modern colonialist politics. She finds this epistemology to have its roots in the notion of universality, detecting its key elements in the "idea that there is one form of reasoning, which is absolutely true and universally valid and can operate independently of historical, social, economic, and hegemonic conditions."[4] This book talked in Sect. 3.1 about the temptation of canonical jurisprudence, with its roots in Neo-Scholastic theology, to rely on the idea of the universal. By mistaking the centralist view of the law for a universal approach to the law, it has cultivated an epistemology that revolves around one form of reasoning made into an absolute by ignoring its historical, social, economic, and hegemonic embedding. Colonialist politics, as Gruber explains, revolve around the very strategies of "concealing the historical, cultural, and economic conditions of their emergence".[5] It is therefore a necessary step in a postcolonial revision of current canon law to address the fact that the Roman view of the law is not a universal perspective but a deeply cultural one. As a cultural view, it is of major value—in the same way as alternative views of the law. Revealing the cultural foundations of canon law does not therefore devalue the law; but it exposes the colonialist patterns that emerge whenever global law is presented as universal to justify its worldwide range of application. Consequently, postcolonialism, as Gruber maintains, is tasked with investing in "de-absolutising" strategies, revealing the historicity and culturality of hegemonic concepts, as the "exposure of their contingency undermines their sovereignty".[6] At the same time, this revelation of the contingency of hegemonic concepts allows for alternative approaches to resurface. What was formerly dismissed as merely a historical, cultural, and local perspective on an issue is now given equal standing alongside all the other views on the matter. With regard to canon law, this means integrating alternative interpretations of the law into the canonical discourse and giving them an equal voice in debates about the development of canon law.

8.1.3 Uncovering Diversity

Postcolonialism's exposure of the contingency of many universal claims also results in the "unsilencing of the interculturality of Christian tradition",[7] as Gruber suggests. By showing that many universal claims are contingent propositions that managed to silence other competing claims in support of a strong uniform Catholic

[4] Ibid.

[5] Ibid.

[6] Ibid.

[7] Ibid., p. 123.

identity, postcolonial criticism does not merely deconstruct the dominance of universal propositions, it also reveals the diversity of coexisting traditions. The Christian tradition, thus, cannot be viewed as the development of one line of tradition throughout history but as the coexistence of manifold and sometimes conflicting traditions. Gruber finds: "Unsilencing interculturality, in other words, denaturalizes and de-essentializes the normative texts of ecclesial tradition and reveals the contingent histories of their formation."[8] This approach might also help canon law rediscover the contingent and historical conditions that determined its formation. For instance, exploring the historical development of the current constitution of the church reveals that its hierarchical organisation with its clear distinction between clergy and laypeople reflects the social class divisions of pre-modern societies. Studying the history of canon law reveals how the Roman view of law triumphed over competing perspectives, such as Germanic legal concepts, to become the dominant Catholic understanding, deriving its identity from suppressing rival approaches. Thus, by revealing the plurality of alternative approaches to the law, the narrative of a uniform Catholic identity is called into question.

Yet postcolonial criticism of universal claims reveals not merely the existence of suppressed competing claims but also the processes of their exclusion. Gruber speaks of a "host of conflictive narratives out of which the normative delineations of ecclesial identity have been forged in powerful processes of inclusion and exclusion."[9] The production of universal claims requires these claims to be demarcated by setting them apart from other competing propositions as mere contingent, relativist, historical, and cultural variances of minor value. Deconstructing these narratives of identity creation via exclusion involves removing the clear distinction between universal and contingent claims. This demonstrates that all of them are equally contingent and calls into question both the hegemony of the universal claims and the practices of deriving them by suppressing others. Gruber notes: "Unsilenced interculturality thus becomes a resource that allows theology to resist the temptations of a 'strong' identity politics."[10]

Based on these findings one can ask if concepts that were formerly regarded as universal still have a place in the discourse after they have been exposed to postcolonial criticism. With Gruber, one can argue that they do. She argues that a deconstruction of the hegemonic traditions of the church does not call for new processes of exclusion but grants all alternative claims a voice in the discourse. However, as she also notes, the hegemonic traditions have a particular role to play, as they, more than other approaches, allow the disputants to understand the past processes of creating Catholic identity. Postcolonialism, in this vein, "puts a spotlight on them [the hegemonic traditions, addition by the author] as crystallization points in the ongoing discursive negotiation of ecclesial identity."[11] Gruber also calls them "privileged

---

[8] Ibid.

[9] Ibid.

[10] Ibid., p. 124.

[11] Ibid., p. 123.

sites for scrutinizing the contingent histories in the forging of tradition through powerful inclusions and exclusions".[12] Current Catholic canon law, in this respect, can serve as such an example of a hegemonic tradition in which a Roman view of the law has created Catholic identities by suppressing alternative views and by excluding approaches to the law derived from alternative traditions. It is helpful to study the law in this light to discover how its success came about. In future lawmaking, the Roman view of the law should have its share, as should other alternative perspectives. In a truly global church constituted of local churches from all over the world, no single view can be allowed to dominate the debate.

8.1.4 Deconstructing the Law

Subjecting present canon law to postcolonial criticism ultimately raises the question of whether a global concept of law has a future in the church. Whilst it has deconstructed the existing law, this book has not given an answer to whether its *re*construction is an option, as colonialist patterns will re-emerge with each advance of global legislation. With his studies on international law, Antony Anghie directed his readers' attention to the dilemma that truly global orders come with an inherent inclination to develop imperialist structures, as it is their "civilising mission"[13] which makes them successful. Without its colonialist course of action, international law could not have become a global phenomenon. As mentioned in Sect. 7.2.2, one can therefore assume that canon law, with its aspiration to serve the global church, has a tendency to embark on a civilising mission too and is naturally tempted to force the local churches under its unifying roof. Whilst one can subject the law to postcolonial criticism to reveal this problem, Anghie's argument might make one wonder how quickly a new body of rules would secure its global success by employing colonialist strategies.

Similar to the debates on international law, scholarly voices that have outlined the necessity to reform canon law have proposed different strategies. Some have called into question the future of a uniform body of global rules. Francis Morrisey, for instance, raised doubts as far back as 1986: "As time goes on it will become increasingly more difficult for the Church to have a universal law. The 1983 Code might well be one of the last such instruments the Church will have if it wishes to remain truly catholic."[14] As early as 1969, Ladislas Orsy proposed: "The conception of full codification should be abandoned",[15] arguing in favour of partial codifications of relevant legal matters. To these critical voices on the current top-down politics of legislation, other voices have added the bottom-up perspective which

[12] Ibid.

[13] Anghie (2006), p. 742.

[14] Morrisey (1986), p. 36.

[15] Orsy (1969), p. 74; see also Orsy (1996b), p. 15.

anticipates the emergence of decentralised rules as the necessary consequence of the establishment of local theologies. The African bishops made such a proposal in 1978, when they argued in favour of an African Canon Law based on African theology, as they found canon law with its roots in Western theology unsuitable for the African churches.[16] Steven Bwana agreed: "Hand-in-hand, there is a well-observed … African traditional system of settling disputes, or worshipping, etc. It is no surprise, therefore, that an African theology is evolving. The next step, I believe, will be the evolution of an African Canon Law emanating from this theology."[17] This thought has gained traction in the debates, as Salvatore Mancuso stated "that the idea of an African canon law tempts a certain number of African (and also non-African) canonists and theologians."[18] Patricia Goler similarly concludes with regard to Black Catholicism in the United States that the advance of a law responding to the needs of Black communities would be a necessary step if canon law wants to have more significance among Black Catholics: "If black Catholics were generally more conscious of canon law, some of the same kinds of questions might be raised about a need for a black canon law as are now being raised about the need for a black liturgy—to give them a legitimacy and relevance to black life styles."[19] These scholars recognise that a church that supports the development of local theologies must also encourage the growth of local liturgies and independent decentralised legal rules. Consequently, from an African perspective, canonist Robert Mwaungulu believes it is necessary to expand the legislative authority of diocesan bishops and bishops' conferences.[20] Francis Morrisey observes that this request is connected with many former mission churches becoming more confident and discovering their own Catholic identity: "The awakening of true self-identity in the newer churches will necessarily call for some type of adaptation of Church law to particular situations."[21]

However, Morrisey's ambiguous words leave it unclear whether this calls for reducing global legislation in favour of more decentralised legislation or for making global law more sensitive to local issues. One may detect a similar ambiguity in many canonists' statements that emphasise the necessity of making canon law more adaptive to cultural issues, yet without clarifying the way in which to achieve this. Ladislas Orsy, for instance, suggests including other traditions besides the continental tradition as foundations of canon law: "This may mean that canon law will have to broaden its base beyond the inheritance that we have received from the ancient

[16] See Symposium of Episcopal Conferences of Africa and Madagascar (1978), p. 225; for this demand in the context of the 1994 African Synod, see Orobator (1996), p. 10.

[17] Bwana (1986), p. 104; see also Busugutsala (1987), pp. 57–62; for an outline of such an endeavour of an African canon law following African ecclesiology, see Okeke (1998), pp. 397–414; Nsomwe Ntambwe (2010), pp. 245–262.

[18] Mancuso (2024), p. 80.

[19] Goler (1972), p. 295.

[20] See Mwaungulu (1996), p. 82.

[21] Morrisey (1986), p. 36.

Roman iurisprudentes!"[22] Hence, he evidently agrees with Aylward Shorter who demanded "to make a radical break with the old monocultural Church of the past."[23] Whilst this claim is undisputed among many scholars, they nevertheless seem less certain of whether it can include a body of global rules or whether the legal future of the church lies in plural and independent legal systems. John Huels seems to express a preference for abiding by a comprehensive body of rules when reminding his fellow canonists of "the critical need for a cross-cultural hermeneutic that has the adaptability to apply a universal Catholic law in cultures that do not share the language, legal system, philosophical presuppositions, or perhaps even the way of looking at reality that are found in the culture that produced the canonical system."[24] Yet it is also Huels who, with his example of Confucian traditions and their distaste for the law as a medium of social regulation,[25] raises the fundamental question of whether a legal framework is an adequate solution for organising the church as a social body always and everywhere. Whilst many Catholics from the Global North tend to accept the law as an essential structure of the earthly church, it is unclear if and how this can apply to contexts where the law is regarded as a subordinate instrument of social engineering. Huels, for his part, is open to the idea that taking plural Catholic identities seriously might result in the finding that canon law is unsuitable for organising each and every local church: "We must also acknowledge that no legal system, including the canonical, is entirely and uniformly suitable for every culture."[26]

8.2 Broadening Local Legislation

The critical voices on current canon law share the opinion that it is essential to cut back global legislation to allow decentralised regulations—legal or non-legal—to flourish in its place. Global rules need to leave more room for the growth of decentralised rules. Huels therefore proposes a greater freedom accorded to the local churches in deciding how to adopt global rules: "If Christianity is truly open to all cultures, it seems that the local church is [sic] such a society needs to 'interpret' the canonical requirements in a way that disruption to the people's language and way of thinking is minimized."[27] Hence, he relies on a broader concept of interpretation, not restricting it to the local reconstruction of meaning but conceiving of it, in a broader sense, as the assessment of whether and how global rules should be given meaning in a local church: "'Interpretation' of canon law, as used here …, is not

[22] Orsy (1996a), p. 22.

[23] Shorter (1988), p. 71.

[24] Huels (1987), p. 262.

[25] See ibid., p. 274.

[26] Ibid., p. 290.

[27] Ibid., p. 260.

limited merely to understanding the meaning of the words of a law in its text and legal context. Interpretation, rather, involves broader skills that include making judgements about the way that a law should be observed or whether it should be observed."[28] This authority to decide whether and how a global rule should impact a local church can include the authorities' decision to discard the law, as Huels maintains: "In some cases the best interpretation of a law might be that it should not be observed due to the particular circumstances of a culture or situation."[29] In its stead, decentralised legislation can aim to establish adequate rules. This shift in focus is required for the aforementioned reasons. First, it is necessary out of respect for the autonomy of local groups to leave them space to legislate for themselves. This corresponds with the principle of subsidiarity, which prioritises self-regulation on the local level and accords centralised intervention a supportive function which only comes into play in those cases in which decentralised regulations fail to meet the regulative demands. A more subsidiary shaping of canon law was already demanded in the 1983 reform of the Code,[30] but failed to have a notable impact on legislation. Second, cutting back on global law in favour of decentralised legislation increases the chances that the law will be accepted, as sociological observations suggest. Third, from a theological perspective, the stronger role of decentralised legislation more accurately reflects the ecclesiological value of the local churches.

8.2.1 Diversity and Autonomy

Understanding the local churches more as independent agents in the development of their own rules will give rise to a greater degree of legal diversity. From this finding arises the question of how to deal with this increase in diversity in light of its limits. Theological considerations often connect this issue with the debate about how to avoid relativism, syncretism, and particularism. Judith Gruber asks: "After the anti-colonial diversification of theology, how can the universality and unity of the church, which are two crucial and normative landmarks of the theological tradition, be sustained?"[31] Robert Schreiter refers to the challenge of syncretism as "a dilution and loss of the Christian message in the local context",[32] where contextualisation transcends the point to the extent that a message can no longer be considered an expression of the Christian message. He therefore warns of a "cultural romanticism, whereby any cultural form is automatically accepted as a vehicle of Christ in culture."[33] In a similar vein, Francis Morrisey perceives: "The fact that something is

[28] Ibid., p. 260 fn. 33.

[29] Ibid.

[30] See Pontifical Commission for the Revision of the Code of Canon Law (1969), pp. 80–82.

[31] Gruber (2018), p. 26.

[32] Schreiter (1985), p. 102.

[33] Ibid., p. 103.

part of a culture does not necessarily make it right or wrong."[34] This explains a certain Catholic reservation towards culture, as John Huels adds, noting that "not all the beliefs, values, and institutions that make up a culture are good ones, at least not from a Christian perspective. Many are in need of redemption; many aspects of cultures, including our own, are contrary to gospel values."[35] As an institution concerned with the idea of one truth that culminates in Christ, the church faces the dilemma that plurality also appears to challenge this concept in favour of relativism, syncretism, and particularism. Whenever ecclesiastical praxis allows for the plural cultures to impact it to any great extent, this raises the question of how to avoid the relativisation that accompanies contextualisation. The Second Vatican Council acknowledged this tension when holding in *Gaudium et Spes*: "Although the Church has contributed much to the development of culture, experience shows that, for circumstantial reasons, it is sometimes difficult to harmonize culture with Christian teaching."[36] The council, consequently, posed the question of how to recognise the legitimate autonomy of cultures "without generating a notion of humanism which is merely terrestrial, and even contrary to religion itself."[37] In asking for the *legitima autonomia* of cultures, it indicated that there might be an illegitimate autonomy, too, promoting culture purely for worldly purposes, whilst neglecting the supercultural value of the Christian message. The council drew the line between a legitimate and an illegitimate endorsement of culture by interpreting legitimate autonomy as the just liberty ("*iusta libertas*") of cultures in responding to their need for development, originating in the essential spiritual and social character of humanity.[38] Cultures, thus, justly push for development when they do so to support the common good, while protecting the rights of the local individuals and the community, both in spiritual and social matters.

8.2.2 *Universalism and Relativism*

Marc de Mûelenaere portrayed the tension of conciliar teaching as holding culture in high esteem as the medium for incarnating and contextualising the Catholic faith, while at the same time raising concerns with regard to relativism, syncretism, and particularism.[39] It is not far from the "antimodernist conception of theology"[40] of the nineteenth century with its supercultural and ahistorical identity politics which relies on universal truths and refers to history and culture merely as the relativist

[34] Morrisey (1986), p. 36.

[35] Huels (1987), pp. 265–266.

[36] Second Vatican Council (1965c), no. 62. Acta Apostolicae Sedis (1966), p. 1082.

[37] Ibid., no. 56. Acta Apostolicae Sedis (1966), p. 1077.

[38] See ibid., no. 59. Acta Apostolicae Sedis (1966), p. 1080.

[39] See de Mûelenaere (1985b), particularly pp. 32–35.

[40] Gruber (2018), p. 91.

other from which to distinguish a universal identity, as Judith Gruber explained. Dramatic hyperboles, such as the danger of a "dictatorship of relativism",[41] have supported this connection. However, besides these polarised opinions, there is reason to ask whether there are cultures that defy incarnating the faith. Schreiter's caveat of a cultural romanticism that blindly accepts all cultures as equally capable of expressing the Christian message challenges theologians to discuss how to deal with the "unchristian" side of cultures which seems incompatible with embodying the faith. John Huels states in a similar vein: "We belong to a Church and we profess certain basic beliefs and uphold fundamental values that are central to our faith and our view of the cosmos, and they cannot be compromised even if people in some cultures do not accept them."[42]

Michael Angrosino underscores this tension between universalism and cultural relativism as a pressing issue from the perspective of anthropology, noting that social scientists are similarly faced with the problem of how to respond to those cultural elements that seem intolerable from their particular point of view.[43] Whilst social studies as descriptive disciplines study cultures without evaluating the value of particular practices and for that reason rely on the hermeneutics of cultural relativism for professional reasons, they also cannot avoid making certain judgements. As a result, most scholars would agree that there are what Angrosino calls "moral limits to a philosophy of cultural relativism."[44] He localises these limits whenever fundamental principles of human dignity are concerned, for instance with regard to practices such as infanticide, child labour, or female circumcision. It is here that most social scientists depart from their methodology of cultural relativism. Angrosino therefore finds it relatively unproblematic that the church ties the ability of a culture to convey the Christian message to certain conditions, such as a culture supporting the common good and the protection of individual and communal rights with regard to spiritual and social matters. One could now debate Angrosino's position in light of the question of whether human dignity is a universal principle; this essentially contested debate was discussed at some length in the introduction. As there is no way to resolve the conflict between universalism and relativism, Boaventura de Sousa Santos suggests "to transcend the debate on universalism and cultural relativism", as he reckons: "The debate is an inherently false debate, whose polar concepts are both and equally detrimental to an emancipatory conception of human rights."[45] For him it is clear that all cultures are relative. Nevertheless he considers cultural relativism to be unhelpful, as he finds all cultures to be concerned with the universal. Yet cultural universalism is also an inadequate conceptual framework. He therefore suggests overcoming this opposition by turning to a *tertium*, cross-cultural cosmopolitanism:

---

[41] Ratzinger (2005). Acta Apostolicae Sedis (2005), p. 687.

[42] Huels (1987), p. 289.

[43] See Angrosino (1994), p. 828.

[44] Ibid.

[45] De Sousa Santos (2020), p. 323.

> Against universalism, we must propose cross-cultural dialogues on isomorphic concerns. Against relativism, we must develop cross-cultural procedural criteria to distinguish progressive politics from regressive politics, empowerment from disempowerment, emancipation from regulation. Neither universalism nor relativism must be argued for, but rather cosmopolitanism, that is to say, the globalization of moral and political concerns with and struggles against social oppression and human suffering.[46]

For theology, Bernard Lonergan made a comparable observation when discussing what unity of the faith means. Lonergan levels criticism at the "classicist assumptions" which attempt to preserve the faith by defining the "universal" aspects of Christianity and protecting them from cultural influences:

> On classicist assumptions there is just one culture. That one culture is not attained by the simple faithful, the people, the natives, the barbarians. None the less, career is always open to talent. One enters upon such a career by diligent study of the ancient Latin and Greek authors. One pursues such a career by learning Scholastic philosophy and theology. One aims at high office by becoming proficient in canon law. One succeeds by winning the approbation and favour of the right personages. Within this set-up the unity of faith is a matter of everyone subscribing to the correct formulae.[47]

Lonergan disregards this approach. He calls it a "shabby shell of Catholicism".[48] In its stead he suggests an alternative view of unity: "The real root and ground of unity is being in love with God".[49] It is evident that this unity can take on multiple forms in which individuals and groups express their communion with God. However, in their various approaches one can see a universal motif at work and discover unity in plurality.

The question remains of how to discover this unity. With regard to the human rights debates, Boaventura de Sousa Santos has a suggestion. Unlike Angrosino, who sees a need to draw an essential bottom line at human dignity where descriptive scholarly interest turns into normative concern and marks the boundary that cultural relativism should not cross, de Sousa Santos suggests engaging in a cross-cultural debate on what is essential to human flourishing and to avoid human suffering:

> Because the question of universality is the answer to an aspiration of completeness, and because each culture 'situates' such an aspiration around ultimate values and universal validity, different aspirations to different ultimate values in different cultures will lead to isomorphic concerns which, given the adequate hermeneutical procedures, may become mutually intelligible and mutually translatable. At best, it is even possible to achieve a mixture and interpenetration of concerns and concepts. The more equal power relations among cultures are, the more probable it is that such *mestizaje* might occur. A balanced cross-cultural *mestizaje* of concerns and concepts is the multicultural correspondent of single-culture universality.[50]

---

[46] Ibid.; in a similar vein, see also Berman (2005), pp. 1112–1115.

[47] Lonergan (1972), pp. 326–327.

[48] Ibid., p. 327.

[49] Ibid.

[50] De Sousa Santos (2020), pp. 320–321.

With regard to the church, his approach can be adapted to accommodate what is essentially Christian. Thus, cosmopolitanism could prevent Christians from establishing a threshold that distinguishes plural expressions of the Christian faith from unchristian beliefs and practices. Instead they could engage in cross-cultural discussions about which beliefs and practices support faith and religious life, and which do not.

8.2.3 Values and Identity

With regard to discerning which laws support Catholicism, John Huels—though evidently thinking in dialectic terms of universalism and relativism—comprehends this task as one of weighing and balancing. He opts to critically work around the crucial core of the Christian faith, with the purpose of finding legal solutions that do not compromise the faith but also respond to plural cultures in the best possible way; Anscar Chupungco discusses the same necessity and difficulty of differentiation with regard to the liturgy.[51] Huels understands this delineation as one principal hermeneutical task of identifying matters essential for the faith and those which are dispensable by asking the question: "What practices, beliefs, values, structures, and institutions are truly necessary and indispensable for church life, and which ones may be modified or abandoned for the sake of values in the culture of the local church?"[52] With regard to the law, this raises the issue of differentiating between its necessary and variable aspects by discerning its divine and contingent sources, as Huels maintains: "A chief hermeneutical task for canon law is to discover which are the abiding gospel values enshrined in the laws, and distinguish these values from whatever is nonessential and changeable."[53] In terms of local legislation, the challenge lies in identifying laws that conflict with the Christian message. Whilst local rules deserve recognition as the independent self-regulation of the local churches, it remains vital to engage in cross-cultural discussion about those cases in which they are unsuited to serve as signs of the church. Boaventura de Sousa Santos, for his part, reminds his readers in his theory of cosmopolitanism that cross-cultural dialogue on what is apposite to serve human flourishing might sometimes have the character of a competition between ideas, norms, and principles that are more or less suitable. However, it is important to make sure "that such competition induces cross-cultural dialogues and transnational coalitions to race to the top rather than to the bottom—What are the absolute minimum standards? The most basic human rights? The lowest common denominators?"[54] Similarly, identifying common

[51] See Chupungco (1992), p. 44.

[52] Huels (1987), p. 266.

[53] Ibid., p. 268.

[54] De Sousa Santos (2020), p. 323.

grounds of Christian identity is not about the lowest common denominators but about finding agreement on beliefs and practices that support Christian life.

It is interesting to read Robert Schreiter in this light, as he tries to define markers of Christian identity that race to the top rather than to the bottom. He discusses this topic when he asks how to assess whether a local theology is truly Christian.[55] In deliberating how to identify these theologies, Schreiter develops five criteria: their coherence with ecclesiastical tradition, their compatibility with liturgy and worship, their reflection in Christian praxis, their coherence with the theologies of other local churches, and their contribution to a global theology of the whole church. Most interestingly, Anscar Chupungco tackles a similar question when asking which rituals can become sacramentals in a local church. According to Chupungco, there exist three major theological principles which guide this evaluation, which are "the liturgical nature of sacramentals as actions of Christ and the Church; their purpose in relation to the sacraments; and the place they hold in the various turning points of human life as well as in the events both great and small that happen in the life of individual Christians and their communities."[56] Since the liturgy and the law can be compared as forms of Catholic practice, it is pertinent to discuss these criteria in relation to the law. The following section therefore begins with a discussion of the principles that assess the appropriateness of theologies, signs, and laws for a local church by relating them to the local praxis itself *ad intra*; this reveals that only theologies, signs, and laws which materialise in local practices can be regarded as authentic expressions of the Christian faith. It then addresses criteria of coherence which assess the suitability of local theologies, practices, and laws *ad extra* by demanding their consistency with the beliefs and practices of other churches and of the church as a global body.

8.2.4 Sparking Local Practices

A criterion for the Catholicity of a local theology, which Schreiter discusses, is that it has an impact on the local community.[57] For him it is evident that theologies that have no repercussion within the local churches cannot be true local theologies. Stephen Bevans observes in a similar vein that theological contextualisation always entails the risk of relativism, syncretism, and particularism, but a greater peril is that theologies which defy contextualisation end up with no relevance for the local communities: "There is no doubt that when a theologian takes context seriously, he or she can fall into the danger of taking these realities more seriously than the Judaeo-Christian tradition as expressed in scripture and church tradition. But even more dangerous is a theology that speaks to no one, that has no power because it has no

[55] See Schreiter (1985), pp. 117–121.

[56] Chupungco (1992), p. 64.

[57] See Schreiter (1985), p. 119.

real audience."[58] This study considers this criterion to be directly applicable to the law. As mentioned in Sect. 5.2.5, ecclesiastical jurisprudence developed the doctrine of *receptio legis* to describe the idea that legal messages require some response to become and remain law. In a similar vein to Schreiter identifying the effectiveness of a theology as proof of its Catholicity, one can therefore argue that ecclesiastical laws need to impact the life of local churches to pass as laws. As also mentioned, an unsolved problem is those laws that receive some response but largely fail to have an impact on a group. As laws that suffer from non-reception for the most part seem to be unsuitable for shaping ecclesiastical reality to any greater degree, one needs to discuss whether it is adequate to limit the invalidating effect of non-reception to cases such as *Veterum Sapientia* where a law fully fails to generate any response. Drawing a parallel to Schreiter's idea of local theologies bearing fruit in their communities supports the idea of understanding legal reception more as a holistic process in which laws shape the social reality of a group. In this case, one might have to take far more seriously those manifold instances in which rules, while being observed by a handful of Catholics, largely fail to impact the life of a church. Section 7.2.5 referred to cool encounters, where Catholics widely ignore a global regulation due to its incapacity to respond to a local need; in the same vein, Catholics can disregard local laws that fail to produce local meaning. Their neglect might even be an articulation of their *sense of law* as a practical subtype of their sense of faith. Whilst not every act of non-reception is a manifestation of the sense of faith, one should not overlook those cases in which non-reception communicates that a law is detrimental in a particular context. Theologically speaking, non-reception can be viewed as the work of the Spirit. It is therefore not an option to simply dismiss cases where a widespread non-reception signals that there is some deficit in the laws.

When considering whether a theology is truly Christian, Robert Schreiter links his idea that authentic theologies should bear fruit with the notion that such a theology should also have an impact on the liturgies, Catholic worship, and local rituals. This thought connects with Anscar Chupungco's proposition on the qualities of rituals that are suitable to become local sacramentals.[59] According to their view, practices, rituals, and rules conducive to celebrating the Catholic faith may become local practices, rituals, and rules. In contrast, as Schreiter notes, local beliefs that make no sense with regard to worship seem to miss the essential ritual dimension of Christianity. Their failure to make any sense with regard to worship may indicate that they do not assist the church and its faith. In a similar vein, other practices, rituals, and rules that fail to convey a meaning to local Catholics and to support their identity formation demand closer scrutiny to determine whether they are fit to become part of Catholic praxis. Rules that do not, explicitly or implicitly, serve the church as a community of worship and prayer seem to miss the point. By saying this, this study is not stating that all legal rules need to refer to the liturgies expressly.

[58] Bevans (2002), p. 24.

[59] See Chupungco (1992), p. 64.

The majority of ecclesiastical rules do not make explicit mention of worship. However, in a broad perspective one might find that it is the purpose of canon law to foster the church as a ritual community, inter alia by providing the community with regulations on liturgical offices and functions, sacred places, and temporal goods. Canon 1254 §1 CIC/1983 helps to illustrate this by way of example. The canon is the first of the Code's regulations on the administration of ecclesiastical goods. It claims the innate right of the church to own and administer assets of all sorts "to pursue its proper purposes". In its list of the three main purposes pursued by the church, §2 of the same canon mentions liturgical purposes first when defining: "The proper purposes are principally: to order divine worship, to care for the decent support of the clergy and other ministers, and to exercise works of the sacred apostolate and of charity, especially towards the needy". In analogy to Schreiter's criterion for evaluating what an authentic Christian theology is, one can therefore state that proper laws are those rules that sustain the local churches as Catholic ritual communities.

8.2.5 Coherence and Concordance

Complementing the fact that local theologies, rituals, and rules spark a praxis is the criterion that the local expressions of Catholicism build bridges with other local manifestations of the faith. Robert Schreiter discusses this criterion as one of coherence. Local theologies must demonstrate their consistency in relation to the church's tradition and theologies developed within other churches. He acknowledges that it is difficult to evaluate which new theologies concord with the ecclesiastical tradition. However, "if the theological formulation finds itself clearly at odds with the rest of Christian doctrine or requires a radical shifting of large parts of it, there is a very good chance that it is not a well-formed Christian performance."[60] This observation alludes to manifest cases of non-compatibility. But it is less helpful when it comes to identifying more ambiguous cases where it is less certain whether a theology is Christian. In a similar vein, it is easy to identify some legal rules as being clearly in opposition to Christian purposes. Yet in most cases it is disputable if this is the case. Thus, whilst coherence is an appropriate standard by which to judge the suitability of rules for serving the church, this criterion leads one swiftly to the problem of *who* should decide which laws are coherent with ecclesiastical tradition. As tradition is always invented tradition,[61] as indicated in Sect. 6.2.6, it is not merely debatable who should decide which rules show a coherence with ecclesiastical tradition, but also who should decide in the first place what tradition is. John Huels likewise seems to acknowledge that tradition is a matter of authority when asking: "What is essential in theology and canon law that cannot be compromised, no matter

[60] Schreiter (1985), p. 118.

[61] For a closer look at the concept, see Hobsbawm and Ranger (1983).

how strange it may seem to a foreign mentality? Who can best make these determinations?"[62] Typically, it is the supreme authority of the church who is to decide what tradition is and, consequently, which rules concord with tradition. This study has argued, in any case, that the Roman supremacy in deciding these issues has led to the problems diagnosed in this book. Hence, it seems adequate to rethink whether it is wise to entrust the Roman authorities alone with the power to discern which signs are fit to constitute Catholic identity. It is clear that the Apostolic See in its function of protecting the unity of the Catholic Church has a particular role to play in these discernments. Yet it has also become evident that a reshaping of legislation that attempts to overcome colonialist patterns requires the local churches to be granted a place at the table. As a result, the assessment of whether a local rule is coherent in the light of ecclesiastical tradition requires a dialogue between the supreme authority and the local churches.

Some of Schreiter's other criteria for assessing whether a local theology is an authentic expression of the Christian faith help to substantiate this idea. He identifies the willingness of local churches to subject their theologies to the evaluation of others as a shibboleth of whether a theology articulates the shared faith. As Christianity is about communion, churches that refuse theological communication with other churches cannot be considered to be following the Gospel message. Furthermore, he regards it to be an essential criterion for a Christian theology that it is not fully content with exclusively focusing on the concerns of the local church but also attempts to support the church as a whole. A local theology, thus, endeavours to contribute to theology in general and to other local theologies, be it in the form of addition or challenge. Accordingly, the relationship between local theologies is not essentially harmonious. Schreiter, in any case, is convinced that adding their views to the comprehensive picture of global theologies is an energy driving authentic local theologies. In a similar vein, one can assume that local rules have something to offer to other legislations as well as to ecclesiastical legal knowledge in general. Regulations that help a church to fulfil its mission could benefit other churches, too. This finding suggests that it might be a natural inclination among the churches to exchange legal experiences and present each other with concepts that have proven useful in their particular context.

Schreiter finds that the desire to add local approaches to the overall picture of Catholic theologies goes hand in hand with the desire to learn from others. As authentic local theologies aim to build the church as a unity out of plurality by giving and receiving from others, local Catholics invite other Christians to assess their theologies. This thought can be applied to the law, too. In this light, local rules make themselves plausible as adequate regulations when they allow for external scrutiny. In comparing local with alternative regulations provided by others, they are subjected to examination to show that they are appropriate legal signs within ecclesiastical systems of meaning. Thus, subjecting the law to mutual interchurch criticism prevents it from losing its coherence with other laws. This dynamic of mutual

[62] Huels (1987), p. 265.

scrutiny could also reduce the current tendency to evaluate the consistency of local regulations solely through a Roman lens. Schreiter explicitly addresses this problem by noting that the other churches' criticism of local theologies does not justify the unilateral and systematic targeting of new local theologies. In the same way, the coherence argument is not an invitation for a unidirectional centralist scrutiny of local laws and does not imply that all local churches have to adjust their rules to be coherent with centralist legislation. Instead, it implies that all rules, including those made in Rome, have to correspond with the standards agreed upon by the local churches.

8.3 Reconstructing Global Law

The previous section expounded that it is necessary to reduce centralist legislation to give decentralised rules room to flourish in its place. This argument in favour of local legislation raises the question of whether it makes sense to pursue the idea of a global body of Catholic canon law for the future. The following section will argue why there is some sense in endowing the worldwide church with a common legal framework, even though this remains a disputable issue. One sociological argument in favour of it connects with the observation that law is a major reducer of complexity in pluralist societies and communities, as Niklas Luhmann elaborated.[63] Centralised rules can help to reduce the difficulty of communicating across a complex system such as the worldwide Catholic Church. And it appears to be a viable option in many ways. As the local churches require a structural backbone to organise membership issues, grant basic rights and duties, and provide regulations on ecclesiastical offices, functions, and institutions, establishing a constitutional law to ensure a certain homogeneity of ecclesiastical structures seems sensible. Shared arrangements in church organisation and procedures make interchurch communications easier. The churches also profit from basic regulations that set out how to deal with ecclesiastical goods. They benefit from disciplinary law for their ministers as well as procedural law to sanction them in cases where their behaviour is detrimental to church life.

Such rules could have even greater merit than merely reducing complexity, as they could also touch upon identity issues. By endowing Catholics all over the globe with a uniform legal frame, canon law could become a marker of identity. As mentioned in Sect. 3.3, law is a major producer of cultural codes and a powerful cultural identifier, as it is essentially concerned with issues of belonging.[64] Some of the identity-shaping experiences that individuals have when belonging to social groups result from being members of legal communities. It is particularly the experience as legal subjects—as individuals with rights and duties—that shapes many modern

[63] E.g. Luhmann (1970), p. 177.

[64] See Burgess (1997).

individuals' self-perception beyond the Global North. In this sense, Catholic canon law could serve as a producer of codes and rules with which Catholics identify in one way or another and which could become a cultural marker of Catholicism. In any case, this would require canon law to become a legal framework offering signs and symbols that make sense to local Catholics from various backgrounds.

8.3.1 Reversing the Perspective

It is therefore reasonable to conclude that shared legal rules could serve as effective identifiers of Catholicism and as an expression of unity among the different churches. Yet at the same time this body of rules must be reduced to provide the local churches merely with a frame-like structure to avoid the pitfalls which this study has encountered in its analysis of the present law. There is a natural inclination for global rules to reproduce hegemonic structures and a continuous risk of neo-colonial relapse connected with global legislation. This temptation seems even stronger in systems that aim at unity through uniformity. Whilst unity in church is desirable, it has become apparent that the current method of enforcing it through uniform global rules is theologically unjustifiable, procedurally questionable, and practically ineffective. As a result, canonists who argue that the church might profit from global regulation are challenged to explain how future lawmaking might prevent the re-emergence of unjustified asymmetries. The following sections will discuss which aspects—theoretical, practical, and procedural—require attention in the development of global rules that are more sensitive to the problem that global claims tend to establish asymmetrical power relations as a way of embarking on a "civilising mission",[65] in Antony Anghie's words.

It is helpful to start with a theoretical shift of perspective on the unifying effect of global law. The current theory of canon law is most concerned with protecting the unity of the church by submitting the plural churches to uniform rules. An alternative could consist of replacing the top-down approach of legitimising centralist legislation with a bottom-up view. A starting point is the recognition that all legislative power should be with the local churches as true realisations of the Church of Christ. This is not a paradigm shift, bearing in mind that the current law already attributes the diocesan bishops with all legislative authority in their dioceses "except for cases which the law or a decree of the Supreme Pontiff reserves to the supreme authority or to another ecclesiastical authority" (canon 381 §1 CIC/1983). This norm was a paradigm shift after the 1917 Code, which still understood episcopal power according to the concept of concession to derive from the pope. The new system follows the idea of reservation, presenting the bishops as genuine powerholders within their jurisdictions, lacking only some of the competence reserved to other authorities to protect the unity of the church. This conception of episcopal power indicates a

[65] Anghie (2006), p. 742.

theological rethinking of the bishops' role after the Second Vatican Council. Legislation, for its part, embraced it only halfway. Whilst the exception clause of canon 381 §1 CIC/1983 implies that it limits the bishops' power only marginally in favour of minor reservations of competence for other authorities, these reservations are in fact enormous; they inter alia cover the whole of centralist legislation. Hence, in practice replacing concession with reservation has not brought much change. Yet it is possible to rework this. Realising the theoretical change from concession to reservation on the practical level could attribute decentralised legislation with maximum power, merely reserving authority to centralised legislation with regard to matters which essentially require a uniform regulation to preserve the unity of the church. To substantiate the need for this transformation ecclesiologically, it helps to return to the argument posed in Sect. 7.1.5 on the problematic restriction of the bishops' right of remonstration. In this context, this study has recalled that the local churches, unlike the Apostolic See, are true realisations of the Church of Christ and participate in the universal church.[66] Therefore, they have an ecclesiological dignity that the Apostolic See does not. One can consequently see why centralist legislation should not dominate the local churches by imposing global rules on them. However, the Apostolic See serves the universal church. It does so also with the help of legislation endowing the universal church with a unifying legal frame. Global rules, thus, as one may argue, may legitimately bind the local churches and restrict the local authorities' power insofar as a uniform legal framework protects the unity of the universal church. Yet, this also means that global rules for the local churches are only legitimate if they support the unity of global Catholicism. In those cases in which legal uniformity does not contribute to unity, it seems hardly justified to subject the local churches to global legislation.

8.3.2 Developing a Criteriology

Certainly, it seems easy to demand this—and complicated to determine which issues require a global regulation to preserve the unity of the universal church. Whilst one might come to agree that law assists the universal church when it fosters the flourishing of the local churches, their communication with the other churches, and the growth of a common faith and identity shared among Christians, it is difficult to transform these purposes into a criteriology to identify issues that call for a uniform regulation. Robert Schreiter nevertheless offers some ideas. When discussing which preconditions the ecclesiastical tradition must fulfil in order to be meaningful for the local churches, he noted that tradition has a meaning for Christians whenever it provides them with resources for identity building, for creating cultural cohesion, and for integrating new elements into their church, life, and faith.[67] Borrowing his

[66] See Second Vatican Council (1964), nos. 23, 26. Acta Apostolicae Sedis (1965), pp. 27–29, 31–32.

[67] See Schreiter (1985), p. 105.

criteria to apply them to canon law, one might find, first of all, that a uniform legal frame has a meaning for Catholics when it provides them with resources from which to build a Catholic identity. Rules that grant Catholics the right to receive the sacraments, help them to build reliable structures to organise their communal life, and legally pre-structure their path to achieve ecclesiastical offices and functions, for instance, can aid their identity formation. Second, global legislation facilitates the unity of the church when it benefits cultural cohesion. This is the case when it preserves the plural cultures as systems of meaning while assisting them to effectively connect with other cultures. Global law could enable the local churches to establish structures that support church life and the celebration of the faith by specifying rules on ministry, preaching and teaching, worship, and sacramental life, and by establishing procedures for dealing with local challenges. A centralised legal framework which contributes to cultural cohesion also supports interchurch collaboration and supplies the local churches with concepts and a legal language that allows them to share their legal experiences. Third, a global legal frame might promote unity when it fosters the integration of new elements into the plural cultures by furthering mutual legal learning. Mutual learning is the free acceptance of legal goods provided by others. It requires autonomous decision and is incompatible with imposed reception. A global law sustaining the unity of the universal church, thus, must accept the freedom of the local churches and curb its impulse to create unity through enforced uniformity. This includes strengthening the instruments with which the local churches can resist legal colonisation through unsuitable laws.

In short, one can find that whenever global legislation aids the local churches in fostering Catholic identities, cultural cohesion, and mutual learning, it contributes to the unity of the universal church. Whenever decentralised rules achieve these goals better, they have priority over centralised ones. Whenever global laws impede the achievement of these goals, they do not serve the unity of the church and are unjustified. And yet again, while all this is easily said, it is difficult to determine how global law can fulfil its role of providing resources for identity building, cultural cohesion, and integration of new elements into the plural cultures. It is, once again, of help to study Schreiter's considerations in this respect. He tackles a similar question when discussing which preconditions tradition must fulfil in order to achieve its purpose. He introduces several prerequisites that a tradition must possess in order to sustain the local churches: it requires credibility, intelligibility, authority, openness for change, and affirmation.[68] These criteria are also of help in establishing how legislation could proceed.

[68] See ibid., pp. 107–109.

8.3.3 Credibility and Acceptance

A Catholic tradition tends to be regarded as credible when the Catholics widely accept it, as Schreiter determines. Most individuals are fairly tolerant in this respect, as they do not expect the tradition to answer fully to all of their needs: "The tradition may not be able to solve all the problems of a culture, but it must be evident to the members of a culture that their concerns are the tradition's concern."[69] One can apply Schreiter's observation to the law as it ties in with the finding of the sociology of law that legal subjects do not expect legal rules to address all their concerns. However, they must feel that their concerns are shared by the law to some extent. This concords with the conditions under which laws stand a chance of finding approval, which Niklas Luhmann observed; reference was made to his approach in sections 7.1.1 and 7.1.2. Luhmann noted that new rules are usually accepted when they derive from transparent lawmaking which absorbs the shock effect of legal development, and when they allow for participation in decision making which endows the legal subjects with a fair chance of impacting legislation.[70] So even deficient rules can receive approval when they result from transparent lawmaking which encourages the legal subjects' participation, giving them hope that they might influence legislation to the effect of improving it in the future. As already mentioned, canon law at present does not meet these conditions. And jurisprudence fails to address the non-reception and non-acceptance of the law in many contexts. While the doctrine of *receptio legis* provides a valuable idea in theory, it has only a limited relevance in practice. Yet if rules require at least some tacit acceptance in a community to have an impact on the group, it can hardly be irrelevant if they are widely ignored. Patricia Goler made some suggestions about how to approach this problem. In her 1972 article, in which she criticised canon law for being white law, she also suggested ways in which it could be developed in the US-American context to address racism and racial segregation. A legal system living up to the expectation of being credible needs to establish an advocacy system, as she demanded:

> We have no tribunals examining the conscious and unconscious habits which have led to separate and unequal Catholicism based on race. We have no procedures for removing pastors or bishops who perpetuate dual parish or school systems. I am not, initially at least, suggesting procedures. What I am suggesting is an advocacy role for canon lawyers and a usage for canon law to promote social justice while the Church still has any possibility of being 'universal' in America.[71]

Goler's proposal makes it clear that she does not expect canon law to be perfect or to deliver complete justice. However, as a Black Catholic she demands that her community's concerns be recognised by the law. And she suggests giving these concerns a voice through an advocacy framework. Hence, if canonical legislation

---

[69] Ibid., p. 107.

[70] See Luhmann (1969), p. 232.

[71] Goler (1972), p. 299.

wants to be credible to Catholics from different backgrounds, it must consider and consult with those affected by the law.

8.3.4 Transparency and Participation

Reforming legislation to meet the demand of transparency entails laying open who is part of the legislative bodies. It calls for information about how the representation of the local churches is organised and the publication of the criteria for choosing the representatives. In major reform projects that last several years or decades, it seems expedient to give the church members substantive information from time to time about where the reform is heading and to publish the draft law at several stages of the debate. The 1983 reform of the Code invested considerable effort in conducting a global consultation process—asking not solely the dicasteries of the Roman Curia, but also all of the bishops' conferences, the Union of Superiors General of the religious orders, and the ecclesiastical universities and faculties all over the globe for their critical opinion on the draft of the Code. However, the relevance of the global consultation and how it influenced legislation remained largely unclear. It seems advisable in any future reform to publish information on the return of the consultative process and to make known how the local churches' responses affect the draft law, including reasons why reform bodies follow up on some suggestions and leave others aside. Likewise, transparent procedures should include publishing the reasons why the pope decides to depart from legislative proposals as suggested by expert commissions when promulgating the law. It could contribute to the credibility of the law if legislation avoids surprise effects such as the sudden disappearance of the administrative procedure from the 1983 Code in the final papal promulgation, to which Sect. 7.1.1 referred.

As mentioned, more participation in legislation requires greater involvement by the ecclesiastical stakeholders from all over the globe. John Huels hinted at this need when demanding that legislation "requires listening to the people of God in the local churches."[72] This entails diversifying the bodies of legal reform by consistently involving representatives of the churches, clergy and laypeople alike, and also by selecting members who were not educated in Roman universities or institutes. Also feasible might be the option to limit the number of representatives of the Roman Curia in bodies of legal reform. Besides having representatives selected by the pope, as was the practice in the reform of 1983, the bishops' conferences could be entrusted with naming or selecting experts from the churches, thereby ensuring that plural voices are heard and hegemonic imbalances are reduced.

Ecclesiastical reform projects require greater consultative involvement, including not only legal experts who share their opinions but also representatives of the various stakeholders. It seems particularly necessary to revise the consultation

[72] Huels (1987), p. 289.

process to integrate the perspective of the local churches. This idea is not new; as early as 1969, Ladislas Orsy made the proposal to organise a broad and transparent process when global rules are concerned.[73] Canonist Richard Puza requested that the right of the local churches to be consulted in every act of global legislation be established as part of the law.[74] He proposed entrusting the Dicastery for Legislative Texts with organising the respective consultations for global legislation. In addition to the consultation of official ecclesiastical stakeholders, such as representatives of the local churches, which he strongly endorsed, Orsy also suggested consulting public opinion, both inside and outside the church. He recommended the reception of this practice of common law legislation in canonical legislation. Against voices disqualifying the value of public opinion he argued: "This is not to reduce the laws to the lowest common denominator but to trust human nature and in particular human intelligence inside and outside the Church."[75] Orsy referred to the experience with global legislation which political organisations such as the United Nations bring to the table. He proposed investing effort in a dialogue with these organisations in order to learn from their expertise.

8.3.5 Increasing Intelligibility

Returning to Robert Schreiter's thoughts on what makes a tradition meaningful for the local churches, one further criterion that he discusses is that a tradition must be intelligible. This is the case when Catholics are able to interpret its signs to derive meaning from them. To allow for this, signs used in a tradition must relate to signs common in local systems of meaning so that individuals can make sense of them based on their knowledge of other systems of meaning: "The sign system and codes in the tradition must be close enough to those in other semiotic domains in the culture (especially economic and familial domains) to be understood."[76] Applying Schreiter's observation to the question of what makes canon law intelligible to legal subjects, one can suppose that it is its correspondence to similar signs used in other systems of meaning, such as secular law. Ecclesiastical legal subjects, hence, stand a good chance of deciphering canonical signs when they have some legal knowledge and can therefore derive meaning out of legal terminology and concepts. As shown, there are in any case several challenges connected with this for canon law. Catholics with a sound knowledge of the law in their home countries may find it even particularly difficult to make sense of canon law, as their experience of modern secular law often conflicts with the terminology, concepts, and institutions of canon law.

---

[73] See Orsy (1969), p. 74.

[74] See Puza (1993), p. 16.

[75] Orsy (1969), p. 74.

[76] Schreiter (1985), p. 107.

Deriving from this is that canon law requires more intelligibility to convey meaning to Catholics. This said, this study does not argue in favour of submitting all Catholics to canonical education. Instead, canon law has to draw closer to secular law to meet the legal subjects' expectations and gain their understanding. This is because in the modern age, in most contexts secular law has become the primary reference for what individuals understand as law. Canonist and legal historian Stephan Kuttner described this finding in its historical development as follows: "Gallicanism, mortmain statutes, *praemunire*, concordats with the princes: they all contribute to establishing the doctrine and practice of the secular ruler's *iura circa sacra*, and to reduce the universal canon law to a set of domestic by-laws of a cultic association chartered by the omnipotent State."[77] This diminished standing of canon law in society is reflected in the way it is perceived. As most individuals think of state law first and foremost when they come across the term "law", it is unrealistic to expect Catholics to interpret canon law without drawing on their experience of secular law. One can discover this, for instance, by studying procedural law, the example referenced in Sect. 2.1, where conflicts derive from different procedural standards in secular and ecclesiastical adjudication. American Catholics have grappled with deficits of due process in church since the nineteenth century, as John Beal noted.[78] Over the past years, the German debates have focused on different standards in secular law and canon law, particularly with regard to the procedural right to be heard. That alleged victims and witnesses are often not invited to testify in person in the administrative penal procedures undermines many Catholics' trust in the ecclesiastical procedures. Yet there is no way to regain that trust by emphasising that canon law differs from secular law. As ecclesiastical legal subjects are members of different legal orders and thus experienced legal pluralists, they compare legal systems with each other. And they assess issues of justice and fairness in the light of the legal system in which they feel most at home, which is frequently secular state law.

One example relating to legal terminology can help to clarify this point. In an interview with a canonist on the 2021 reform of penal law, the interviewer asked why the reformed law still speaks of "a sin against the sixth commandment of the Decalogue" (canons 1385, 1395, and 1398 CIC/1983), even though many Catholics, including canonists, have repeatedly criticised this choice of words as being unclear and inappropriate to describe the nature of sexual transgressions.[79] The canonist responded by alluding to the tradition of using this expression in canon law and moral theology. In response to the question of why the legislator did not change ecclesiastical terminology to correspond with secular legislation, for instance by speaking of "offences against sexual self-determination", the canonist dismissed this expression as lacking a history in canon law. He thus emphasised the autonomy of canonical terminology. While one might see it that way, it certainly does not

77 Kuttner (1990), pp. 208–209.

78 See Beal (1996), pp. 51–52.

79 See Juchem (2021).

foster the legal subjects' understanding. Many Catholics will continue to criticise that the law speaks of *sin*, even though sins have no place in modern penal law. They will wonder why the penal rule pertains to sexual abuse, while the sixth commandment of the Decalogue speaks of adultery. And they might even suspect that legislation strategically uses unclear terms to facilitate cover-ups. Consequently, if canon law loses touch with secular legal terminology, it jeopardises the legal subjects' acceptance. In order to gain their approval, it would benefit from different terminological choices.

8.3.6 Language and Terminology

As suggested, drawing canon law closer to secular legal concepts and terminology where possible increases its intelligibility and acceptance. This could include abandoning the priority of Latin in legal communications and promulgating global laws in the world languages. This decision would promote understanding but also change the power relations between the Latinised Roman church and the local churches. Translations are always connected with power and knowledge, as Judith Gruber emphasises, a power of "selection, interpretation, and rewriting in hegemonic cultural relations."[80] Translating the law into the languages of the plural churches would symbolise a divestment of the Apostolic See's power over the churches and a more equal share of power among the churches. Undoubtedly, providing official translations of the law is an arduous task. Yet it is not unprecedented. For instance, the law can learn from the liturgies. Similarly to how liturgical translations require the collaboration between the bishops' conferences and the Congregation for Divine Worship and the Discipline of the Sacraments, as specified by Pope Francis in his 2017 Motu Proprio *Magnum Principium*,[81] translations of the law could be accomplished through cooperation between the bishops' conferences and the Dicastery for Legislative Texts. With regard to the challenge of producing authentic multilingual rules binding in several languages, the church can learn from examples such as the European Union. The case of the European Union demonstrates how difficult it is to deal with a multitude of authentic legal languages. However, it also reveals that forming a union of equal partners necessitates treating language issues as power issues and therefore involves treating them on equal terms. If the local churches are true representations of the Church of Christ, the languages in which these churches express their faith and celebrate their liturgies should be treated with the same seriousness in legal matters. This ecclesiological argument in favour of a multilingual law is accompanied by pragmatic arguments. Translating global rules into the world languages, for instance, helps to uncover tensions between legal cultures. That certain legal ideas do not translate well into another language is often a symptom of

[80] Gruber (2018), p. 69.

[81] See Francis (2017). Acta Apostolicae Sedis (2017), pp. 967–970.

cultural issues that impede legal communication. Peter Shannon, for instance, refers to terms such as *express*, *explicit*, or *virtual*, the meaning of which is significantly different in canonical terminology compared to their common law use,[82] which makes word-by-word translations misleading. He also relates to the difficulty of expressing canonical *dominium* with the help of common law *ownership* terminology or of harmonising *juridic persons* of canon law with secular *corporations*. Gunther Teubner's example of the difficulty of implementing *good faith* in British law alludes to the complications of importing a principle of continental European civil law into a common law context, as discussed in Sect. 7.3.2.[83] In translating the rules, these difficulties can be identified and addressed before they become major irritants in other legal cultures.

8.3.7 Revising Interpretation

That global laws need to be intelligible to be meaningful attributes particular relevance to their interpretation. As discussed in Sect. 7.3, the local generation of legal meaning is at present suffering particularly from the legislator's decision to subject the interpretation of global canon law to a distinct methodology laid down in the canons of interpretation (see canons 6, 17, and 18 CIC/1983). Acknowledging this problem, Ladislas Orsy remarks somewhat helplessly: "I know of no secure and universal guidelines which could tell the interpreter how the transition of a law from one culture to another can best be made; I know only that persons at home in both cultures (where the law originates and where it is to be applied) can do a great deal to facilitate the transition."[84] His doubts are well-founded. There are no rules to ensure that an effective (re)construction of meaning takes place in the receiving culture. As Orsy suggests, the only way in which legal transfers succeed is by relying on legally versed receivers who attribute the received rule with a new meaning which makes sense in its new environment. This finding calls for the revision of ecclesiastical interpretation theory and the canons of interpretation. Whilst the content of canon 18 CIC/1983, containing the ecclesiastical variant of the rule of lenity, might prove to be undisputed across the borders of civil and common law cultures alike, canons 17 and 6 §2 CIC/1983 seem more debatable. These canons in their current form leave little room for independent local reconstructions of global rules. They promote a highly centralist approach to interpretation, urging interpreters to apply textualist and intentionalist methods to discover the Roman meaning of legal concepts and suppressing local methodologies in favour of a uniform methodology. Orsy has taken a critical stance towards this and has argued in favour of restricting

[82] See Shannon (1985), p. 618.

[83] See Teubner (1998), pp. 11–32.

[84] Orsy (1983), p. 122 fn. 28.

the legislator's relevance for interpretation.[85] This includes that none of these canons of interpretation should be part of the law itself. Legislation could allow for greater freedom of interpretation by abstaining from codifying the rules of interpretation. This would enable interpreters to proceed in accordance with their local methodologies.

8.3.8 Legitimising Power

When describing the conditions under which traditions can be meaningful for local churches, Robert Schreiter refers to authority as a third criterion. In his view, one can understand a tradition as having authority when it is capable of introducing new elements into a culture and connecting them with local identities.[86] One can apply his thoughts to global legislation. It has authority in the local churches when it is capable of introducing legal rules into a local church in such a way that they connect with the Catholics' experiences and identities to generate meaning. Following Schreiter, one can also understand authority as the power to speak on behalf of the law. This alludes to the power of the law to endow individuals and groups with the authority to exercise legislative, judicial, and executive power accepted in the local churches. Modern individuals, in any case, tend to accept power merely as authority and, thus, as legitimate domination when they find it to be based on tradition, charisma, or the law, as Max Weber argued.[87] Tradition, however, has ceased to serve as a consistent foundation for authority in modernity, as Schreiter notes in line with Weber. It reappears now and then to legitimise power, particularly in times of crisis, in a similar vein to charisma. Yet both tradition and charisma have lost much of their influence in legitimising power in modern times. It is interesting to note though that Schreiter stops at this point and does not refer to the law as Weber's most reliable source for legitimising power. According to Weber, it is the law that in modernity largely eclipses charismatic and traditional authority. Following Weber, power is primarily considered legitimate authority when it is subject to the law and thus controlled and restrained by the law. This idea of legitimising power and domination by subjecting it to the law includes the power of the legislator, courts and tribunals, and administrative bodies. Their power to govern a group is regarded as legitimate particularly in those cases in which it is tied to rules restricting it and controlling its exercise.

Hence, legal subjects tend to accept decisions made by these authorities because their power is constrained by the law. Poor checks and balances, on the other hand, can undermine their legitimacy. This is a problem in church. A rule of law that proves porous in light of instruments such as equity and dispensation casts doubt on

[85] See Orsy (1984), pp. 67–68.
[86] See Schreiter (1985), p. 108.
[87] See Weber (1978), pp. 219–220.

the capacity of canon law to restrict power. As abundant equity and dispensation undermine legal certainty, equality, and justice as principles connected with the rule of law, many Catholics from civil law and common law traditions alike have grown sceptical about the ability of canon law to transform domination into legitimate authority. Hence, if the law is to be a meaningful source of authority for local churches, it must be reformed to meet the common standards associated with the rule of law, in line with Schreiter's approach. With regard to agents in church, the rule of law demands that they be subject to the law; that there be a separation of powers; that public offices be bound to selection procedures such as elections which enjoy widespread acceptance; and that the power connected with offices be controlled, for instance by limiting the time periods for which offices can be held. Substantive criteria associated with the rule of law include guarantees of fundamental rights, such as equality before the law and freedom of speech and assembly. These rights allow for public criticism of officeholders and their subjection to public scrutiny through a free press and both public and academic discourse. As mentioned in Sect. 7.2.6, global canon law at present restricts freedom of speech (see canon 212 §3 CIC/1983) and freedom of theological research (see canon 218 CIC/1983). These regulations require reform if they are to support a rule of law in church which helps to legitimise legal authority.

8.3.9 Reallocating Authority

The question of authority with regard to global legislation becomes particularly pertinent in cases of conflict where the issue of authority itself is at stake. As mentioned, one approach to revising current legislation would consist of the reallocation of authority, moving the focus from the top down. Hence, instead of locating all power to legislate for the global church at the Apostolic See, it should primarily reside with the local churches, with the exception of those issues that require a uniform regulation to preserve the unity of the universal church. Yet deciding which matters should be subjected to centralised regulation proves to be difficult. This is because legal issues are regularly mixed matters, consisting of elements that call for local variances but also of elements that demand a certain degree of uniformity. The law of the sacraments illustrates this complex blend. As discussed in Sect. 7.2.8 with regard to the Eucharist, the current decentralised rule on the Eucharistic species is problematic (see canon 924 CIC/1983). Providing alternatives to wheat bread and grape wine in regions in which these matters are uncommon could support the symbolic value of the Eucharistic species to represent real food to local Catholics. Yet it is plausible that the sacraments as effective signs for conveying God's grace to Christians all over the globe necessitate some uniform provisions. So it is difficult to draw a line between decentralised and centralised responsibility in regulating these matters. John Huels's suggestion for how to deal with the Eucharistic substances reveals this uncertainty. Whilst he argues in favour of improving the law of the Eucharist by allowing local ingredients to be used to produce the Eucharistic species,[88] he does not specify how to achieve this. Technically, Huels's idea can be realised in two ways. One option is to maintain centralised rules which, in any case, need to be more sensitive to local circumstances. This would require revising canon 924 CIC/1983 to allow for greater flexibility in choosing appropriate ingredients. Another option would be to allocate the power to regulate these matters on the level of decentralised legislation, merely reserving some indispensable elements to centralised legislation, such as the rule to use two species, a matter representing Christ's body and a matter representing Christ's blood, when celebrating the Eucharist. These two alternative approaches reveal the difficulty of differentiating between global and local responsibilities. Yet behind this problem stands the issue of authority itself, of who is entitled to determine which matters call for a uniform regulation.

It is interesting to study William Blackstone's thoughts on related problems, which he posed in his 1765 *Commentaries on the Laws of England*, when discussing who should decide the fate of English law in the colonies when its rules fail to answer adequately to the local circumstances:

> What shall be admitted and what rejected at what times, and under what restrictions, must, in case of dispute, be decided in the first instance by their own provincial judicature, subject to the revision and control of the king in the council; the whole of their constitution being also liable to be new-modeled and reformed by the general superintending power of the legislature in the mother-country.[89]

Blackstone, accordingly, suggested a mixed model for resolving these disputes, bringing all stakeholders' views in front of the provincial judicature, which remains under the control of the king. Blackstone, thus, seems to prioritise local decisions, yet in coordination with the king. And he found that profound constitutional change required consent from the mother country. The analogy between Blackstone's considerations and legislation in church is evidently limited. But it contains helpful ideas. First, it proposes that cases of conflict should be decided locally, which would realise subsidiarity. Second, it suggests that fundamental decisions should be subject to critical revision by others. Third, it proposes that constitutional issues should be discussed with the wider community. More specifically, one could consider a mechanism for the church whereby decentralised legislators independently resolve issues within their own church. Where decentralised regulation affects the universal church, local legislation may be required to consult the Dicastery for Legislative Texts. In cases in which consultation does not lead to an adequate solution, the matter could be subjected to a broader debate. Ladislas Orsy seems to have the Synod of Bishops in mind as the context for debating conflictive topics, as he asks: "[C]ould the Roman Synod of Bishops become a forum where proposals for change in the laws could be introduced and debated?"[90] Synodal structures bringing together the bishops as well as representatives of clerics and laypeople from all over the globe

[88] See Huels (1987), p. 281.

[89] Blackstone (1893), p. 107.

[90] Orsy (1996b), p. 15.

might be the framework for debating critical issues in the intersection of decentralised and centralised legislation and for discussing constitutional questions.

8.3.10 Challenging Change

In his considerations, Robert Schreiter goes on to explain that ecclesiastical traditions require constant renewal if they want to become and remain meaningful for the local churches. As cultures are continuously facing transformation, traditions must develop to avoid losing touch with local sources of meaning.[91] The churches are interwoven into a social environment. As a result, change in society has a major impact on them. This is naturally critical for the churches, as Schreiter maintains, as the Gospel message and Christianity always have a counter-cultural side to them. Throughout Christian history, it has been one of the great challenges to integrate the Christian faith into concrete contexts and yet retain a certain distance from them. John Huels also emphasises this tension: "To be Christian, in the fullest sense, means always being counter-cultural, living in society but being sufficiently distant from it to see its faults and seek changes that promote human and gospel values."[92] This tension might stimulate development on both sides, affecting the social environment as much as the church itself. Schreiter contends with regard to new encounters between a local culture and the Christian faith: "If Christianity is alive at all in a situation, it will certainly change things about the culture. The Christian message, after all, is about change: repentance, salvation, and an eschatological reality to be realized. To think that Christianity will not change a situation is to rob the Christian message of its most important part."[93] Hence, the Gospel when received in a new context impacts established sign systems: "From a semiotic perspective, one cannot introduce a new message into a culture without creating change in the sign systems."[94]

Cultural transformation can be more or less conflictual, as Schreiter discerns.[95] It is frequently less conflictual when transformation merely integrates new signs into a culture. It is more conflictual when new signs replace old ones. This can even undermine cultural cohesion. In these cases, transformations damage a culture to the extent that it fails to provide the group members with any more meaning, as "the codes, unable to accommodate the signs and the basic message to one another and to the tradition as a communication network, cease to provide cohesion and continuity to a culture, resulting in its breakdown."[96] This often causes individuals and

---

[91] See Schreiter (1985), p. 108.

[92] Huels (1987), p. 266.

[93] Schreiter (1985), p. 29.

[94] Ibid., p. 150.

[95] See ibid., p. 71.

[96] Ibid., pp. 106–107.

groups to turn their backs on their tradition, as Schreiter observes. This corresponds with observations made by the sociology of law that the development of the law is risky when attempting too much too rapidly. Niklas Luhmann's approach proves useful for explaining why this is difficult. For Luhmann law is *expectation*, as the legal community connects the law with certain behavioural expectations.[97] Change therefore tends to disappoint the legal subjects and risks their allegiance. As a result, it presents legislation with the challenge of effectively converting the legal subjects' expectations "to adapt expectations and actions to other norms."[98] This is easy to accomplish with minor adjustments to widely unknown rules,[99] but challenging with major reforms of well-known rules. When replacing prominent laws, legislation must seek to align the legal subjects' expectations with the new rules without causing significant disappointment. With regard to canon law, John Huels discerns that "change can only fully come about when the people themselves accept and integrate the change".[100] Gradual change is more likely to be accepted because it allows legal subjects' expectations to evolve slowly over time, thereby minimising disappointment. The example of the papal law *Traditionis Custodes* might serve to illustrate this challenge—this book already referred to it in Sect. 7.1.1 to exemplify that legal subjects do not appreciate unexpected surprise legislation. The same case might also show that a sudden transformation can destabilise groups. By disestablishing the Latin Tridentine Mass as a *lex orandi* of the Roman Rite, *Traditionis Custodes* disrupted the cohesion of cultures celebrating the old liturgy as their symbol of authentic Catholicism.[101] This transformation unsettled traditional liturgical systems of meaning as it challenged the connection between the Latin liturgy and Catholic identity. In consequence, many traditional Catholics were deeply disappointed. Some groups even called for resistance and considered a schism. One can understand their reaction as one way of defending their culture from breakdown by rejecting the new rules and insisting on the old rules as continuous bearers of meaning. Other traditional Catholics decided to abide by the papal command but felt that their Catholic identity had been damaged. Their reaction is a typical example of disappointment in the expectation of the law as a reliable expectation caused by legislation developing rules too abruptly and too radically.

[97] E.g. Luhmann (2014), p. 77.

[98] Ibid., p. 243.

[99] See ibid., p. 196.

[100] Huels (1987), p. 289.

[101] See Francis (2021b). Acta Apostolicae Sedis (2021), pp. 793–796.

8.3.11 Small Big Changes

The example of *Traditionis Custodes* also illustrates that bringing change by replacing old signs with new ones is particularly risky when it is enforced upon a culture. The imposition of signs onto a group is a critical interference with local sign systems and established webs of meaning. However, not all conflicts in transformation processes result from external influence, as Robert Schreiter realises. He mentions examples of change brought about from within a society, such as the French Revolution. During this period, groups within society came to reject specific signs that had previously played a key role in creating meaning. One might likewise perceive many demands for change within the church as being fostered by groups from within the church. When Catholic laypeople opt for more participation and speak out against clericalism, one can understand their claims as demands for a cultural transition of the church from within. This change, if successful, would affect full sign systems, as it would touch the constitution of the church and the law serving as its structural backbone. One example from Germany can illustrate in which sense the internal struggle over single signs, such as the ministers' clothing, can affect whole sign systems. Many liberal German Catholics view clerical attire, such as clerical collars, critically. They do not see the collar as a symbol of clerical identity but rather as a symbol of conservatism and clericalism. Therefore, it was very uncommon for liberal clergy to wear a collar after the Second Vatican Council. Over the past two decades, however, the collar has become popular again among the younger, more traditional clergy as a marker of clerical identity. Many liberals, clerics and laypeople alike, find this provocative. They interpret it as signifying a return to elitism and clericalism. As a result, they connect their demands for reform of the German Church with the removal of these symbols that distinguish the clerics from the laity. They want to remove the old signs because they are identified with a system of meaning that represents clericalism, male elitism, and the oppression of women. At the same time, many voices demand the introduction of new signs that express the church members' equality. Many German Catholics, for instance, welcome liturgical clothing for laypeople when taking on liturgical roles as signs acknowledging their service. Lay ministers presiding over worship often wear white albs to signify their liturgical function. For many, this means that they are recognised as ministers, and this has become an important part of their identity. These debates show that the demands for reform, as voiced in the German Church, sometimes pertain to apparently small signs, such as the ministers' clothing, but in fact touch upon whole systems of meaning reaching deep into the constitution of the church. Hence, replacing old signs with new ones can be a sensitive issue when it touches upon fundamental matters, such as identity.

However, replacing signs can destabilise some cultures while allowing others to flourish, as the example of *Traditionis Custodes* shows. Whilst this law distressed some traditional Catholics, other groups have embraced the reform as an urgent step towards modernising the church. Many of these groups find that it is only through the abolition of signs incompatible with modern Christianity that Catholicism continues to be meaningful. This ambiguity highlights a common issue with all legal reforms, which must strike a balance between stability and change in order to address the concerns of stakeholders who are disappointed by transformation and those who are disappointed by stagnation. Since reform and stagnation alike can lead to legal subjects feeling disappointed, legislators must address change as an ongoing project, continuously adapting the law to its evolving environment.

8.3.12 Trust and Consent

In considering what is needed for tradition to be meaningful for the local churches, Robert Schreiter also notes that it requires constant affirmation, particularly as a living tradition is continuously changing. As "a tradition continually needs to incorporate innovation and weave it into a culture's identity … it can find its credibility always at stake."[102] Tradition must therefore constantly regain the trust of local Catholics, for example by reassuring them that, despite its constant change, it successfully responds to local needs. Yet in addition to this, as Schreiter perceives, traditions also require a broader level of trust to carry the local Catholics through times when positive experiences are lacking. He understands myth and ritual as resources for establishing this fundamental trust. Myths as narratives on the roots of a tradition and rituals that engage the group in celebrating its tradition and the identity derived from it both affirm a tradition by reinstating and reviving it.[103] Similarly, the sociology of law recognises that laws require public legal rituals in order to maintain their status as living law.[104] When laws shape the social praxis of a group, even if only to a small extent, they are effective. This affirmation is not necessarily given freely. Coercion is also a way to keep the law effective. However, as Robert Schreiter's considerations on tradition help to illustrate, retelling and reviving a tradition is different from enforcing traditional behaviour. It is connected with embracing a tradition as a source of meaning and identity. This is similar with regard to the law, as paradoxical as this may seem. That the law requires consent might seem puzzling for the reason that law, in the Weberian tradition, is often seen as coercion.[105] Yet coercion plays a much smaller role in the law than one might assume, and an even smaller role in canon law.[106] Canon law has limited means to coerce its subjects to abide by its rules. Whilst church authorities have some influence over the clerics and religious who are dependent on them, they can barely coerce other Catholics into following the law. Instead, in many contexts global canon law is often only adopted to the extent to which the local

[102] Schreiter (1985), p. 108.

[103] See ibid., p. 109.

[104] With regard to canon law, see Hahn (2022a), pp. 179–222.

[105] See Weber (1978), p. 313.

[106] See Hahn (2022a), pp. 41–42.

Catholics—ecclesiastical authorities, legal practitioners, and legal subjects—welcome it and integrate it into their culture. Reception is an intellectual and a practical action. It requires the receivers' decision to turn mere law on paper into living law by allowing it to impact the local praxis and by fostering the growth of local rules and customs which give substance to the global framework. Yet, while customs and customary law play a major role in canonical literature, canon law, in practice, tends to restrict the emergence of customary law, as mentioned in Sect. 7.1.6. Ladislas Orsy criticised the fact that, while legislation praises custom as a community's affirmative response to the law, it takes pains to avoid customary law where possible.[107] If customs are useful in helping global laws be accepted in the local churches, it would be beneficial to give local churches greater freedom to establish them.

8.4 Summary

The observation that current legislation transfers a body of culturally rather insensitive rules into the local churches through asymmetrical law planting and imposed reception raises the question of how to deal with global canon law in a postcolonial perspective. Based on studying canon law in the light of intercultural theology, this chapter has proposed a revision of the law subjecting it to postcolonial criticism. On a practical level, the scope of decentralised legislation must be expanded, granting local agents more autonomy in the creation of culturally adequate rules. Fundamentally, a discussion is needed whether a uniform set of rules for the whole global church is justifiable and has a future. Taking into account the principle of subsidiarity and the autonomy of groups to legislate for themselves, the sociological finding that decentralised legislation increases the chances of rules finding acceptance, and the theological demand to strengthen the role of the diocesan bishops in governing their churches, there is reason to reverse the perspective. Rather than imposing uniform rules on the worldwide church through top-down legislation while allowing for some exceptions, the focus should be on decentralised legislation, allowing for the bottom-up creation of shared rules where uniform regulation is essential for the unity of the church. These shared rules must respect subsidiarity, be the result of transparent and participatory lawmaking, be intelligible, and invite local consent.

[107] See Orsy (1992), p. 116.

Chapter 9
Conclusion and Outlook

This study has examined the supercultural, transcultural, cross-cultural, and multicultural claims of current canon law. Whilst global ecclesiastical legislation identifies canon law as transcultural law permeating easily through cultures because of its supercultural foundation, the law is seldom truly transcultural—not even with regard to those norms which legislation refers to as universal due to their being grounded in divine law. Global canon law is rather cross-cultural law, acknowledging some diversity of the local churches while allowing centralised rules and a certain view of the law to dominate over alternative views of the law. The law is also multicultural in some respects, insofar as it leaves some room for multiple regulations under the roof of the one church and its legal framework. Yet it is still far from being intercultural, respecting all local cultures not merely as media for expressing the faith, but also as legal cultures with a distinct view of the law. An intercultural approach to canon law would include the reciprocal exchange of cultural goods—legal ideas, concepts, and rules—between the churches, which, by allowing for a mutual transmission and reception of legal knowledge, would trigger change in all ecclesiastical cultures. At present, this intercultural potential of the law is impeded by an antagonistic dualism which dominates the debates: Shifting between the law as a universal and a contingent reality, a global and a local phenomenon, the current debates on reforming the law move back and forth between two daunting prospects: the Scylla of losing the unifying function of global legislation and the Charybdis of neglecting the cultural idiosyncrasies of the local churches. This chapter attempts to outline what an alternative might look like.

9.1 Glocal Legislation

This study suggests that adopting a glocal approach to law might help reconcile the church's global ambitions with its plural local cultures. When sociologist Roland Robertson introduced the term *glocalisation* into the sociological debates, he did so

J. Hahn, *The Cultures of Canon Law*, Law and Religion in a Global Context 6,
https://doi.org/10.1007/978-3-032-14812-4_9

to overcome dichotomies implied by speaking of the global versus the local, the universal versus the particular, and the homogenous versus the heterogeneous. Instead, he suggested "the debate about global homogenization versus heterogenization should be transcended. It is not a question of either homogenization or heterogenization, but rather of the ways in which both of these two tendencies have become features of life across much of the late-twentieth-century world."[1] Robertson called endeavours to reconcile both tendencies strategies of glocalisation. However, as he also noted, glocalisation is not so much the dialectical attempt to reconcile the global and the local; rather, it is a redefinition of the global, encouraging scholars to view globalisation through the lens of its local mechanisms and effects. The global is a glocal reality, as no global phenomenon exists that has no local origins or effects. In this vein, Boaventura de Sousa Santos describes glocality as consisting of two dimensions: *globalised localism* as the globalisation of local facts and events, and *localised globalism* as the local reception and processing of global occurrences.[2]

Receiving this theoretical impulse of rethinking the global in terms of the glocal, legal scholars over the past years have posed the question of what glocalisation means for the law. Legal anthropologist Christoph Eberhard, for instance, writes: "Our world is shrinking. Frontiers get blurred. A sense of 'globality' emerges. … At the same time the diverse 'locals' reaffirm themselves. The reality that we have to deal with as lawyers and as anthropologists becomes increasingly a reality of 'in-betweens'."[3] As the legal reality is becoming a hybrid reality existing in the intersection of the global and the local, he finds glocalisation a helpful concept to describe "the complex dynamics and interactions between diverse 'globals' and diverse 'locals' in the contemporary world."[4] In a similar vein, legal scholar Werner Menski poses the question of "whether the phenomenon of globalisation should and can be premised on a vision of global uniformisation, or whether a vision that emphasises legal pluralism and the pluralising effects of globalisation is more realistic, so that globalisation ends up as almost unlimited diversity, indeed as 'glocalization'".[5] These debates on the glocality of modern global law pave the way for scholars of canon law to deconstruct the claim of canon law to be universal law and to rediscover canon law as global—or rather glocal—law. Normatively speaking, interpreting canon law as glocal law emphasises that it only receives its justification in its function of serving the local churches as a framework supporting the growth and development of their mutual relationship to become one church. Factually, understanding canon law as glocal law emphasises that it is created for global Catholicism but only becomes effective law when received in the local churches. It is then both global and local at the same time. As rules born in a particular legal context, global

---

[1] Robertson (1997), p. 27.

[2] See De Sousa Santos (2020), p. 215.

[3] Eberhard (2009), p. 67.

[4] Ibid.

[5] Menski (2006), p. 4.

laws are *globalised localisms*, in de Sousa Santos's terms. But they are also *localised globalisms*, as it is merely the local responses that bring them to life. Canon law, thus, depends on a productive relationship between globalised localism and localised globalism.

9.2 Alternative Discourses

But de Sousa Santos also reminds his readers that this is not all one can learn from applying the analytical tool of *glocalism* to approach ecclesiastical legislation. His considerations also help to address the challenge that global canon law, as a law that spans global Catholicism, requires constant scrutiny due to its tendency to reproduce asymmetrical patterns of domination in the local churches. De Sousa Santos perceives that the dominant forms of global action are accompanied by powerful alternatives which keep hegemonic globalisation, as expressed in the dynamic of globalised localism and localised globalism, under critical observation. These alternative discourses of *counterhegemonic globalisation* undermine or confront the dominant patterns, insofar as "two kinds of globalization meet and clash in the global political arena: on the one hand, globalization from above, or hegemonic globalization comprising globalized localisms and localized globalisms, and, on the other, globalization from below or counterhegemonic globalization."[6] Two important expressions of counterhegemonic globalisation, as he finds, are *subaltern cosmopolitanism* and a growing concern in the *common heritage of humankind*. As alternative views of global acting, these strategies offer individuals and groups ways to question and challenge dominant globalism with the help of "confrontational politics",[7] as de Sousa Santos proposes: "They … create the space for social practices that transcend the hierarchies established by asymmetric globalisms, and for credible emancipatory discourses beyond the confines of capitalist reasoning and reasonableness."[8]

De Sousa Santos uses the term *cosmopolitanism*, which was already mentioned in Sect. 8.2.2, to refer to alternative intercultural politics undermining or opposing dominant modes of globalisation. He has in mind subordinate nations, regions, or social groups, such as NGOs, international movements, and human rights initiatives, which network with each other to promote their common interests. These institutions or groups distance themselves from dominant forms of globalisation but use the established structures to organise their own cross-cultural exchange and interaction.[9] Their alternative politics have a major impact in the political realm, insofar as "cosmopolitanism has become a fundamental component of the global

[6] De Sousa Santos (2020), p. 218.

[7] Ibid., p. 545.

[8] Ibid., p. 218.

[9] See ibid., p. 216.

political agenda."[10] This study suggests that cosmopolitanism can have a similar function in church. Local agents can use the structures established by centralised politics to connect with each other to voice and defend their interests, and also to oppose dominant ecclesiastical globalisms. One can think of structures such as the bishops' conferences, synods and synodal processes, or the diverse bodies of participation established by canon law. These institutions could connect with each other to develop alternative intercultural politics undermining or even opposing dominant politics. The alliance between the German Bishops Conference and the Central Committee of German Catholics (ZdK) when establishing the Synodal Path is an example of subaltern cosmopolitanism on a more regional level. In a similar vein, but different from reality, one could have imagined the German Synodal Path and the Australian Plenary Council joining forces to promote their common interests for how the church might develop in light of its current challenges in increasingly secular contexts. One might also imagine a politics of subaltern cosmopolitanism with regard to developing canon law. As strategies for using established paths to propose alternative ways to organise the church, a subaltern cosmopolitanism of ecclesiastical bodies, interest groups, and alliances from different backgrounds might challenge the law and suggest how to improve it in light of local needs. For instance, the German Synodal Path produced a whole catalogue of proposals for legislative reform with regard to church organisation, lay participation, the role of women in the church, and clerical discipline, which was submitted to the Apostolic See with the request for consideration. It is doubtful that these demands will find Roman approval. However, the procedure reveals that the organisers recognised that using established channels, such as requesting Roman approval, could help disseminate alternative ideas and bring them to the attention of the plural churches for discussion. Following cosmopolitanism, these alternative intercultural politics do not oppose the fact that the church is both a global and a local player but present an alternative to the dynamic of globalised localism and local globalism. Legal scholar Paul Schiff Berman interprets this view as a dialectic that unites the personal and the global perspectives on the world: "The cosmopolitan worldview shifts back and forth from the rooted particularity of personal identity to the global possibility of multiple overlapping communities."[11]

9.3 Shared Concerns

A second perspective, which de Sousa Santos adds to globalised localism and localised globalism as dominant forms of global politics, is the shared concern in "the common heritage of humankind"[12] as the growing awareness that humanity needs to

[10] Ibid.

[11] Berman (2005), p. 1115.

[12] De Sousa Santos (2020), p. 217.

respond to facts and events which pertain to the globe as such, such as climate change, environmental problems, or the nuclear threat. De Sousa Santos uses these examples to show that there are issues which affect humanity globally. They therefore also rekindle an interest in global rules and transnational regulations. These observations can also be applied to the church, as it is here that Catholics worldwide share concerns that they perceive as being of major relevance to the future of their church. For instance, one can understand ecumenism as a common interest of many Catholics all over the globe. Catholics engage in ecumenical dialogue driven by a desire for Christian unity, aiming to achieve mutual understanding and cooperation in order to overcome historical divisions. Many support projects that foster interfaith communion and shared interests, such as a common commitment to justice and peace. It is interesting to read that de Sousa Santos also addresses ecumenism in relation to the law when he asks in one of his chapter titles whether it is possible to hope for the law to develop "From Legal Diaspora to Legal Ecumenism".[13] He connects this idea with the hope for a law that is supportive of tolerance, global solidarity, and cosmopolitanism, against intolerance, chauvinism, and imperialism, as proposed by other forms of the law.[14] Adopting his thoughts for canon law implies embracing social practices that undermine established and dominant forms of asymmetrical globalism by promoting global discourses from below which work in favour of developing rules that support tolerance, global solidarity, and cosmopolitanism among Catholics all over the world and among the local churches. These politics are not counter-hegemonic because they oppose the established ways of acting globally, as de Sousa Santos reminds his readers, "but because they challenge the conception of general interest underlying the latter and propose an alternative conception."[15] In a similar vein, the constant questioning of whether global canon law is in the best interests of all Catholics and whether it is the most appropriate way to organise the church is a perpetual source of contention for global legislation. This constant challenge can be a perpetual source of irritation. Yet as long as hegemonic law feels the sting of counter-hegemonic criticism, this is proof that the law is still a relevant factor in global Catholicism's search for meaning and identity.

[13] Ibid., p. 196.

[14] See ibid., p. 206.

[15] Ibid., p. 545.

Bibliography

Abu-Lughod L (2006) Writing Against Culture. In: Moore H L and Sanders T (eds), Anthropology in Theory: Issues in Epistemology. Malden, MA, Blackwell Publishing, pp 466–479
Aguilar F S (1997) Closing Session. The Jurist 57: 445–453
Althaus R (2020) Das Kirchenrecht—ein überzeitlicher Fels in der Brandung oder Wegbereiter der Veränderung?. In: Kopp S (ed), Kirche im Wandel: Ekklesiale Identität und Reform. Freiburg im Breisgau, Herder, pp 313–335
Anghie A T (2006) The Evolution of International Law: Colonial and Postcolonial Realities. Third World Quarterly 27: 739–753
Angrosino M V (1994) The Culture Concept and the Mission of the Roman Catholic Church. American Anthropologist 96: 824–832
Aymans W (1983) Einführung. In: Sekretariat der Deutschen Bischofskonferenz (ed), Einführung in das neue Gesetzbuch der lateinischen Kirche. Bonn, Sekretariat der Deutschen Bischofskonferenz, pp 7–28
Beal J P (1996) The Inculturation of Canon Law: Made in the USA. In: Provost J H and Walf K (eds), From Life to Law. London, SCM Press, pp 48–56
Beinert W (1991) Die Rezeption und ihre Bedeutung für Leben und Lehre der Kirche. In: Beinert W (ed), Glaube als Zustimmung: Zur Interpretation kirchlicher Rezeptionsvorgänge. Freiburg im Breisgau, Herder, pp 15–49
Beinert W (1997) The Subjects of Ecclesial Reception. The Jurist 57: 321–346
Berkmann B J (2016) Inculturation and Evangelization in the Catholic Canon Law. Kritische Zeitschrift für überkonfessionelles Kirchenrecht 3: 29–38
Berman H J (1993) Faith and Order: The Reconciliation of Law and Religion. Grand Rapids, MI, William B. Eerdmans Publishing
Berman P S (2005) Conflict of Laws, Globalization, and Cosmopolitan Pluralism. The Wayne Law Review 51: 1105–1145
Betengne J P (2019) Culture canonique et cultures juridiques en Afrique. In: Miñambres J (ed), Diritto Canonico e culture giuridiche nel centenario del Codex Iuris Canonici del 1917. Rome, EDUSC, pp 639–656
Bevans S B (2018) Essays in Contextual Theology. Leiden, Brill
Bevans S B (2002) Models of Contextual Theology: Revised and Expanded Edition. Maryknoll, NY, Orbis Books
Bier G (2009) Kirchliche Rechtskultur: Vom Umgang mit dem Recht der Kirche. In: Böhm T (ed), Glaube und Kultur? Begegnung zweier Welten?. Freiburg im Breisgau, Herder, pp 203–228
Blackstone W (1983) Commentaries on the Laws of England in Four Books. vol. 1. Philadelphia, PA, J. B. Lippincott Company

J. Hahn, *The Cultures of Canon Law*, Law and Religion in a Global Context 6,
https://doi.org/10.1007/978-3-032-14812-4

Blankenburg E (1988) Zum Begriff "Rechtskultur". In: Hoffmann-Nowotny H-J (ed), Kultur und Gesellschaft: Gemeinsamer Kongreß der Deutschen, der Österreichischen und der Schweizerischen Gesellschaft für Soziologie. Zürich, Seismo, pp 292–297

Blicharz G J (2022) Global Law and Christianity: Discussion with the book Christianity and Global Law. Oxford Journal of Law and Religion 11: 170–174

Bray S L (2020) Form and Substance in the Fusion of Law and Equity. In: Klimchuk D, Samet I, and Smith H E (eds), Philosophical Foundations of the Law of Equity. Oxford, Oxford University Press, pp 231–248

Burgess J P (1997) Law and Cultural Identity, ARENA Working Papers 14. www.sv.uio.no/arena/english/research/publications/arena-working-papers/1994-2000/1997/wp97_14.htm

Burke C (1988) Marriage and the Family in Africa. Position Papers, April 1988. www.cormacburke.or.ke/node/288

Burkhard J J (2016) The Sensus Fidelium: Old Questions, New Challenges. In: Phan P C and Hinze B E (eds), Learning from All The Faithful: A Contemporary Theology of the Sensus Fidei. Eugene, OR, Pickwick Publications, pp 125–142

Busugutsala G G (1987) Vers un droit canonique africain?. Praxis Juridique et Religion 4: 46–62

Bwana S (1986) The Impact of the New Code in Africa. In: Provost J H and Walf K (eds), Canon Law—Church Reality. Edinburgh, T. & T. Clark, pp 103–109

Carty A (1991) Critical International Law: Recent Trends in the Theory of International Law. European Journal of International Law 2: 1–27

Casanova J (2019) Asian Catholicism, Interreligious Colonial Encounters and Dynamics of Secularism in Asia. In: van der Veer P and Dean K (eds), The Secular in South, East, and Southeast Asia. Basingstoke, Palgrave Macmillan, pp 13–35

Chupungco A J (1992) Liturgical Inculturation: Sacramentals, Religiosity, and Catechesis. Collegeville, MN, The Liturgical Press

Connolly P (2023) The Current Canonical Legislation of the Catholic Church on Marriage with Particular Reference to the Major Changes of the Last Century. Marriage, Families & Spirituality 29: 233–264

Coriden J A (1982) Rules for Interpreters. The Jurist 42: 277–303

Coriden J A (1990) The Canonical Doctrine of Reception. The Jurist 50: 58–82

Coughlin J J (2012) Law, Person, and Community: Philosophical, Theological, and Comparative Perspectives of Canon Law. Oxford, Oxford University Press

Dammert Bellido J (1986) The New Code in an Andean Diocese. In: Provost J H and Walf K (eds), Canon Law—Church Reality. Edinburgh, T. & T. Clark, pp 110–117

Deckers D (2019) Marx weist römischen Kardinal in die Schranken. 14 September 2019. www.faz.net/aktuell/politik/inland/marx-weist-roemischen-kardinal-in-die-schranken-16384249.html

De Mûelenaere M (1985a) The Canonical Significance of Marital Fidelity among the Bantu of South Africa. Dissertation submitted to the Faculty of Canon Law, Saint Paul University, Ottawa, Canada, in partial fulfillment of the requirements for the Degree of Doctor of Canon Law. Ottawa, University of Ottawa

De Mûelenaere M (1985b) Cultural Adaptation and the Code of Canon Law. Studia Canonica 19: 31–59

De Sousa Santos B (2020) Toward a New Legal Common Sense: Law, Globalization, and Emancipation. 3rd edn. Cambridge, Cambridge University Press

Doe N (1992) Toward a Critique of the Role of Theology in English Ecclesiastical and Canon Law. Ecclesiastical Law Journal 2: 328–346

Doe N (1994) Canonical Doctrines of Judicial Precedent: A Comparative Study. The Jurist 54: 205–215

Domingo R, and Witte J (2020) Introduction. In: Domingo R and Witte J, Christianity and Global Law. Abingdon, Routledge, pp 1–13

Dreßing H, Salize, H J, Dölling D, Hermann D, Kruse A, Schmitt E, and Bannenberg B (2018) Sexueller Missbrauch an Minderjährigen durch katholische Priester, Diakone und männliche Ordensangehörige im Bereich der Deutschen Bischofskonferenz. Mannheim/Heidelberg/

Gießen. www.dbk.de/fileadmin/redaktion/diverse_downloads/dossiers_2018/MHG-Studie-gesamt.pdf
Dworkin R (1998) Law's Empire. Oxford, Hart Publishing
Eberhard C (2009) Law and Anthropology in a "Glocal" World: The Challenge of Dialogue. In: Freeman M and Napier D (eds), Law and Anthropology, Oxford, Oxford University Press, pp. 67–88
Eckert J (2010) Von der Universalisierung und Partikularisierung von Normen: Sozialanthropologische Überlegungen zu Normgeltung als sozialem Prozess. In: Ernst G and Sellmaier S (eds), Universelle Menschenrechte und partikulare Moral. Stuttgart, Kohlhammer, pp 115–130
Fögen M T, and Teubner G (2005) Rechtstransfer. Rechtsgeschichte—Zeitschrift des Max-Planck-Instituts für Europäische Rechtsgeschichte 7: 38–45
Foljanty L (2013) Recht oder Gesetz: Juristische Identität und Autorität in den Naturrechtsdebatten der Nachkriegszeit. Tübingen, Mohr Siebeck
Foljanty L (2015) Legal Transfers as Processes of Cultural Translation: On the Consequences of a Metaphor. Frankfurt am Main, Max Planck Institute for European Legal History
Froehle B T, and Gautier M L (2003) Global Catholicism: Portrait of a World Church. Maryknoll, NY, Orbis Books
Funk K R (2024) Sect and Superstition: The Protestant Framework of American Codification. American Journal of Legal History 64: 190–213
Geertz C (1973a) Thick Description: Toward an Interpretive Theory of Culture. In: Geertz C, The Interpretation of Cultures: Selected Essays. New York, Basic Books, pp 3–30
Geertz C (1973b) The Impact of the Concept of Culture on the Concept of Man. In: Geertz C, The Interpretation of Cultures: Selected Essays. New York, Basic Books, pp 33–54
Geertz C (1973c) Ritual and Social Chance: A Javanese Example. In: Geertz C, The Interpretation of Cultures: Selected Essays. New York, Basic Books, pp 142–169
Geertz C (1973d) The Politics of Meaning. In: Geertz C, The Interpretation of Cultures: Selected Essays. New York, Basic Books, pp 311–326
Geertz C (1973e) Person, Time, and Conduct in Bali. In: Geertz C, The Interpretation of Cultures: Selected Essays. New York, Basic Books, pp 360–411
Geertz C (1973f) Deep Play: Notes on the Balinese Cockfight. In: Geertz C, The Interpretation of Cultures: Selected Essays. New York, Basic Books, pp 412–453
Goldmann M (2019) Decolonizing Intertemporal International Law. 13 November 2019. https://voelkerrechtsblog.org/de/decolonizing-intertemporal-international-law
Goler, P A (1972) Must Canon Law Be Color Blind? Catholic Lawyer 18: 293–299
Grabmeier J (2012) Kirchlicher Rechtsweg—vatikanische Sackgasse! Kirchliches Rechtssystem in der römisch-katholischen Kirche endgültig gescheitert—dargestellt am konkreten Fall eines hierarchischen Rekurses von Regensburg bis Rom zur Mitwirkung der Laien in der Kirche. Schierling, Animus
Griffin B F (1984) Introduction to the Jargon of Canon Law. The Jurist 44: 19–27
Gruber J (2013) Theologie nach dem Cultural Turn: Interkulturalität als theologische Ressource. Stuttgart, Kohlhammer
Gruber J (2018) Intercultural Theology: Exploring World Christianity after the Cultural Turn. Göttingen, Vandenhoeck & Ruprecht
Haering S (2003) Lateinische Sprache und Kanonisches Recht. Seminarium 43: 237–256
Hahn J (2019) Church Law in Modernity: Toward a Theory of Canon Law between Nature and Culture. Cambridge University Press, Cambridge
Hahn J (2022a) Foundations of a Sociology of Canon Law. Cham, Springer Nature
Hahn J (2022b) Sex Offenses—Offensive Sex: Some Observations on the Recent Reform of Ecclesiastical Penal Law. Religions 13. https://doi.org/10.3390/rel13040332
Hahn J (2023) The Language of Canon Law. Oxford, Oxford University Press
Hahn J (2024) The Language Games of Canon Law: Strategic Ambiguity between Law and Religion. Oxford Journal of Law and Religion 13. https://doi.org/10.1093/ojlr/rwae004

Hall G, and Muonwe K (2017) Towards Integrative Christian Theology and Experience: Missiology, Inculturaton & Practical Theology. In: Wolfteich C E and Dillen A (eds), Catholic Approaches in Practical Theology: International and Interdisciplinary Perspectives. Leuven, Peeters, pp 49–69

Hartmann C P (2021) Das System Vatikan ist träge und intransparent. 23 December 2021. www.katholisch.de/artikel/32457-das-system-vatikan-ist-traege-und-intransparent

Hebblethwaite P (1994) Synod on Africa a World Away from Real Life African Church. National Catholic Reporter, 8 April 1994, p 8

Hobsbawm E, and Ranger T (eds) (1983) The Invention of Tradition, Cambridge, Cambridge University Press

Hogan L, and Heyer K (2019) Beyond a Northern Paradigm: Catholic Theological Ethics in Global Perspective. Journal of the Society of Christian Ethics 39: 21–38

Huels J M (1987) Interpreting Canon Law in Diverse Cultures. The Jurist 47: 249–293

Huels J M (1996) From Practice to Law. In: Provost J H and Walf K (eds), From Life to Law. London, SCM Press, pp 22–28

Huizing P J (1982) Reflections on the System of Canon Law. The Jurist 42: 239–276

Ignatieff M (2001) Human Rights as Politics and Idolatry. Princeton University Press, Princeton, NJ

Joncheray J (1997) The Agents of Reception from a Sociological Perspective. The Jurist 57: 347–361

Juchem R (2021) Kirchenrechtler Graulich: Neues Strafrecht braucht Mentalitätswandel. 7 December 2021. www.katholisch.de/artikel/32271-kirchenrechtler-graulich-neues-strafrecht-braucht-mentalitaetswandel

Kämmerer J A (2016) Introduction—Imprints of Colonialism in Public International Law: On the Paradoxes of Transition. Journal of the History of International Law 18: 239–247

Keenan J F (2020) Pursuing Ethics by Building Bridges beyond the Northern Paradigm. In: Stephens D W (ed), Reenvisioning Christian Ethics, Basel, MDPI, pp 99–112

Kisembo B, Magesa L, and Shorter A (1977) African Christian Marriage. London/Dublin, Geoffrey Chapmann

Komonchak J A (1986) Vatican II and the New Code. Archives de Sciences Sociales des Religions 62: 107–117

Krämer P (1999) Universales und partikulares Kirchenrecht: Zur Mehrstufigkeit im kirchlichen Rechtssystem. In: Krämer P, Demel S, Gerosa L, and Müller L (eds), Universales und partikulares Recht in der Kirche: Konkurrierende oder integrierende Faktoren?. Paderborn, Bonifatius, pp 47–69

Kuttner S G (1990) Reflections on Gospel and Law in the History of the Church. In: Kuttner S G, Studies in the History of Medieval Canon Law. Aldershot, Routledge, pp 199–209

LaBelle J-P (2002) Le Code de Droit Canonique de 1983, en raison du phénomène de l'inculturation, est-il adapté au Japon?. Studia Canonica 36: 487–495

Lamb C (2021) Catholic Church must embrace "synodality". 26 March 2021. www.thetablet.co.uk/news/13985/catholic-church-must-embrace-synodality

Lassak S (2020) Free from Burdens? Cultural and Social Aspects of the Concept of Reconciliation in Latin America. In: Hahn J and Werner G (eds), Mercy and Justice: A Challenge for Contemporary Theology. Leiden/Boston, MA, Brill, pp 173–185

Lederhilger S (2000) Universale Einheit und partikulare Vielfalt: Zur Bedeutsamkeit eines kontextuellen Kirchenrechts. Theologisch-Praktische Quartalschrift 149: 375–387

Legrand P (1997) The Impossibility of "Legal Transplants". Maastricht Journal of European and Comparative Law 4: 111–124

Lehnen R (2019) Ein Urteil, das von sich reden macht. 29 May 2019. www.kirchenzeitung.de/doris-wagner-urteil

Lonergan B J F (1972) Method in Theology. New York, Herder and Herder

Lonergan B J F (2016) The Transition from a Classicist Worldview to Historical Mindedness. In: Doran R M and Dadosky J D (eds), Collected Work of Bernhard Lonergan: A Second Collection. Toronto/Buffalo/London, University of Toronto Press, pp 3–10

Lüdecke N (2011) Globales Kirchenrecht—Chance des Katholischen?. In: Ozankom C (ed), Katholizität im Kommen: Katholische Identität und gegenwärtige Veränderungsprozesse, Regensburg, Friedrich Pustet, pp 49–62
Lüdecke N, and Bier G (2012) Das römisch-katholische Kirchenrecht: Eine Einführung. Stuttgart, Kohlhammer
Luhmann N (1969) Legitimation durch Verfahren. Neuwied/Berlin, Luchterhand
Luhmann N (1970) Positivität des Rechts als Voraussetzung einer modernen Gesellschaft. Jahrbuch für Rechtssoziologie und Rechtstheorie 1: 175–202
Luhmann N (1986) Die soziologische Beobachtung des Rechts. Frankfurt am Main, Suhrkamp
Luhmann N (2004) Law as a Social System. Oxford, Oxford University Press
Luhmann N (2014) A Sociological Theory of Law. London/New York, Routledge
Mancuso S (2024) African Law(s): Comparative Insights on the African Lawscape. Leiden, Brill
Mannion M F (1990) Liturgy and Culture. In: Fink P E (ed), The New Dictionary of Sacramental Worship. Collegeville, MN, The Liturgical Press, pp 307–313
Marattil J (2009) Reverential Fear as a Ground of Marriage Nullity with Special Reference to the Indian Culture. Studia Canonica 43: 431–486
Martens K (2019) Canonical Culture and Legal Systems in Common Law. In: Miñambres J (ed), Diritto Canonico e culture giuridiche nel centenario del Codex Iuris Canonici del 1917. Rome, EDUSC, pp 713–730
Mendonça A (1995) Recent Rotal Jurisprudence from a Sociocultural Perspective. Studia Canonica 29: 29–83, 317–355
Menski W (2006) Comparative Law in a Global Context: The Legal Systems of Asia and Africa. 2nd edn. Cambridge, Cambridge University Press
Merry S E (1991) Law and Colonialism: Review Essay. Law & Society Review 25: 889–922
Merry S E (2009) Legal Transplants and Cultural Translation: Making Human Rights in the Vernacular. In: Goodale K (ed), Human Rights: An Anthropological Reader. Malden, MA, Wiley-Blackwell, pp 265–302
Miñambres J (ed) (2019) Diritto Canonico e culture giuridiche nel centenario del Codex Iuris Canonici del 1917. Rome, EDUSC
Monteiro E (2004) Church and Culture: Communion in Pluralism. Delhi, ISPCK
Moore S F (1973) Law and Social Change: The Semi-Autonomous Social Field as an Appropriate Subject of Study. Law & Society Review 7: 719–746
Morrisey F (1986) Is the New Code an Improvement for the Law of the Catholic Church?. In: Provost J H and Walf K (eds), Canon Law—Church Reality. Edinburgh, T. & T. Clark, pp 32–41
Mörsdorf K (1967) Die Rechtssprache des Codex Juris Canonici: Eine kritische Untersuchung. 2nd edn (reprint of the 1937 edn). Paderborn, Ferdinand Schöningh
Mwaungulu R T (1996) Possibilities of Inculturating the Roman Law in Africa. In: Provost J H and Walf K (eds), From Life to Law. London, SCM Press, pp 81–87
Mwiti M E (2015) The Reception of Canon Law and its Challenges in Africa. Long Essay Submitted in Partial Fulfilment of the Requirements for the Bachelor of Theology, Tangaza University College. Catholic University of Eastern Africa, Nairobi
Neumann F (2020) Kardinal Stella will nicht mit Laien über Pfarreien-Instruktion reden. 26 October 2020. www.katholisch.de/artikel/27357-kardinal-stella-will-nicht-mit-laien-ueber-pfarreien-instruktion-reden
Novak D (1998) Natural Law in Judaism. Cambridge, Cambridge University Press
Novak D (2014) Natural Law and Judaism. In: Emon A M, Levering M, and Novak D, Natural Law: A Jewish, Christian, and Islamic Trialogue. Oxford, Oxford University Press, pp 4–44
Nsomwe Ntambwe C Y (2010) Le droit ecclésial et la "canonisation" du droit coutumier en Afrique subsaharienne: Pour un droit canonique africain. Revue des Sciences Religieuses 84: 245–262
Ohly C, Haering S, and Müller L (eds) (2020) Rechtskultur und Rechtspflege in der Kirche: Festschrift für Wilhelm Rees zur Vollendung des 65. Lebensjahres. Berlin, Duncker & Humblot
Okeke H O (1998) Church-as-God's Family: From African Ecclesiology to African Canon Law. Studia Canonica 32: 397–414

Ombres R (2016) Justice and Mercy: Canon Law and the Sacrament of Penance. In: Cranmer F, Hill M, Kenny C, and Sandberg R (eds), The Confluence of Law and Religion: Interdisciplinary Reflections on the Work of Norman Doe. Cambridge, Cambridge University Press, pp 131–143
O'Reilly J T, and Chalmers M S P (2014) The Clergy Sex Abuse Crisis and the Legal Responses. Oxford, Oxford University Press
Orobator A E (1996) Reassessing Canonical Attitudes Towards African Marriage Practices: Based on a Study of the African Synod. Hekima Review 14: 9–18
Örücü E (2002) Law as Transposition. The International and Comparative Law Quarterly 51: 205–223
Orsy L M (1969) The Spirit of Common Law and the Reform of Canon Law. The Catholic Lawyer 15: 65–76
Orsy L M (1983) The Interpretation of Laws: New Variations on an Old Theme. Studia Canonica 17: 95–133
Orsy L M (1984) Reception and Non-Reception of Law: A Canonical and Theological Consideration. Canon Law Society of America Proceedings 46: 66–70
Orsy L M (1992) Theology and Canon Law: New Horizons for Legislation and Interpretation. Collegeville, MN, The Liturgical Press
Orsy L M (1995) The Reception of Laws by the People of God: A Theological and Canonical Inquiry in the Light of Vatican Council II. The Jurist 55: 504–526
Orsy L M (1996a) The Theological Task of Canon Law. Canon Law Society of America Proceedings 58: 1–23
Orsy L M (1996b) Classical Philosophy and the Legal Life of the Church. In: Provost J H and Walf K (eds), From Life to Law. London, SCM Press, pp 11–21
Otaduy Guerin J (2018) Unidad y pluralidad en la Iglesia. Ius Canonicum 58: 1–36
Otaduy Guerin J (2019) Igualdad y diversidad, unidad y pluralismo, universal y particular. In: Miñambres J (ed), Diritto Canonico e culture giuridiche nel centenario del Codex Iuris Canonici del 1917. Rome, EDUSC, pp 237–274
Panikkar R (1982) Is the Notion of Human Rights a Western Concept?. Diogenes 30: 75–102
Pihlajamäki H (2010) Canon Law and European Legal Culture: Reviewed Book Der Einfluss der Kanonistik auf die europäische Rechtskultur. Rechtsgeschichte 17: 177–179
Potz R (1986) The Concept and Development of Law According to the 1983 Code. In: Provost J H and Walf K (eds), Canon Law—Church Reality. Edinburgh, T. & T. Clark, pp 14–22
Pree H (1999) Universales und partikulares Kirchenrecht—die Mehrstufigkeit im kirchlichen Rechtssystem. Erster Diskussionsbeitrag. In: Krämer P, Demel S, Gerosa L, and Müller L (eds), Universales und partikulares Recht in der Kirche: Konkurrierende oder integrierende Faktoren?. Paderborn, Bonifatius, pp 71–89
Provost J H, and Walf K (1986) Editorial: Church Law—Church Reality. In: Provost J H and Walf K (eds), Canon Law—Church Reality. Edinburgh, T. & T. Clark, pp IX–XVI
Provost J H (1992) Local Church and Catholicity in the Constitution Pastor Bonus. The Jurist 52: 299–334
Provost J H (1996) Strategizing the Application of Life to Church Order. In: Provost J H and Walf K (eds), From Life to Law. London, SCM Press, pp 116–124
Pudumai Doss J (2019) Cultura canonica e cultura giuridica Indiana. In: Miñambres J (ed), Diritto Canonico e culture giuridiche nel centenario del Codex Iuris Canonici del 1917. Rome, EDUSC, pp 619–637
Pulte M (2006) Das Missionsrecht—ein Vorreiter des universalen Kirchenrechts: Rechtliche Einflüsse aus den Missionen auf die konziliare und nachkonziliare Gesetzgebung. Nettetal, Steyler Verlag
Puza R (1993) Katholisches Kirchenrecht. 2nd edn. Heidelberg, UTB
Rahner K (1962) Über den Begriff des "Jus Divinum" im katholischen Verständnis. In: Rahner K, Schriften zur Theologie. vol. 5. Einsiedeln, Benziger, pp 249–277
Riedel-Spangenberger I (ed) (2006) Rechtskultur in der Diözese: Grundlagen und Perspektiven. Freiburg im Breisgau, Herder

Robertson R (1997) Glocalization: Time—Space and Homogeneity—Heterogeneity. In: Featherstone M, Lash S, and Robertson R (eds), Global Modernities. London, Sage Publications, pp 25–44
Robinson G (1983) Law in the Life of the Church. Studia Canonica 17: 47–61
Robitaille L A (1999) Consent, Culture and the Code. Studia Canonica 33: 125–138
Salinas Araneda C (2019) Codificación civil hispanoamericana y codificación canónica. In: Miñambres J (ed), Diritto Canonico e culture giuridiche nel centenario del Codex Iuris Canonici del 1917. Rome, EDUSC, pp 657–676
Schmitz H, and Rhode U (2011) Einführung. In: Katholische Theologie und Kirchliches Hochschulrecht: Einführung und Dokumentation der kirchlichen Rechtsnormen. 2nd edn. Bonn, Secretariat of the German Bishops' Conference, pp 19–186
Schmitz H (2015) Codex Iuris Canonici. In: Haering S, Rees W, and Schmitz H (eds), Handbuch des katholischen Kirchenrechts. 3rd edn. Regensburg, Friedrich Pustet, pp 70–100
Schockenhoff E (2007) The Challenge of Pluralism. In: Keenan J F (ed), Catholic Theological Ethics in the World Church: The Plenary Papers from the First Cross-Cultural Conference on Catholic Theological Ethics. New York, Continuum International Publishing Group, pp 212–220
Schreiter R J (1985) Constructing Local Theologies. Maryknoll, NY, Orbis Books
Shannon P M (1985) Canon Law/Civil Law. The Jurist 45: 618–630
Sharma A (2006) Are Human Rights Western? A Contribution to the Dialogue of Civilizations. Oxford, Oxford University Press
Shorter A (1988) Toward a Theology of Inculturation. Maryknoll, NY, Orbis Books
Smits J M (2003) Import and Export of Legal Models: The Dutch Experience. Transnational Law & Contemporary Problems 13: 551–574
Sobański R (1986) Erwägungen zum Ort des Kirchenrechts in der Rechtskultur. Archiv für katholisches Kirchenrecht 155: 3–15
Tamanaha B Z (2017) A Realistic Theory of Law. Cambridge, Cambridge University Press
Teubner G (1998) Legal Irritants: Good Faith in British Law or How Unifying Law Ends up in New Divergences. The Modern Law Review 61: 11–32
Tillard J M (1996) Ecclesiology of Communion and Canon Law: The Theological Task of Canon Law—A Theologian's Perspective. Canon Law Society of America Proceedings 58: 24–34
Thull P (2024) Kontextuelle Kanonistik. Herder Korrespondenz 78: 47–48
Von Savigny F C (1840) System des heutigen Römischen Rechts. vol. 1. Berlin, Veit und Comp.
Watson A (1993) Legal Transplants: An Approach to Comparative Law. 2nd edn. Athens, GA, The University of Georgia Press
Watson A (1995) From Legal Transplants to Legal Formants. The American Journal of Comparative Law 43: 469–476
Watson A (2000) Legal Transplants and European Private Law. In: The Ius Commune Lectures on European Private Law, Ius Commune Research School. http://awf.ius.bg.ac.rs/legal_transplants.pdf
Weber M (1978) Economy and Society: An Outline of Interpretive Sociology. Berkeley, CA, University of California Press
Whorf B L (1956) The Relation of Habitual Thought and Behavior to Language. In: Whorf B L, Language, Thought, and Reality: Selected Writings of Benjamin Lee Whorf, edited by John B. Carroll. Cambridge, MA, The Technology Press of Massachusetts Institute of Technology, pp 134–159

Source Texts

Aristotle (350 BCE) The Nicomachean Ethics. In: The Nicomachean Ethics (1966) Translated and Introduced by David Ross. London, Oxford University Press

Augustine (396) Letter 36. In: Migne J P (1865), Patrologia Latina. vol. 33 part 2. Paris, Excudebat Sirou, pp 136–151

Justinian (530–33) Digest. In: The Digest of Justinian (1998) Translation edited by Alan Watson. vol. 2. Philadelphia, PA, University of Pennsylvania Press

Thomas Aquinas (1265–73) Summa Theologiae II–II. In: Editio Leonina (1897) Sancti Thomae Aquinatis Doctoris Angelici opera omnia iussu impensaque Leonis XIII P. M. edita. vol. 9: Secunda Secundae Summae Theologiae a questione LVII ad questione CXXII. Rome, Typographia Polyglotta

Pius IV (1564) Bull *Benedictus Deus*. 26 January 1564. In: Canons and Decrees of the Council of Trent (1851) Translated into English by Theodore Alois Buckley. London, George Routledge and Co., pp 268–273

Von Bismarck O (1872) Circular-Depesche. 14 May 1872. Deutscher Reichs-Anzeiger und Königlich Preußischer Staats-Anzeiger. 29 December 1874. no. 304, pp 1–2

Pius X (1906) Encyclical *Vehementer Nos* on the French Law of Separation. 11 February 1906. Acta Sanctae Sedis (1906). 39: 3–16

Pius XI (1981) Encyclical *Quadragesimo Anno* on the Reconstruction of the Social Order. 15 May 1931. Acta Apostolicae Sedis (1981). 23: 177–228

John XXIII (1962a) Apostolic Constitution *Veterum Sapientia* on the Promotion of the Study of Latin. 22 February 1962. Acta Apostolicae Sedis (1962). 54: 129–135

John XXIII (1962b) Opening Speech to the Council. 11 October 1962. Acta Apostolicae Sedis (1962). 54: 786–796

Second Vatican Council (1963) Constitution *Sacrosanctum Concilium* on the Sacred Liturgy. 4 December 1963. Acta Apostolicae Sedis (1964). 56: 97–138

Second Vatican Council (1964) Dogmatic Constitution *Lumen Gentium* on the Church. 21 November 1964. Acta Apostolicae Sedis (1965). 57: 5–71

Paul VI (1964) *Tempus Eucharistici ieiunii servandi reducitur*. 21 November 1964. Acta Apostolicae Sedis (1965). 57: 186

Second Vatican Council (1965a) Decree *Christus Dominus* on the Pastoral Office of Bishops in the Church. 28 October 1965. Acta Apostolicae Sedis (1966). 58: 673–696

Second Vatican Council (1965b) Decree *Ad Gentes* on the Mission Activity of the Church. 7 December 1965. Acta Apostolicae Sedis (1966). 58: 947–990

Second Vatican Council (1965c) Pastoral Constitution *Gaudium et Spes* on the Church in the Modern World. 7 December 1965. Acta Apostolicae Sedis (1966). 58: 1025–1120

Pontifical Commission for the Revision of the Code of Canon Law (1969) Principles guiding the Revision of the Code of Canon Law. Communicationes (1969). 1: 77–85

Congregation for the Discipline of the Sacraments (1973) Instruction *Immensae Caritatis* on Facilitating Sacramental Communion in Particular Circumstances. 29 January 1973. Acta Apostolicae Sedis (1973). 65: 264–271

Congregation for the Clergy (1973) Letter of the Cardinal Prefect to the President of the German Bishops' Conference. 20 November 1973. Prot. no. 144823/I. Archiv für katholisches Kirchenrecht (1973). 142: 480–482

Symposium of Episcopal Conferences of Africa and Madagascar (1978) Acts of the Fifth Plenary Assembly of the Symposium of Episcopal Conferences of Africa and Madagascar. Nairobi, SECAM Publication

Pontifical Commission for the Revision of the Code of Canon Law (1981) Relatio complectens synthesim animadversionum ab Em.mis atque Exc.mis Patribus Commissionis ad novissimum Schema Codicis Iuris Canonici exhibitarum, cum responsionibus a Secretaria et Consultoribus datis. Vatican City, Libreria Editrice Vaticana

John Paul II (1983) Apostolic Constitution *Sacrae Disciplinae Leges* for the Promulgation of the new Code of Canon Law. 25 January 1983. Acta Apostolicae Sedis (1983). 75 II: pp VII–XIV

Preface to the Code of Canon Law (1983) Acta Apostolicae Sedis (1983). 75 II: pp XV–XXX

Secretariat of State (1983) Norms *Necessitas Ipsa* on the Translation of the Code of Canon Law. 28 January 1983. Communicationes (1983). 15: 41

John Paul II (1986) Address to the Aborigines and Torres Strait Islanders in Blatherskite Park. Alice Springs, 29 November 1986. Acta Apostolicae Sedis (1987). 79: 973–979

John Paul II (1988) Apostolic Constitution *Pastor Bonus* on the Roman Curia. 28 June 1988, Acta Apostolicae Sedis (1988). 80: 841–934

International Theological Commission (1988) Faith and Inculturation. www.vatican.va/roman_curia/congregations/cfaith/cti_documents/rc_cti_1988_fede-inculturazione_en.html

Congregation for the Doctrine of the Faith (1989) Profession of Faith and Oath of Fidelity on Assuming an Office to be Exercised in the Name of the Church. Acta Apostolicae Sedis (1989). 81: 105–106; republication: Acta Apostolicae Sedis (1998). 90: 542–544

Catechism of the Catholic Church (1992). In: United States Conference of Catholic Bishops (ed), English translation for the United States of America (1994). Vatican City, Libreria Editrice Vaticana

John Paul II (1995) Post-synodal Apostolic Exhortation *Ecclesia in Africa* on the Church in Africa and its Evangelizing Mission towards the Year 2000. 14 September 1995. Acta Apostolicae Sedis (1996). 88: 5–82

John Paul II (1996) *Universi Dominici Gregis* on the Vacancy of the Apostolic See and the Election of the Roman Pontiff. 22 February 1996. Acta Apostolicae Sedis (1996). 88: 305–343

John Paul II (1999a) Post-synodal Apostolic Exhortation *Ecclesia in America* on the Encounter with the Living Jesus Christ: The Way to Conversion, Communion and Solidarity in America. 22 January 1999. Acta Apostolicae Sedis (1999). 91: 737–815

Pontifical Council for Culture (1999) Towards a Pastoral Approach to Culture. 23 May 1999. www.vatican.va/roman_curia/pontifical_councils/cultr/documents/rc_pc_pc-cultr_doc_03061999_pastoral_en.html

John Paul II (1999b) Post-synodal Apostolic Exhortation *Ecclesia in Asia* on Jesus Christ the Saviour and his Mission of Love and Service in Asia. 6 November 1999. Acta Apostolicae Sedis (2000). 92: 449–528

John Paul II (2001) Post-synodal Apostolic Exhortation *Ecclesia in Oceania* on Jesus Christ and the Peoples of Oceania: Walking His Way, Telling His Truth, Living His Life. 22 November 2001. Acta Apostolicae Sedis (2002). 94: 361–428

John Paul II (2003) Post-synodal Apostolic Exhortation *Ecclesia in Europa* on Jesus Christ Alive in his Church, the Source of Hope for Europe. 28 June 2003. Acta Apostolicae Sedis (2003). 95: 649–719

Ratzinger J (2005) Homily: Mass "Pro Eligendo Romano Pontifice". Vatican Basilica, 18 April 2005. Acta Apostolicae Sedis (2005). 97: 685–689

Benedict XVI (2005) Address to the Roman Curia Offering them his Christmas Greetings. 22 December 2005. Acta Apostolicae Sedis (2006). 98: 40–53

Congregation for the Clergy (2006) Dekret über die Änderung der Mitwirkungsorgane in der Diözese Regensburg (Decree on the Changes made with respect to the Bodies of [Lay] Participation of the Diocese of Regensburg). 10 March 2006. Prot. no. 2006/0224. Archiv für katholisches Kirchenrecht (2006). 175: 156–158

Congregation for the Doctrine of the Faith (2010) Normae de delictis Congregationi pro Doctrina Fidei reservatis seu Normae de delictis contra fidem necnon de gravioribus delictis. 21 May 2010. Acta Apostolicae Sedis (2010). 102: 419–430

Benedict XVI (2011) Post-synodal Apostolic Exhortation *Africae Munus* on the Church in Africa in Service of Reconciliation, Justice and Peace. 19 November 2011. Acta Apostolicae Sedis (2012). 104: 239–314

German Bishops' Conference (2011–15) Documents of the Discussion Process "Living in Faith Today" 2011–15. www.dbk.de/themen/gespraechsprozess/wichtige-dokumente

Francis (2015) Address during the Ceremony Commemorating the Fiftieth Anniversary of the Institution of the Synod of Bishops. 17 October 2015. Acta Apostolicae Sedis (2015). 107: 1138–1144

The Roman Missal: The Order of Celebrating Matrimony (2016) English Translation According to the Second Typical Edition for use in the Dioceses of the United States of America, approved by the United States Conference of Catholic Bishops and confirmed by the Apostolic See. Collegeville, MN, The Liturgical Press

Apostolic Signatura (2016) Circular Letter *Inter Munera* on the State and Activity of Tribunals. 30 July 2016. Prot. no. 51712/16 VT. Acta Apostolicae Sedis (2016). 108: 948–953

Francis (2017) Apostolic Letter Issued Motu Proprio *Magnum Principium* by which Canon 838 of the Code of Canon Law is Modified. 3 September 2017. Acta Apostolicae Sedis (2017). 109: 967–970

Royal Commission into Institutional Responses to Child Sexual Abuse (2017) Final Report. 15 December 2017. www.childabuseroyalcommission.gov.au/final-report

Prefect of the Congregation for Bishops (2019) Letter to the President of the German Bishops' Conference. 4 September 2019. Prot. no. 485/2019. www.dbk.de/fileadmin/redaktion/diverse_downloads/dossiers_2019/2019-09-04-Schreiben-Rom-mit-Anlage-ital-Original.pdf

Plenary Assembly of the German Bishops' Conference/Plenary Assembly of the Central Committee of German Catholics (ZdK) (2019) Statutes of the Synodal Path. 25 September/22 November 2019, www.synodalerweg.de/fileadmin/Synodalerweg/Dokumente_Reden_Beitraege/2019_Satzung-des-Synodalen-Weges-englisch.pdf

Diocesan Bishop of Trier (2019) Gesetz zur Umsetzung der Ergebnisse der Diözesansynode 2013–16. 9 October 2019. www.bistum-trier.de/no_cache/bistum-bischof/bistumsverwaltung/amtsblatt/details/amtsblatt/gesetz-zur-umsetzung-der-ergebnisse-der-dioezesansynode-2013-2016

Prefect of the Congregation for the Clergy (2019) Letter to the Bishop of Trier. 21 November 2019. Prot. no. 20194939. www.bistum-trier.de/fileadmin/user_upload/docs/SchreibenRom_Nov2019.pdf

Synodal Assembly (2020) Rules of Procedure of the Synodal Path. 31 January 2020. www.synodalerweg.de/fileadmin/Synodalerweg/Dokumente_Reden_Beitraege/Synodaler_Weg-Geschaeftsordnung-des-SW-engl.pdf

Francis (2020a) Apostolic Exhortation *Querida Amazonia*. 2 February 2020. Acta Apostolicae Sedis (2020). 112: 231–273

Congregation for the Clergy (2020) Instruction: The pastoral conversion of the Parish community in the service of the evangelising mission of the Church. 20 July 2020. https://press.vatican.va/content/salastampa/en/bollettino/pubblico/2020/07/20/200720a.html

Prefect of the Congregation for Divine Worship (2020) Letter to the Presidents of the Episcopal Conferences "Let us return to the Eucharist with joy!". 15 August 2020. Prot. no. 432/20. Osservatore Romano. 25 September 2020. pp 7–8

Prefect of the Congregation for the Doctrine of the Faith (2020) Letter to the President of the German Bishops' Conference. 18 September 2020. Prot. no. 1230/2019-78677. www.dbk.de/fileadmin/redaktion/diverse_downloads/Dossiers_alt/dossiers_2020/2020-09-18_Kard.-Ladaria_Lettera-Vorsitzender-DBK.PDF

Australian Catholic Bishops' Conference (2020) Fifth Plenary Council of Australia: Statutes and Regulatory Norms (Can. 94 and Can. 95). Amended 6 November 2020. https://plenarycouncil.catholic.org.au/wp-content/uploads/2021/02/Plenary-Council-Statutes-and-Regulatory--Norms.pdf

Francis (2020b) Catechesis. General Audience, Library of the Apostolic Palace. 25 November 2020. www.vatican.va/content/francesco/en/audiences/2020/documents/papa-francesco_20201125_udienza-generale.html

Congregation for the Doctrine of the Faith (2021a) *Responsum to a Dubium* regarding the Blessing of the Unions of Persons of the Same Sex. 15 March 2021. www.vatican.va/roman_curia/congregations/cfaith/documents/rc_con_cfaith_doc_20210222_responsum-dubium-unioni_en.html
Francis (2021a) Apostolic Constitution *Pascite Gregem Dei* Reforming Book VI of the Code of Canon Law. 23 May 2021. Acta Apostolicae Sedis (2021). 113: 534–537; 537–555
Diocese of Tucson (2021) Australia's plenary council: Listening brings liberation, archbishop says. 3 June 2021. https://news.diocesetucson.org/news/australias-plenary-council-listening-brings-liberation-archbishop-says
Francis (2021b) Apostolic Letter issued *Motu Proprio Traditionis Custodes* on the Use of the Roman Liturgy prior to the Reform of 1970. 16 July 2021. Acta Apostolicae Sedis (2021). 113: 793–796
Congregation for the Doctrine of the Faith (2021b) Norms regarding Delicts Reserved to the Congregation for the Doctrine of the Faith. 11 October 2021. www.vatican.va/roman_curia/congregations/cfaith/documents/rc_con_cfaith_doc_20211011_norme-delittiriservati-cfaith_en.html
Francis (2022) Apostolic Constitution *Praedicate Evangelium* on the Roman Curia and its Service to the Church and to the World. 19 March 2022. Acta Apostolicae Sedis (2022). 113: 375–455
Dicastery for the Doctrine of the Faith (2023) Declaration *Fiducia Supplicans* on the Pastoral Meaning of Blessings. 18 December 2023. www.vatican.va/roman_curia/congregations/cfaith/documents/rc_ddf_doc_20231218_fiducia-supplicans_en.html
German Bishops' Conference (2023) Press Release no. 194 "Bischof Bätzing zum römischen Dokument *Fiducia supplicans*". 18 December 2023. https://www.dbk.de/presse/aktuelles/meldung/bischof-baetzing-zum-roemischen-dokument-fiducia-supplicans
Catholic Bishops Conference of Nigeria (2023) Declaration concerning *Fiducia Supplicans*. 20 December 2023. www.nigeriacatholicnetwork.com/cbcn-on-fiducia-supplicans-on-fiducia-supplicans-2

MIX
Papier aus verantwortungsvollen Quellen
Paper from responsible sources
FSC® C105338

If you have any concerns about our products,
you can contact us on
ProductSafety@springernature.com

In case Publisher is established outside the EU,
the EU authorized representative is:
Springer Nature Customer Service Center GmbH
Europaplatz 3, 69115 Heidelberg, Germany

Printed by Libri Plureos GmbH
in Hamburg, Germany